Property and the German Idea of Freedom

Studies in Central European Histories

VOLUME 75

The titles published in this series are listed at *brill.com/sceh*

Aufrührerischer Bauer. Flugblatt aus dem Bauernkrieg. (Rebellious Farmer: Broadsheet print from the Peasants' War.) Reproduced from Emil Rosenow, *Wider die Pfaffenherrschaft: Kulturbilder aus den Religionskämpfen des 16. und 17. Jahrhunderts* (Berlin: Buchhandlung Vorwärts, 1904)

Property and the German Idea of Freedom

From the End of the Thirty Years' War to the Eve of the French Revolution in Germany

By

Colin F. Wilder

BRILL

LEIDEN | BOSTON

Cover illustration: *Repraesentatio Rep[ublicae] Germanicae*. Representation of the German Republic or Commonwealth. (Also reproduced in this book as Figure 27.)

Library of Congress Cataloging-in-Publication Data

Names: Wilder, Colin, author.
Title: Property and the German idea of freedom : from the end of the Thirty Years' War to the eve of the French Revolution in Germany / by Colin F. Wilder.
Description: Leiden ; Boston : BRILL, 2024. | Series: Studies in Central European histories, 1547-1217 ; 75 | Includes bibliographical references and index.
Identifiers: LCCN 2023042779 (print) | LCCN 2023042780 (ebook) | ISBN 9789004685161 (hardback) | ISBN 9789004685178 (ebook)
Subjects: LCSH: Freedom (concept)–History. | Law–Germany–History. | Property–Germany–History. | Natural law–Germany–History. | Germany–Politics and government, 1648-1815. | Property–Philosophy. | Possession (Law)–Germany–History. | Enlightenment (Germany)–History. | Constitutional history–Germany. | Pluralism–History.
Classification: LCC KK433 .W55 2024 (print) | LCC KK433 (ebook) | DDC 346.4304/09032–dc23/eng/20231002
LC record available at https://lccn.loc.gov/2023042779
LC ebook record available at https://lccn.loc.gov/2023042780

Typeface for the Latin, Greek, and Cyrillic scripts: "Brill". See and download: brill.com/brill-typeface.

ISSN 1547-1217
ISBN 978-90-04-68516-1 (hardback)
ISBN 978-90-04-68517-8 (e-book)
DOI 10.1163/9789004685178

This book is printed on acid-free paper and produced in a sustainable manner.

There are many forms of life, some better than others, and everyone is free to choose from these what pleases him.

HUGO GROTIUS (1625)

•••

[Hessian subjects] are all too accustomed to freedom.

LANDGRAVE WILHELM IX OF HESSE-CASSEL (1780)

∵

Contents

Preface

The chief goal of the chapters which follow is to understand what Germans meant when they spoke of their freedom in the era between the Thirty Years' War and the arrival of the French Revolution in the Rhineland a century and a half later. To answer that, of course I look back at that time period, and back further to earlier ideas, institutions, and trends which influenced it such as older myths, ideas, and state structures.

But here by way of a high-level orientation, it may be helpful first instead rather to look *forward*, *from* the period ca. 1648–1789 *toward* the era of *the modern liberal state.*

In political science and economics, personal freedom has been closely tied to economic development.[1] But in the late eighteenth century, the linkage was rather looser and less certain. Some writers in Germany did tie freedom and economic growth together – for instance the German Physiocrats, importers of Adam Smith, and critics of monopoly. And there were also *other schools of liberal thought* – understood as *writers who theorized the value and importance of freedom as one of the highest goods in society.* For Romantics like Novalis or Goethe, personal freedom was the germ for self-realization. Wilhelm von Humboldt was unusual in combining both foundations – freedom both led to prosperity and enabled human flourishing. There were also ancient-constitutionalists like Justus Möser for whom imperial federalism and old law were the guarantees of republican freedom.

This book suggests that there was also a lot of important, as yet little recognized *protoliberal* thought in Germany, or perhaps variously *liberal, semiliberal,* and *illiberal* thought, which contributed to the foundation of the later *liberal* legal order. Modern liberal legal systems, defined as focusing preeminently on preserving individual freedom however understood, are characterized by universalism and uniformitarianism.[2] That is, their regulatory power

1 David S. Landes, *The Wealth and Poverty of Nations: Why Some are so Rich and Some so Poor* (New York: Norton, 1998); Hernando de Soto, *The Mystery of Capital: Why Capitalism Triumphs in the West and Fails Everywhere Else* (New York: Basic Books, 2000); Douglass C. North and Robert Paul Thomas, *The Rise of the Western World: A New Economic History* (Cambridge: Cambridge University Press, 1973); Friedrich August Hayek, *The Constitution of Liberty* (Chicago: University of Chicago Press, 1960). See also below Ch. 3, Section 3, p. 102.

2 Carl Schmitt, *Constitutional Theory* (Durham: Duke University Press, 2008 [orig. 1928]), Part 2, §13, §14, pp. 181–219. The terms universalism and uniformitarianism are mine but are based on Harold Berman, *Law and Revolution II: The Impact of the Protestant Reformations on the Western Legal Tradition* (Cambridge: Belknap Press, 2003). See also discussion in Glossary below, p. 316.

reaches everywhere and they apply one set of rules and procedures to all civil subjects; there are no special jurisdictions and no status privileges. By contrast, rather than universalism, an early modern German state might have a number of carved out jurisdictions within it controlled by special old right, so-called patrimonial courts. Rather than uniformitarianism, early modern states typically recognized and/or created special privileges great and small. The legal order of, say, the western German imperial estates in Hesse, Solms, or Frankfurt am Main did not as such treat all legal subjects uniformly. States prized their collective autonomy, peace, order, power, and prosperity far more than they did their individual subjects' freedom.

Still, illiberal legal conditions were giving way to more liberal ones during the eighteenth century. Regard first the considerable, widespread substantive inequality among people's material wealth and social estate. Yet in the second half of the eighteenth century, estate-based legal status was becoming desiccated into the concrete order of property rights. Most estates were increasingly being transformed into transferable wealth (with transferable legal privileges such as tax freedom or right of higher first court instance) in the second half of the century. Privileges, even those of rulers and great lords, were regarded by jurists as "odious" and were interpreted narrowly.[3] The concrete order of rights was governed almost exclusively by open-market transactions. I use the latter term in a somewhat novel way to refer to voluntary transactions between free actors, in cash or through new contract, with ever fewer and weaker unwind conditions or restrictions (e.g. retraction, estate restriction, fief, custom, or exclusions based on gender or religious estate). Protections of old lordly rights such as hunting, serf-lordship, and family property were withering away under the pressure of modernizing, universalistic civil law, proceduralism of possession as the highest form of title, and nigh-indefeasible financial law. Consent was a powerful element in law and most things could be consensually transferred to others. "Every right and every action can be ceded to someone," wrote Gottfried Fibigius in 1638,[4] and everyone's money spent as good as everyone else's. Further, rules of possession and prescription strengthened all this by

3 Bernhard August Gaertner, *Meditationum practicarum ex jure communi et Hassiaco secund. ord. pandectarum specimen primum* (Marburg: Johann Christian Krieger jr., 1785), Caps. 30, 32, 33, 35. The growth of easy transferability is discussed in Ch. 4.

4 Gothofredus Fibigius, praeses, Godofredus Scheffer, respondans, *De iure venandi, aucupandi et piscandi ... Von Wildvogel-, Fischfang- und Forst-Rechten, auch wie man und wer sich dessen anzumassen befugt* (Jena: Heller; Steinman, 1756 [orig. 1638]), §88–89. Consent is discussed below in Ch. 7, pp. 296–299.

interpreting dubious or obscure complexes of right and obligation as based on consensual transactions i.e. well-formed property rights within liberal legal order. Procedural equality was also increasingly the order of the day, though by no means universal. Adjudicatory institutions like the princely chancery in Marburg and the Hessian High Appellate Court treated individuals as formally equal subjects at law, enjoying to a great extent equal application of universalistic black-letter civil laws and procedures.

This may all sound rather pat – as though we just happen to have noticed this protoliberal political-legal system quietly growing up in some of the German lands (the Hessian and Rhine-Main region to be exact). No, anything but. I think we can indeed make out a protoliberal legal order, but for all that, it was an unstable order, if that is not an oxymoron, constantly changing, and I do not think that there was a very clear trend line of change in a uniform direction. Also, many diverse forces were at work. Still, I have developed three main interpretive perspectives on causality in studying these phenomena, and I alternate between them. To use concise, colorful terms, these three views of causality could be called anarchism, systems theory, and managerialism, although these are not meant as technical terminology.

One way of thinking about causality, favored by many current historians, could be called (perhaps too dramatically) anarchism. By this I merely mean that people acted for lots of different, diverse reasons, not all of which can be reconstructed. When push comes to shove, people often seek power, freedom, or escape from negative outcomes. The scattered debris of people's actions and ideas might, partially, get aggregated into later ideas and structures. But much gets lost. Sometimes people seem to have been moved, indeed driven, by ideas, whether abstract or personal. Much of the time we can assume self-interest as a powerful motive. In fact, ideas and interests usually grow together in symbiosis, the bond forming at 98.6° about midway between the human brain and heart.[5]

Sometimes people play roles in pre-established games or designs of controlling principals such as projectors or state ministers. This leads to the second interpretive perspective I often take, systems theory (loosely along the lines of Talcott Parsons), here meaning to look for ways that people's historical actions and ideas cohere into systems. In this way, I sometimes model activity in terms

5 Various parties' motives and strategies are examined below throughout the book. For individuals' and families' motives and strategies, see e.g. Ch. 4, p. 128; Ch. 7, Section 2, p. 291; and Ch. 7, Sections 7–8, pp. 304–312 especially pp. 308–309.

of games, grammar, and institutions, which are all systems.[6] I fit historical elements in this book variously into systems of interaction among independent agents (e.g. the competitive interstate system including the states in the Holy Roman Empire), legal systems (e.g. the "body" of modern Roman civil law, the feudal system, the law merchant), administrative organizations (e.g. the Protestant German bureaucratic *Rechtsstaat*), and even modern social scientific systems (e.g. neoclassical economics with curving supply and demand for resources and services). Systems like these are used at times by period actors, period observers, or later observers to understand people's motives or, alternatively, broader impersonal causes of events.[7]

Negative outcomes and dogs that didn't bark can also reflect systems, absences (e.g. disenfranchisement) indicating acceptance of an expectable outcome within a given system. Administrative projects were all too often ill-fitting grids which projectors and managers tried to superimpose over variegated local practices which had grown up "in the wild" (Bruno Gebhardt). Here I think of Hernando de Soto's developmental economics theory or James Scott's understanding of state-building as system-building.[8] The anarchy of ideas and methods develops as people's individual or self-organized local community life. Such evolutionary orders might best be thought of as more like workable patois than as systems. Functionalism is a privileged, *ex post facto* way of modeling steady-state activities as a system of smoothly interacting roles. This somewhat resembles the arguments made by such economic historians as Douglass North and David Landes that widespread individual freedom and well-functioning property rights have usually co-developed (and the two also frequently linked to a third thing, namely prosperity, though your mileage may vary).

Third, in some cases the best way to understand what was happening and why things changed could be called managerialism – where we identify particular interventions by state actors in pursuit of state interests. Examples here vary from creating or changing statutes, civil law procedures, and

---

6 The approach to understanding personal interaction and meaning-making in terms of games was pioneered in Thomas Szasz, *The Myth of Mental Illness: Foundations of a Theory of Personal Conduct* (New York: Hoeber-Harper, 1961), albeit with reference to work also by Eric Berne and similarities to Ludwig Wittgenstein.

7 Institutions are the theme of Ch. 3. The influence of political economy ideas is discussed below in Ch. 1, Section 5, p. 25 and Section 7, pp. 28–29; Ch. 6, pp. 223–228; and Ch. 7, Section 4, p. 293 and Section 5, p. 298.

8 See de Soto, *Mystery of Capital* and James C. Scott, *Seeing Like a State: How Certain Schemes to Improve the Human Condition Have Failed* (New Haven: Yale University Press, 1998). For the Gebhardt reference, see Chapter 4 below.

administrative rules, to tax rectification schemes or public institutions such as universities. Sometimes interventions apparently had quite unintentional downstream consequences – e.g. the Saxon rule of 1699 discussed in Chapter 6 appears to have been the key ingredient in the birth of freely circulating paper currency (in Germany), itself a major element of freedom in modern liberal society. More generally, we have to separate plans, motives, and unintended consequences in examining the actions of political entrepreneurs and managers. Sometimes patterns emerge without intentional design and plans often miscarry and create not the desired outcome but instead chaos or something else altogether. Even the creation of theoretical systems is part of this. Protoliberal bureaucrats believed that "the system of natural liberty" (liberal property law) was beneficial, so they would interpret existing things in that way or amend laws to more resemble that ideal system. What resulted was not exactly natural but rather the outcome of an administrative project. In the nineteenth century, such systems thinking had become hegemonic in the liberal version of the natural law theory of the state and in the new social sciences.[9]

9 "The system of natural liberty" was a phrase Adam Smith used to describe the set of laws, institutions, and *mores* which he saw as conducive to creating freedom and prosperity. See also below, e.g. Ch. 7, Section 7, p. 306. For a critique which historicizes Smith's naturalistic arguments, see Joyce Appleby, *The Relentless Revolution*, Chs. 1–4. For the medieval roots of the natural law theory of the state, see Otto von Gierke, *Political Theories of the Middle Age* (Beacon Hill: 1959), e.g. Section v, pp. 33–35. For the claim about social science systems, see Immanuel Wallerstein, *World-Systems Analysis: An Introduction* (Duke University Press, 2004), Chapter 1: Historical Origins of World-Systems Analysis. State actors' concerns to encourage economic growth, including through adjusting legal frameworks, are discussed in *passim* below including at Ch. 1, Section 5, p. 25 and Section 7, pp. 28–29; Ch. 4, p. 128; Ch. 6, p. 223; and Ch. 7, Section 4, p. 293, Section 5, p. 298, Section 7, p. 306, and Section 8, pp. 309–312. Managerial concern to restore a certain vision of lost or faltering older order is discussed at Ch. 6, p. 223. and in Ch. 7, Section 4, p. 293 aforereferenced.

Acknowledgements

In the process of writing this book, I have received help from many people. I am deeply indebted to my wife Christina Andrews, who helped me greatly with editing and conceptual clarification in some very trying times. She now involuntarily knows more about early modern German history than she ever cared to. I have presented versions of chapters of this book at the Consortium on the Revolutionary Era, the Sixteenth Century Society and Conference, the European Forum for Young Legal Historians, the History Center at the University of South Carolina, and other venues. I thank participants at all of these events for their questions and suggestions. Michael Lobban was very generous with his time in suggesting revisions to this book. Mary Woolsey did fantastic editing. Early inspiration for some of the book's main ideas came from my experiences in the Prefecture of the Old Regime of Political Union at Yale University in the 1990s. The dissertation project on which this book is more proximately based was inspired by many teachers, peers, and friends at the University of Chicago and elsewhere. Some of my greatest individual debts are to my doctoral advisor Constantin Fasolt, doctoral committee members Michael Geyer and William H. Sewell, jr., and other teachers including Ralph Lerner, Fredrik Jonsson, Irad Kimhi, Marc Lilla, Steven Pincus, and Richard Epstein. Constantin Fasolt and Susan Karr helped me understand the role of canon law in the development of natural rights thought. Susan also helped me to see this study as a contribution to the history of human rights and consequently encouraged me to present it to the Chicago Human Rights and History Group, chaired at the time by Michael Geyer. Early versions of many of this book's arguments were developed in discussions at Chicago. I will always be grateful for those. Many of my ideas were influenced by the great war that always seemed to be raging at Chicago between liberals and Marxists. I was a super liberal at the time, though this has abated somewhat since. I wish also to thank my friends at the Club in Five Points and the Lizard's Thicket Reading Fellowship.

Figures

CHAPTER 1

Introduction

In 1758, in the small German town of Kothen, the tavern keeper Lorenz Dillsberger sued a party of townspeople over wine. Kothen (or Köthen) lay a few kilometers south of the larger regional town of Motten, which like Kothen was part of the imperial estate of the abbey of Fulda in the western Holy Roman Empire of the German Nation. Dillsberger held a monopoly license from the bishopric of Fulda to serve wine in the tavern. His monopoly would have been uncontroversial: rulers and community governments commonly awarded alcohol concessions to favorites and to those who paid fees. But Dillsberger also claimed that his concession gave him the right to compel everyone who attended festive occasions such as weddings and baptisms occurring at places other than the tavern to purchase his wine as well. People customarily drank a great deal on such occasions, he contended, and custom and civil law supported his claim. The court of the Fuldan government decided in favor of Dillsberger. Although the Fuldan court's reasoning is unknown, it does not seem surprising that the appellate court of the regime that granted him the license would back his claim.

The townspeople of Kothen, however, dissatisfied with the lower court's decision, appealed to one of the imperial appellate courts, the Imperial Chamber Court, seated in Wetzlar, about two to three days' travel away. The imperial court reversed Fulda's decision. In the words of Johann Ulrich Cramer, one of the Wetzlar judges,

> Natural right permits each and every subject to buy and drink as much wine and beer as he wishes. Therefore, he who wishes to deny such a right to subjects must prove either that they consent to it, or that it is done by the authorities in a manner allowed by law.[1]

---

1 "Das Recht der Natur erlaubet einem jeden Unterthanen den Wein und Bier zu kauffen, und Zechen zu halten, wo Er will. / Wer also denen Unterthanen solches Recht absprechen will, der muß erweise, daß Sie sich dessen entweder gutwillig begeben, oder daß Ihnen solche von der Obrigkeit Rechts erlaubet Weß entzogen worden." Johann Ulrich Cramer, "Ob das Bann-Recht einer Schenk-Statt dahin sich erstrecken lasse, dass die gebannte Ehren Zechen bey Hochzeiten, oder Kindtauffen zu halten, und dabey an ein gewisses Getraenck, auch an eine determinirte Anzahl der Mensur adstrigiret werden koennen?," in *Wetzlarische Nebenstunden*, Vol. 12 (Ulm: Johann Conrad Wohler, 1758), §5, p. 88.

 | DOI:10.1163/9789004685178_002

Furthermore, continued Cramer,

> Interpretation of this type of individual right must be done so as to cause as little injury as possible to another [person] and minimally injure his remaining natural freedom [*libertatem naturalem*] … and indeed there should always be a presumption on behalf of [his] remaining natural ability [*facultate naturali*], unless it be proven that one party has made a contradiction or prohibition and that the other party has accepted [i.e. suffered] it.[2]

With "contradiction or prohibition," Cramer refers to prescription, a key concept in this book. We will get into the weeds with prescription in Chapters 4 and 5, but for present purposes we can think of it as a (notional) naturalistic process which creates, changes, and/or destroys real rights. Through peaceful exercise, rights might be gained (acquisitive prescription) and through non-exercise they might be lost (extinctive prescription). In the present example, Cramer meant that the court should assume that the Kotheners retained their natural freedom (to not buy and consume food and beverage) unless a process of prescription had taken place to create in them an obligation to do so.[3] The Kotheners could enjoy their natural freedom to buy and drink as much or as little wine and beer as they wished in the tavern as long as they hadn't given in to Dillsberger's asserted restriction.

In a rare flourish, Cramer even added a joke to the later, published version of the court's decision: Since people might get hungry while drinking wine and had in the past bought bratwurst while celebrating, could Dillsberger also claim the right to compel each person to buy a ring of sausage?[4]

---

2 "Quod interpretation ejusmodi singularis juris its fit facienda, ut minime vergat in alterius Injuriam, ut minime laedat libertatem naturalem in tantum relictam, ut nemo duplici onere gravetur: cum potius exceptio firmet regulam in casibus non exceptis; adeoque semper praesumendum fit pro relicta facultate naturali, domex contrarium, donec prohibition ex una, & patientia ex altera parte probetur." Ibid, §15, pp. 97–98, quoting Christian Ludwig Scheidt, praeses, Johann Rudolph Wendeborn, respondans, *De iure erigendi cauponas et hospitia publica tam in genere quam in specie in terrris Brunsuico Luneburgicis von wirthschaffs-und krug-nahrung* (Göttingen: Typis Hagerianis [Johann Friedrich Hager], 1739).

3 See glossary for major terms used in this book including dominion, lordship, ownership, possession, prescription, property rights, and law among others.

4 "Zu 2. Maas Wein muß man doch auch etwas zu essen haben; gesetzt nun, der Mann habe 2. Ring und die Frau 1. Ring Bratwürsten darzu gegessen, und die 3. Zeugen hätten solches gleichfalls bekräfftiget, daß es von Alters her gebräuchlich gewesen, könnte dann nicht der Wirth ein *possessorium immemoriale* daraus machen, und die Manutenenz davon

Joh. Ulr. Freyherrn von Cramer
Kayserl. und des Reichs-Cammer-Gerichts-Assessoris,
Wetzlarische
Nebenstunden,
worinnen
auserlesene beym Höchstpreißlichen
Cammergericht entschiedene Rechts-
Händel
zur
Erweiter- und Erläuterung der teutschen
in Gerichten üblichen Rechts-Gelehrsam-
keit angewendet werden.
Zwölfter Theil.
Nebst einem Register vom IX. bis XII. Theil.

Ulm, 1758.
Verlegts Johann Conrad Wohler.

FIGURE 1 Title page of Cramer's *Wetzlarische Nebenstunden*, Band 12, the serialized collection of legal decisions from which this chapter's opening vignette is taken

---

eben sowohl praetendiren?" See Cramer, "Ob das Bann-Recht einer Schenk-Statt dahin sich erstrecken lasse," §17, p. 99. The Court gave several further grounds for its decision, such as customary Saxon law, which do not concern us here. See ibid., §16, p. 98.

• • •

Germans in the late seventeenth and eighteenth centuries had a lot to say about freedom and freedoms.[5] They spoke regularly of national freedoms they enjoyed as "German freedom." This seems to have encompassed a variety of things loosely associated with what historians are accustomed to label political, economic, and legal liberalism in the Anglo-American world of the same period. In researching this topic, I came quickly to perceive that a great deal of what contemporaries seem to associate with freedom was connected with property law, property rights, and property jurisprudence in one form or another. This book therefore has taken the more specific shape of an inquiry into the relationship between property law and "German freedom," both as a suite of ideas and in concrete practices and guarantees of rights and civil lib-

5 I use the term *Germans* generously in this book. I treat as historically German or a German anyone who called himself such or was or would have been typically called such by his contemporaries. Usually this would be in German *teutsch* and in Latin not infrequently *germanicus*. The Germanized Latin form *germanisch* tended to be used to refer to ancient Germans, meaning roughly prior to the Carolingian period. In that most Latin usage was somewhat antiquarian, usually context was required to determine whether *germanicus* referred to ancient "Germans" ("Germanic" peoples, we might today say) or modern (seventeenth- and eighteenth-century) Germans. By default, Germans would be most or all subjects in the empire excluding people from commonly recognized other nationalities, especially Bohemian, Hungarian, Slavic, Burgundian, Dutch, etc. According to Peter Wilson, however, when eighteenth-century Germans spoke of Germanness, they typically used the older, folksy term *teutsch*, which was generally understood to mean those people north of the Alps and east of the Rhine, not all of whom even spoke versions of German. I encounter the Swiss rarely in this book, only occasionally in reference to specific towns such as Geneva or Basel, where there seems to have been no confusion that such people were German. My sense is that Germanness was in no sense a racial concept as it would be understood today and I do not think I have ever encountered racial terms in my sources. Germanness seems to have been allowed through adoption, as say Americanness would usually be today, say for a person or family who had settled in a German state and adopted self-identity, language, and customs after a couple of generations. Wilson also notes that "official documents" were fifteen times more likely to refer to Germans' super-polity as the "Holy Roman Empire" rather than use the full name of "Holy Roman Empire of the German Nation." Also, neither "of the German Nation" nor "Holy" were often used after the sixteenth century, although they are used ordinarily in this book because they are standard historical terms in modern scholarship. Indeed in the seventeenth and eighteenth centuries, simply "empire" was three times more likely to be said than anything else. So, in direct contrast to the conceptions and interests of many modern scholars, Germans of the day thought their self-conception neither problematic nor particularly worthy of attention. See Peter H. Wilson, *The Holy Roman Empire, 1495–1806*, 2nd ed., Studies in European history (Houndmills, Basingstoke, Hampshire: Palgrave, 2011 [orig. 1999]), pp. 103–107 and Georg Schmidt, *Geschichte des Alten Reichs: Staat und Nation in der Frühen Neuzeit, 1495–1806* (Munich: Beck, 1999), p. 296.

erties.[6] Personal freedom,[7] such as it existed in Germany in the seventeenth and eighteenth centuries, developed within the legal institutions governing private property rights. In support of this argument, the following chapters examine the mechanics of law regarding real property (that is, real estate and rights connected with land), extractions such as tithes and taxes, and the use of money and moveable commercial goods. These specific inquiries help us discover what rights existed, how they were applied, and how they changed over time. In the nineteenth century in England, Lord Acton, famous for his contention that power corrupts, devoted much scholarship to writing what he called "the history of freedom." His research agenda into the history of freedom was very wide, encompassing antiquity, the early Christian period, and medieval and modern Europe, By focusing on freedoms related to the control of property in early modern Germany, I hope to add to that history.

Within the German context, freedoms developed not from discourse in the public sphere or changes in public law but rather from the resolution of conflicts over property in Germany's emerging commercial markets. Presented with disputes among and initiatives originating with a range of actors – from serfs, merchants, burghers, and bureaucrats to noble country lords, princes, and imperial officials, jurists generated new interpretations and in a real sense, new law. In the process, they began to establish a well-defined set of personal freedoms governing individuals' basic rights to enjoy, exploit, buy, sell, leverage, and borrow property.

1 The Consensus and Revisionist Views of German Freedom

The ideas of "natural" rights, freedom, and abilities that Cramer cited were discussed frequently in law books and used in legal arguments and court decisions throughout the eighteenth century. Yet most scholars persist in believing that premodern Germany was characterized by authoritarian states, with lit-

6 See glossary: civil liberties; concrete order of law.

7 Here and in some other places, I use the term "personal freedom" in contrast with other kinds of freedom sometimes discussed in the early modern period, namely those of estates within a realm, as in the freedom-as-autonomy of the imperial German estates like Hesse or Brandenburg-Prussia vis-à-vis the imperial government in Vienna. Elsewhere below I shall use the term "personal" in its more technical legal meaning of something held be a person, in contrast to rights appurtenant to real estate and disposable as such. I try to make clear in each section of this book whether I mean personal freedom as "personal" *qua* individual or personal in contrast to real.

tle in the way of rule of law, constitutionalism, or personal freedom. This 'consensus' view was articulated by Leonard Krieger in his classic 1957 work, *The German Idea of Freedom*.[8] According to Krieger's thesis, similar to the broader "Special Path" (*Sonderweg*) school of thought, freedom had developed only anemically in Germany right up to the era after the Second World War. Krieger drew primarily from sources in the realm of political theory, texts that informed how Germans thought about political authority and freedom from Luther to Kant to Hitler. He argued that, while liberal currents of thought existed in the period of the Second German Empire (1871–1918), the predominant political institutions in Germany before, during, and after that period were authoritarian, with little personal freedom other than set legal procedures and basic protections for religious minorities. In this view, only "thoughts were free" (Schiller) prior to the modern era.

In opposition to the thinking of Krieger and his heirs stands the body of scholarship which has been developed by liberal and revisionist historians. The latter two cliques have argued that liberal governmental structures were more present in parts of Germany than has widely been believed, as much by other historians and politicians as in popular memory. In the nineteenth century, scholars such as Rudolph Olden and Gottfried Dietze presented histories of liberal political thought from the Rheinbund Era to the Second Empire (1806–1871). They demonstrated that there were lively liberal currents in German popular culture, intellectual circles, and government throughout the nineteenth century.[9] More recently, Diethelm Klippel demonstrated that there was significant political diversity of thought in the eighteenth century, including not only varieties of conservatism but also liberalism, including physiocracy and constitutionalist thought, as well as policies of religious toleration.[10] Investigating the rise of representative government in Germany, Margaret Anderson made a compelling case that the advent of important freedoms in Germany began not in the twentieth century, but the nineteenth, contra Krieger and others. Anderson focused on parliamentary democracy, political pluralism, and dissent, rather than other more palpable, individual

8 Leonard Krieger, *The German Idea of Freedom: History of a Political Tradition* (Chicago: University of Chicago Press, 1957).

9 Rudolf Olden, *The History of Liberty in Germany* (London: V. Gollancz Ltd., 1946 [orig. 1939]); Gottfried Dietze, *Two Concepts of the Rule of Law* (Indianapolis: Liberty Fund, 1973).

10 Diethelm Klippel, *Politische Freiheit und Freiheitsrechte im deutschen Naturrecht des 18. Jahrhunderts* (Paderborn: Ferdinand Schöningh, 1976).

freedoms, such as personal conduct, taxes, labor, or movement.[11] Karl Otmar von Aretin, Horst Dreitzel, and Georg Schmidt have argued that, at the latest from 1648 onward, the Holy Roman Empire and many of its constituent states were constitutional monarchies and in most cases firmly grounded in rule of law (*Rechtsstaaten*).[12] "Absolutism" was more a political myth or program, an aspiration of rulers and their servants, than a reality. There was in fact much evidence of talk of freedom during the "age of absolutism" (approximately 1648 to 1803) in a context of federalism and pluralistic dialogue.[13] Germans, including jurists, spoke of civil liberty, criticized serfdom, praised liberal and physiocratic political economy, even talked of something called "German freedom" ("teutsche Freyheit"). We are then left with the question of what freedoms Germans actually enjoyed during the seventeenth and eighteenth centuries. Joachim Whaley has made a great contribution to the understanding of "German Liberties" in the Holy Roman Empire; I hope to advance further in this direction.

Perhaps the most powerful revision of our view of the politics of early modern Germans and freedom thus far was the work of Peter Blickle. Blickle painted a colorful, epic panorama of successful political activism by common Germans against oppression from the sixteenth through the eighteenth centuries. He transformed the paradigm of the "Peasants' War" of 1525 in Germany into that of "the Revolution of 1525," a struggle for the freedom of the common man. Blickle went so far as to argue that the love of, and striving for, freedom

---

11 Margaret Lavinia Anderson, *Practicing Democracy: Elections and Political Culture in Imperial Germany* (Princeton: Princeton University Press, 2000). Anderson's work picked up a line of argument first initiated in David Blackbourn and Geoff Eley, who had broken the Marxist orthodoxy about German history by arguing that there had been indeed no classic "bourgeois revolution" as required by Marxist theory for middle-class capitalism to emerge. Instead, Germany had slowly achieved bourgeois, capitalist modernity despite varying periods of socialism, parliamentarism, capitalism, and militarism. See David Blackbourn and Geoff Eley, *The Peculiarities of German History: Bourgeois Society and Politics in 19th Century Germany* (Oxford: Oxford University Press, 1984).

12 Karl Otmar Freiherr von Aretin, *Das Alte Reich, 1648–1806* (Stuttgart: Klett-Cotta, 1993); Horst Dreitzel, *Absolutismus und ständische Verfassung in Deutschland: Ein Beitrag zu Kontinuität und Diskontinuität der politischen Theorie in der frühen Neuzeit* (Mainz: Verlag Philipp von Zabern, 1992).

13 Diethelm Klippel, "The True Concept of Liberty: Political Theory in Germany in the Second Half of the Eighteenth Century," in *The Transformation of Political Culture: England and Germany in the Late Eighteenth Century*, ed. Eckhart Hellmuth (London: Oxford University Press, 1990); Maiken Umbach, *Federalism and Enlightenment in Germany, 1740–1806* (2000); Georg Schmidt, *Wandel durch Vernunft: Deutschland, 1715–1806* (Munich: C. H. Beck, 2009).

was a powerful driver of political action throughout German history since at least the Reformation, even helping to drive serf emancipation.[14] According to the revisionists, therefore, not only did Germany for several centuries have diversity of thought, but a notable portion of German society enjoyed – and sometimes fought for – substantial freedom and equality under law. Coming back around to the beginning of this chapter, however, I believe that historians have generally not yet argued that *personal* freedom was either widespread or greatly valued or respected in German society before about 1800. Such is this book's task.

Other scholarship has focused on other elements related to the theme of freedom. One was political Aristotelianism, as in the work of Samuel Pufendorf, Hermann Conring, and Christian Thomasius. Pufendorf's critique of the state form of the Holy Roman Empire of the German Nation is probably the best-known example of this, but also important were anti-absolutist polemics.[15] Frank Grunert, Ian Hunter, T. J. Hochstrasser, and Knud Haakonssen have reconstructed the growth of natural law from the reception of Grotius in Germany to the period following the Peace of Westphalia (1648), the blossoming of German universities, and the heyday of so-called Enlightened Absolutism. Natural law became a cornerstone of political and ethical thought in Germany and influenced policy issues including toleration and codification. Enlightenment has ever been associated with liberalization of one form or another, for instance including toleration or limitation of inhumane and unaccountable police procedures in torture and imprisonment.[16] Finally, the principal understanding of Enlightenment in Germany as human liberation (Kant) has been reconsidered most recently by Georg Schmidt and

14 Peter Blickle, *Die Revolution von 1525 i.e. Fünfzehnhundertfünfundzwanzig* (Munich; Vienna: Oldenbourg, 1975); Peter Blickle, *Von der Leibeigenschaft zu den Menschenrechten: Eine Geschichte der Freiheit in Deutschland* (Munich: Beck, 2003).

15 Robert von Friedeburg, "Natural Jurisprudence, Argument from History and Constitutional Struggle in the Early Enlightenment: Gottlieb Samuel Treuer's 1719 Anti-Absolutist Polemic," in *Early modern natural law theories: Contexts and strategies in the early Enlightenment*, ed. T. J. Hochstrasser and Peter Schröder, Vol. 186, *Archives internationales d'histoire des idées; International archives of the history of ideas* (Dordrecht; Boston: 2003). Constantin Fasolt's interpretation of Hermann Conring's historical and political thought in the former's *The Limits of History* (Chicago: University of Chicago Press, 2004) is both clear and highly stimulating.

16 Christian Thomasius has been regarded as a key figure of the early German Enlightenment not for any great worship of reason but for his critique of torture and calls for reform of institutions. See Franz Wieacker, *A History of Private Law in Europe with Particular Reference to Germany*, trans. Tony Weir (Oxford: Clarendon Press, 1995 [orig. 1952]), pp. 239b–240t, p. 251t–252.

others, who have turned the focus back from religion, science, technology, agriculture, and manufacture, toward freedom. Enlightenment, declared Kant in 1784, about when this book's treatment ends in fact, was "man's liberation from self-imposed tutelage." Schmidt contends that by the late Enlightenment, German thinking focused heavily on individual self-improvement, responsibility, and perfectionism, with concomitant "limits of state action."[17]

2 This Book's Contribution

I wish to push in the same general direction as the liberal and revisionist historians mentioned above, trying to reconstruct and understand what seventeenth- and eighteenth-century Germans meant when the boasted of their national freedom(s). Although the phrase "German freedom" may have been used differently and even inconsistently by different actors, it was a meaningful national rallying cry for Germans at all levels of society, from common subject to prince. In order to fill out our understanding of what "German freedom" actually meant in the seventeenth and eighteenth centuries. I set myself the task of rediscovering ideas, theories, and stories (or myths) about freedom as well as legal developments in property rights that expanded people's freedom. (I will henceforth drop the quotation marks from German freedom but it should be understood that I always use the term to indicate the phrase as used in the period, rather than a modern conception of my own.)

German freedom was and is often associated with constitutionalism, imperial federalism, a reverence for law and impartial courts, and strong property law and property rights. Germans at all levels of society enjoyed, created, and expanded their rights in real property and in the use of reliable, circulating paper money during the late seventeenth and eighteenth centuries. These developments increased freedom for both individuals and communities by

17 See respectively Immanuel Kant, "What is Enlightenment?," in *Philosophical Writings*, ed. Ernst Behler (New York: Continuum, 1986 [orig. 1784]); Schmidt, *Wandel durch Vernunft*; Wilhelm von Humboldt, *Ideen zu einem Versuch, die Grenzen der Wirksamkeit des Staats zu bestimmen* (Berlin: Deutsche Bibliothek, 1841 [orig. 1792]); and Ian Hunter, *Rival Enlightenments: Civil and Metaphysical Philosophy in Early Modern Germany*, Ideas in Context (Cambridge: Cambridge University Press, 2001). Other important revisionist accounts of the German Enlightenment include those of Barbara Stollberg-Rilinger, *Des Kaisers alte Kleider: Verfassungsgeschichte und Symbolsprache des Alten Reiches* (Munich: Beck, 2008); Ursula Goldenbaum, *Appell an das Publikum* (2004), Martin Mulsow, *Radikale Frühaufklärung in Deutschland*, 2 vols., 2002 and 2018); and Steffen Martus, *Aufklärung* (2015).

permitting people and communities a greater ability to secure and control their lives and resources.

The idea of German freedom was informed by older concepts or myths of ancient Germanic freedom and the "Free German Empire," but my focus is on its evolution in the seventeenth and eighteenth centuries. I define freedom in multiple ways, as did Germans of the period. In the region studied in this book, the ability to secure and transfer real estate property grew much stronger after the Thirty Years' War, as jurists came to connect immunities – freedom from certain taxes, dues, and labor impositions – directly with natural freedom. A person could, they argued, recover his natural freedom and gain immunities as actual civil rights (*iura civilia*). As the older, paternalistic society of estates was gradually undone in the eighteenth century, people also gained a new and different kind of freedom in the increasingly widespread use of paper money. Although Germans did not achieve a classical liberal structure of politics and economy of the kind gained in Britain or the new United States, one can see the beginnings of important ideas and institutions of freedom, consent, economic dynamism, and the transformation of earlier privileges into essentially private and fungible rights – in addition to the constitutionalism, federalism, and appellate courts already explored by other scholars. Many factors drove these developments, including the expansion of courts, publishing, and universities. I contend that, in the period under study, freedoms were expanded through the operations of modern legal institutions – the resolution of conflicts in law, theoretical debates, adversarial courtroom structures, and the needs of policymakers to solve perceived problems or achieve new goals of political economy.

What made many Germans free was not the spread of open, popular government as developed in Britain and later in France. Instead, in most of Germany, broadly speaking, there was toleration, and relatively free discussion of new ideas. And – while this is controversial among German historians – I would suggest there was something that looked much like what is called in the Anglophone context "the rule of law," both public and private. Certainly German liberals and republicans in the nineteenth century looked back on what they thought was a heritage of freedom and rule of law.[18] Estates and

18 As Delegate Wagner put it in the 24th session of the diet of the North Rhine Confederation in 1866, "As if the rule of law [*Rechtsstaat*] were something which we had to figure out, something we had not already lived for centuries!" "Als wäre der Rechtsstaat Etwas, was Sie sich auszudenken hätten und worin wir nicht schon seit Jahrhunderten lebten!" Quoted in D. Merten, "Friedrich der Grosse und Montesquieu. Zu den Anfangen des Rechtsstaates im 18. Jahrhundert," in *Verwaltung im Rechtsstaat. Festschrift für Carl Hermann Ule* (Cologne: 1987), p. 187.

diets in Germany long before the French Revolution had sought, often successfully, to limit the powers of rulers. And rulers created court systems which were increasingly able to enforce uniform rule of private law, and guarantee of private rights, throughout a realm.[19] Probably a majority of German states in the late Holy Roman Empire could be classified as constitutional monarchies. These exercised restrained enforcement of clear property rights on a large scale throughout society.

This early form of freedom found in Germany, the focus of this book, encompassed the ability to acquire, "use, abuse," and dispose of property as one saw fit. In modern theoretical terms, this freedom is complex – it could either be individual or collective, natural or civil. In all cases, these property freedoms encompassed a large part of a person's quotidian concerns – what they could control, what they were going to be made to do by someone else, what they might have to suffer, and what value they could realize from resources they controlled. How much of their crop did they have to yield to a seigneur or ruler? How many days' labor did they have to perform for public works? Were their old rights in commons like fishing ponds or timbering forests protected? And so on.

I ask the reader to bear in mind that my goal is to recover and interpret semi-forgotten or poorly understood German concepts of freedom. I could not claim that "German freedom" *precisely and always encompassed all* of the ideas which have been presented by *other scholars* (such as constitutionalism or the early rule of law) as well as *all* of the ideas *I* present (such as freedom to use real property or freedoms from extractions). But I argue that these ideas together constitute most of what many people were thinking of when they believed their empire was peculiarly free. Our goal will be to reconstruct ambiguous usages of freedom, common among people from all social estates, only some of whom themselves worried about theories of freedom. Some of my examples were theorized by jurists as matters of a natural law of freedom ("natural freedom," "pure natural abilities"), while others were not. In many examples, although freedom is mentioned by a party at suit, no connection is made to a theory of natural freedom.

Beyond the usage of the term freedom there is another difficulty: things which seem like freedom in substance to modern eyes, but were not so called three centuries ago, and conversely things which were called freedom then, but fit into very different linguistic or conceptual usage today. For instance, one of my arguments concerns paper money. Its extension into more cor-

19 See glossary: private law.

ners of society involved a recognizable kind of liberalization: the removal of earlier estate restrictions, which prevented serfs, women, priests, and (sometimes) nobles from engaging in certain commercial practices, such as using bills of exchange. But the lifting of restrictions was not sufficient: the privilege to use bills with all their power had to be sanctioned by the prince and estates or recognized by the courts. That privilege was extended out among increasingly greater parts of the population. No one in the period spoke of this as a freedom, though today it looks like a combination of negative and positive freedom: estates' restrictions were lifted, and the state authority took positive action to allow groups to use bills (paper money) in a way previously impossible.[20]

The kinds of freedom presented in this book bear only a broad family resemblance to each other. Implicit in ancient Germanic freedom was strong royal authority and subsidiary, household-level patriarchy. The Reformation idea of a Free German Empire was a pluralistic vision of the empire as a confederation whose basic law was the protection of the rights, freedoms, and privileges of its thousand member parts, from village to archduchy. Free disposal of real estate and freedom from extractions were what today we call negative rights – the right to stop someone or some power from making you do or give something. The liberation of serfs sometimes involved a conflict of jurisdictions rather than any formal change in law. Some kinds of freedoms began as illegality or legal fictions but were in time blessed by jurists for practical reasons. In modern terms, we can find different concepts of freedom: negative freedom, positive freedom, and freedom as non-domination.

I take a pluralistic approach to explaining how and why changes occurred. I will propose several factors or mechanisms which fostered ideas of freedom and helped transmit them through institutions. Some of these, alluded to briefly above, were entrenched, powerful ideas or myths that appear to have influenced courts, legislators, and free-range jurists. As I will explain below, some factors were more a matter of opportunity or circumstance, such as the destruction and information loss resulting from the Thirty Years' War. The acquisitiveness or other motives of private parties can also be seen as

20 There is a negative (liberatory) element, but also a positive (privileging) element. By the mid eighteenth century, most social estates including serfs were much freer in a negative sense than ever before in the Hessian and Rhine-Main region, where this study is focused. But that does not as such mean that they could do all the things that other people could do. Some kinds of freedom were powers which required privileges not yet widely granted. This is the subject of Chapter 6.

the causes of certain kinds of changes or pressures. High legal theory, drawing on ideas of natural freedom and the public-law authority of the state, was frequently cited in argumentation, even over very quotidian or humble matters such as liquor licensing (discussed earlier) or urban easements. But state policy may also have motivated change – to solve problems involving the circulation of money, to increase investment and lending, and to grow the resources on which regimes could then levy dues or taxes. While actors sometimes seemed to champion freedom and individual or communal rights, in other cases their interests lay elsewhere, in the service of other goals. Hence in many cases the legal outcomes concerning freedoms in the cases I discuss were not closely related to the goals or intentions of actors involved.[21]

3 Legal Operators

The German states teemed with jurists. Borrowing a term from Bruno Leoni, one could call them *legal operators* – people trained in law who used the law.[22] Some of these jurists' names are well known today, such as Hugo Grotius (Dutch, but highly influential in Germany), Samuel Pufendorf, or Christian Thomasius.[23] But this book is mostly based on the writings of a larger set of German legal operators not so well known anymore, including private lawyers, representatives of the prince's and the state's interests, university law professors, chancellors, regime court and supreme court justices, and even state regents. Law was made not only by "legislators" such as rulers and diets, but also by these more humble legal operators, who fashioned new arguments that later became dominant interpretations. New ideas came up from below, out of

21 This is consistent with the evolutionary-pluralist model of legal development presented in Colin F. Wilder, "Teaching Old Dogs New Tricks: Four Motifs of Legal Change from Early Modern Europe," *History and Theory* 51 (2012), itself just a model of older ideas from Adam Ferguson and Carl Friedrich von Savigny.

22 Bruno Leoni, *Freedom and the Law*, 3rd ed. (Indianapolis: Liberty Fund, 1961).

23 For Grotius's German followers, see Frank Grunert, "The reception of Hugo Grotius's *De jure belli ac pacis* in the early German enlightenment," in *Early modern natural law theories: contexts and strategies in the early Enlightenment*, ed. T. J. Hochstrasser and Peter Schröder, Vol. 186, *International Archives of the History of Ideas* (Dordrecht: Kluwer, 2003) and Knud Haakonssen, "German Natural Law," in *The Cambridge history of eighteenth-century political thought*, ed. Mark Goldie and Robert Wokler (Cambridge: Cambridge University Press, 2006). For Thomasius, see Ian Hunter, *The secularisation of the confessional state: the political thought of Christian Thomasius*, Ideas in Context (Cambridge; New York: Cambridge University Press, 2007).

a churn of conflict in classroom and courtroom. While the great and famous natural law of Grotius, Pufendorf, or Thomasius was important and studied and not infrequently cited, what one encounters much more on an everyday basis could better be called low natural law, the casual, everyday reasoning about comparative law which made up the court decisions and dissertations produced by the hundreds every year in every region of the empire.[24]

This development of the law most often emerged through legal operators' efforts to resolve conflicts over what today are often simply called property rights (although legal historians put them into several distinct categories) – contests over ownership, use, dues, payments, prices, contracts, and related matters connected in most cases to "real" "estate" – immovable land or other land-related rights like drawing water, timbering, or lordship over serfs. In addition to these rights which already look rather modern, freedoms from having to pay certain dues or perform labors were also treated as property and could be alienated or encumbered. Did someone have to perform certain labor, seek permissions, or pay a tax? How might one build structures on his land? Were several villagers free to use a common pasture, or did another person try to exclude them from it? With whom could you do business, and on what terms? Could you divest yourself of certain property, perhaps in order to emigrate, or invest in some new emergent capitalistic enterprise?[25] Jurists of the day asked deep and consequential questions like, Were serfs fundamentally free or more like slaves? (The German term for *serf*, *Leibeigene*, means "owned body.") The legal operators I present here articulated ideas about freedom, natural rights, equality, and the limits of political and social oppression, particularly within the context of property rights. Legal operators took up earlier ideas about freedom and equality and transformed them into modern theories with practical application in courts of law.

Over the course of the seventeenth and eighteenth centuries, important freedoms developed and expanded through such conflicts. First, people gained more freedom to dispose of their real estate – to buy, sell, use, encumber, or give its use to others. New freedoms also developed in the form of immunities connected to land (real rights on real estate): freedoms from paying

---

24 See glossary: natural law.

25 The kernel of "capitalism," in word as well as in concept, dates back earlier than is usually supposed. For instance, Carl Gottfried Fürstenau, *Versuch einer Apologie des physiokratischen Systems gegen die Einwuerfe im Deutschen Museum 1778. 10. St. und Hannoeverschen Magazin 48–51 St. desselben Jahrs* (Cassel: J. J. Cramer, 1779), p. 32, mentions that in one contemporary view, "capitalists [*Kapitalisten*] who invest their capital either in foreign lands or in production or trade which is made for foreign lands" are one of the three groups in the "sterile class," according to "economic reason."

tax, from performing customary services, or from having to seek certain special permissions. Freedoms also emerged in the use of cash and of chattels. Rulers, anxious to increase territorial wealth and revenue, encouraged new industry, patented banks to lend money, and liberalized restrictions on both usury and on use of paper money (bills of exchange). Jurists and rulers in the mid eighteenth century progressively tolerated and later encouraged use of bills by non-merchant members of society, such as professionals, farmers, artisans, and women. The oppression of serfs by one lord, or defense of them by another, not infrequently figured into inter-polity conflict, as in the conflict between Solms and Hesse-Darmstadt in 1750. Indeed, sometimes in our region of study one polity would make a policy of protection of sheltering serfs who had run away from a neighboring county or principality, probably not so much out of humanitarianism and early love of human rights, but rather as a measure to weaken a neighboring opponent. But we also see jurists of the seventeenth and eighteenth centuries debating serfdom. They would argue about whether serfs were slaves, whether their choice of marriage could be controlled by their lords, and how to reconcile their status as (nominally) free human beings with the control that lords lorded over them.

4 Significance

The findings of this work challenge several common narratives in European history. First, they show that significant strides in the development of personal freedom came about in Germany as much as a century earlier than has previously been recognized – during the Enlightenment, but well before the time of Kant, Schiller, or Humboldt. Many ordinary Germans enjoyed personal freedoms, initially in the Renaissance, increasingly in the sixteenth and seventeenth centuries, and certainly during the eighteenth, suggesting that the German Enlightenment was less illiberal than is usually supposed, nor did it solely concern religious toleration and progress in the arts and sciences. The history of freedom in Germany can no longer jump discontinuously from the autonomy of medieval German towns and lordships in the thirteenth century to the rise of liberal political movements in the 1820s, as it did in Lord Acton's telling.[26] Although historians already know that forms of feudal property could be transferred in various ways, the modes and scope of this transfer are not

26 I make this jump only for the sake of brevity. As mentioned above, about half a dozen scholars, most notably Peter Blickle, have argued that both ideas and political activism around freedom and liberation dot German history and began to be political significant

widely understood. I contend that these property rights expanded faster and earlier than in the common narrative, principally through the expansion of the appellate court system and law faculties. Not only could nobles transfer fiefs, but so could many common people, and they could also transform the terms of tenure – whether holding land or holding certain freedoms appurtenant to land such as not paying taxes or performing certain associated labors.

My findings also contradict the common modern, legal positivist assumption that formal governance structures were the primary mechanism through which freedoms were established. Not only statutes but also court decisions, legal ideas from universities, and even independent partisan action in disputes could all serve to create new rights and legal relationships.[27] In the late seventeenth and eighteenth centuries, these mechanisms together led to people gaining property rights, and therefore a kind of freedom, rather than to new structures of domination. In a nutshell, German freedoms developed as jurists sought to resolve hotly contested claims to property and commercial rights including custom, lawyers' arguments, judicial decisions, and negotiation in the marketplace.

Regarding the relationship between property and freedom, my argument involves two closely related threads. First, I show how key property rights relating to land use, freedoms from extractions (taxes, dues, and labor), and the use of money and commercial instruments, all expanded during the period 1648–1768, and the enjoyment of them spread more broadly in society. Second, I contend that these developments constitute, and were in most cases understood at the time as, expansions of personal freedom, raising the question of why scholars have not interpreted the considerable personal and communal control over property as a great expansion in freedom, rather than primarily focusing on religious toleration or federalism.

My argument also suggests a place in German history for political, economic, and legal themes which scholars have identified in other European countries. One example is how law either constrained or encouraged commercial activity.[28] Another is how both private and public civil law influenced

---

by the early sixteenth century. For Acton, see John Emerich Edward Dalberg Acton, "The History of Freedom in Christianity," in *The History of Freedom and Other Essays*, ed. John Neville Figgis and Reginald Vere Laurence (London: Macmillan, 1907).

27 This argument builds on my earlier article, Wilder, "Teaching Old Dogs New Tricks."

28 For application in Anglo-American and generalized legal settings, see Harold Demsetz, "Toward a Theory of Property Rights," *American Economic Review* 57, no. 2, Papers and Proceedings of the Seventy-ninth Annual Meeting of the American Economic Association (1967); Richard Posner, "The Economic Approach to Law," *Texas Law Review* 53

political thought, including the construction of constitutions such as that of the US. But because of the longstanding predominant opinion among historians that Germans had little freedom during the early modern period, German political thought has not been as broadly explored as comparable work in other countries in the same period, whether by German historians (other than a few, as mentioned above) or those writing in other languages.[29] Like scholars elsewhere in Europe around the same time, German thinkers such as Johann Georg Estor and Johann Ulrich Cramer were engaged in intellectual, legal, and policy problems, part of a transnational project of legal comparison (*usus modernus*).

5 Context

This book focuses chiefly on the work of jurists and institutions located in the Hessian and Rhine-Main region, western lands in the Holy Roman Empire of the German Nation. The region comprised primarily Upper and Lower Hesse, but more broadly the region around Frankfurt am Main. This is the area where the Rhine River and the Main River are close to one another (connecting in Wiesbaden), north, east, and south of the Taunus Forest. This region is near the Rhineland, south of what was to become the Ruhr industrial region. The whole area was part of Franconia or Franken, the land of the ancient Eastern Franks, some of whom were called "*Chatti*" (or *Hassiae*, Hessians). (See Figures 2, 3.)

Most of the jurists here studied were principally active in the courts, governments, and universities in this area – particularly in Cassel, Darmstadt, Frankfurt, Giessen, Hanau, Marburg, and Solms, although other, smaller locales such

(1975); Todd Zywicki, "The Rise and Fall of Efficiency in the Common Law: A Supply-Side Analysis," *Northwestern University Law Review* 97 (2003). For German applications, see Oliver Volckart, "Politische Zersplitterung und Wirtschaftswachstum im Alten Reich, ca. 1650–1800," *Vierteljahrschrift für Sozial- und Wirtschaftsgeschichte* 86, no. 1 (1999); Jürgen G. Backhaus, ed., *Christian Wolff and Law & Economics: The Heilbronn Symposium* (Hildesheim; New York: Georg Olms, 1998); Backhaus, "Otto von Gierke (1841–1921)," in *The Elgar Companion to Law and Economics*, ed. Backhaus (Cheltenham; Northampton: Edward Elgar, 2005); and David J. Gerber, "Law and Economics in Wilhelmine Germany: Examining the Dynamics of the Relationship," in *Grundlagen des Rechts: Festschrift für Peter Landau zum 65. Geburtstag*, ed. R. H. Helmholz, Paul Mikat, Michael Stolleis, and Jörg Paul Müller (Paderborn: F. Schöningh, 2000).

29 The volume of studies of British, French, and American political thought from roughly the same period, in English and in other languages, dwarfs that of German thought, including by German writers.

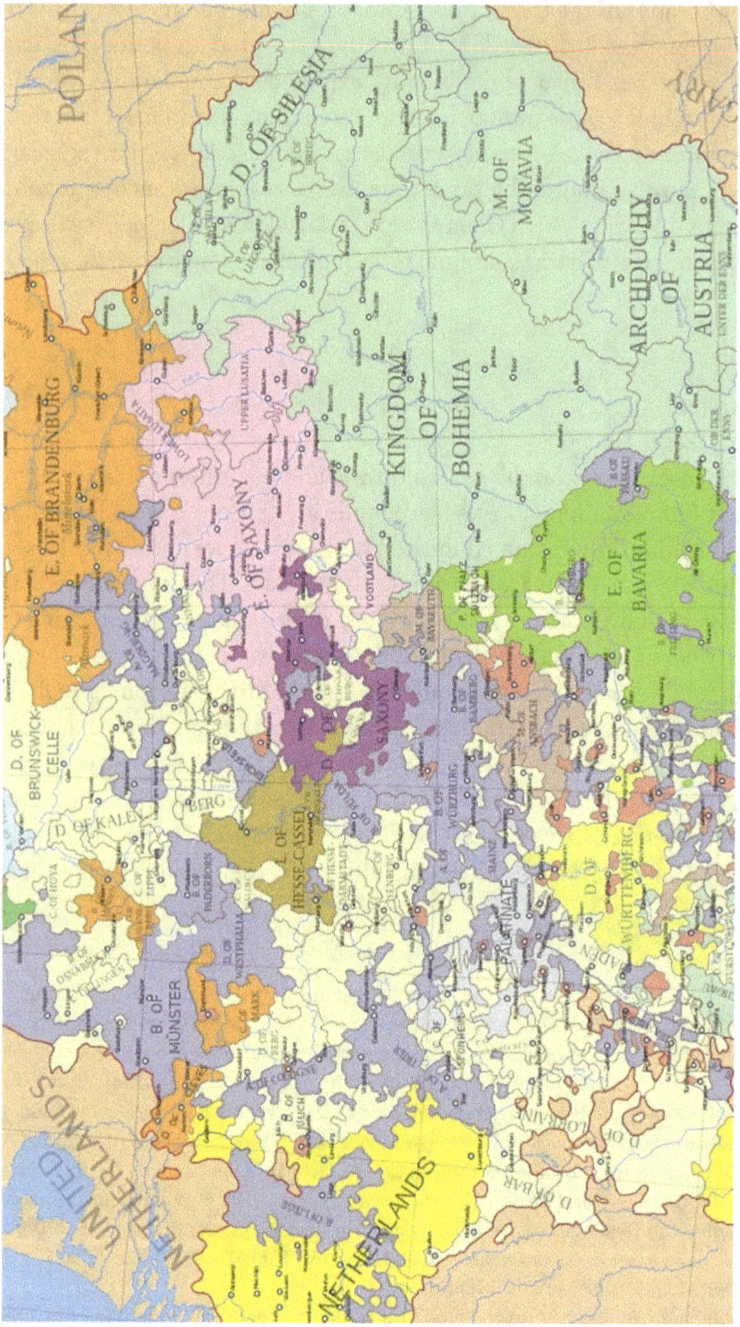

FIGURE 2 The Holy Roman Empire of the German Nation after the Peace of Westphalia 1648. Hesse-Cassel is depicted in dark brown in the middle. Hesse-Darmstadt is south of Hesse-Cassel. See also Figure 3

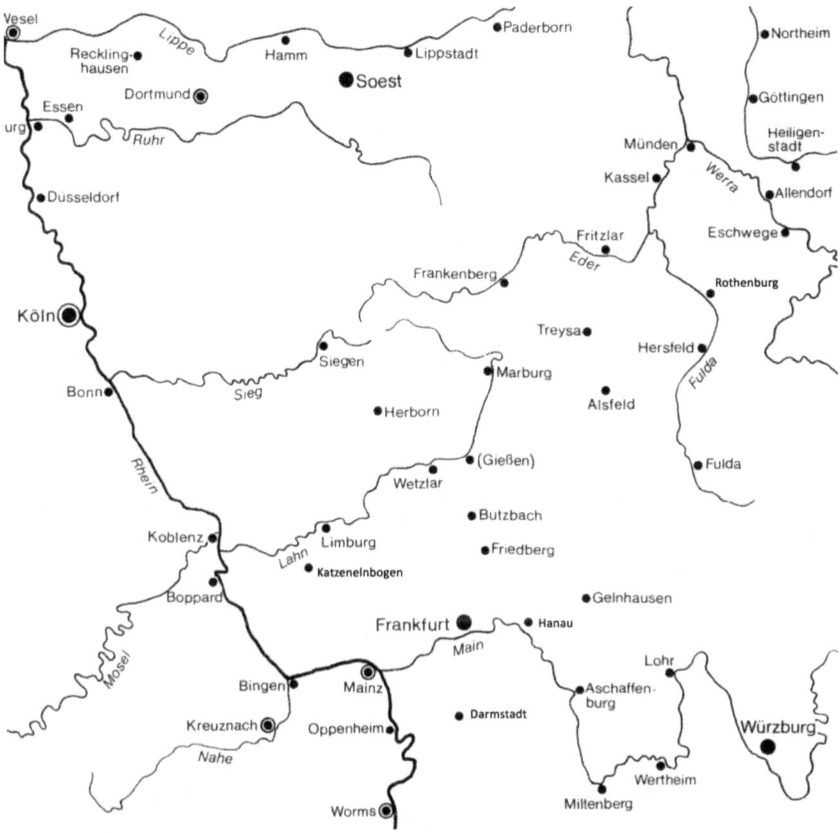

FIGURE 3 The major towns of Hesse, the Wetterau, and the other regional lordships e.g. counties in the period. Rinteln is the only major administrative or educational center mentioned in this book but not shown here; it lies north of Paderborn. Rothenburg, Eschwege, and Fulda, discussed in Chapter 6, are in the eastern area of the map

as Offenbach, the Wetterau, and Ysenburg are occasionally noted. Early in the eighteenth century, this region was comprised of many small states – a number varying between perhaps ten and fifty, depending on what counted as a "state" at the time. There were other significant communities and free powers in the region, almost too numerous to name:

- the smaller but enduringly important comital powers – Nassau, Solms, and Waldeck;
- free imperial towns and villages, including Frankfurt and Offenbach;
- a small but persistently indomitable episcopal seat: Mainz;
- the Freigericht (free court) Kaichen;
- the free imperial knightly communities, including the local order of the Teutonic Knights in Marburg and the free imperial castle of Friedburg;

- large noble condominia, notably the "republic" of the Riedesel zu Eisenbach or what can only be described as the joint-stock company of the estates of Staden;
- self-governing serf communities of old around Breidenbach and Gladenbach; and
- the old free region of the Wetterau, where, perhaps not coincidentally, sat one of the two imperial supreme courts (the *Reichskammergericht*) in the free city of Wetzlar.

Was the heterogeneity of this region of the German-Roman empire typical? There was hardly any "typical" region in the empire. This heterogeneity of state form is sometimes exaggerated but bears consideration. There were many Germanies, some with greater freedom of estates, some with more muscular absolutist programs; there were free cities, small free communities, confederations, and so on. It is a famous conundrum even to measure how many polities, let alone how many actual laws, there were in the broader federated empire. The Hessian and Rhine-Main region appears to have been freer than Brandenburg-Prussia or the Austrian crown lands in the same era.[30] Its complexity and political pluralism somewhat resembled early Swiss federation polities, though by the late eighteenth century most of these small Hessian and Rhine-Main region polities would be folded into the two dominant Hessian states centered in Cassel and Darmstadt.[31]

A focus on this regionally delimited network of thinkers and actors, rather than a single person, court, or state (all more popular approaches among historians), yields some advantages. For one thing, sources from the region exhibit a relative coherence because the actors and regimes were in frequent communion and communication. Second, the Hessian and Rhine-Main region was a region of what Bismarck later derided as "Kleinstaaterei": the many small states each had their own policies and interests. As a consequence, they had their own laws, courts, chanceries, archives, and libraries, and several had their own law schools. These many courts and law schools produced a great deal of legal literature. It was *a region rich in law*. In terms of professional legal writing, this abundance included dissertations, police codes, and law codes. In terms of

30 Two recent works contradict the received view of Prussia: William W. Hagen, *Ordinary Prussians: Brandenburg Junkers and Villagers, 1500–1840*, New Studies in European History (Cambridge: Cambridge University Press, 2002) and Sean A. Eddie, *Freedom's Price: Serfdom, Subjection, and Reform in Prussia: 1648–1848* (Oxford: Oxford University Press, 2013).

31 Thomas A. Brady, Jr., *Turning Swiss: Cities and Empire, 1450–1550*, Cambridge Studies in Early Modern History (Cambridge; New York: Cambridge University Press, 1985).

actual practice, more courts heard more lawsuits and produced more judicial decisions. This high volume was important. *More (if smaller) regimes* produced *more juristic activity* – that is, *more law*.[32] (Figure 4.) While precedent in the English sense (*stare decisis*) did not formally operate, nevertheless jurists reverently cited decisions made by major courts and consilia penned by famous jurists, even state courts were likely to follow the previous judgments of those more famous or revered than they, and local courts were likely to follow the high courts above them in their territory. Jurisprudence was not so much a sharpening of rules implied by earlier sources (like English precedent) as it was a thriving, polyvocal tradition (in the sense of handing down and building on earlier work), replete with disagreement and change, but also with concurrence, refinement, and extension.[33] Much of this development happened in relation to university law faculties, where faculty members were consulted on difficult local legal issues in the sixteenth and seventeenth centuries.

I draw partial inspiration from Jean Baechler's argument about the origins of capitalism in Europe, though of course my quarry here is freedom, not capitalism. According to Baechler, the ultimate (deepest, oldest) cause of the development of capitalism in Europe was the fact that, more or less, Europe was a largely homogenous cultural space but one in which there had never been hegemonic, unitary, monarchical control, unlike in Byzantium or eastern Asian empires. Cultural homogeneity (or at least affinity) produced trust and understanding, while continuous pluralistic rivalry prevented ossification or the exclusion of innovative technologies and products.[34]

32 Comparison might be made here to the idea that the diverse, semi-independent American states are "laboratories of federalism." Different states now and then try new policies, different ways of living and governing. I am indebted to Tom McSweeney for pointing this out. As I remark elsewhere, there is actually a direct connection from the Holy Roman Empire to American federalism through Montesquieu, who somewhat admired the federalist structure of the Empire and made a point much like this. The American Founding Fathers were influenced by Montesquieu's conception of federalism.

33 Wilder, "Teaching Old Dogs New Tricks."

34 See Jean Baechler, *The Origins of Capitalism* (New York: St Martin's Press, 1976), Chapter 7. A comparable argument was made more recently by Richard Davis: "Though the empires of the East had highly developed civilizations and cultures, their centralized political systems discouraged economic experimentation and thus the creation of a range of options that might have been employed to meet new economic challenges. In the West, in contrast, the lack of a large-scale political, and therefore economic, system at the beginning of the Middle Ages not only allowed experimentation, but actually encouraged it because of competition among the fragmented political bodies that made up western Europe. By creating a wide range of options, the system promoted economic growth. At the same time, it encouraged an independence of mind and spirit that would complement the later

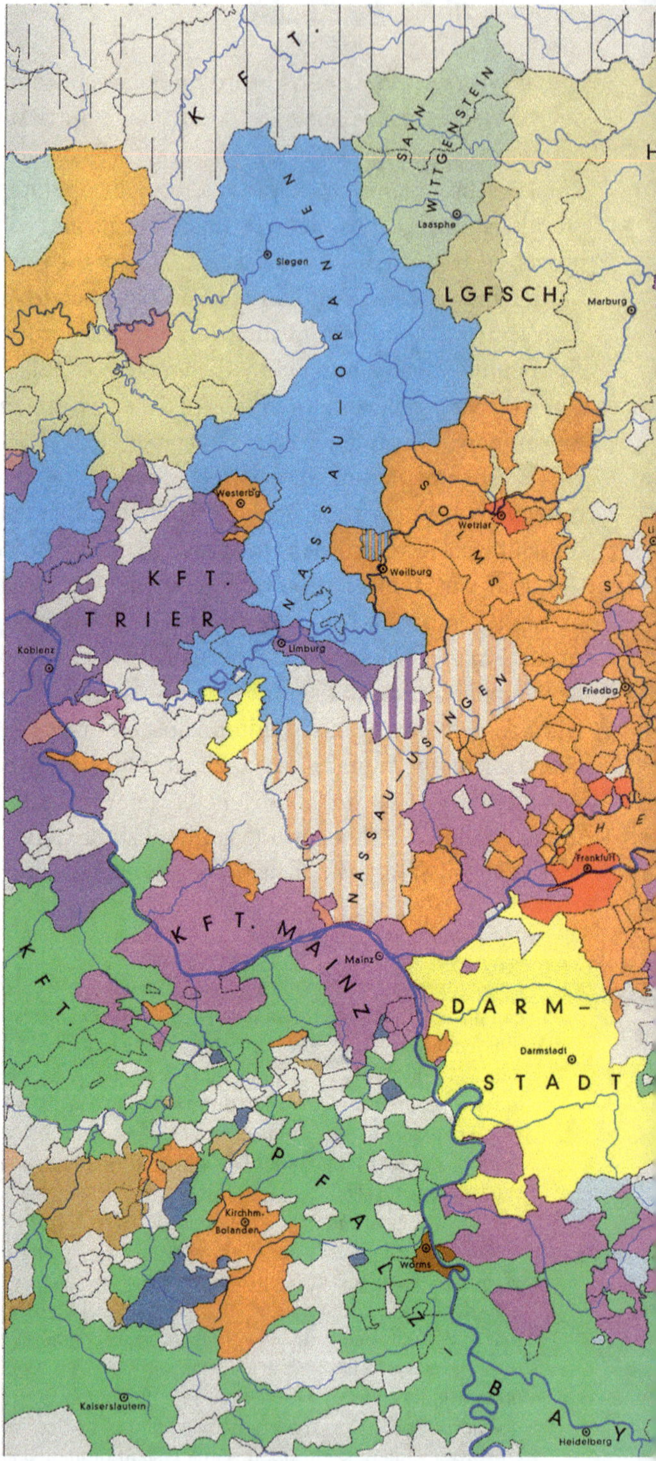

FIGURE 4 Map of some of the many sources of law in the region. The many different laws applicable in different regional locales are listed in the caption box, with the small horizontal boxes indicating the significance of the given law in the given area

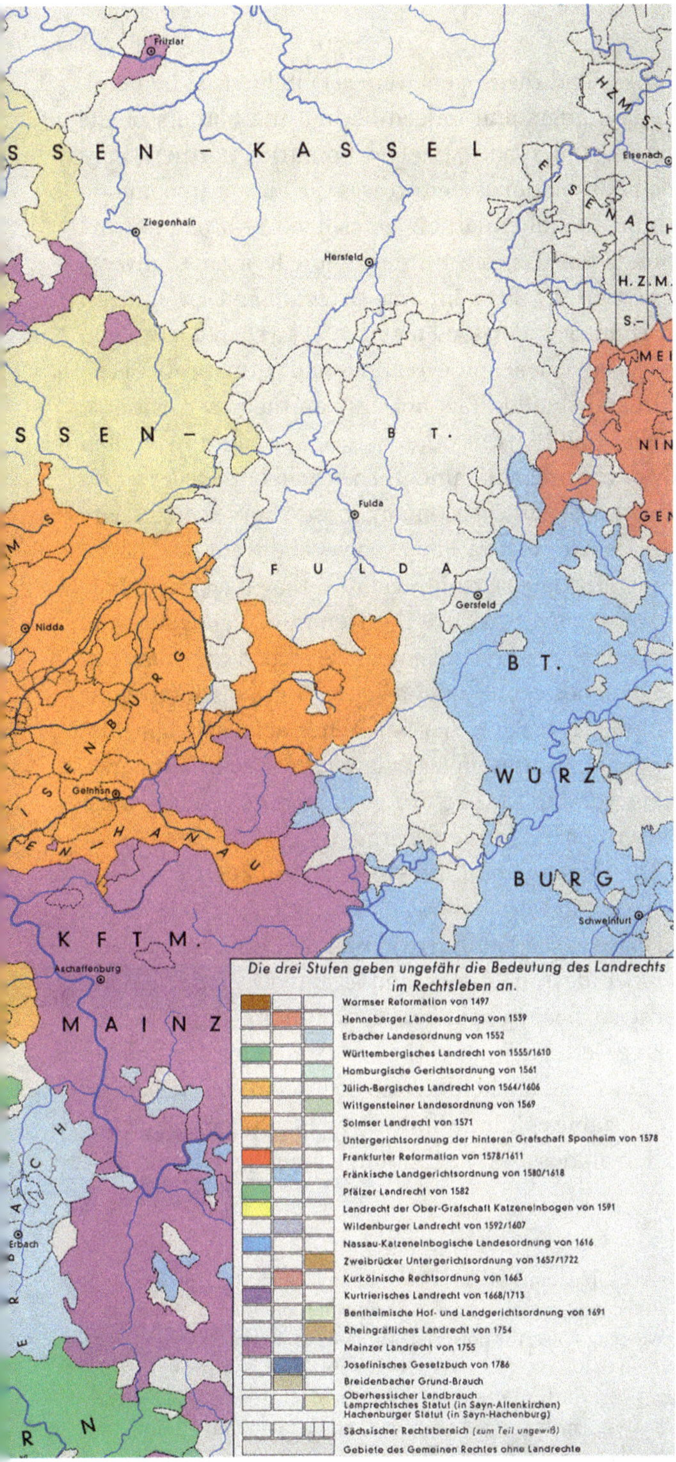
Fritzlar
Eisenach
Ziegenhain
Hersfeld
H. Z. M.
Fulda
Gersfeld
Nidda
Gelnhausen
Schweinfurt
Aschaffenburg
Erbach
KFTM. MAINZ
FULDA
BT. WÜRZBURG
Die drei Stufen geben ungefähr die Bedeutung des Landrechts im Rechtsleben an.
Wormser Reformation von 1497
Henneberger Landesordnung von 1539
Erbacher Landesordnung von 1552
Württembergisches Landrecht von 1555/1610
Homburgische Gerichtsordnung von 1561
Jülich-Bergisches Landrecht von 1564/1606
Wittgensteiner Landesordnung von 1569
Solmser Landrecht von 1571
Untergerichtsordnung der hinteren Grafschaft Sponheim von 1578
Frankfurter Reformation von 1578/1611
Fränkische Landgerichtsordnung von 1580/1618
Pfälzer Landrecht von 1582
Landrecht der Ober-Grafschaft Katzenelnbogen von 1591
Wildenburger Landrecht von 1592/1607
Nassau-Katzenelnbogische Landesordnung von 1616
Zweibrücker Untergerichtsordnung von 1657/1722
Kurkölnische Rechtsordnung von 1663
Kurtrierisches Landrecht von 1668/1713
Bentheimische Hof- und Landgerichtsordnung von 1691
Rheingräfliches Landrecht von 1754
Mainzer Landrecht von 1755
Josefinisches Gesetzbuch von 1786
Breidenbacher Grund-Brauch
Oberhessischer Landbrauch
Lamprechtsches Statut (in Sayn-Altenkirchen)
Hachenburger Statut (in Sayn-Hachenburg)
Sächsischer Rechtsbereich (zum Teil ungewiß)
Gebiete des Gemeinen Rechtes ohne Landrechte

In our context here, jurists and their peers were also influenced by developments beyond territorial borders and indeed beyond the borders of the empire in such realms as England, France, the Low Countries, northern Italy, and the Levant. The broad, international context was the European common law (*ius commune*), meaning the inherited Roman civil law as it had evolved between about the tenth and fourteenth centuries, before it began to diverge significantly in different countries.[35] Even into the sixteenth and seventeenth centuries, jurists in every country understood that this was a shared law based on shared inheritance, so despite divergent evolutions and antipathy between specific states, they could and should draw not only on their own national law but also on the parallel traditions in other states. German jurists often traveled abroad for study or cultural enrichment. They read both *belles lettres* and prominent, current works of political economy, mostly from Scotland and France. Some dabbled in science (natural philosophy) and were part of the Republic of Letters. Through the late sixteenth century, they traveled to Italy to study or to copy rare, celebrated texts like the Florentine Pandects, or to Switzerland to train with Calvin or Hotman. They spoke French or Italian. Not until perhaps the mid eighteenth century did a sense of the distinctiveness of German institutions and ideas begin to develop. While acknowledging the international context, this book focuses on legal developments in Germany – that is, involving Germans working for German governments, reading Latin and German sources, and writing in Latin and German.

My arguments about the Hessian and Rhine-Main region and the empire are focused on a particular period from about 1648 to 1786 (the date of the latest of my sources, and close to the Kantian explosion of German idealism). During this time, many older ideas, doctrines, and legal tools were still operative, including many received, heavyweight conceptions of freedom (ancient Germanic freedom, the Free German Empire, the Protestant idea of Christian Freedom, etc. – Chapter 2) as well as the doctrine of prescription (Chapters 4–5). But the importance of stable cultural affinity as an incubator for borrowing, imitation, and mutation of ideas and institutions cannot be overstated.

---

emergence of other kinds of freedom, associated, for example, with the growth of self-government in towns, the emergence of representative institutions, and the Protestant Reformation. In a less sweeping sense, the powerful economic component in the making of modern freedom assured that among its earliest elements would be a strong association between liberty and the security of property." See Richard W. Davis, ed., *The Origins of Modern Freedom in the West*, The Making of Modern Freedom (Stanford: Stanford University Press, 1995), Epilogue, p. 314m.

35 See glossary: common law or imperial common law.

To understand the interrelation of arguments about property and freedom presented here, it may help to show the means, motive, and opportunity (to borrow terminology from modern US criminal law) for freedoms to be developed as they did. First, people had the *means* to change their lives, change property rights, and potentially expand their freedoms. Such means included ideas, institutions like courts and law schools, and various legal strategies used by interested parties (Chapters 3–6). Individuals' *motives* may well have been acquisitiveness or pursuit of power or freedom, but states also had motives – to implement a certain sumptuary policy, restore a previous order governed by religion or ideology, or increase wealth and productivity in the land. Finally, I contend that the *opportunity* that precipitated the developments discussed in this book was the highly unusual situation of the Thirty Years' War and its aftermath. The War was not short, like the Schmalkaldic War a century earlier, but long and extremely destructive; in Hesse alone, it was twice as long and more devastating than World War Two (relatively speaking). The Thirty Years' War provided a very unusual opportunity for new freedoms to be developed. Altered circumstances gave thoughtful people a chance to imagine a more personalized freedom, which they assimilated into "German Freedom."

6 Commercialization

To understand property law in this period, we must understand how commercialization was changing. By commercialization I mean a complex phenomenon of increasing levels of agricultural production, with surplus beyond subsistence intended for sale at market; increasingly systematic exploitation of real estate for said production; and refinement of paper financial instruments to improve their transferability and security. The term overlaps semantically with what is often called the development of capitalism.[36]

The growth of commercialization in Europe during the early modern period was closely associated with contests over property rights, which grew in number, intensity, and precision over the seventeenth and eighteenth centuries (Chapter 3). The resolutions of these disputes both helped to change the system of commerce and production and to transform legal systems. Property law became more individualistic, describing and safeguarding fungible individual

36 There were other aspects of the emergence of capitalism such as its mysterious acquisitive "spirit" (Weber), motor power, commodity production, standard of living, and changing supply and demand. These are beyond the scope of this book or its sources.

property rights under a broad paradigm of equality and civil liberty on a scale, and with a uniformity, previously unseen in Europe except in the few shining, commercial city republics like Amsterdam, Florence, or Genoa.

The credit world of early modern Europe expanded over the centuries for several reasons (Chapter 6). One was the growth of inter-regional long-distance trade with agents in far-away trading centers – such as Bruges and Champagne earlier on, and later London, Amsterdam, or Frankfurt am Main. Another stimulus to overall trade came from the massive increase in liquidity (circulating money) around Europe that resulted from the Spanish extraction of silver and gold from Central and South America, followed later by increased monetary velocity associated with clearing banks. Demand for other kinds of investments and luxuries in monarchical and seigneurial courts across Europe also stimulated increase in production and discovery of new sources of both raw and finished goods. Both supply and demand dynamics were made more simple and secure and less expensive with the increase in the use of bills of exchange in the seventeenth and eighteenth centuries, especially with the spread of discounting and endorsement.[37]

With parallels to the mid-twentieth century, Germany's political and economic situation in the seventeenth century comprised apocalyptic war and economic collapse followed by "miraculous" economic recovery and modernization.[38] This was epitomized by lavish Baroque courts across the empire just as elsewhere on the continent. Such courts were centers of patronage of new arts, schools, and universities.[39] The political-military side saw the growth of expensive new fortifications and of large, powerful standing armies. Although France was the Continental heavyweight, numerous smaller powers such as the dozens of waxing German principalities followed suit with their courts, universities, and armies. For these reasons, historians have seen the eighteenth century as a period of economic modernization. Rulers were under pressure to "make comprehensive reforms" in the areas of agricultural and financial regulation, import and export rules, and taxation. The period also "revealed

37 Anja Amend-Traut, *Wechselverbindlichkeiten vor dem Reichskammergericht: Praktiziertes Zivilrecht in der Frühen Neuzeit*, Vol. 54, Quellen und Forschungen zur höchsten Gerichtsbarkeit im Alten Reich (Cologne; Weimar; Vienna: Böhlau, 2009), pp. 108–110.

38 Emmanuel Kreike, *Scorched Earth: Environmental Warfare as a Crime Against Humanity and Nature* (Princeton: Princeton University Press, 2021).

39 Bruce T. Moran, *The Alchemical World of the German Court: Occult Philosophy and Chemical Medicine in the Circle of Moritz of Hessen, 1572–1632*, Vol. 29, Sudhoffs Archiv. Beihefte. (Stuttgart: F. Steiner, 1991); Hans Philippi, *Landgraf Karl von Hessen-Kassel: Ein Deutscher Fürst der Barockzeit*, Vol. 34, Veröffentlichungen der Historischen Kommission für Hessen (Marburg: Elwert, 1976).

a growing divergence of interests in society through the rise of the urban classes."[40]

Commercialization accelerated in Germany after the Thirty Years' War. Sources for this book reveal elements of forms of commercialization which economic historians tend to associate with the growth of early capitalism: investments in large-scale agriculture, natural resources, and industrial production; changes in law facilitating the mobilization of real estate wealth; and the growth of paper money, which made the transfer of large amounts of money easier and more secure over long distances, whether the equivalent of a few days' ride or all the way across continental Europe or the oceans.

Investment in resources expanded dramatically, consistent with Adam Smith's contemporary analysis of what he called the growth of trade within a "system of natural liberty," and his work was translated into German and published in Leipzig *the first year it appeared* (London: 1776; Leipzig: 1776) and became widely read in the empire. There are ample examples of Germans seeking to liquidate real property and to make the law give them maximal flexibility and security in how they could use the issuing "capital." Common farmers struggled to wrestle free of old seigneurial obligations such as labor service. Landlords fought to turn common lands into solely owned estates they could privately control and harvest. Joint owners of common estates similarly sought to retain joint control of those estates for their own benefit, rather like shareholders.[41] Sometimes one person's freedom was another's or others' loss or subjection. As the use of bills of exchange spread, they afforded people additional freedom and security, although until the late eighteenth century bills were restricted by traditional rules about who could use them and how transferring them was limited by what previous bearers had owed other parties.

The legal changes described in this book – namely, the emergence of legally consequential ideas about natural right and stronger, more broadly held property rights – helped to tear down the estate and collective protections of the old society of orders and to uproot traditional sources of authority (especially

---

40 Dreitzel, *Absolutismus und ständische Verfassung in Deutschland*, p. 15. Reconstruction after 1648, the author further argues, "led to a kind of economic miracle [*Wirtschaftswunder*] for nobles and princes" whose high point was "the period of Baroque princely power in the decades of the transition from seventeenth to the eighteenth centuries."

41 For commons theory, see Elinor Ostrom, *Governing the Commons: The Evolution of Institutions for Collective Action*, Political Economy of Institutions and Decisions (Cambridge: Cambridge University Press, 1990). In this German context, see Colin F. Wilder, "Property, Possession and Prescription: The Rule of Law in the Hessian and Rhine-Main Region of Germany, 1648–1776" (Ph.D. thesis, University of Chicago, 2010), pp. 214–265.

the seigneurie), and created the property law and commercial institutions fostering capitalism's emergence in Germany around the end of the eighteenth century and into the post-Napoleonic period. In the Hessian and Rhine-Main region, as in England and Scotland, this was done while preserving older forms and appearance, giving the illusion of tradition and continuity.[42]

7 Political Economy

Jurists' views were often influenced by the political economic ideas of their day when governments made concerted efforts to increase production and trade. By the same token, not a few jurists also penned studies of and influenced economic policy.[43] In this as in other contexts, affairs in Germany paralleled those elsewhere. The Central European variant of mercantilism, cameralism, focused on domestic production and accumulation, as Germany lacked foreign markets and produced mostly for regional trade. Cameralist policy makers also sought to create liquidity through experimental patented bank monopolies. Cameralist writers often served regimes either as ministers or as university professors. Molded by German princely paternalism, they promoted the growth of the resources – and the tax base – of the *Land*, all of which in some sense belonged to the territorial prince.[44] The programs of mercantilists and cameralists aimed to enrich societies, especially in the form of the supply

42 It is common for legal doctrines to justify themselves in terms of their predecessors. European law (including all its derivative imperial jurisdictions such as white colonial North America) employs both rhetoric and justificatory strategies which connect new law to old law, thus creating continuity (some superficial, some substantial). Good accounts of tradition include Alasdair C. MacIntyre, *Whose justice? Which rationality?* (Notre Dame: University of Notre Dame Press, 1988), p. 12, and Pier G. Monateri, "Black Gaius: A Quest for the Multicultural Origins of the 'Western Legal Tradition'," *Hastings Law Journal* 51, no. 3 (2000), pp. 27–28, based on ideas in Harold Berman, *Law and Revolution: The Formation of the Western Legal Tradition* (Cambridge: Harvard University Press, 1983).

43 Karin Nehlsen-Von Stryk, "Die Monopolgutachten des rechtsgelehrten Humanisten Conrad Peutinger aus dem frühen 16. Jahrhundert," *Zeitschrift für Neuere Rechtsgeschichte* 10 (1988); Fritz Blaich, "Die hessische Antimonopolpolitik unter Landgraf Moritz," *Hessisches Jahrbuch für Landesgeschichte* (1966); Johann Hermann Fürstenau, "De meritis Lutheri in oeconomiam publicam et privatam," ed. Carl Gottfried Fürstenau (Rinteln: Johannes Godofredus Enax, 1749); Fürstenau, *Versuch einer Apologie des physiokratischen Systems*.

44 Cameralism developed out of "house father" literature, i.e. the tradition of household economy traceable through writers like Becher, Seckendorf, Hohberg, or Sonnenfels all the way back to Xenophon. For scholarship see the earlier Albion W. Small, *The Cameralists: The Pioneers of German Social Polity* (Chicago: University of Chicago Press, 1909),

of valuable resources like bullion, other ore, timber, or manufactured commodities. Increasing trade was a means toward this goal, to be sure, but so was the extraction of forced labor, compelled through domination. More wealth and resources across society meant that society was richer, therefore the tax base bigger, tax revenue higher, and finally the government therefore stronger.

Until about the 1760s, when jurists wrote about political economy their ideas tended to reflect cameralist thought, with discussion of harmony, balance, flourishing, productivity, and the paternalistic duty of the ruler over "his" domain. Some cameralists like Joseph von Sonnenfels called for the abolition of serfdom and stronger property rights for serfs and small farmers. But most jurists, working as they did for a variety of interest groups, tended to defend the order of concrete (that is, actually existing) rights and vested interests. They might argue that in theory serfs were free, but few called for radical land reform. Physiocratic and liberal ideas became popular in Germany soon after they appeared in France and Scotland in the 1760s. Publications soon appeared, including in Hesse, that critiqued rentiership, monopolies, and other privileges, and advocated that serf labor be reduced and serfs granted stronger property rights on their farmlands.[45] The Hessian regime in Cassel had long been experimenting with economic stimulus policies which fell halfway between cameralism and liberalism, such as granting tax incentives to industrious new settlers, trying to expand the grain market, and patenting banks to put more money into circulation.[46] Such pro-growth policies were aided through the strengthening of property rights (i.e. in land

---

Otto Brunner, "Johann Joachim Bechers Entwurf einer '*Oeconomia ruralis et domestica*'," in *Festgabe an das Österreichische Staatsarchiv zur Feier des 200-jährigen Bestandes des Haus-, Hof- und Staatsarchives*, ed. Richard Meister, Otto Brunner, and Alphons Lhotsky (Vienna: R. M. Rohrer, 1949), and Otto Brunner, *Adeliges Landleben und europäischer Geist: Leben und Werk Wolf Helmhards von Hohberg, 1612–1688* (Salzburg: O. Müller, 1949). More recently for Hesse, see Peter K. Taylor, *Indentured to Liberty: Peasant Life and the Hessian Military State, 1688–1815* (Ithaca: Cornell University Press, 1994). See also the recent and very helpful André Wakefield, *The Disordered Police State: German Cameralism as Science and Practice* (Chicago: University of Chicago Press, 2009).

45 Blickle, *Von der Leibeigenschaft zu den Menschenrechten*.

46 Hans-Joachim Braun, "Economic Theory and Policy in Germany, 1750–1800," *Journal of European Economic History* 4 (1975), p. 302–311; Fürstenau, *Versuch einer Apologie des physiokratischen Systems*, p. 32; Ulrich Friedrich Kopp and Claus Wittich, *Handbuch zur Kenntnis der Hessen-Casselischen Landes-Verfassung und Rechte* (Cassel: 1796–1808), Th. 11, "Capitalisten," pp. 271–272; Friedrich Wilhelm Strieder, *Über die Monopolien. Nebst Bemerkungen über die in dieser Materie von dem Herrn Probst und Prälaten Quirl und Herrn Kammerrath Klippstein zum Vorschein gekommene Schriften* (Hannover: Helwingische Hofbuchhandlung, 1779).

and appurtenant rights), emancipating of marginal social figures like serfs, and enhancing of capital mobility. I suspect that, just as Napoleon would later free the serfs in order to draft them, here cameralist elites sought to free common people in order to tax them and their produce. Enrich the elites by enriching the base.

8 Sources

The sources for this book are the publications and other professional writings of jurists in the Hessian and Rhine-Main region from the seventeenth and eighteenth centuries. Most of these jurists or legal operators had studied law at a university law faculty and had written and defended jurisdoctoral theses. Most obtained their license to practice law, after which their careers while varied tended to advance through a *cursus honorum* (a course of increasingly high honors and positions in a typical career). This was not exactly one-dimensional, but it proceeded roughly as follows: student, private practitioner of law, lower instructor at a school or university (*Privatdozent*), professor. More advanced strata included serving as dean, vice chancellor, state's attorney (that is, representative of the prince's or state's interests), judge, chancellor, and perhaps even regime regent or a bench on the imperial supreme court. Most legal operators were bourgeois – men from prominent or rising families who could afford to enter the professions. Legal training was highly concentrated; there were only a few dozen esteemed university law faculties in the entire German-speaking part of the empire, though one could train at many lesser institutions.

Perhaps a tenth of these jurists could be called *gentleman jurists*, lower nobility who trained in law and used their training to serve in aristocratic associations, such as the Burg und Stadt Friedberg, Reichsganerbschaft Lindheim, or the Riedesel republic. These associations and groups like them were tightly organized local clans or networks of clans. Such gentleman jurists had been schooled in the *belles lettres*, speaking French or Italian and going on tours to gain culture, technical knowledge, and professional experience. Members of the intelligentsia of the day, they were familiar with current literature and conversant with new theories from the sciences, especially political economy. They produced legal arguments, *ex parte* for their clients, which were generally valid (in the sense of *well formed*). They were trained enough and rounded enough to be, on average, able legal operators.

The best way to classify jurists' writings is by the career stage at which they were produced. A *law student* produced lecture notes but more importantly a jurisdoctoral thesis, which was published, collected, read, and cited as a source of law. These were printed by a privileged printer and sold both locally and in bigger crossroads of learning like Frankfurt am Main or Leipzig. A *private lawyer* assembled documents supportive of the party or cause he was employed to serve and then formulated arguments in *lites* (documents submitted in connection with the hearing of a lawsuit). *Judges* produced decisions, combining their own research with a rearticulation of the arguments of one or more party to a suit. At higher levels, the work was more synthetic: *Law professors* furnished their treatises with documents and arguments they had encountered earlier as students, as lawyers, and as judges, as well as archival material discovered on research trips or original research materials they discovered while on legal business for their client at suit. As *government officials such as councilors*, jurists considered reports and requests and issued new policies. Law professors, especially more senior ones and "primary chairs," were usually the most authoritative jurists in a territory or regime, and they frequently rose from there to be the highest judges or *chancellors* or even *regents*. So senior professors' opinions mattered enormously. This book is based on reading several hundred such sources (most of them connected somehow to the Hessian and Rhine-Main region). All of these have informed my arguments, though I have selected about a dozen for closer reading and explication. Most were written by members of what we might call the lower German Enlightenment[47] – lesser figures known to some specialist historians, but not as famous as prominent Enlightenment jurists whose work is still read today as philosophy or political theory, like Grotius, Pufendorf, Thomasius, or Christian Wolff. Those major figures play a smaller role in this story because they do not address the level of detail I deal with here. My source jurists were educated, active, effective, and well-known and respected in their time – they were the men who made and used the law that is the subject of this book.

What bodies of law did these jurists study and draw upon? The Holy Roman Empire of the German Nation, comprising most of Central Europe, recognized a combination of ancient Roman law, modern (seventeenth- and eighteenth-century) theory, and local custom. (Although this book will make reference to local custom, it is in no way an exhaustive exploration of it.[48]) In discussions of

47 This is a play on the clever phrasing of Robert Darnton, "The High Enlightenment and the Low-Life of Literature in Pre-Revolutionary France," *Past and Present* 51 (1971).

48 The most exhaustive compilation of German custom was that performed by Jacob Grimm two centuries years ago: Jacob Grimm, ed., *Weisthümer* (Göttingen: Dietrich, 1840–1878). And indeed the subject of what local custom was, how stable and explorable it was, whether we have sources which allow us to discover it, and how it was influenced and

governing law, public law is usually distinguished from private law, and several main areas or bodies are also distinguished – civil law, sometimes criminal law, canon law (or other law of the church), and special bodies like merchant law or feudal law. The discovery and uses of various sources of law, especially ancient Roman civil law from the Pandects, are generally described as the reception of Roman law, a long process extending from about 1200 to 1800 in which ancient and medieval ideas, specifically about civil law from ancient Rome, influenced the legal practices of modern polities, for example Germany.[49] Two concepts, central to this book, that emerged from this legal evolution concerned *natural* freedom and modern jurisprudence of *civil* liberty.

While most of the legal writings I use cited and discussed law derived from or connected to Roman civil law, they also occasionally would cite and discuss the law of the Roman Catholic church hierarchy (canon law) and what was widely taken to be folk custom (Germanic law).

For most of the nineteenth and twentieth centuries, historians would have considered the subject matter of this book (the growing sphere of freedom created by property law) as a matter of private, civil law. The distinction between private law and public law persists in some form today, although scholars also suggest that historically it is open to some doubt. Public law is a category of

---

interpreted by the technical jurists of modern (German) Roman law in the sixteenth, seventeenth, and eighteenth centuries, is a fascinating and difficult problem.

49 The reception of Roman law generally refers to the idea that at a certain point, a version of the ancient Roman civil law was adopted (hence "received") into the Roman-German empire, where previously it had not been used. Contrary to this old idea, it seems clearly to rather have been the case that Roman civil jurisprudence had been continuously learned and brought to German governments since at latest the thirteenth century, and probably hundreds of years prior to that. I discuss the reception of Roman law briefly again at Ch. 3, p. 93, n. 24. A good primer on the topic is Manlio Bellomo, *The Common Legal Past of Europe: 1000–1800*, Vol. 4, Studies in Medieval and Early Modern Canon Law (Washington, D.C.: Catholic University of America Press, 1995). More detailed, older, and authoritative is Wieacker, *History of Private Law*. For the broader geography of the receptions of Roman law, see Douglas J. Osler, ed., *Bibliographica iuridica* (Frankfurt am Main: Vittorio Klostermann, 2000–2009). A sample primary source of this in the Hessian context is the autobiography of Marburg humanist professor, jurist, and regime servant Hermann Vultejus (1555–1634), published later as "Vita Hermanni Vulteji ab ipso descripta," in *Auserlesene kleine Schrifften*, ed. Johann Georg Estor, Vol. (i.e. Band) 2 (Giessen: Johann Philipp Krieger, 1746 [orig. 1735]). A classic study of the reception of Roman is P. Legendre, *La pénétration du droit romain dans le droit canonique classique: recherche sur le mandat (1140–1254)* (1957). A recent study of the medieval Roman and canon view of property law is Emanuele Conte, "Modena 1182: The Origins of a New Paradigm of Ownership: The Interface between Historical Contingency and the Scholarly Invention of Legal Categories," *Glossae: European Journal of Legal History* 15 (2018).

law descending from ancient Roman jurisprudence. It is the law of the state, meaning such things as legislation, officeholding, constitutions as fundamental law of the whole land, and any rights or duties assigned generally to citizens by virtue of their membership in the polity. Private law is usually understood to be that set of laws governing the creation and use of private rights – essentially property rights – held by individual members of society privately, including ownership of land, entry into contracts, and the use of money. This is one of several meanings of private law. Thus democratic decision-making, separation of powers, state authority, and civil liberties are elements of public law, while debts to landlords and easements are matters of private law. (In and after the sixteenth century, there also developed a distinctive, new field of public law in Europe, called police law (the *Polizeistaat*), which described regulations of public order, morals, public safety, obeisance to religious rules including public church functions, and sometimes relations between different social estates such as lords and tenants.[50]) Roman public and private law would take curious paths in the middle ages and early modern period. Most significant was the way jurists used private law to interpret the rights of kings, princes, and sometimes clerics. The understanding of corporations (*universitates*) in Roman law drew from both public and private law, and ultimately was used to interpret churches, the Church, monarchies, cities, noble unions, and indeed universities and other organizations. Most of these developments are seen in both German and broader European contexts.

The distinction between public law and private law sits uneasily, however, in the pre-modern German context. Since the earliest days of settled, codified German political organization eleven centuries ago, public and private authority have been mixed. The distinction between public law and private law was an artificial imposition from Roman jurisprudence which could not be cleanly applied either to German legal custom or to the developing practices of kings, emperors, princes, counts, and even seigneurs from the high middle ages onward.[51] The example of landlordship can quickly illustrate the point: even into the eighteenth century, one finds local landlords exercising elements of what look like both public and private authority – levying taxes and dues, supervising courts, exercising legitimate monopoly on violence, collecting dues on landholding, supervising morals, owning (or quasi-owning) serfs, and so on. To be sure, the extent and contents of the suite of rights and

---

50 Marc Raeff, *The Well-Ordered Police State: Social and Institutional Change through Law in the Germanies and Russia, 1600–1800* (New Haven: Yale University Press, 1983).

51 See, e.g., Otto Brunner, *Land and Lordship: Structures of Governance in Medieval Austria*, 1st ed. (Philadelphia: University of Pennsylvania Press, 1984 [orig. 1931]).

prerogative authorities belonging to landlords changed over the centuries and varied by region, mode of holding, etc. But, even in the eighteenth century, when one speaks of freedom and property rights, there are elements of both public law (freedom and authority *vis à vis* the state) and private law (bilateral, non-universal, unequal, fungible rights and obligations). We cannot, therefore, categorize the phenomena in this book as merely private.

We tend to think of modern public law as generated by state authority, in opposition to private law arising from market transactions and contracts. In the seventeenth and eighteenth centuries, things which look like public law (such as jurisdictional and tax authority) could arise from activities which look to modern eyes like matters of private law. In some circumstances, rulers and their councilors could enact statutes. But valid law was created in many other ways – for example, by new interpretations of rules including court decisions and new teachings of law faculty. There were also other, subtler ways law was made, such as when a party to a dispute advanced an interpretation of laws and rights that was later affirmed and generalized by the court judges. New law was in effect produced when jurists discovered, edited, and studied heretofore unknown local customs. Law could also be created through what would today be considered private law, in the sense of actions between individual persons at a sub-state level, recorded as the concrete order of vested rights and interests, altered slowly through prescription.[52]

•••

The history of freedom being an exciting and attractive theme, at least in my mind, it is not surprising that numerous other books have been written touching on it in one way or another, in one or another context. Excellent tokens from several close fields can be mentioned (in addition to the works mentioned earlier such as those of Diethelm Klippel and Georg Schmidt), if just to underline the saliency of this investigation. John Phillip Reid's *Rule of Law* (2004) makes a similar argument for *England*, and indeed readers familiar with *English legal history* will find many affinities between the master narratives of that field and my arguments here. Several of the essays in Dale Van Kley's anthology *The French Idea of Freedom* (1994) sought to trace the *origins of liberal ideas in France*, specifically influences on the *Déclaration des droits de*

52 Just as court precedent in common law-based countries has the effect of creating new law, there was a similar process of law production from many sources in civil law countries like the Holy Roman Empire. For a preliminary extension of the theory of how law is created, see Wilder, "Teaching Old Dogs New Tricks."

l'homme et du citoyen of 1789. Another work on *property rights, freedom, and the French Revolution* is Rafe Blaufarb, *The Great Demarcation* (2016). Several contributions to Richard Davis's anthology *The Origins of Modern Freedom in the West* (1995) seek the *origins, on a broad European scale, of well-recognized liberal political elements* such as judicial protection of both person and property, free elections and habeas corpus. The recent anthology by Mary Lindemann and Jared Poley (2017) speaks to the *growth of ideas about money in German history* during the period considered here. Some recent work has excavated *elements of liberal politics in the German ancien régime, such as republicanism and federalism* (which while allies of individual civil liberty are not the same thing). James Sheehan's *German Liberalism in the Nineteenth Century* (1978) "[attempted] a synthesis which would describe how German liberalism looked when all of its components were seen together." Some historical studies of the institutional features of Western exceptionalism, such as Nathan Rosenberg and L. E. Birdzell, *How the West Grew Rich* (1986) also plough close to our fields.[53]

Where to start then? Chapter 2 presents three influential ideas of freedom which laid the theoretical and legal foundations for the jurisprudence of property and freedom in the late seventeenth and eighteenth centuries: the idea of "ancient Germanic freedom" during the period from Tacitus to the Renaissance; the Free German Empire of the sixteenth century; and the concept of "German freedom" that emerged during the seventeenth century. Chapter 3 presents changes in institutions: the expansion of courts, law faculties, printing, and library collections, as well as the *usus modernus* and ideas of possession and prescription. The next two chapters focus on real rights: Chapter 4 on immovable property (lands, houses, etc.), and Chapter 5 on freedoms (or immunities) from lordly extractions such as taxes, dues, and labor.

53 John Phillip Reid, *Rule of Law: The Jurisprudence of Liberty in the Seventeenth and Eighteenth Centuries* (Dekalb: Northern Illinois University Press, 2004); Dale K. Van Kley, ed., *The French Idea of Freedom: The Old Regime and the Declaration of Rights of 1789*, The Making of modern freedom (Stanford: Stanford University Press, 1994); Rafe Blaufarb, *The Great Demarcation: The French Revolution and the Invention of Modern Property* (Oxford: Oxford University Press, 2016); Davis, *The Origins of Modern Freedom in the West*; Mary Lindemann and Jared Poley, eds., *Money in the German-Speaking Lands*, Vol. 17, Spektrum: Publications of the German Studies Association); Jürgen Heideking and James A. Henretta, eds., *Republicanism and Liberalism in America and the German States, 1750–1850*, Publications of the German Historical Institute (Cambridge: Cambridge University Press, 2002); Umbach, *Federalism and Enlightenment in Germany*; James J. Sheehan, *German Liberalism in the Nineteenth Century* (Chicago: University of Chicago Press, 1978), p. 2; Nathan Rosenberg and L. E. Birdzell, *How the West Grew Rich: The Economic Transformation of the Industrial World* (New York: Basic Books, 1986).

Both were considered "real" rights connected to estates, rather than "personal" rights tied to individual persons or social classes such as widows, farmers, or Jews. Chapter 4 shows how people gained greater freedom to dispose of their real estate – to buy, sell, use, encumber, or give its use to others. Chapter 5 presents evidence that, during and after the Thirty Years War (which ended in 1648 with the Peace of Westphalia), common rural people as well as nobles had stopped paying taxes or dues or performing labor obligations, and that this phenomenon of extraction-avoidance and non-compliance apparently continued for at least several decades. Jurists wrestled with this problem, developing the existing concepts of possession and prescription to justify non-performance, while grounding their arguments in an ultimately scholastic concept of natural freedom. Chapter 6 focuses on a different kind of property, money. Governments in the Hessian and Rhine-Main region including Frankfurt am Main introduced and promulgated the use of bills of exchange (the major form of pre-modern paper money). This enhanced people's ability to borrow and lend in an easy and secure way, whether over short or long distances. All of these developments contributed to advancing an idea of natural freedom not directly tied to ownership of spaces or of things, but rather what we might today call self-ownership – freedom over one's own body and freedom of movement, association, and commerce.

CHAPTER 2

The Core Stories and Ideas of German Freedom

> The people of ancient Germany lived in the greatest freedom.
>
> BEATUS RHENANUS (1551)[1]

∵

Two ideas inherited from the past formed the core of the concept of German freedom in the seventeenth and eighteenth centuries: *Ancient Germanic Freedom* and the *Free German Empire*. These two threads, the focus of this chapter, were woven into the later idea of German freedom and influenced seventeenth- and eighteenth-century jurists. They are perhaps best characterized as myths in the anthropological sense – stories containing ideas which reflect a received, collective teaching, often about a group's identity, similar to what Charles Taylor calls "social imaginaries."[2] The first concerned German identity and national inheritance; the second focused on what the imperial constitution spelled out for Germans of different classes (or estates).

Ancient Germanic Freedom was a depiction of ancient Germans, comparable to the Rousseauean idea of the "noble savage" – simple, proud, fierce, honorable people untouched by the corrupting *mores* and laws of modern civilization and commerce. In this telling, ancient Germans lived in tribes, were free, and guarded their independence with arms. This myth was taken up and circulated in in the sixteenth and seventeenth centuries thanks to the modern publication of Tacitus's ancient treatise *Germania*. Tacitus's depiction of ancient Germans became a commonplace among German readers. Six centuries after Tacitus began to recirculate, we need not weigh

1 "Populi Germaniae ueteris in summa libertate uixerunt." Quoted in Donald R. Kelley, "*Tacitus noster*: The *Germania* in the Renaissance and Reformation," in *Tacitus and the Tacitean tradition*, ed. T. James Luce and A. J. Woodman (Princeton University Press, 1993), p. 160.

2 Charles Taylor, *Modern Social Imaginaries* (Duke University Press, 2004).

 | DOI:10.1163/9789004685178_003

in on the veracity of the story of Ancient Germanic Freedom as a characterization of the legal status or character of barbarian peoples in contact with ancient Rome almost a thousand years prior. What matters here is how the story was *received, interpreted,* and *employed* by legal operators in our period of consideration. As I will show in later chapters, where modern law was vague or inconclusive, jurists and other readers drew on this idea in positing that modern Germans – especially rural farmers, including serfs – were *by birthright* free and that a presumption of individual freedom for them should prevail, in the absence of clear evidence to the contrary.

The term *Free German Empire* was a propagandistic or political slogan used by the Protestant Schmalkaldic League in their military conflict with Catholic estates and emperor in the 1530s. Another way of describing the Holy Roman Empire of the German Nation, the term was meant to identify the German nation-state (as it was imagined) and to indicate that it was free. However, the asserted freedom of the name referred not to the empire's independence from other powers (such as from the kingdom of France), but rather to a novel constitutional vision of the empire. Protestant rulers who allied together in the League advanced the idea that the empire was, by its constitution, a federation of free, largely independent political units such as Hesse, Saxony, and Brandenburg. They argued that the emperor's chief duty was to guarantee the freedoms of the empire's component units such as their realms. As I will show, other political actors of the same period (towns, villages, and knights) set forth a similar vision of the empire and its constitution. In a manner complementary to that of Ancient Germanic Freedom, the Free German Empire served as a new conception of law and politics for legal operators after 1550 in two salient ways. One was that the empire was presumed to be a political space filled with many *smaller, free, component polities* at all levels of governance. Second, the Free German Empire presented a normative political theory according to which the chief duty of the ruler (the emperor) was to protect the freedoms of domains and communities within the realm. This was not to imply that the ruler might not have other rights or duties, or that other laws or constitutions did not apply, but the ruler's fundamental duty was to defend his subjects' rights. Whereas Ancient Germanic Freedom focused primarily on the freedoms of the individual, the idea of the Free German Empire expanded notions of autonomy by asserting that polities have a right to basic freedoms as well.

Finally, I also suggest that the notions of Ancient Germanic Freedom and the Free German Empire had evolved by the seventeenth century into a loose set of political ideas that has been referred to simply as *German freedom*. An umbrella term that arose as a rallying cry in the Thirty Years' War, *German freedom* referred to the two aforementioned myths/imaginaries but also to other related or derivative political concepts, including property rights and protections. German freedom also seems to have included the normative superiority of written laws and constitutions over mere custom or claims of personal authority as well as the toleration of religious minorities. Moreover, according to early modern German constitutionalism, higher magistrates and even rulers who had abused their position could legally be, and if possible should be, removed from office.[3] In bringing together personal freedom and federalistic pluralism, German freedom became a generative concept that showed jurists (and other intellectuals) how natural *society* looked (or might look). This image of a free, pluralistic society led them to focus often on freedoms when thinking about conflicts of law. The story of German freedom predisposed them to believe that *German subjects – even serfs – were essentially free both by natural law and by their birthright.*

1 Ancient Germanic Freedom

> Who is prior in time is stronger in law.
>
> FÜRSTLICH-HESSISCHE LANDESORDNUNG IN DER OBERN GRAFSCHAFT KATZENELNBOGEN (1579)[4]

3 Estates could and did limit rulers' powers via intransigence, avoidance (Chapter 4), or siding with a rival to actually replace the ruler, for instance with a pretender from a cadet line of the ruling house. What makes the example of Prussian absolutism so striking is that it was an unusually successful collaboration between ruler and elites. The norm was more of a tradeoff between ruler and estates. For the latter, see Werner Trossbach, "Power and Good Governance: The Removal of Ruling Princes in the Holy Roman Empire, 1680–1794," in *The Holy Roman Empire, Reconsidered*, ed. Jason Philip Coy, Benjamin Marschke, and David Warren Sabean, *Spektrum: Publications of the German Studies Association* (Berghahn Books, 2011).

4 "Qui prior tempore, potior jure." Fuerstlich-Hessische Landesordnung in der obern Grafschaft Katzenelnbogen, in *Magazin für die teutschen Rechte und Geschichte*, ed. Johann Heinrich Christian von Selchow, Vol. 1 (Göttingen: Meyerische Buchhandlung, 1779), Von der Priorität der Gläubiger, p. 554. This Landesordnung, often called the Catzenelnbogen Landrecht, was a well-respected, much imitated early territorial law code in the region. The specific passage concerns priority of creditors, but the idea that temporal priority grants greater legal force is very old and very widely held in Western law, deriving ultimately from D.50.17.98. I thank Michael Lobban for this citation.

The story of what has usually been called "ancient Germanic freedom" (*altdeutsche Freiheit*)[5] was that the Germans,[6] before they became incorporated into the Roman Empire, had enjoyed a primitive form of freedom.[7] Because this story had a profound influence on Germans' ideas about their society, traditions, and birthright in the sixteenth through eighteenth centuries, I examine its influence in some detail. Like other myths of national origin, it would become a source of national pride, providing latter-day Germans with a story not only about their ancestral heritage, but also implicitly about their

---

5 The best treatment, though dated, is Erwin Hölzle, *Die Idee einer altgermanischen Freiheit vor Montesquieu; Fragmente aus der Geschichte politischer Freiheitsbestrebungen in Deutschland, England und Frankreich vom 16.-18. Jahrhundert* (Munich: R. Oldenbourg, 1925). Wolfgang Samtleben, *Die Idee einer altgermanischen Volksfreiheit im vormärzlichen deutschen Liberalismus* (Hamburg: 1935) treats the myth's reconstruction in the thought of nineteenth-century liberals and *Rechtsstaat* theorists in Germany. Examples of philological reconstruction of ancient Germanic *mores* are Andreas Heusler, *Germanentum. Vom Lebens- und Formgefühl der alten Germanen* (Heidelberg: C. Winter, 1934) and Jan de Vries, *Die geistige Welt der Germanen* (Darmstadt: Wissenschaftliche Buchgesellschaft, 1963 [orig. 1943]). For remarks by each about ancient Germanic freedom, see respectively their p. 38 and pp. 71–72. The more recent Kelley, "*Tacitus noster*" is helpful for the broader Tacitus reception as a process of reading and appropriation, with useful overview of the Tacitean-Germanic virtues and how they related to contemporary German concerns.

6 The question may arise whether ancient "Germans" were Germans. If Germans like Johann Wilhelm Waldschmiedt, writing in 1716, mentioned their ancient Germanic ancestors, were they simply mistaken in the characterization? Perhaps. Tacitus's "Germans" are best understood as the earliest of the many "Germanic" peoples who moved into Europe from what is now Russia and Central Asia during the first through ninth centuries of the common era. By long-standing convention, sources and scholars call these peoples "Germans" and other tribal names such as Goths, Vandals, etc. Thus the "ancient constitution" of England was called the "Gothic constitution," and German, French, English, and Dutch writers looked back to ancestors whom they variously called "Germanic" and "Frankish" (as well as Anglo-Saxon, Visigothic, Saxon, etc.). "[Hugo] Grotius saw in the Netherlands an unbroken continuity" of ancient Germanic law, such that "for him the old freedom and the new freedom were one and the same." Hölzle, *Idee einer altgermanischen Freiheit*, p. 36mb. For doubt about essential tribal identity, see Patrick J. Geary, *Before France and Germany: The Creation and Transformation of the Merovingian World* (New York: Oxford University Press, 1988). One might further say that the ancient Germans were actually something other than German, that Germanness was an evolving identity, that it came from other sources, and/or that the problem lay in Tacitus's possibly loose use of sources in his original account. Since the nineteenth century, the meaning of *Germanic* as a historical or anthropological term has been confused because of romantic and nationalist-motivated research programs (in Germany as well as elsewhere).

7 An influential synthesis of scholarly views of what the life of ancient Germans was like, from Arminius's day to the century following Charlemagne, is Perry Anderson, *Passages from Antiquity to Feudalism* (London: Verso; *Humanities Press; NLB*, 1974), Part One, Section II, pp. 107–142.

birthright – and therefore providing a program about how the world *should* be. The story of ancient Germanic freedom became widely disseminated after the rediscovery in the early fifteenth century of the Roman historian Tacitus's study (long known of but presumed lost) of the ancient "Germans," a work now known as the *Germania*.[8] The *Germania* was an anthropological study, based on others' reports, of the Germanic tribes of Tacitus's day. The work had been discovered in the Hersfeld monastery library in 1425, and after circulating privately, was published a couple of decades later, achieving its greatest popularity in the sixteenth century although it continued to inspire Germans long after its reappearance.

Before the reading public encountered Tacitus's *Germania*, there had been traces of the myth of ancient Germanic freedom in other antique and pre-reception sources. The Roman poet Lucan, for example, wrote of "freedom beyond the Rhine." Machiavelli, who wrote during the first phase of the Tacitus reception but never mentions the work, identified the Germans with freedom in several places.[9] But prior to the dissemination of Tacitus, most Germans and non-Germans alike had a rather *different* conception of German history and of Germans' relationship to other political orders. It was believed that the political structures of the modern *Holy* Roman Empire were continuations of the ancient forms of the Roman empire, from Augustus and Romulus Augustus to Charlemagne and Otto I and beyond, right up to the present. The modern imperial electors were imagined to be the continuation of the ancient Roman senate.[10] In this view, German tribes who arrived at the borders of the Roman empire, later settled within it, and haltingly integrated into Roman society and government were initially not *subjects of the history of that empire*, but outsiders, opponents at its fringes. Roman history was not *their* story until the great Germanic king Charlemagne created the Frankish empire, which Pope Sylvester declared in 800 to be a "translation" of the Roman empire. The legendary *translatio* would be more precisely understood as a transference of authority, somewhat like the changing of the king's political body (as opposed to his natural body) in medieval political theology. According to this narrative,

---

8 The story was closely related to other stories of ancient freedom which became popular in France and England in the same era. See on this Hölzle, *Idee einer altgermanischen Freiheit*, pp. 47–112.

9 Ibid., p. 6. Machiavelli worked and wrote in the late fifteenth and early sixteenth centuries. Neither his *Prince* nor *Discourses on Livy* cite the *Germania* or discuss the "primitive Germans" in their mythical form exemplified in Tacitus prior to their incorporation into the Roman empire. See *The Prince*, 2nd ed. (Chicago: University of Chicago Press, 1998 [orig. 1513]) and *Discourses on Livy* (Chicago: University of Chicago Press, 1996).

10 Hölzle, *Idee einer altgermanischen Freiheit*, p. 10.

only when they either *became* Romans or at least became the Romans' *rightful heirs* did Germans become subjects of imperial history. As Erwin Hölzle wrote, "The primitive age of the Germans prior to the Frankish empire had no place in the history of the Holy Roman Empire of the German Nation."[11]

With the reception of Tacitus, however, an attractive, alternative conception of the ancient Germanic past became available, rich with implications. Tacitus gave German humanists a sketch of their (notional) ancient ancestors, a picture of great virtue from their perspective: The ancient Germans demonstrated an "original rude simplicity" and cared more for "good manners [*guten sitten*]" than the ancient Romans did for their famous laws. Chastity, liberality, integrity, loyalty, constancy, fortitude, genius (*ingenium*), and nobility were their ordinary virtues, and they were in turn "free from usury, avarice, fraud, and trickery." These virtues helped make them "invincible" militarily, which in turn supported their crowning virtue: love of freedom. As Donald Kelley put it, "The defining trait around which all these virtues were gathered was the German love of freedom."[12]

Sixteenth-century writers began to use this myth in contemporary political and ideological struggles. In the Reformation era, Protestant writers like Ulrich von Hutten fused Luther's concept of Protestant Christian freedom with the growing resonance of the Tacitus-inspired myth of ancient Germanic freedom. In both, a negative image of Rome was contrasted with a positive image of Germany. In religion, Roman (i.e., Roman Catholic) tyranny over the conscience was contrasted with Christian freedom. In politics, the tyranny of the Roman Empire was set against ancient Germanic freedom, with implications

---

11 Ernst Hartwig Kantorowicz, *The King's Two Bodies: A Study in Mediaeval Political Theology*, 7th ed. (Princeton: Princeton University Press, 1997 [orig. 1957]); Hölzle, pp. 9–10. Where Hölzle wrote "Kaiserreich," I give "Holy Roman Empire of the German Nation"; from the context I take him to make a clear identification consistent with the ambiguous ways that German intellectuals spoke of the "first empire" (Holy Roman Empire of the German Nation) and "second empire" (deutsches Reich, Kaiserreich). See also Emanuele Conte, "The order and the *Volk*. Romantic roots and enduring fascination of the German constitutional history," De rebus divinis et humanis*: Essays in Honour of Jan Hallebeek* (2019), p. 43. The purpose of the the discussion of the empire, in the body of the chapter above, is not of course to discern the finer points of arguments about imperial authority. But it may briefly be said that there were several different arguments about why and whether a transfer of authority had legitimately happened. See for example Gierke, *Political Theories of the Middle Age*, p. 41.

12 Hölzle, *Idee einer altgermanischen Freiheit*, pp. 2, 4, 11–15; Kelley, "*Tacitus noster*," pp. 152–153, pp. 158–160, quoting sixteenth-century commentaries on Tacitus. See also Hajo Holborn, *Ulrich von Hutten and the German Reformation* (New York: Harper Torchbooks, 1966 [orig. 1937, 1929]).

for the current political conflict between the modern Roman emperor and German princes. The myth of ancient Germanic freedom was often deployed as a tool of clarification and critique: a depiction of a virtuous ancient society, implicitly revealing the vices of a modern society.[13] A similar function was served by other contemporary fabulist critiques involving quasi-mythical lands such as Montaigne's America, Montesquieu's Persia, and Voltaire's China.[14]

Humanistic writers found support for their Tacitus interpretation in other sources they were beginning to study, especially earlier German law codes. Hutten's presentation of the Tacitean character resembles how other humanists such as Beatus Rhenanus and Martin Bucer saw the revived ancient story. First and foremost, they claimed, the ancient Germans were virtuous, free, and strong. "From all times the Saxons have been free ... from all times invincible," Hutten wrote, "in our German land, we have been born the most free among all peoples of the earth."[15] At this time an antipathy toward Roman law was also developing among Protestant German humanists.[16] Hutten's animosity toward Roman law is well known. He and others saw lawyers and legal scholars as shysters who made law and lordship overly complex, a labyrinth of dubious, foreign rules which disadvantaged good, simple, pious Germans. This aversion to Roman law grew in conjunction with the German Reformation, a salient element of which was Luther's "hatred of Judaic and canon law."[17] Hatred of Old Testament law, hatred of canon law, and hatred of Roman law were mutually reinforcing.

Humanists, preachers, and reformers claimed that old codes of German law supported this picture of ancient Germanic freedom. The most famous of them, the "Saxon Mirror" (fourteenth century; see Figure 8) proclaimed that

13 This German-Roman, ancient-modern, virtue-vice contrast was material for many works of fiction, history, and historical anthropology (some of it quite allegorical or fanciful) among the German Romantics and in the Second Empire period, from the work of Heinrich von Kleist to Guido von List.

14 Michel de Montaigne, "Of Cannibals," in *The Complete Essays of Montaigne* (Stanford: Stanford University Press, 1957 [orig. 1580]); Charles le Secondat baron de Montesquieu, *Persian Letters* (London: J. Tonson, 1722 [orig. 1721]); and Voltaire, *Philosophical Dictionary* (Harmondsworth, Middlesex: Penguin Classics, 1972 [orig. 1764]).

15 Respectively these two in the original are as follows: "Wan die Sachsen seint alle zeit frey gewest, alle zeit unuberwindtlich." "das wir unser Teutsch land der under allen nation in der gantzen welt die freyheit am meisten geburt." Kelley, "*Tacitus noster*," p. 159.

16 There were nonetheless many Protestant civilians who continued to study and appropriate the civil law and incorporate it into territorial princely governance. This is a major theme of Berman, *Law and Revolution II*.

17 Hölzle, *Idee einer altgermanischen Freiheit*, p. 15; Kelley, "*Tacitus noster*," p. 160m.

FIGURE 5 Title page of Corvinus's *Jurisprudentia Romana* (1658), a typical condensation and handbook of Roman law

MONIMENTA
HASSIACA
darinnen verschiedene
zur
Hessischen Geschichte
und
Rechtsgelahrsamkeit
dienende Nachrichten und Ab-
handlungen
an das Licht gestellet werden
von
Friederich Christoph Schmincke

Zweiter Theil

CASSEL
bey Johann Bertram Cramer 1748

FIGURE 6 Title page of Schmincke's *Monimenta* (1748) featuring classicizing device

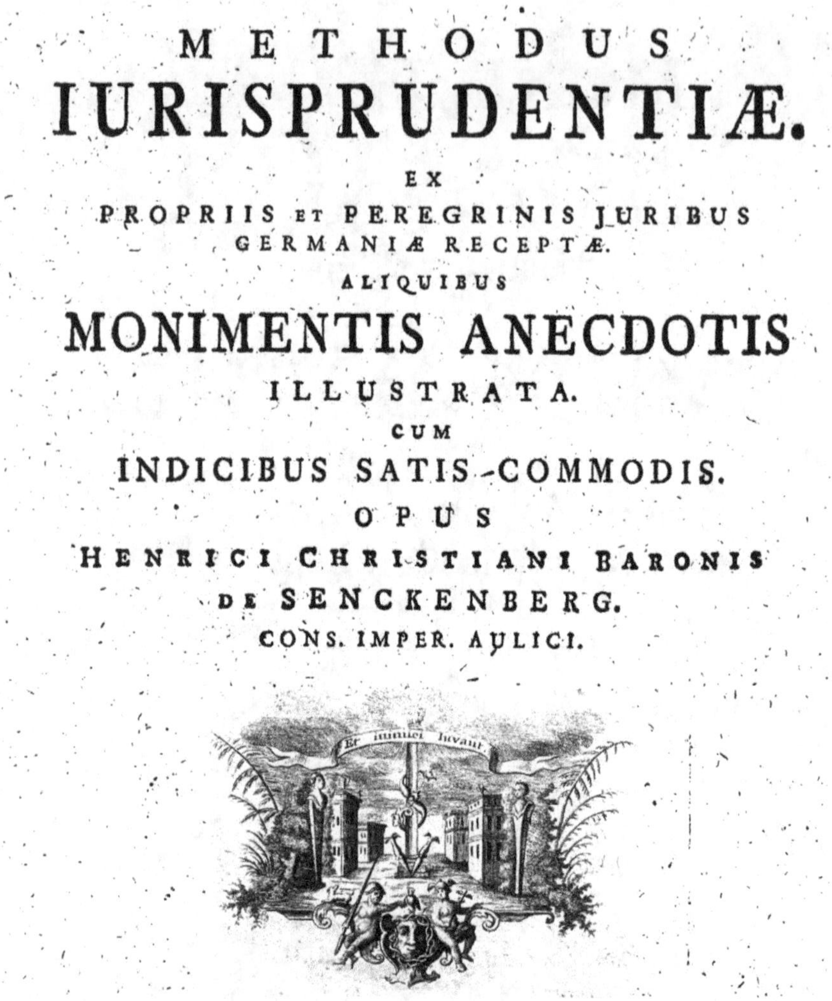

METHODUS
IURISPRUDENTIÆ.
EX
PROPRIIS ET PEREGRINIS JURIBUS
GERMANIÆ RECEPTÆ.
ALIQUIBUS
MONIMENTIS ANECDOTIS
ILLUSTRATA.
CUM
INDICIBUS SATIS-COMMODIS.
OPUS
HENRICI CHRISTIANI BARONIS
DE SENCKENBERG.
CONS. IMPER. AULICI.

FIGURE 7 Title page of the Frankfurt jurist Senckenburg's *Method of Jurisprudence* (1756), featuring classicizing printer's device typical for the period – a Roman-German cityscape. The book's very title indicates the same approach: "… received into Germany from both authentic and foreign laws." The adjectives *propriis* and *peregrinis* signal the Roman categories of *ius proprium* and *ius peregrinum*

all men are by nature free, based on Christ's redemption of humanity.[18] The extent to which the Mirror really reflected common native custom has been

18 Jochen Bleicken, Werner Conze, Christof Dipper, Horst Günther, Diethelm Klippel, Gerhard May, and Christian Meier, "Freiheit," in *Geschichtliche Grundbegriffe: Historisches Lexikon zur politisch-sozialen Sprache in Deutschland*, ed. Otto Brunner, Werner Conze, and Reinhart Koselleck, Vol. 2 (Stuttgart: E. Klett, 1975), p. 448; Peter Blickle, *From the*

Sachsen-Spiegel/
oder
Das Sächsische
Land-Recht/
in
Der Alt-Teutschen/ Lateinischen und ietzo gebräuchlichen Hoch-Teutschen Sprache/
nebst
Nöthigen Auszügen aus der Glosse/ so weit selbige zum Verstande des Teutschen Rechts etwas beyträget/ und gegeneinanderhaltung der Zobelischen und Loßischen hochteutschen edition,
Wie auch
Einer Vorrede/
Darinnen die Historie/ wie und wann das Teutsche Recht zu erst in Schrifften verfasset worden, wie auch derer verschiedenen Ausleger und glossatorum desselben, enthalten ist.
Herausgegeben von
Jacob Friederich LVDOVICI, ICto,
Königl. Preuß. Hoff-Rath und Prof Iur. P. ord
HALLE/ in Verlegung des Wäysenhauses, M DCC XX.

FIGURE 8 Title page of a printing of the Saxon Mirror from 1720

Communal Reformation to the Revolution of the Common Man, Vol. 65, Studies in Medieval and Reformation Thought (Leiden; Boston: Brill, 1998), p. 174. Rather than reflecting common national German customary law, the Saxon Mirror (*Sachsenspiegel*, *Speculum Saxonum*) is better understood as the recording by a learned juror of customs as he knew them, fit into the categories he knew from Roman civil and criminal law (*ius commune*), subject to some doubt, but we can say for sure that many Germans over the centuries believed that the Saxon Mirror and other customary law connections like it constituted an inheritance of law and freedom. A remarkable example reflecting this view of ancient German law can be found in a 1543 letter from the preacher Martin Bucer to Landgrave Philipp of Hesse, one of the leaders of the Protestant Schmalkaldic League (1531–1547). In 1542, the League's army and allies defeated and captured one of the leading Catholic princes, Heinrich, duke of Braunschweig-Wolfenbüttel, and imprisoned him in Ziegenhain in Hesse.[19] Bucer wrote to Philipp,

> [There] is no doubt in my mind that our group was in the right, when we drove this faithless, inhuman tyrant [sc. Heinrich] from the land, never to let him return. Here I look to God's law, natural law, and the ancient free Frankish law, which God gave the German people, though which for a long time now they have held to be evil and put away.

After invoking ancient Germanic law which was understood to guarantee Germans' freedom, Bucer went on to articulate how he and his comrade reformers contrasted this law with the advance of Roman law (the *ius commune*) in imperial courts:

> Nowadays ... the doctors [i.e. civilian jurists] have become all-powerful tyrants ... They look only in the written, Roman, tyrannical law and set their reputation and pride in that law ... This law has become so devel-

---

rather like the work of Philippe de Beaumanoir in France. A contemporarily published *Sachsenspiegel* was Eike von Repgow, *Sachsen-Spiegel oder Das Sächsische Land-Recht in Der Alt-Teutschen, Lateinischen und ietzo gebräuchlichen Hoch-Teutschen Sprache*, ed. Jakob Friedrich Ludovici (Halle: Wäysenhaus, 1720); a low *Frankenspiegel* from Hesse was Johann Emerich, "Samlung der alten Rechten und Gewohnheiten der Stad Franckenberg," in *Monimenta Hassiaca*, ed. Friedrich Christoph Schmincke, Vol. 2 (Cassel: Johann Bertram Cramer, 1748 [orig. ca. 1476]).

19 Letter from Bucer to Landgrave Philipp of Hesse, December 4, 1543. Max Lenz, ed., *Briefwechsel Landgraf Philipps des Großmüthigen von Hessen mit Bucer*, Vol. 2, Publicationen aus den k. preussischen Staatsarchiven (Leipzig: K. Archiv-Verwaltung; Verlag von S. Hirzel, 1887), p. 213. Heinrich of Braunschweig was duke of Braunschweig-Wolfenbüttel and one of the leading opponents of the Schmalkaldic League. The League's army and allies defeated and captured Heinrich in 1542 and imprisoned him in Ziegenhain in Hesse. After Charles v and his allies turned around the conflict with the Battle of Mühlberg in 1547, Heinrich was released.

> oped and is so buried in books that no one besides them can make anything of it. [It] has been captured by the emperors, who by themselves alone made all law, and interpreted and enforced it as they pleased. Following this law, the judges of the Imperial Chamber Court put everything into the emperor's hand. And so it is that these doctors occupy the highest court, so that all princes and estates are obliged to ask the doctors about the law.[20]

… or in the pithy proverb that pleased Martin Luther and was still studied as an example of folk wisdom centuries later, "Juristen, böse Christen" (jurists are bad Christians).[21]

The features of German society depicted in the Tacitean story were taken seriously by early modern jurists and historians. They used it not only as a source of political legitimacy for the cause of "freedom" against "Rome," but also to try to understand the nature of their society. They wondered, for instance, whether there was slavery in ancient Germany and whether modern serfdom was justified. The first law professor at the University of Marburg, Johannes Ferrarius Montanus (r. 1527–1558), wrote that in his day, "slaves are

---

20 The complete text of the two passages translated here together read: "In der braunschweigischen sachen hab ich kein zweifel, unsere stende haben ubrig recht, das sie diesen sogar glaublosen und beharrenden, onmenschlichen wutrich von land und leuten vertriben haben und in dazu niemer komen lassen. Ich sehe aber in dem Gottes, der natur und das alt frei frenckisch recht an, das Gott deutscher nation gegeben hatt, sie aber nun ein lange zeit ubel helt und bewaret. Die doctoren aber, die nun des rechten in deutscher nation von varlessigkeit und eigenutzigkeit wegen der anderen verstendigen leuten, von herren, adel und burgeren, gantz mechtige tyrannen worden sind, sehen allein an ire geschribne romische, tyrannische recht, und in demselbigen ire reputation und hochtragen bei allen stenden; dieweil soliche recht so verwicklet und in den großen buchern so vergraben sind, das sie nieman, dann sie, anstellen kan. Dasselbige recht ist von keisern eingethon, die monarchen waren und durch sich selb allein alle recht macheten, außlegten und exequireten ires gefallens. Nach diesen rechten stellen und treiben die camerbeisitzer alles in des keisers handt, und so diese doctoren das höchst gericht besitzen, mussen alle fursten und stend die doctores umb recht fragen. Die geben dann demnach iren rath, wie sie das gegen iren herren verhoffen zu genießen, doch das sie auch ir handtwerck mit ontheur machen."

21 For Luther, see Kelley, "*Tacitus noster*," p. 160m; a later early modern example is Johann Nikolaus Hertius, "De Paroemiis Juris Germanicis Libri Tres," in *Commentationum atque opusculorum de selectis et rarioribus ex jurisprudentia universali, publica, feudali et Romana, nec non historia Germanica, argumentis tomi tres*, Vol. 3 (Frankfurt am Main: Johannes Davidus Zunnerus, 1700), paroemia 1 (!), pp. 386–390.

not known to the Germans." Turning to a colorful legal proverb, this was because "our Germany" lay "under a more free sky" (or heaven) than did other polities. For, he continued, everyone knew that "even Cornelius Tacitus recognizes this ..."[22] Scholars in Hesse-Cassel in the eighteenth century embraced the ancient story, true or not, even as they sought to reconcile it with medieval accounts of war and subjugation. They also carefully distinguished between slavery, semi-servitude, and serfdom.

2 The Free German Empire

A famous controversy in earlier German history was over the structure and constitutional nature of the empire. This was quite aside from such peculiarities as whether the empire was "holy," or "Roman," or an "empire," or how a Roman empire could be "of the German nation" in the first place. (Which added up to alleged problems with every aspect of its fullest official name.) What, one asked, was the empire's constitutional form? In his book on "the state of the German empire" Samuel Pufendorf had called the empire's form "monstrous," meaning of unnatural shape, chimerical. He alleged this because the empire had what political scientists in the Polybian tradition of Aristotelian political science called a mixed constitution, meaning that it blended elements of democracy, aristocracy, and monarchy. Its specific confederated composition was also both heterogeneous and in a way heterogenous: It had many different kinds of component estates (towns, counties, duchies, archduchies, and multiple kingdoms), of extremely different size and power, which were of quite diverse origins (some like Bohemia not "teutsch" at all). Pufendorf crafted this argument while in Palatine service and it served what we might call a contemporary "kleindeutsch" or "small German" agenda by

22 "Servilis conditionis homines, quemadmodum jure Gentium esse coeperunt, Germania nostra, liberioris coeli, non ita agnoscit, etiam Cornelio Tacito de moribus Germanorum teste ... servi Germanis non sunt cogniti." Quoted in Johann Wilhelm Waldschmiedt, praeses, Christian Fridericus Goy, respondans, *De hominibus propriis Hassiacis. Von Hessischen Leibeigenen* (Marburg: 1716), Cap. III, §11, p. 38. The phrase *liberioris coeli* is a Latinization of the customary German notion of convening "unter dem freien Himmel" (under the open sky), playing on a double meaning of free as *open* in the idiom. Custom was that community meetings, including diets, were held outdoors.

criticizing the role of the great Austrian power as well as the politics of the prince bishops.[23]

The tension between Protestant and Catholic views of the imperial constitution or the nature of the empire found expression earlier as well, in the sixteenth century, although this story is less well known than that of Protestant polemics in Pufendorf's day. In the early sixteenth century, the Tacitean discourse about an ancient birthright of Germanic freedom was at first just a recently rediscovered ancient story, though an inspiring one. But in the heady, violent early decades of the Protestant Reformation and the wars it quickly engendered, Germans named for themselves a new freedom, or a new kind of freedom, one that built on the "ancient Germanic freedom" that had become all the rage among humanists in those days.

In this new vision, articulated first by Protestant princes and their publicists, the Holy Roman Empire had a constitution which guaranteed the laws, rights, and freedoms of the component parts of the empire – from great duchies to small towns and free cities, baronies, bishoprics, abbeys, and even villages.

This new understanding of the empire as a guarantor of freedoms of its corporate member units actually had older origins in canon law (as did several other later, secular or liberal ideas often associated with Protestant political thought).[24] During the Investiture Conflict of the eleventh century, the reforming / papal monarchist party led by Pope Gregory VII fought to assert the independence of the Latin Christian churches from control by lords whom it labeled as merely temporal or lay or worldly. This was the origin of the peculiarly Western distinction between Church and state. Gregory and his party described their struggle as one for the "freedom" of the church.[25] Two features

---

23 Samuel Pufendorf, *The Present State of Germany*, ed. Michael J. Seidler, trans. Edmund Bohun (Indianapolis: Liberty Fund, 2007 [orig. 1667, 1696]); on the intellectual controversies in the mid seventeenth century as to the nature of the empire's constitution, see Stollberg-Rilinger, *Des Kaisers alte Kleider*, Chapter 4, esp. pp. 140–146.

24 For discussions of natural rights theories and the importance of consent, see Brian Tierney, "Hierarchy, Consent, and the "Western Tradition"," *Political Theory* 15, no. 4 (1987) and Constantin Fasolt, "Quod omnes tangit ab omnibus approbari debet: the words and the meaning," in *In iure veritas: Studies in Canon Law in Memory of Schafer Williams*, ed. Steven Bowman and Blanche E. Cody (Cincinnati: University of Cincinnati College of Law, 1991). Consent is also discussed below briefly in Ch. 7, pp. 291–294. For election of leader-representatives, see Brian Tierney, "Freedom and the Medieval Church," in *The Origins of Modern Freedom in the West*, ed. Richard W. Davis (Stanford: Stanford University Press, 1995). Other examples could be given.

25 Gerd Tellenbach, *Church, State, and Christian Society at the Time of the Investiture Contest* (Oxford: Basil Blackwell, 1940 [orig. 1936]), pp. 1–25, 64, 126–161.

of the Investiture Controversy would prove lasting models for Germans in the centuries ahead. First, the negative and positive conceptions of freedom of the church applied not to individuals but to a hierarchical monarchy. The papacy's program was based on the premise that individuals find freedom through their membership in a larger, active political unit which declares independence.[26] Second, the church's demand for freedom from the emperor, regardless of the arguments on which it was based, provided a model for how other, increasingly independent polities came into being within the empire[27]: the secular and ecclesiastical princes. Seen from this perspective and in retrospect, the struggle of the popes to assert the freedom of the church was but the first assertion or eruption of a new unit of authority within the empire.[28] In the long term, through the gaining of widespread princely rights in the thirteenth century, this resulted by the sixteenth century in the conception of the "Free German Empire" – a pluralistic space of small powers who demanded that the emperor guarantee their freedoms. Thus the story of the freedom of the church must be considered one touchstone of German identity, even in a way for Protestants.[29]

According to the new sixteenth-century story, the empire was a realm of freedom, vividly described by Protestant princes of Hesse and Saxony as a

26 This feature accords with Leonard Krieger's argument that freedom for pre-modern Germans was subsumed within the state.

27 To be clear: Bishops, kings, emperors, and of course their clerks had many arguments about the perfection of the church's authority over all worldly institutions, or the perfection of imperial authority respectively, or of royal authority as same within a limited royal realm. These were not arguments for independence of a federalistic nature. Particularly clear on this is Otto von Gierke, *Political Theories of the Middle Age*, transl. Frederic Maitland (Beacon Hill: 1959), Sections I–V, especially pp. 1–22, 24–27, and 34. But when these ideas clashed, in the arms of their partisans during the Investiture Conflict, they resulted in the eruption of new authority structures.

28 I take the language of the eruption of political authority from Eric Voegelin, *The New Science of Politics: An Introduction* (Chicago: University of Chicago Press, 1952).

29 This story about the struggle over authority and freedom between pope and emperor may not seem wholly German. That is, it is not a story specifically of German freedom, to the exclusion of other nations, because other European nations were involved and affected. It may not be a national story in the same way that the English myth of England's "ancient constitution" was said to be the foundation of English freedom, as in the phrase "rights of Englishmen." But the Investiture Controversy, about the struggle of Roman-German emperors against the papacy, occupied a central place in the political imagination of Germans for almost a millennium, in a way it did not for the English or French. The Germans (however defined) were the protagonists of the stories that Germans told about Christian freedom in Europe (except when specifically speaking about other nations).

"free German empire." Although this term itself emerged amidst the Catholic-Lutheran military conflicts in Germany in the 1530s, similar or complementary ideas were also articulated by the imperial knights, free cities, towns, and common farmers in the sixteenth century (discussed below). These ideas about the imperial constitution incorporated powerful earlier stories about freedom – the freedom guaranteed Germans in the present empire was the modern, evolved version of their ancient freedom. Protestants were galvanized through their fight against the emperor both to free churches from outside interference (other than their own) and to free the conscience of Protestant Christians from the interference of imposed rituals and laws (most immediately, those of the "Roman" church hierarchy). Towns and villages articulated communalist visions that echoed this "constitution of liberty," but their focus was usually on preserving their "ancient liberties" against neighboring princes looking to expand their control at the smaller powers' expense. The endeavors of these smaller powers sometimes succeeded and sometimes failed. Notably, while the idea that the empire should guarantee the freedoms and rights of estates was initially ignited in confessional and local conflict, it became a pan-confessional heritage for Germans, much as freedom of conscience would become in several European countries and colonies.

The first act in this drama was the fight between Protestant princes supporting the Reformation and the Catholic princes and emperor who opposed it. Although earlier imperial laws had arguably functioned as a constitution by governing the conduct, duties, and rights of imperial offices and units,[30] when the Schmalkaldic League rebelled against the emperor and his Catholic allies, their articulation of an imperial constitution must have seemed new. They and their comrades in arms began talking about the empire in terms of freedom. Kurfürst Johann Friedrich of Saxony and Landgraf Philipp of Hesse proclaimed in 1539 that "The German nation is a free empire and, justly, the freest in the world. Grudgingly would it give itself into servitude" to the Catholic powers.[31] While Protestant rulers "called on the old constitution of the empire which

30 The best-known formal provision of the imperial constitution was the Golden Bull of 1356, which regulated the election of the emperor by seven prince-electors. Settlements between emperor and princes in the thirteenth century are also seen as earlier constitutional structures. For earlier documents, see Geoffrey Barraclough, *The Origins of Modern Germany*, 2nd ed. (New York: Capricorn Books, 1962 [orig. 1946]), p. 237, p. 240.

31 "Die teutsche Nation ist ein frey Reich und billich das freyeste auf der Welt, das wird sich in solch Dinstbarkeit ungerne begeben." Friedrich Hortleder, *Der Römischen Keyser- Und Königlichen Majestete[n], Auch deß Heiligen Römischen Reichs Geistlicher und Weltlicher Stände, Churfürsten, Fürsten ... Handlungen und Außschreiben, Send-Brieffe* (Gotha: Endter, 1645), quoted at Schmidt, *Wandel durch Vernunft*, p. 82tm.

secured freedom," their vision of the empire was novel. In the words of historian Georg Schmidt, it was:

> a *res publica*, a commonwealth with free will and pluralist division of power. Its patriotic citizens (meaning only the imperial estates ...), made their own laws and recognized no absolute authority other than God. They set themselves firmly against any and all monarchical supremacy ...[32]

This constitutional theory associated freedom with *federalism*, advancing the underappreciated idea that the autonomy or independence resulting from a protected separation of different units within a greater polity constitutes a form of freedom. Keen observers of European politics from the sixteenth through the eighteenth centuries like Machiavelli, Montesquieu, and the framers of the American Constitution all appreciated the relationship between German federalism and German freedom.[33] Another way to understand what the imperial constitution was is to think of it in terms of its form and its substance. The late medieval constitution was, in form, "as multitude of individual laws" (such as the Golden Bull), and thus a "relative" constitution. By contrast, the Reformation vision articulated by the Protestant rebels and others typified an "ideal concept of a constitution," in that it was identified with "a certain content," namely freedom.[34]

So far, this is a story of the great powers – the monarch and the more powerful princes. And on some level, this princely-aristocratic view would persist until the end of the old empire in 1806. After 1648, the Peace of Westphalia guaranteed both older princely rights and certain key new ones, notably territorial sovereignty, particularly in matters of alliances and confession, albeit with accompanying religious toleration among the three Christian confes-

---

32 Schmidt, *Wandel durch Vernunft*, p. 82.

33 However, the interpretation of the empire as of "monstrous" shape pioneered by Samuel Pufendorf in the service of his Saxon and Prussian patrons, combined with Whiggish teleology suggested by nineteenth- and twentieth-century Special Path partisans, have cast this older view as obscure, naïve, or even somehow dangerous. In a wider European perspective, German federalism was not particularly original. Federalist Swiss constitutional visions predated German federalism by at least one century. And mixtures of towns, villages, and lordships were accustomed to creating confederations (*Einungen, Genossenschaften, Bunden*). The German federalist constitutional vision persists in the present structure of the *Bundesrepublik*. See Umbach, *Federalism and Enlightenment in Germany*, p. 6t, pp. 189–200.

34 Schmitt, *Constitutional Theory*, Part 1, Sections 2 and 4, pp. 67–74, 89–93.

sions. In the eighteenth century, the aggressive Prussian king Frederick the Great would say the empire was a "republic of princes." Among Frederick's offices was that of prince-elector (a margrave) of the empire; he was not much of a federalist or believer in the old imperial constitution, but he recognized that this remained a salient idea to his princely peers.[35] In addition to its deployment in opposition to Vienna and Rome, the constitutional formula was over time also marshalled against the Germans' other continental enemy, France.[36]

This constitutional theory was not limited to the princes. The lesser nobility, commonly called the imperial barons or imperial knights, articulated a similar constitutional vision slightly earlier in the same period – against the princes. In 1523–1525, Franz von Sickingen and Ulrich von Hutten led a spectacular revolt of imperial knights, essentially a failed reactionary coup attempt. Sickingen's strategy was to galvanize a large confederacy of knights into becoming a significant power within the empire, capable of countering the great princes, especially those of Trier, Hesse, and Saxony, who were the threatening neighbors of the majority of the knights' usually small and poor domains.[37] The knights argued that the empire must constitutionally guarantee the freedom of its immediate estates (dukes, bishops, and certain counts, knights, and abbots), with the emperor himself serving as protector of their rights. Thus much like the princes against the emperor and the Catholic estates in the same period, here were smaller powers organizing and rebelling in the

35 The king contended that Emperor Joseph sought to disadvantage the imperial estates through a reform of the Imperial Chamber Court. Frederick issued an ultimatum: "… since the Viennese Court has undertaken to injure that which should be most holy for men, to topple the German empire, this republic of princes (which the emperor has the duty to preserve), the king [Frederick, king in Prussia] has resolved to forestall the mournful consequences which these dark plans must have. This prince declares that the freedoms of the German empire will only be buried in a grave with Prussia alongside them." Hapsburg plans would, he argued, "endanger" the "freedoms and privileges" of the other estates. The conflict would lead to the Seven Years' War in 1756, in which Frederick emerged victorious and in possession of Silesia. Artur Brabant, *Das Heilige römische Reich teutscher Nation im Kampf mit Friedrich dem Grossen* (Berlin: G. Paetel, 1904), pp. 72–73. It is common to interpret this as an instrumental piece of rhetoric – serving the aspirations of a rising power (Prussia) struggling against the hegemon (Austria). See further T. C. W. Blanning, *Frederick the Great: King of Prussia* (New York: Random House, 2016), pp. 322–325.

36 Schmidt, *Wandel durch Vernunft*, pp. 81–83.

37 See Hillay Zmora, *State and Nobility in Early Modern Germany: The Knightly Feud in Franconia, 1440–1567*, Cambridge Studies in Early Modern History (Cambridge: Cambridge University Press, 1997).

name of defending their traditional freedoms. [38] As Hutten put it, their battle cry was that "we must risk all, and suffer all, for freedom."[39] While the knights were decisively defeated by the forces of Hesse and Trier in 1523, they ultimately, achieved one of their goals. In 1532–1542, they changed their strategy and offered their services to the emperor directly in exchange for imperial immediacy, the legal guarantee that they would never be subjected to the jurisdiction of the princely courts, whether bishop, landgrave, margrave or anyone else. This guarantee would give the knights tremendous autonomy for the subsequent 250 years. The growth of the imperial courts over the same period would increase the value of this guarantee: Other small imperial powers consumed one another or were gobbled up by bigger ones, but all the while the imperial knights successfully maintained their independence with the help of the two imperial appellate courts.[40] Their security was a major buttress for imperial federalist pluralism over the ensuing centuries.

As historian Georg Schmidt put it, in the sixteenth century, "the topos of ancient Germanic freedom, which already had performed good services for the growth of territorial states, was ... expanded to cover the whole structure of the empire." That is, the idea of an ancient inheritance of freedom was applied broadly to all polities in the empire from the sixteenth century onward. Germany was almost as famous as Renaissance Italy for its many proud, free cities (*Städte*, which can also be translated as "towns"). They often allied themselves in regional coalitions to secure their interests against threats. The freedom claimed by imperial cities consisted in the same right the princes and knights claimed for themselves: imperial immediacy, meaning that they should answer only to the emperor himself, not to any other magistrate or power in the empire. For lords such as dukes or knights, this meant quasi-monarchical administration of their domains. For cities, immediacy entailed not only this administration but also republican features such as control over

38 These and subsequent remarks emphasize proximities and functional similarities among movements by princes, knights, and towns, but I would not wish to overstate the case. For example, the knights' military revolt took place a decade before the Protestant princes formed the militant Schmalkaldic League. Similarly it is not a research object of this book to establish that there was some precise common source of the ideas about constitutional freedom animating these different estates; perhaps there was, or perhaps there was just something in the air.

39 "Nos omnia dura et adversa facere et pati, ut constet libertas, par est." Letter to Erasmus, 1523, quoted at Holborn, *Ulrich von Hutten*, p. 194.

40 Karl E. Demandt, *Geschichte des Landes Hessen*, 2nd, expanded ed. (Cassel: Bärenreiter, 1972), pp. 468–469; for background, see ibid., pp. 223–224.

membership in their bodies, choice of leaders, and legislative autonomy.[41] Some cities like Frankfurt am Main held on to their freedom for centuries, while others like nearby Gelnhausen, Burg Friedberg, and the Freigericht Kaichen lost some or all of their independence.[42] Toward the south, some towns managed to "turn Swiss," that is, join the Swiss Confederation, giving them defensive security against hostile neighbors (and emperors).[43]

A distinct claim of freedom, derived from natural liberty, arose from lower social ranks. Almost at the same time as the Knights' Revolt, a series of other, equally spectacular local conflicts erupted, also in the western and southern lands of the empire – conflicts long called the Peasants' War or, more recently by Peter Blickle, the Revolution of the Common Man (*der gemeine Mann*). In 1523–1525, thousands of farmers and burghers primarily in Franconia, Swabia, and Hesse revolted against local lords. The simple slogan of their revolts was often "freedom." The peasants' posters and pamphlets articulated their claim that they were defending their freedoms, theirs by "natural freedom" and tradition (the "good, old law"), against new impositions by their landlords. (See Figure 9.) They alleged that landlords were trying to enclose common pastures and forests, arbitrarily raise rents, and impose new labor services. While some farmers and sympathetic bourgeois publicists connected these militant ideals to the nature of the empire (comparable to the rhetoric of the princes and knights discussed above), the salient point is that "the common man" saw himself as free and in possession of old rights, a heritage of ancient freedom. The rebelling farmers and burghers also connected their freedoms to what modern political theorists would call republicanism – free, communalistic, self-government.[44] Like all collectivities, German towns and cities of the day were characterized internally by hierarchy, privilege, and inequality, though

41 Schmidt, *Geschichte des Alten Reichs*, p. 79; Beat A. Kümin, *Imperial Villages: Cultures of Political Freedom in the German Lands, c. 1300–1800*, Studies in Central European Histories (Boston: Brill, 2019).

42 Friedrich von Thudichum, *Wettereiba. Eine Gau-Geschichte* (Giessen: Alfred Töpelmann, 1907), pp. 35–40, also discussing the similar cases of Butzbach, Gedern, Hanau, Münzenberg, Rodheim vor der Höhe, Schotten, Staden, Windecken, and Weilburg, all of which received significant imperial freedoms in the twelfth or thirteenth centuries but steadily lost them afterward, either by selling or pawning them or losing them in military conflict with powerful neighbors.

43 Brady, *Turning Swiss*.

44 Peter Blickle, *The Revolution of 1525: The German Peasants' War from a New Perspective* (Baltimore: Johns Hopkins University Press, 1981 [orig. 1975]), pp. 23–86. The term "communalism" was coined by Peter Blickle to name what he perceived as a communitarian ideology which prized self-government combined with the belief that common or public issues should be solved through collective town decision-making (usually by male

the gulf was not as great as the separation between seigneur and tenant or prince and subject. Most burghers would have readily characterized urban life as free, even if they themselves lived within a hierarchy of subordination. This view resembles the modern political model of freedom as non-domination.[45]

Freedom was not just on the minds of political leaders and rebels in the sixteenth century. It also became a concern of jurists working in the new and expanding university law faculties as well as growing regime chanceries (Chapter 3). As princes consolidated their growing territories with courts to rule them, jurists studied local customs. Among the "freedoms" the jurists found were an immunity from a tithe or from serf dues, the right to hold local courts and select local leaders, limitations on labor service, and specific property rights, such as holding fields or shared use of commons like forest or fisheries.[46] Such rights could, needless to say, mean the crucial difference between sustenance and starvation, or freezing due to insufficient firewood in winter. Beginning in the sixteenth century, but much more in the seventeenth and eighteenth centuries, jurists learned about, recorded, quoted, and marveled at such local freedoms, mostly claimed by rural families and communities. These freedoms made up the fabric of the "free German empire." The kinds of freedoms people held and sought varied by social class. Farmers and burghers cared most about not paying dues, rights of marriage and inheritance, use of commons, and terms of property holding, especially for natural resources like timber or fishing. Townspeople were more likely to have rights to

---

heads of household and larger stakeholders). Towns and cities themselves were made up of internal corporate bodies, chiefly guilds, and other forms of associative life. Communalist ideology mobilized communities to fight for their autonomy in decision making with regard to keeping the peace, land distribution, and management of parish religious matters. Blickle contended that communalism was vigorous across Europe for many centuries until it was clipped in the eighteenth and nineteenth centuries by the growth of the modern technocratic, central state. See Peter Blickle, *Kommunalismus: Skizzen einer gesellschaftlichen Organisationsform* (Munich: R. Oldenbourg, 2000). A good historiographical review is R. W. Scribner, "Communalism: Universal Category or Ideological Construct? A Debate in the Historiography of Early Modern Germany and Switzerland," *The Historical Journal* 37, no. 1 (1994).

45 The way that the importance of communal independence outweighed internal inequality constitutes the functional similarity between communalism and the modern concept of republicanism. For the latter, see e.g. Quentin Skinner, *Liberty before Liberalism* (Cambridge: Cambridge University Press, 1998 [orig. 1997]) and Phillip Pettit, *Republicanism: a theory of freedom and government*, Oxford political theory (Oxford; New York: Oxford University Press, 1997).

46 For a comparative example, see Peter Linebaugh, *The Magna Carta Manifesto: Liberties and Commons For All* (Berkeley: University of California Press, 2008), on thirteenth-century England.

FIGURE 9 A famous symbol of German freedom: a farmer from the Revolution of 1525 waving a flag emblazoned "freedom"

simply alienable tenure (burgage, *Burgrecht*).[47] The nobility cared about their old rights of immunity, patronage, and judicial lordship. Nobles also sought be directly subject only to the prince or only to the emperor. Princes thought of themselves as the first among equal nobles, of, by, and for whom the imperial government served.

47 Wilhelm Brauneder, "Burgrecht," in *Handwörterbuch zur deutschen Rechtsgeschichte*, ed. Albrecht Cordes and Wolfgang Stammler, Vol. 4 (Berlin: E. Schmidt, 2004); Michael E. Tigar and Madeleine R. Levy, *Law and the Rise of Capitalism* (New York: Monthly Review Press, 1977), pp. 170–171.

Across the empire, diverse "ancient" freedoms were claimed by people from all estates and by thousands of polities–a certain peasant clan, a specific town or village, a noble family, a bishopric, and so forth. And while each estate (princes, knights, towns, common people) probably cared most for its own freedom, it at least paid lip service to the idea that other estates enjoyed great freedom as well.

Many of these freedoms do not exactly resemble what we think of as freedom today. For example, in the fifteenth century, the "little people" of the village of Egloff enjoyed the right that the children of mixed serf-free marriage should themselves be free.[48] In that example, freedom meant that a person was not subject to certain kinds of authority of a serf lord, such as labor service, onerous taxes (dues in produce), or control over marriage. In fifteenth-century Hesse, the people of Allendorf had become free from paying the *Besthaupt* serf tax and the Lent tithe and from doing labor service to the landgrave.[49] In this case, the freedom specifically meant a freedom from extractions alone (see Chapter 5 below). The burghers of Nidda had enjoyed "remarkable freedoms" from their lord the count of Ziegenhain since 1311.[50] Sometimes emancipatory documents even invoked the language of natural freedom.[51]

While Germans were certainly proud of their diverse freedoms, by the eighteenth century they did not think that their empire was much more free than

48 "The free hand shall lead the unfree," stated the deed. Children go "with the better hand." Egloff is a village close to the town of Ytzin in the Allgäu. See Heinrich Christian Senckenberg, ed., *Senckenbergische Sammlung von ungedruckt- und raren Schriften. Zu Erläuterung derer Rechte und Geschichten von Teutschland; Vier Theile samt Vorrede und General-Register*, Vol. 4 (Frankfurt am Main: Johann Friedrich Fleischer, 1751) §15, pp. 261–268.

49 "Henry landgrave of Hesse ... gives to our townsmen of Allendorf and their descendants forever that they are free and clear [*frey ledig und loß*] of *Besthaupt* and the Lent tithe ..." also "freed them from labor [*Dienst und Schatzung*]" for the coming six years. See Heinrich Christian Senckenberg, ed., *Selecta iuris et historiarum*, Vol. 3 (Frankfurt am Main: Johann Friedrich Fleischer, 1735), §28–29, pp. 616–620.

50 Thudichum, *Wettereiba*, p. 40 n. 2.

51 When the king of France freed serfs in 1315, he wrote that "as according to the law of nature everyone should be born free, but by certain usages and customs ... many persons of our common people have fallen into the bonds of servitude ... which much displeased us ... we have ordered that these servitudes shall be brought to freedom." Berman, *Law and Revolution*, p. 331b. For classical Roman discussion of the idea of natural freedom, one can start with Ernst Levy, "Natural Law in the *Institutes*," in *Proceedings*, ed. Alfred L. Scanlan (Indianapolis: University of Notre Dame Press, 1948) and, for the early modern period, Johannes Calvinus, *Lexicon Iuridicum Iuris* (Colonia Allobrogum [Geneva]: Excudebat Matthaeus Berjon, Sumptibus Caldorianae Societatis, 1612).

other realms, or at least we do not read such boasting.[52] But they believed they enjoyed freedoms, and I argue that they said so and believed it and we can generally concur with their self-assessment.

3 German Freedom

Roughly in the first half of the seventeenth century, especially in connection to the Thirty Years' War, the expression "German freedom" (*teutsche Freyheit*) entered the discourse. This is a difficult term because it was widely used, deceptively simple in sound, and manifold in meaning. "German freedom" became a rallying cry for the Protestant German princes (in alliance with France and Sweden), echoing the earlier ideas of ancient freedom and the freedom-constitution of the empire itself. With the Peace of Westphalia, imperial estates (principalities great and small) generally gained considerable autonomy, in some cases almost to the point of sovereignty. The new theological-political settlement of "*cuius regio, eius religio*" enabled a new widespread religious toleration which became one of the pillars of "German freedom," especially among the many small powers in the empire. A local prince or lord could decide to give toleration or asylum to some minority such as Calvinists or Jews.[53] This created a more stable peace among the Christian confessional states than during the era of religious civil war which preceded it. Even if the rebel princes were concerned primarily for their own rights as rulers, their propaganda resonated with the concerns of other estates as well, including eventually even Catholic princes. Over the seventeenth and eighteenth centuries, the idea the princes expressed came to be dubbed simply *German freedom*.

---

52 More typical was the story Luther told in his table talk (*Colloquia Mensalia*): "When the emperor Maximilian made a league with the Venetians, he said, 'Three kings are in the Christian world; himself, the French king and the king of England. Himself [he said] was a king of kings; for what he imposed upon his princes, if they were pleased therewith, then they accomplished his will, otherwise they let it alone, thereby showing that the princes never were in obedient subjection under the Emperors, but did what they pleased. The French king was a king of asses, for they did everything that he commanded them. But the king of England was a king of people, for what he laid upon them, the same they did willingly, and loved their king like obedient subjects.'" See Adam von Bartsch, *The Triumph of the Emperor Maximilian I*, ed. Hans Burgkmair and Alfred Aspland (Holbein Society, 1875), p. 28.

53 Dietmar Willoweit, *Rechtsgrundlagen der Territorialgewalt: Landesobrigkeit, Herrschaftsrechte und Territorium in der Rechtswissenschaft der Neuzeit* (Cologne: Böhlau, 1975).

The concept of German freedom grew to include not only the religious toleration enshrined in the treaty, but also strong property rights and appeal against unjust action of magistrates. Schmidt goes so far as to argue that Protestantism and Germanic freedom had become fused in the sixteenth and seventeenth centuries. Appeals to Germanic liberty animated the sympathies not only of the nobility but also of the common man as well. The very idea played a profound role in the formation of German identity (it was "identity-forming," *identitätsbildend*).[54]

By roughly around 1700, "German freedom" came to enjoy a more generalized usage. Germans spoke of such diverse freedoms that it is genuinely difficult to keep count of them all or argue that they even cohere into one great unity. It was an embarrassment of riches. Germans in many states were proud of what we would call written constitutions or constitutionalism, the idea that government is restrained by a written, fixed, fundamental law or laws. In English legal tradition, Magna Charta is looked back to as the first great constitutional agreement between ruler and estates (or ruler and ruled, ruler and represented). Jurists of every European country have agreed that many other agreements fit the same bill – they functioned like Magna Charta – and were written constitutions in every meaningful sense. Some of these were made within the empire, others in Spain, England, and elsewhere. Among such agreements have been listed the Peace of Constance (1183), the Constitution of Leon, from Alphonso IX (1188), the Territorial Peace of the Holy Roman Empire (1152), the Confoederatio cum principibus ecclesiasticis (1220), the Statutum in favorem principum (1231), the Mainz territorial peace (1235), the Privilegio general of Aragon (1283, more in 1287), the Castilian constitution of Valladolid (1307), the charter of Kortenberg (Brabant, 1312), French charters of liberty by Philip the Fair (1314–1315), the Joyeuse entrée of Brabant (1356), the Golden Bull (1356), the oath of Jean de Valenrose of Liege (1418), the agreement between margrave and estates of Brandenburg (1472), and the pact of Tübingen (1514). This list could be multiplied probably a *hundredfold*, at a smaller scale of political organization, that of constitutional settlements between princes and territorial estates. The common feature is that, whatever the diverse *names* of such instruments, they *functioned* as records of leaders guaranteeing certain rights toward their constituents.[55] The German form of

54 Schmidt, *Geschichte des Alten Reichs*, p. 79, p. 99.

55 See Morongiu (orig. 1968), Altamira (orig. 1917), Stevens (orig. 1971) and editorial notes by Holt, all in James Clarke Holt, ed., *Magna Carta and the Idea of Liberty* (New York: Wiley, 1972). Naturally not every German jurist was aware of every one of these agreements. My point is to point to a broad array of ruler-estates constitutional documents, many instances of which would have been familiar to most jurists.

the rule of law – the *Rechtsstaat* – also has its beginnings in this time, as legal operators of every stripe usually said that only known, valid, authoritative laws could be legally enforced (though this, like much involving magisterial authority, was subject to exceptions, as in the case of "police" ordinances[56]). The imperial constitution was, we might say, faintly praised with clear damnation by Carl Schmitt in 1927, when he wrote that the old empire was so fixed in its rule of law that it was politically impotent and vulnerable to dissolution from within and attack from without – dangerously so, he contended. As Schmitt put it,

> Every state that respects unconditionally valid objective law and existing subjective rights could be designated a *Rechtsstaat*. That would mean that the status quo that is in force would be legitimated and perpetuated and that vested interests, whether of individuals or of some associations and corporations, are considered more important than the political existence and security of the state. In this sense ... the Roman Empire of the German Nation ... was an ideal *Rechtsstaat* in the period of its dissolution ...[57]

56 German *Polizeiordnungen* or police ordinances refer to public safety regulations, sumptuary and morals regulation, rules about holidays and public conduct, etc. While novel edicts regulating such matters might seem to contravene what is today thought of as the rule of law, no jurist of the period viewed them that way: legal authority over public safety, public morals, and so on was reserved by governments on every level. What jurists universally worried about was the regularity, clarity, and settledness of black-letter law governing crime and property (the latter category including taxes and serfdom). Laws regulating crime and property relations should be clear and known, and should change only slowly and predictably. See glossary of terms.

57 Schmitt, *Constitutional Theory*, pp. 172–173. In 1800, Daniel Jenisch wrote that "the German imperial constitution" made it "impossible for the strong state [within the empire] to simply help itself (*Selbsthilfe*) at the expense of the weak ..." For indeed "the subject can bring suit against the abuses of the highest power at an even higher tribunal." Of course after 1648, the empire was weakened by the ebbing of Habsburg power and the growing power of the German princes and France. These probably more than the respect for general law were what really weakened the empire. Indeed Schmitt's point is that the empire was so much governed by the rule of law that it lacked the strong authoritarian (decisionist) element which he argued states need to weather severe political storms. And indeed Schmitt's characterization seems quite sensible given the destructive deluges of the attacks of France under Louis XIV and Napoleon. See Daniel Jenisch, *Geist und Charakter des achtzehnten Jahrhunderts: politisch, moralisch, ästhetisch und wissenschaftlich betrachtet* (Berlin: Königliche Preussische Akademie Kunst- und Buchhandlung, 1800) Bd. 2, p. 47, quoted in Dreitzel, *Absolutismus und ständische Verfassung in Deutschland*, p. 136.

This constitutionalism, if it is not too anachronistic to label it that retroactively, extended to interpreting the powers and duties of magistrates as authorized and fixed and magistrates as serving on good behavior, that is, conditional on proper performance of office. It was not even unheard of (though rare) for rulers themselves to be removed from office by a coalition of estates led by an alternate claimant (say from a cadet line).[58] Overall, in the seventeenth and eighteenth centuries, the idea of the "Free German Empire" remained popular and serviceable, under various signs. The German empire, or empire-state, was a diverse patchwork of rights and immunities enjoyed by thousands of dominions and communities at all levels. Preferring this pluralism to universal subjection under powerful kings characteristic of other countries, Germans saw their constitution as exhibiting an ideal power balance, akin to that of England, halfway between excessively strong monarchy (as in France and Russia) and anarchy and paralysis (Poland-Lithuania).

No less famous a jurist than Johann Wolfgang von Goethe (1749–1832), articulated and praised this interpretation of German freedom as sheltering in the empire's peculiar combination of homogeneity, openness, stability, and plurality. Goethe was no stranger to Germany's "small-state politics" (*Kleinstaaterei*). A government administrator as well as poet and polymath, Goethe celebrated the empire's numerous small states as friendly rivals in patronizing arts, culture, and widespread learning. He praised the empire's federalist pluralism, which he identified with freedom. An extended remark he made to his conversation partner Eckermann is worth presenting here at length. He said,

> [May] Germany be one in love! ... May it be one so that German dollars and groschen may be of equal value throughout the whole empire ! one so that my travelling-chest may pass unopened through all the six-and-thirty states! ... May there be no more talk about inland and outland among the German states ! In fine, may Germany be one in weight and measure, in trade and commerce, and a hundred similar things which I will not name! / But if we imagine that the unity of Germany consists in this, that the very great empire should have a single great capital, and that this one great capital would conduce to the development of great individual talent, or to the welfare of the great mass of the people, we are in error. / A state has been justly compared to a living body with many limbs, and thus the capital of a state may be compared to the heart, from

58 Trossbach, "Power and Good Governance: The Removal of Ruling Princes in the Holy Roman Empire, 1680–1794."

FIGURE 10 The Imperial Court. A stylized almost schematic depiction of the Imperial Court. The emperor presides, though jurists advise and books are consulted. Freedom (*libertas*) consists in the separation of sacred and secular powers (depicted in the foreground figures), both of them equal before the court to have their grievances heard

which life and prosperity flow to the individual members, near and far. But if the members be very distant from the heart, the life that flows to them will become weaker and weaker … / Whence is Germany great, but by the admirable culture of the people, which equally pervades all

> parts of the kingdom? But does not this proceed from the various seats of government …? / And now think of such cities as Dresden, Munich, Stuttgart, Cassel, Brunswick, Hanover, and the like; think of the great elements of life comprised within these cities; think of the effect which they have upon the neighboring provinces; and ask yourself if all this would have been the case if they had not for a long time been the residences of princes? / Frankfort, Bremen, Hamburg, and Lubeck are great and brilliant j their effect upon the prosperity of Germany is incalculable. But would they remain what they are, if they lost their own sovereignty and became incorporated with any great German kingdom as a provincial town? I see reason to doubt this.[59]

Indeed, theorists of both federalism and pluralism in the generations before Goethe, in the days of Montesquieu, the Scottish Enlightenment, and the American Founding, have frequently taken the old empire as an object of study and inspiration. As Maiken Umbach writes, "the political diversity which had evolved within the Old *Reich* … [before the eighteenth century] came to be seen by many enlightened reformers as a political achievement in its own right." These came to look favorably on the "political pluralism" because it was favorable to "improvement," "opportunities for new initiatives," and "healthy competition."[60]

---

59 Goethe added (in the middle of these remarks), "Suppose, for centuries past, we had had in Germany only the two capitals, Vienna and Berlin, or only one of these, I should like to see how it would have fared with German culture, or even with that generally diffused opulence which goes hand in hand with culture. Germany has about twenty universities distributed about the whole empire, and about a hundred public libraries similarly distributed. There is also a great number of collections of art, and collections of objects belonging to all the kingdoms of nature; for every prince has taken care to bring around him these useful and beautiful objects. There are gymnasia and schools for arts and industry in abundance, nay, there is scarcely a German village without its school. And how does France stand with respect to this last point! / Then look at the quantity of German theatres, the number of which exceeds seventy, and which are not to be despised as supporters and promoters of a higher cultivation of the people. In no country is the taste for music and singing, and the practice of it so widely spread, as in Germany; and even that is something!" See Johann Wolfgang von Goethe, *Conversations of Goethe with Eckermann and Soret*, Vol. 2 (London: Smith, Elder, & Co., 1850), pp. 104–107.

60 Umbach, *Federalism and Enlightenment in Germany*, p. 5, p. 8. See also Jacob Levy, *Rationalism, Pluralism, and Freedom* (Corby: Oxford University Press, 2014) and Alain de Benoist, "The Idea of Empire," in *Democracy and Populism: The Telos Essays*, ed. Russell A. Berman and Timothy W. Luke (Candor: Telos Press Publishing, 2018). Early modern writers who first trod this path included Johannes Althusius and Montesquieu.

The Old Empire and its member states were, of course, riven by hierarchy and oppression in many places. But the imperial monarchy and many princely states more resembled constitutional monarchies than absolutist regimes or autocracies. There were many champions of "natural freedom" and "natural rights" among Germans in the Old Regime.[61]

We should also consider how widely common people subscribed to the princes' ideal constitutional concept. This is difficult in the earlier period since their voices are not often heard (or at least recorded in documents we still possess). Was "German freedom" anything more than a propaganda program for oligarchs? Here I can only make a conjecture, building on the arguments of historians Mack Walker and Alon Confino. Walker depicted pre-modern German "home towns" as hierarchical and autonomous, combining internal inequality with an appreciation of freedom as independence. Confino argued that in the nineteenth century, Germans projected their feelings and ideas about their home town or home region onto their conception of Germany as a nation.[62] I propose that what Walker and Confino were describing was also at work in jurists' and other intellectuals' conceptions of the relationship between freedom and their beloved empire: They knew of the story of ancient freedom, knew of contests over local freedoms in their home regions, and knew of the princes' and knights' formulation of the empire as a realm of freedom, guaranteed in the empire's (notional) constitution. Drawing on these sources together, a person could well believe – *and project onto his or her own polity* – the idea that the imperial constitution in some way guaranteed the freedom of all subjects (or at least many of them). German intellectuals in the late seventeenth century and the eighteenth century *thought* that their federal polity was a still Free German Empire.

---

61 Klippel, *Politische Freiheit und Freiheitsrechte*, p. 204 and *passim*; Dreitzel, *Absolutismus und ständische Verfassung in Deutschland*. "Personal absolutism," argues Umbach, can be thought of itself as a myth, projected backward in time by "modern totalitarian ideologies." Against this, Umbach writes, "If, however the concept of 'Enlightened absolutism' is taken to refer to a systematic process of state-building, involving the expansion and rationalization of administrative structures as well as cooperation with existing elites, then the term can be regarded as a legitimate description of the aims and objectives (if not always the achievements) of these regimes." Umbach, *Federalism and Enlightenment in Germany*, pp. 7b–8t, citing Nicholas Henshall, *The Myth of Absolutism* (London: Longman, 1992), while noting the latter is principally about France.

62 Mack Walker, *German Home Towns: Community, State, and General Estate, 1648–1871* (Ithaca: Cornell University Press, 1998 [orig. 1971]); Alon Confino, *The Nation as Local Metaphor: Württemberg, Imperial Germany, and National Memory* (Chapel Hill: University of North Carolina Press, 1996).

Another kind of freedom which had common currency from the sixteenth century onward, and which therefore surely must have been close in people's minds when speaking of freedom, was one first articulated by Martin Luther, namely "Christian freedom." (See Figure 11.) This firmly impressed itself on Protestants everywhere (not just the German lands). In one crucial way, this conception resembled that of the medieval Gregorian reformers mentioned briefly earlier: It said that a distinct, and most important freedom of all was not about control of worldly spaces or activities, but instead concerned the soul's access to God. (There the similarity with the medieval Gregorian story ended.) At the heart of Luther's concept of Christian freedom was his argument that personal guilt, penance, and ultimately salvation could not be measured by man-made laws (canons), formulae (such as rituals), and other metrics. The true "freedom of a Christian" consists in being free from impositions that block a person's access to the Gospel.[63] People are "free to do good for God's sake, not for the selfish and demeaning end of achieving their own salvation, a doctrine the Church had recently grossly abused." As Luther himself wrote in his influential pamphlet *On the freedom of a Christian* (1520), no acts, not even meditation and fasting, suffice for "righteousness and freedom," only "the most holy Word of God." That is, personal confrontation with the Gospel is the true and only road to "righteousness and freedom."[64] Unbelievably, Luther's conception was later

63 The Reformation, as Richard Davis writes, "encouraged the belief that [people's] passage to the next [world] was a matter between them and God alone." Davis, *The Origins of Modern Freedom in the West*, Introduction, p. 3mb. See also William J. Bouwsma, "Liberty in the Renaissance and Reformation," in the same volume.

64 Davis, *The Origins of Modern Freedom in the West*, Epilogue, p. 318tm; Martin Luther, *Christian Liberty*, ed. Harold J. Grimm, revised ed. (Philadelphia: Fortress Press, 1957 [orig. 1520]), p. 8. As Roland Bainton explains, for Luther, "The Christian man is of all men the most free, because he is not dominated by rules and does not pretend that he is carrying out laws. He is simply giving expression to his gratitude to God and to his love for his neighbor. The Christian man is … the most bound, but the obligation laid inescapably upon him is from within." In this conception, the Christian is *free* from rules; only his conscience directs his action, where conscience means hearing the Gospel. Roland Bainton, *The Reformation of the Sixteenth Century* (Boston: Beacon Press, 1952), p. 52. To give an example of the words of Luther himself, consider the following passages from his *Christian Freedom* (1520): "Our faith, the Christian liberty … does *not* induce us to live in idleness or wickedness, *but* [*yet*] makes the law and works unnecessary for any man's righteousness and salvation." Since "all earthly lawgivers … [prescribe] laws and works … it is impossible that they should *of themselves* escape from the slavery of works and come to a knowledge of the freedom of faith." Christians therefore want to be taught by God rather than other men – they want Him to "write his law in our hearts" A Christian must

even praised by Friedrich Nietzsche (who however turned it on its ear of course).[65]

Luther's notion of the freedom of a Christian was closely connected theologically yet another component strand or stream of German freedom, also familiar to jurists of the day: *res merae facultatis* or "pure abilities," a theory of natural freedom resembling that theorized by Thomas Hobbes but far older. This was the conception which underwrote the Imperial Chamber Court's decision in the Fulda wine monopoly lawsuit presented at the opening of Chapter 1. It all goes back to the teaching of Paul of Tarsus about the Jewish law in the New Testament of the Bible, and Luther's use of this teaching in his new reformed theology of the 1520s. A pure ability was a natural freedom to do any of a variety of things which one had by natural right and which could not be taken by others without cause or lost through non-use. For that reason it was considered to be a property right when applied to a given circumstance such as way across land or open-market activity.[66]

"not be idle and ... must do such works freely and only to please God." See Luther, *Christian Liberty*, pp. 12–13, [pp. 37b–40], and p. 23, respectively. For more background, see Bleicken et al., "Freiheit," pp. 436–446 and Martin van Gelderen, "Liberty, Civic Rights, and Duties in Sixteenth-entury Europe and the Rise of the Dutch Republic," in *The Individual in Political Theory and Practice*, ed. Janet Coleman, *The origins of the modern state in Europe* (New York, 1996), pp. 101–102.

65 The sage of Basel wrote that "perhaps Luther performed no greater service than to have had the courage of his *sensuality* (in those days it was called, delicately enough, 'evangelical freedom')." Friedrich Wilhelm Nietzsche, *On the Genealogy of Morals* (New York: Vintage Books, 1967), Third Essay, Section 3, p. 98.

66 While *res merae facultatis* was in origin not exclusively use by Germans, and by the nineteenth century was part of Scots law as well, during the seventeenth and eighteenth centuries it was a German exclusive, as it were. I have seen discussion of *res merae facultatis* in works by German jurists as early as 1575, and have been told it shows up early sixteenth-century legal humanism as well. My sense though is that it probably arose in canon jurisprudence not later than the fourteenth century, given its terminological similarity to other legal distinctions from that period (*merum* vs. *mixtum*; *facultas*). No new treatments appeared after 1761 although it is mentioned in passing once in an article discussing the Fulda lawsuit in 1983, but that is all. The concept also shows up in nineteenth- and twentieth-century Scottish civil jurisprudence, where legal historians consider it obscure, apparently being unaware of its earlier life in Central Europe or prior. The concept begs of further investigation. See respectively Matthaeus Wesenbeck, *Tractatus et Responsa, quae vulgo Consilia Juris appellantur* (Colonia Munatiana [Basel]: Episcopius, 1575); Johann Georg Estor, "Die belehnung mit einer sache tilget die *res merae facultatis* und werket ein verbithungs-recht," in *Neue Kleine Schriften*, Vol. 4 (Marburg: Philipp Casimir Müller, 1761); Rainer Polley, "Retraktsrecht und Weinkauf im Hochstift Fulda. Zur Bedeutung des Volksgewohnheitsrechts im 18. Jahrhundert," *Hessisches Jahrbuch für Landesgeschichte* 33 (1983); Roderick Paisley, "Right to Make Roads and *res merae facultatis*,"

FIGURE 11 Allegorical picture featuring Luther liberating the conscience

In many parts of the empire, freedom of discussion was also substantial (measured relative to the period). There have been many *bons mots* concerning this.[67] Goethe and Fichte believed their Germany (perhaps romantically exaggerated) was one of great spiritual and discursive freedom. The speech of royal subjects was famously free in Kant's Königsberg: The great liberal nationalist historian Friedrich Meinecke contended that the liberal conditions of the

---

Edinburgh Law Review 11, no. 1 (2007); and Sheriff Douglas J. Cusine, "Res merae facultatis: Through a Glass Darkly," in *Essays in conveyancing and property law: In honour of Professor Robert Rennie*, ed. Frankie McCarthy, James Chalmers, and Stephen Bogle (Cambridge: Open Book Publishers, 2015), especially p. 202. The New Testament connection was that Paul had argued that, since Jesus had finally fulfilled the Hebrew Law, many matters remain thereafter for Christians morally indifferent (*adiaphoron*). Lutheran and Calvinist writers would take up this tradition. "Adiaphoron" and "indifferent" matters were treated by Philipp Melanchthon, John Locke, Jonathan Swift, and Immanuel Kant as matters in which people are naturally free to choose to do whatever they wish, ungoverned by religion or law, but only morality or conscience (equity).

67 "Thoughts are free," wrote Friedrich Schiller. "God gave the French dominion over the land, the English dominion over the sea, and the Germans dominion over the clouds" (meaning ideas), wrote Heinrich Heine. Quoted in Jorge Luis Borges, *Selected Non-Fictions*, ed. Eliot Weinberger (New York: Viking, 1999).

Old Empire, at least in Brandenburg-Prussia (his focus) were the fertile soil which permitted "idealistic individualism" to grow up and replace the older "rationalistic individualism" (by which he meant the old rationalistic, contractarian individualism rooted in natural law, which was the first cousin across the Channel of English liberalism).[68]

But German freedom also must have implied a tension in political and legal thought after 1650 between *individual freedom* and the *autonomy of domains or communities*. The freedom of a principality vis-à-vis the empire might mean that its lord could oppress his or her subjects. A high level of personal freedom for individual subjects requires a government to guarantee that freedom – if not the local or regional government, then some greater power. (The tensions in modern American federalism, for example around the Civil Rights movement, illustrate this nicely.) Who then was to champion people's rights? German jurists in the eighteenth century did not strongly distinguish between what we would think of as private rights (e.g. property rights) and the public rights of a citizenry (modern "civil liberties" or constitutional protections, such as those found in the English Magna Carta). The enjoyment of any and all such rights, whosoever enjoyed them, was to be guaranteed by counts, princes, and kings of the Free German Empire. Almost all subjects called on the long-suffering emperor to guarantee such rights. Domains (local courts, seigneurs, and principalities) and communal rights (such as freedom from taxes or autonomous choice of leaders) look both like public law rights of governments and like private law rights of estates. This tension between private and public rights emerges in cases examined in this book from appellate courts, including the high appellate court in Hesse-Cassel and especially the Imperial Chamber Court (the major imperial appellate court), throughout the period. Around the French Revolution, soon after the end of the period studied, the *public-private* distinction became better settled in Germany. By that time, princely states had become the German states, seen as the true guarantors of individual freedom.

68 Friedrich Meinecke, *The Age of German Liberation, 1795–1815*, ed. Peter Paret and Helmuth Fischer (Berkeley: University of California Press, 1977 [orig. 1906]), pp. 20–25. See also Schmidt, *Wandel durch Vernunft*, pp. 330–339, 354–360. Two great theoretical works which begin from the historical context of free discussion growing up under German absolutism are Jürgen Habermas, *The Structural Transformation of the Public Sphere: An Inquiry into a Category of Bourgeois society* (Cambridge: MIT Press, 1989 [orig. 1962]) and Reinhart Koselleck, *Critique and Crisis: Enlightenment and the Pathogenesis of Modern Society* (Cambridge: MIT Press, 1988 [orig. 1979]), both in the series Studies in Contemporary German Social Thought.

•••

As Erwin Hölzle put it, in both Germany and in England during the seventeenth and eighteenth centuries, ancient national myth, evolved political and legal institutions, modern national birthright, and natural law came together like a confluence of rivers. The apparently popular conception of a more broad "German freedom" arrived in the later seventeenth century, partially overlapping what came before but also having distinct, additional meanings, including religious toleration and freedoms gained through protection of personal and group property rights. There was something almost democratic about this third element – German freedom suffused the lives of many if not all German subjects. The composite idea of German freedom gave people an understanding of Germans' natural and historical rights. This understanding subtly guided their interpretation of the law in difficult suits or obscure situations. Many people appreciated and expected civil liberty and features associated with limited government, fixed legal procedures including judicial impartiality (due process), rule of general law, free association, religious tolerance, and free discussion.[69] Before examining the mechanics of German freedom in the sphere of property law, however, we will take a closer look at jurists and at the workings of professional legal institutions.

---

69 The anecdote of the "miller of Sanssoucci" in Berlin was a representative and well-known example of this popular belief in the eighteenth century – that German subjects could expect fair and equal protection under the law in their states.

CHAPTER 3

Idea-Generative Institutions

The previous chapter culminated in a parade of different ideas which coexisted under the notion of German freedom in the eighteenth century. I take German freedom to have been one of the key animating spirits of this historical context. Here though we turn to something far more concrete: institutions and how institutional change worked and generated changes in law and jurisprudence. Understanding these two factors – the ideas of German freedom and the institutions which housed jurists and coordinated their creative activity – will best help us understand the developments of civil liberty and civil libertarian jurisprudence of that period, the topics of Chapters 4–6.

This chapter employs a model of *the growth of ideas as being a function of institutional processes*, within which are embedded working, active individuals (legal operators). Why these institutions existed, what they did, how they shaped jurists and juristic ideas, and how they expanded and changed during the seventeenth and eighteenth centuries are the specific topics explored below. This infrastructure produced new law, largely through the courts and the extension of the appellate court system, but also within the growing network of universities.

Institutions can be thought of as the rule-like ways that people regularly organize themselves to perform recurrent activities.[1] Examples in our context here include things as diverse as real estate markets and courts, teaching and study by university law faculty, and libraries. Institutions have stable, persistent roles for people to play, such as plaintiff's attorney, student, librarian, printer, etc. People perform activities and in many cases produce new ideas in performance of their specific roles. Institutional action is a combination of spontaneity and pre-programmed function.

Ideas were not mainly produced in the abstract. Rather they were generated and/or transformed through institutions. Judges, lawyers, professors, students,

1 I loosely follow the definition of institutions used by Douglass North and Paul Thomas, that institutions are "the rules of the game," distinct both from people themselves and from organizations. See North and Thomas, *Rise of the Western World* and Oliver E. Williamson, "The New Institutional Economics: Taking Stock, Looking Ahead," *Journal of Economic Literature* 38, no. 3 (2000).

 | DOI:10.1163/9789004685178_004

privy councilors, members of regime staffs, notaries, printers, booksellers, and even librarians manned these institutions. The latter took texts and ideas in and churned them out changed or put to new applications. Jurists' access to knowledge was itself institutionally channeled, as described above – through the forms of training, use of libraries, and collegial networks.

Behind and above these institutions pressed the superpersonal forces of supply and demand: the supply of books, justice, and training, and the demand for books, justice, and jurists to press one's claims. At the broadest level, the highest sources of causality here, stood state competition, population growth, and commercialization.

This chapter proceeds from the very general and high level and moves down to the concrete and low level. We start with a brief overview of state competition in the Germanies. The sixteenth and seventeenth centuries saw consolidation of states through the amalgamation of smaller territories. New, more complex regimes created appellate courts and universities with law faculties. Population growth and advancing commercialization contributed to a growing demand for jurists. Court activity at the appellate level in the Hessian and Rhine-Main region grew robustly in the second half of the seventeenth century and in the eighteenth century. Courts contributed not only to the spread of important ideas about freedom, but also affected civil liberties, sometimes expanding them, sometimes limiting them. No matter what hat a professional jurist wore, he had by definition been trained at a university law faculty, usually (in this region) a Protestant one. Universities and smaller "high schools" were founded and created law faculties steadily throughout our period, a new one about every one to two generations for almost three centuries with nine faculties training jurists in a region of half a million people by the late eighteenth century. Like courts, the law faculty was another institution which helped transform and generate ideas.

Real estate markets, civil courts, teaching and study by university law faculty, regime chanceries, and the book market can be thought of as agonistic institutions. This is key. By agonistic, I mean they were structured around confrontation between parties, typically resulting in the generation of new ideas. Students studied, teachers taught, judges interpreted, books were created, printed, sold, bought, collected, and consulted, and so on. These activities transmitted new ideas and the new application of ideas. Such idea-production was motivated by competitive pressures within institutional arrangements and the institutions themselves were subject to external forces such as patronage, population growth, and commercialization. For example, in the book trade, printers not only printed books but also commissioned them and sometimes assembled them from pilfered component texts.[2] Book sellers connected this supply with the demand arising among modern professional jurists. Sellers imported books containing highly regarded jurisprudence from places like Genoa all across the Latin Christian legal communion. Lawyers and judges in courts, and professors and students in universities, created new arguments and interpretations of established law. Library collections were a transmission mechanism running in parallel to the book market itself, connecting printers, authors, readers, and other users of law (such as notaries). The growth of courts, universities, the book trade, and library collections was itself brought about by the larger forces of inter-state competition, commercialization, and population increase, themselves interrelated in ways still not fully understood and in any event firmly beyond the scope of this book.[3] State expansion, university faculties, population growth, book trade, libraries – all of these were key elements that transmitted ideas and practices outwards, from urban elites to people in the countryside, thus transforming society across the seventeenth and eighteenth centuries.[4]

1 State Expansion

Law courts are of course the creatures of states, at least in modern Western polities. States created and extended courts and patronized law faculties, which produced the actors in the courts. Beginning in the fifteenth century, German princes increasingly consolidated their dominion over many of the smaller polities in the Holy Roman Empire.[5] Consolidation happened through inheritance, sale, conquest, or a combination of these. State formation and consolidation continued apace throughout the sixteenth and seventeenth centuries, becoming overlain with religious reformation (the "Protestant Reformation" and similar Catholic reform) and reformations of territorial law by the

2 Adrian Johns, *The Nature of the Book: Print and Knowledge in the Making* (Chicago: University of Chicago Press, 1998). The common actors in these spheres of activity were jurists, book printers (and other business agents in the book trade), and assorted clerks in various bureaucracies such as copyists. I focus primarily on the creative writing, as it were, of the jurists alone.

3 Charles Tilly, *Coercion, Capital, and European States, A.D.990–1992*, Revised ed. (Cambridge: Basil Blackwell; Wiley-Blackwell, 1992); Raeff, *Well-Ordered Police State*; North and Thomas, *Rise of the Western World.*

4 In Chapter 4, I will also discuss a unique event which contributed to changes in property rights and jurisprudence in the mid seventeenth century, namely the destruction of the Thirty Years' War.

5 An illustrative study of this process is Zmora, *State and Nobility in Early Modern Germany.*

rulers.[6] In 1500, for example, Upper and Lower Hesse were united formally in the person of the heir of the House of Brabant, Landgrave William. William's son, Landgrave Philipp the Magnanimous, additionally inherited the county of Catzenelnbogen. Philipp introduced Lutheran reforms into the churches in his domains and expropriated most of the monasteries, which were converted to new purposes. Other domains such as Dietz and Ziegenhain came under landgravial control around the same time.

As a rule of thumb, when political dominion changed hands, most legal structures were left unchanged. Even when political units came under the control of a single ruler, as with Hesse, Catzenelnbogen, Dietz, and Ziegenhain, they were usually considered to remain distinct from one another. Pre-existing political and legal structures persisted for centuries, even when stripped of much of their substance. The county of Dietz, a neighbor of the Landgraviate, came permanently under Hessian control after 1479 until its eventual extinction after the Napoleonic Wars. The county of Hanau was created in 1429 and divided and recombined several times over the centuries until its components came permanently under the control of Hesse-Cassel in 1643 and Hesse-Darmstadt in 1736. As an example of how the existing laws, customs, and vested interests of a dominion were preserved amidst change of rulers, the title of the Hessian landgraves in the eighteenth century was "Lord … Landgrave of Hesse, Prince of Hersfeld, Count of Catzenelnbogen, Dietz, Ziegenhayn, Nidda, Schaumburg, and Hanau … etc. etc. etc." – not simply prince of a single-named unitary domain. In other words, rulers bundled together disparate rights rather than recasting them as a single, unitary right. A similar process occurred in most monarchical states of the era, including the House of Austria, the Prussian monarchy, and the Kingdom of Great Britain (formed in 1707). This persistence of ancient orders (or at least the belief in their persistence) was a cornerstone of the doctrine of ancient constitutionalism (*antiqua constitutio* or "ancient constitution").[7]

In most European countries, centralized monarchies were able to expand their power by creating tax and administrative bureaucracies capable of subordinating both local powers (villages and seigneurs) and regional powers

6 Berman, *Law and Revolution II*. For reform movements broadly, see Steven E. Ozment, *The Age of Reform (1250–1550): An Intellectual and Religious History of Late Medieval and Reformation Europe* (New Haven: Yale University Press, 1980).

7 J. G. A. Pocock, *The Ancient Constitution and the Feudal Law* (Cambridge: 1957); Jacob Levy, "Not So *Novus* an *Ordo*: Constitutions without Social Contracts," *Political Theory* 20 (2009). The term "*antiqua constitutio*" is from Nicolaus Hieronymus Gundling, "De iure oppignorati territorii secundum ius gentium et teutonicum," in *Exercitationes academicae* (Halle: Johann Gothfriedus Renger, 1736 [orig. *1705*]), §22, p. 38.

(rich towns and great lords).[8] In the empire, however, the regional powers struggled against the monarchy and achieved considerable power and independence against the emperor. The emperor, while always the most powerful lord in the realm, became more a first among equals and never the liege lord or indisputable master, as in France or Russia. From the late sixteenth century onward, a three-level, federalist political and legal structure developed in the Holy Roman Empire. The counts and dukes who came to predominate were regional magnates such as the dukes of Saxony, landgraves of Hesse, and margrave of Brandenburg. Rulers of great territories – margraves, landgraves, dukes, some counts, and some bishops and abbots – were called princes. Most counts, bishops, and abbots were not princes but were instead subject in some form to the aforementioned territorial princes. What I am calling the local level might include counts, bishops and abbots (in their non-religious tenures), knights, towns, and free common people (*Gemeinfreie*) – that is, all people or collective units of any cut who had become subordinated to the greater magnates calling themselves princes. Princes thus constituted a middle level between local powers and the emperor, titular monarch of the entire realm (Figure 12).

Princes sought to and increasingly were able to draw jurisdiction to themselves, overseeing local affairs while also escaping imperial oversight. Nevertheless, two imperial supreme courts continued to exist and decide civil suits until the abolition of the empire in 1804. These two courts were the Aulic Council (*Reichshofgericht*) and the imperial chamber court (*Reichskammergericht*). These two courts held parallel jurisdiction, meaning that either could take appeals from local matters. In practice, the chamber court convened in the north, first in Speyer and later very close to most of the people and events in this book, in Wetzlar (near Marburg and Frankfurt am Main), while the Aulic Council convened in Vienna. The chamber court primarily heard suits between smaller powers, often villages or towns and lesser princes or lords, while the Aulic Council more often heard disputes between greater imperial powers.[9]

---

8 Richard Bonney, ed., *Economic Systems and State Finance* (Oxford: Oxford University Press, 1995); Tilly, *Coercion, Capital, and European States, A.D.990–1992*.

9 On the activity and jurisprudence of the imperial chamber court, several decisions of which are discussed in the chapters following, see Filippo Ranieri, *Recht und Gesellschaft im Zeitalter der Rezeption: eine rechts- und sozialgeschichtliche Analyse der Tätigkeit des Reichskammergerichts im 16. Jahrhundert*, Quellen und Forschungen zur höchsten Gerichtsbarkeit im alten Reich (Cologne: Böhlau, 1985); Filippo Ranieri, "Die Juristen im Alten Reich des 17. und 18. Jahrhunderts: ein Forschungsprojekt," in *Stände und Gesellschaft im Alten Reich*, ed. Georg Schmidt, *Veröffentlichungen des Instituts für Europäische Geschichte Mainz. Abteilung*

FIGURE 12 The German-Roman Emperor

Universalgeschichte. Beiheft (Stuttgart: Franz Steiner Verlag, 1989); Bernhard Diestelkamp, *Das Reichskammergericht in der deutschen Geschichte: Stand der Forschung, Forschungsperspektiven*, Quellen und Forschungen zur höchsten Gerichtsbarkeit im alten Reich (Cologne: Böhlau, 1990) and Bernhard Diestelkamp, ed., *Die politische Funktion des Reichskammergerichts* (Cologne: Böhlau Verlag, 1993) (both demonstrating the continuing vitality of the court); and in more recent overview Anette Baumann, Peter Oestmann, Stephan Wendehorst, and Siegrid Westphal, eds., *Prozesspraxis im Alten Reich. Annäherungen – Fallstudien – Statistiken*, Vol. 50, Quellen und Forschungen zur Höchsten Gerichtsbarkeit im Alten Reich (Cologne; Weimar; Vienna: 2005) and Wilson, *Holy Roman Empire*, pp. 70–75.

Often, two or more polities claimed authority to adjudicate a given dispute at the same time. By the sixteenth century, local, state, and imperial/federal governments had *concurrent* or parallel jurisdiction in the empire. A count might claim with apparent right high appellate jurisdiction over a local matter, but another prince might too. It was unusual by the eighteenth century for there to be any direct conflict between local government law and imperial law, except when imperial rights were clearly at stake. Such a situation in our region, in particular Hesse-Darmstadt and Solms, occurred sporadically in the late seventeenth and early eighteenth centuries. The counts of Solms were oppressing their subjects in the town of Freienseen. The town claimed to be under the protection of the larger, neighboring principality of Hesse-Darmstadt. Count and landgrave brought their dispute before the Aulic Council.[10]

Local polities like villages, regional towns, and seigneuries had their own laws, meaning rights, duties, and customary rules such as inheritance law. The rising princely states achieved their fullness of power in the late seventeenth century, when the most powerful thirty or so of them (Prussia, Saxony, Bavaria, etc., but also small states like Hesse-Cassel and Hesse-Darmstadt) were largely able to assert juridical supremacy over the localities, exerting authority to give final judgment over local conflicts. By the eighteenth century, these thirty or so states exercised most of the effective state power in the Holy Roman Empire of the German Nation. At the imperial level, the emperor (the imperial court bureaucracy) and the two supreme courts exercised jurisdiction. Although, to a great extent, these jurisdictions remained concurrent or parallel, in the Hessian and other Rhine-Main polities, at least, local custom and rights held strong predominance.

Which law then was to be applied in a given conflict – local custom, seigneurial right, the edicts of princes, the resolutions of diets, or imperial statute? This is perennial problem which jurists call *conflict of laws*. Sometimes one source of law such as a command or rule was widely recognized to have clear authority, but in many situations it was unclear. In the absence of well-established, contravening local custom, any privileges or other laws made by the *state* governments would be recognized as supreme both in *regional* (*local*) court decisions and by *imperial* courts. The emperor could issue an

10 We do not know how it was decided, but some of the arguments are presented in Heinrich Christian Senckenberg, *Unfug des recursus ad comitia in unerheblicher antastung seiner Kayserl. Majestät reservati iuris cognoscendi de suis privilegiis, welcher ab seiten der armen gemeinde Freyenseen gegen des Herrn Grafen zu Solms-Laubach Hoch-Gräfliche Excellence*, ed. Johann Bernhard Christian Hase (Giessen: Johann Müller, 1744).

edict which had the force of law and would apply to all lower jurisdictions – so long as it did not contradict established custom, currently valid law, or vested interests or rights.[11] Beyond these formal considerations, we should keep in mind the legal-sociological considerations addressed in this book: that law is not only a set of norms but also a creature of circumstance.[12]

On the eve of the Reformation, many small, autonomous jurisdictions existed in the Hessian and Rhine-Main region. Broadly, the Hessian regimes of the landgraves in Marburg, Cassel, Darmstadt, and Giessen were the most powerful, followed by a shifting order of the lordships and communal governments in Nassau, Frankfurt am Main, Hanau, Fulda, Herborn, Solms, Ysenburg, Wied, and other power centers in the region. An aspiring ruler called himself or herself a prince or princess, or was dubbed such by his or her publicists, jurists, and other bureaucrats. Episcopal sees and more powerful monasteries and towns often exercised prince-like powers of, for example, independent law-making, adjudication, and alliances.

For the purposes of this book, it must be understood that, on a practical level, the most relevant level of legal authority was probably not the higher principality, but rather the county (*Grafschaft*) – the lordly unit of the count (*Graf*). The reason that the county level was often the most important, even in larger principalities amalgamated from multiple smaller counties such as Hesse, Catzenelnbogen, Fulda, Hanau, etc., is that, as noted above, the original comitial jurisdiction, customs, and especially rights and freedoms were as a rule held to be continuously valid unless they had been formally abolished or changed at some discrete point in modern history (modern = "now," "today," i.e. in the jurists' own present era). Princes emerged as major players from the ranks of counts, dukes, bishops and abbots, frequently by absorbing the local rights and properties of counts in the process. The names of rulers in Hesse and Thuringia were "landgraves," meaning "territorial counts," indicating

11 In cases of necessity (war, public health, catastrophe), however, the ruler was understood to be able to unilaterally undertake any measure needed to preserve the realm. Then as now, public safety or other great necessity was generally understood to have the highest authority. Custom probably on the whole ranked as the second highest level of legal authority, followed by royal rights, court decisions in lawsuits between private parties, police regulations, vested property rights, executive commands (of princes, kings, or emperors), civil law, and finally natural right, in that order. The rank of various legal authorities including matters of public necessity is also discussed below in Ch. 5, p. 202 including in nn. 49-50 and in Ch. 7, p. 299 including in n. 16.

12 For discussion of law as a complex evolutionary order, see Wilder, "Teaching Old Dogs New Tricks" and Pier G. Monateri, "Deep Inside the Bramble Bush: Complex Orders and Humanities," *Rechtsgeschichte* 11 (2007).

that they were counts like other counts as lords of a county (the *Grafschaft* of Hessen), but had expanded their power around a whole region through the processes discussed previously. So all princes were dukes or counts (including different kinds of counts like landgraves, margraves, and burgraves), but only a handful of counts were princes. The ill-defined term *prince* referred to the largely sovereign ruler of a territory, subject really only to the emperor and the emperor's Aulic Council. Barons (*Freiherren*) had legally the same standing and eminence as territorial princes like landgraves or dukes, only subject to the emperor, but substantially less power. Ordinary counts and lords (Herren) had become subject to the territorial prince's jurisdiction, and incorporated into the diet he held, by the seventeenth century.

To modern ears, a "lordship" or "seigneury" suggests sole dominion, which sounds very different from a communal or republican government. However, in addition to sole dominion, there could be group dominion or ownership (as in family co-ownership) as well as communal or corporate dominion (as in town government or abbacy of a monastery). To period observers, these various kinds of ownership, rule, or government shared at least one common legal element: they legitimately governed and were usually cast as *dominium* or *Herrschaft*. The lord, whether sole or collective, exercised lordship or ownership. The incumbent(s) upheld the public peace, settled disputes, and usually had some kind of legislative power.

More important, at that time, than the distinction between lordly or monarchical government and republican government was the distinction between just and unjust rule, or legitimate or illegitimate (tyrannical) authority. God's dominion was supreme, subordinate to which in a great pyramid were the dominions of popes, bishops, priests, emperors, kings, princes, seigneurs, heads of household, small tenants, and even serfs and those with fewer rights than they. Of course, different lords in society might view their relative positions in the hierarchy differently, or only grudgingly accepted the distribution of power. The pope thought himself superior to king and emperor, and vice versa (the "two swords" theory). The German princes and German kings and emperors interpreted their authority and rights differently, leading to constant tensions and conflicts. The balance of power shifted slowly but continuously.

In all of this dynamism among powers in the empire, the task of tracking and analyzing changing the legal order fell to regimes' jurists, including those on law faculties of universities (which were of course sponsored by princes, major players in the very game). Rather than erasing legal orders which got subsumed in the interstate competition, regime bureaucrats gathered and recorded the many individual laws and customs of the new territories. They validated and digested the latter's "ancient constitutions" (their "old

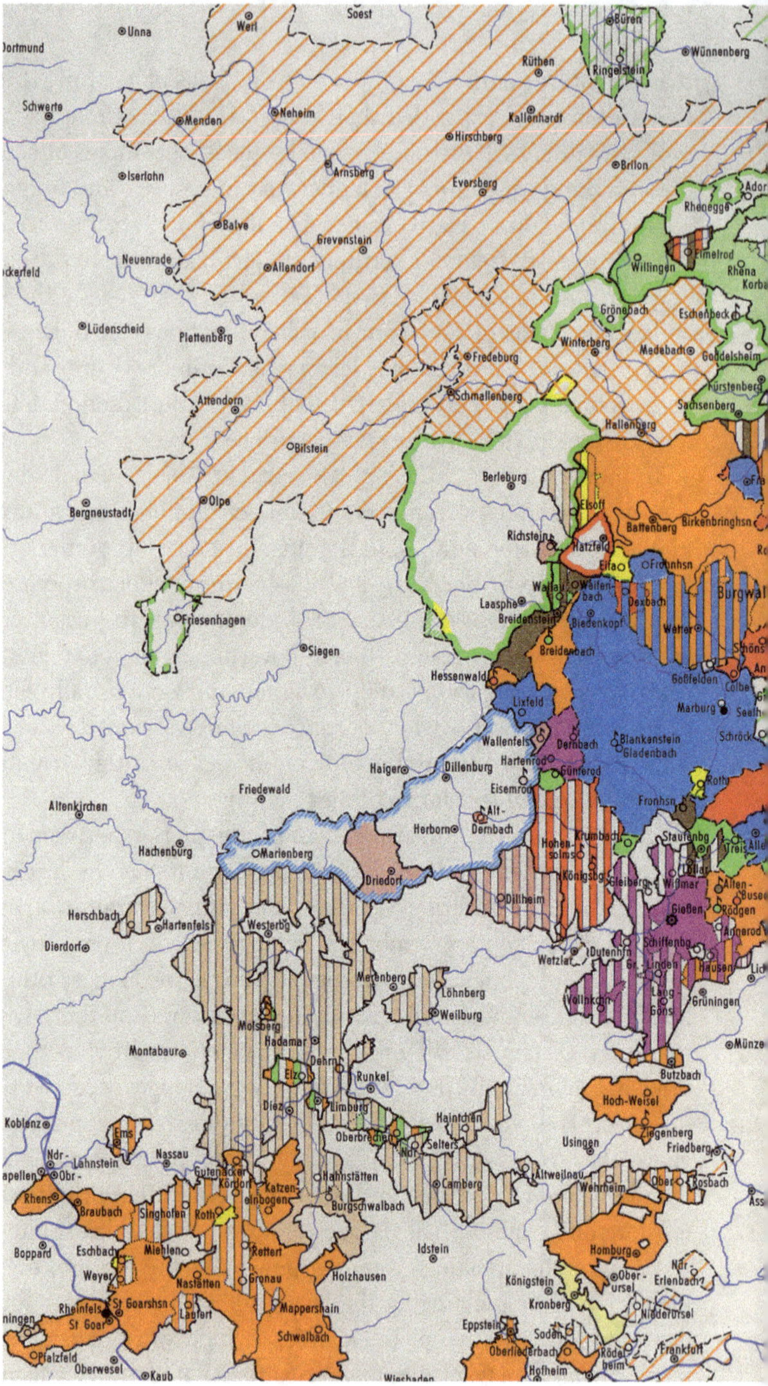

FIGURE 13 The growth of the Hessian landgraviate from 1247 to 1567, most of which happened through inheritance, purchase, and extending protective jurisdiction. After 1567 the landgraviate would be divided and recollected several times, but would not collectively be diminished until after the end of the empire

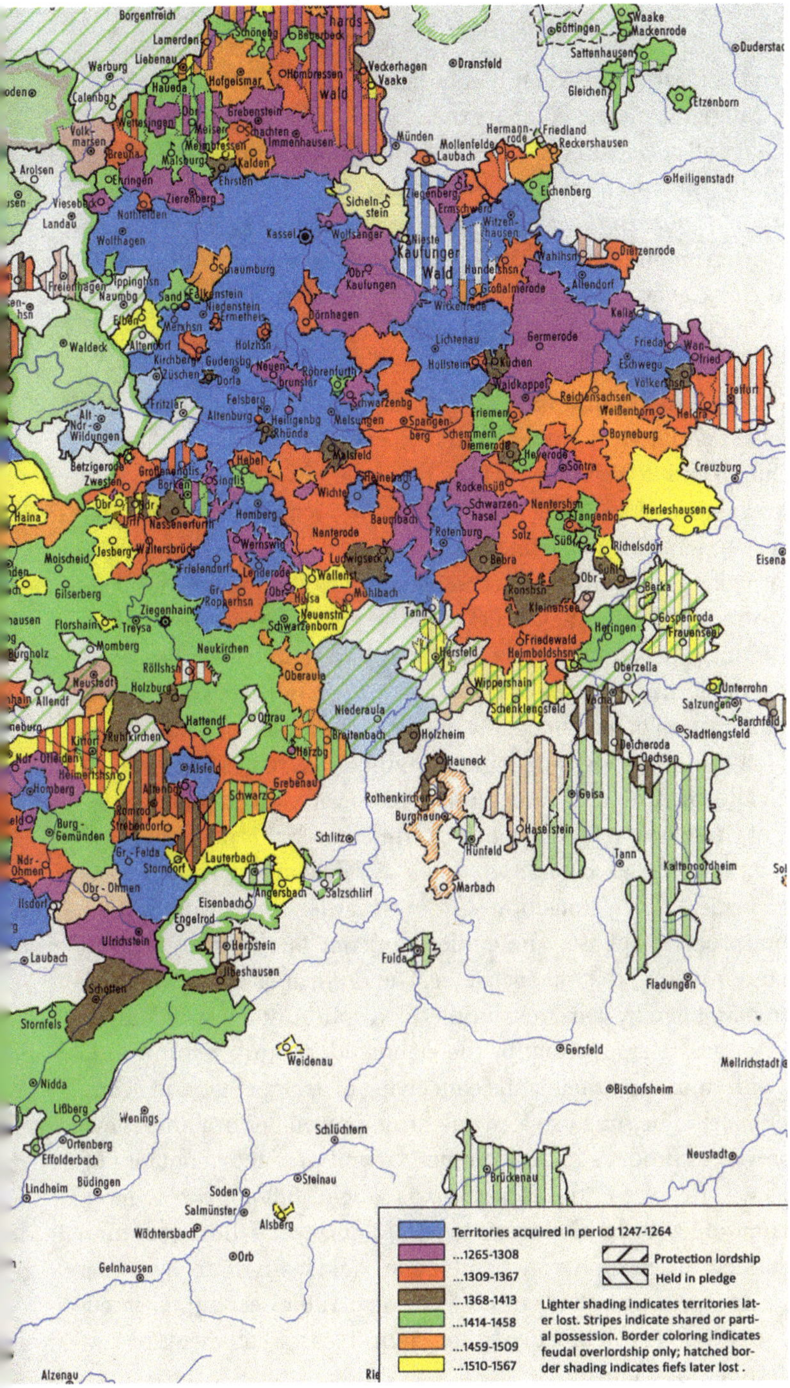
Territories acquired in period 1247-1264
...1265-1308
...1309-1367
...1368-1413
...1414-1458
...1459-1509
...1510-1567
Protection lordship
Held in pledge
Lighter shading indicates territories later lost. Stripes indicate shared or partial possession. Border coloring indicates feudal overlordship only; hatched border shading indicates fiefs later lost.
Kassel
Göttingen
Dransfeld
Münden
Heiligenstadt
Eschwege
Allendorf
Witzenhausen
Kaufunger Wald
Wolfhagen
Waldeck
Fritzlar
Melsungen
Spangenberg
Rotenburg
Bebra
Sontra
Boyneburg
Herleshausen
Creuzburg
Hersfeld
Ziegenhain
Treysa
Homberg
Alsfeld
Grebenau
Lauterbach
Schlitz
Hünfeld
Fulda
Tann
Geisa
Vacha
Salzungen
Niederaula
Neukirchen
Schotten
Ulrichstein
Nidda
Laubach
Büdingen
Gelnhausen
Schlüchtern
Steinau
Soden
Salmünster
Wächtersbach
Orb
Brückenau
Gersfeld
Bischofsheim
Mellrichstadt
Neustadt
Fladungen
Kaltennordheim
Weidenau
Alsberg
Alzenau

law," *antiqua constitutio*). Jurists then had to figure out what all of these old laws, customs, and rights meant, compare them, sometimes weigh one against another, and above all *reconcile them* into a common, plural framework. By the eighteenth century, this common framework had come to be called the "territorial constitution" (*Landesverfassung*).[13] In Germany, this process took place at all levels of government, from the imperial appellate courts to the courts of princes and cities, even to the classrooms of law faculty. Regime courts in each territory brought all pre-existing laws and orders into their construction of this "territorial constitution."

The reconciliation and reform of laws in these growing states often went under the label of *reform*, a term much used in the sixteenth century (the "age of reform"). Church and Reformation history tells us about reforms of ecclesiastical laws governing institutions, church officers, hierarchies, and penitential practices. Legal humanists and regime legal operators of the period sought to simplify, normalize, and standardize the mass of law (and numerous specific sources), correcting what they believed to be messes created over time by abridgement, mistranslation, forgery, and abuse. To that extent they were "reformers" in a modern sense. Hence newly instituted appellate courts were to perfect the application of just procedure and laws as they already notionally existed. Local law was to be inspected and sometimes altered to bring it into alignment with known, just procedure or other, more widespread practice.[14]

In his study of German and Russia police reformations in this period, part of which focuses on the Hessian lands, Marc Raeff argues that the work of legal and religious reformers slowly transitioned from an earlier, conservative phase to a later, more proactive phase. The earlier work sought to (in reformers' minds) shore up or restore the old social, legal, and religious order, buffeted as it seemed to have been by wars, revolutions, corruption, and loss of knowledge of earlier forms. He argued that by the eighteenth century, reform work had changed, with rulers and their staffs conceiving of society, law, and economy as manipulable, to be tuned so to speak for improved performance. Law might be improved to produce better commercial and productive outcomes, for instance, as we often see in this book. The paradigm shift appears to have had much in common with developments in natural science of the day: nature followed mechanical, discoverable laws and if one could learn those laws, one could build machinery to gain ends desired by man. The research presented here certainly supports Raeff's broader contention, at least in the fields of law and administration (not science).

---

13 Berman, *Law and Revolution II*.

14 Ozment, *Age of Reform*; Raeff, *Well-Ordered Police State*.

2 Courts

> We have taken the Schaumburg subjects into our protection and, as is just, have commanded our soldiers to leave them unmolested and not to extract any *Kontribution* from them, and therefore we also demand that they pay us homage and bring cases before no other court than our Chancery ... and appeal to us as their only ordinary authority, whereby we shall represent them.
>
> AMALIE-ELIZABETH, LANDGRAVINE OF HESSE-CASSEL (1640)[15]

In this epigram Amalie-Elizabeth (regent of Hesse-Cassel in exile, r. 1627–1650) encapsulates the classic political contract of protection and obedience: Rulers demand obedience from their subjects and in exchange commit to uphold justice.[16] If a ruler can provide more justice to more people, he or she can reasonably seek more subjection and thus exercise more power. A central feature of early modern state-building was the effective extension of the regime's guarantee of justice to its subject population, a process in which courts and universities played a critical role. This section and the next discuss law faculties and appellate courts in the region and period under study. To understand how law worked locally and at the state level, it is not enough to treat it as a simple system of explicit, fixed norms. Since legal operators created and changed law not only by aiding in actual legislation, but also in crafting court procedures, ad hoc governmental edicts, and most importantly but subtly in crafting new ideas in law schools and in arguments before courts, we also need to understand how they were trained and where they worked – primarily in courts created by the princely regimes. (See a depiction of a court in Figure 20.)

To secure their power against challengers from all levels, princes like Hessian Landgrave William and his son Philipp created and strengthened bureaucracies to raise taxes, enforce order, unify the application of existing law, and subdue potential challengers.[17] It helps us understand legal change to con-

15 Christoph Ludwig Kleinschmid and Christian Gerhard Apell, eds., *Sammlung fürstlich Hessischer Landes-Ordnungen und Ausschreiben etc* (Cassel: Johann Nicolaus Seibert; Johann Martin Lüdicke, 1767–1816), Vol. 2, Patent of December 9, 1640, pp. 162–163.

16 Thomas Hobbes, *Leviathan; or, The matter, forme & power of a commonwealth, ecclesiastical and civil*, ed. Michael Oakeshott (Oxford: Blackwell, 1957 [orig. 1651]), p. 396, discussed famously in Carl Schmitt, *The Concept of the Political* (Chicago: University of Chicago Press, 1996 [orig. 1976, 1932]), p. 52.

17 States extend their aid to the "periphery" of society in order to increase their power: "... a key mechanism of Power's expansion becomes visible, this being the manner in which this central Power naturally makes appeals to the periphery of society as a means to engage in indirect and subversive conflict against its own subsidiaries." See C. A. Bond,

sider that appellate courts resolved disputes and regime chanceries and tried to respond to grievances submitted to them.

One way that regimes worked to settle legal disputes was to supervise local jurisdictions, checking for irregularities, unjust practices, or other biases. Another kind of conflict which would flare up came as principalities grew in size and complexity, as old customs of independence came into conflict with new rulers' ideas of their own authority or notions of justice or the "good, old law."[18] In some cases, the new rulers applying new policies to old problems inadvertently created new freedoms. This was what happened for instance when the Hessian landgraves declared that they would not support extradition of runaway serfs back to their old masters in neighboring Hanau.[19] However, in many places, at least for a time, the old freedoms of communities were protected. For example, in the Wetterau, wrote the great nineteenth-century Hessian historian Friedrich von Thudichum,

> Until 1813, every seven years a "*Land- und Eigengericht*" [court for the region and for serf matters] was held on the Knotenberg bei Obereisenhausen, northwest of Marburg. All of the serfs [*Eigenleute*] subject to the landgrave of Hesse-Darmstadt who lived in the jurisdictions of Blankenstein, Grund Breidenbach, Dautphe, Lohra, Kaldern and Reutzberg had to appear there, as well as all Hessian serfs who were from there, including those from the Wetterau. The local laws and the documents from this court throw a bright light on the nature of serfdom in these areas. They show that in the last three hundred years this relationship can hardly be called one of personal unfreedom ... It was people of the Hessian offices who put on these *Eigengerichte*, at which there never wanted for good food and wine.[20]

Nemesis: The Jouvenelian vs. the Liberal Model of Human Orders (Ellenbrook: Imperium Press, 2019), p. 6.

18 The latter describes some of the conflicts which people complained about leading to the Revolution of 1525. See Blickle, *Revolution of 1525*.

19 While prince and vassal were, legally and morally, deeply bonded, they were usually political rivals and sometimes even enemies, as each vied for more power vis-à-vis the other. It could benefit the ruler to disadvantage his vassal by weakening the latter's control over his tenants, including serfs. This is the classic scenario of the high-low-middle strategy modeled in Bertrand de Jouvenel, *Power: The Natural History of its Growth* (London: Hutchinson, 1948 [orig. 1945]); see for instance p. 344, cited in Bond, *Nemesis*, p. 18 n. 1.

20 Friedrich von Thudichum, *Zur Rechtsgeschichte der Wetterau*, Vol. 2 (Tübingen: H. Laupp, 1874), 1.2. Heft, pp. 29–30.

This picture, perhaps embellished, of the *volkisch* (ethnic-customary) rural past shows how local self-management was largely preserved by the regional princes. The court convened to settle outstanding conflicts involving real rights, sometimes including inheritance and familial relations. Such long intervals between convenings were common. According to Thudichum, the serf court was convened and run by the serfs for their own benefit and had been for centuries. The *Land- und Eigengericht* is a fascinating example of a special customary freedom enjoyed by serfs in the region, in that they apparently had autonomy to settle their own affairs, even though according to the same customary serf law, serfs themselves were not free common people, or were in some interpretations "half free." It was a meaningful and cherished kind of freedom which even unfree people might enjoy and was accepted by the local nobility and guaranteed by the ruling princes.[21]

But local autonomy was also being eroded. Centralizing legal bureaucracies introduced new, professional standards of supervision and legal training, which gradually changed the character of the law and the character of those who made and interpreted it. For instance, when jurists surveyed marriage customs in satellite villages around the main Hessian administrative centers of Cassel and Marburg (Figures 14–15, 17–19), they created typologies of custom, translated them into quasi-Roman legal concepts, fixed them in writing, studied them, and set them into dialogue with the Roman common law (*ius commune*). As the number of princely courts increased and expanded their caseload between about 1500 and 1750, the proportion of their staff who were trained in law schools (trained jurists, as opposed to being local jurors or untrained noblemen) also grew. Equally importantly, regimes lowered the limit of the monetary value of matters at suit for which they heard appeal, thus effectively extending the professional appellate courts' activity further into the local lordship structures of squire, manor, and village. These developments had the effect of tightening princely control over local courts and increasing princely review of decisions, which reduced local jurisdictional autonomy.[22]

21 The level of freedom experienced by serfs over the period no doubt varied from age to age with changes in economic conditions and the character of local leaders, landlords, and regime judges, but serfs in Hesse were subject to less oppressive conditions than in many other places. (They continued to suffer impositions, such as special taxes or inability to legally emigrate.)

22 Examples of such surveys were published as *Stadt- und Landesbrauch des Oberfürstenthums Marburg* (Marburg: 1749) and Almut Nehls, *Alte Gewohnheit und Stadtrecht zu Kassel in Erbfällen: Ein Beitrag zur Rezeptionsgeschichte*, Vol. 6, Hessische Forschungen zur geschichtlichen Landes- und Volkskunde (Cassel: Bärenreiter, 1967). Peter Taylor gives a good account of rural judicial practice in his *Indentured to Liberty*, pp. 132–133.

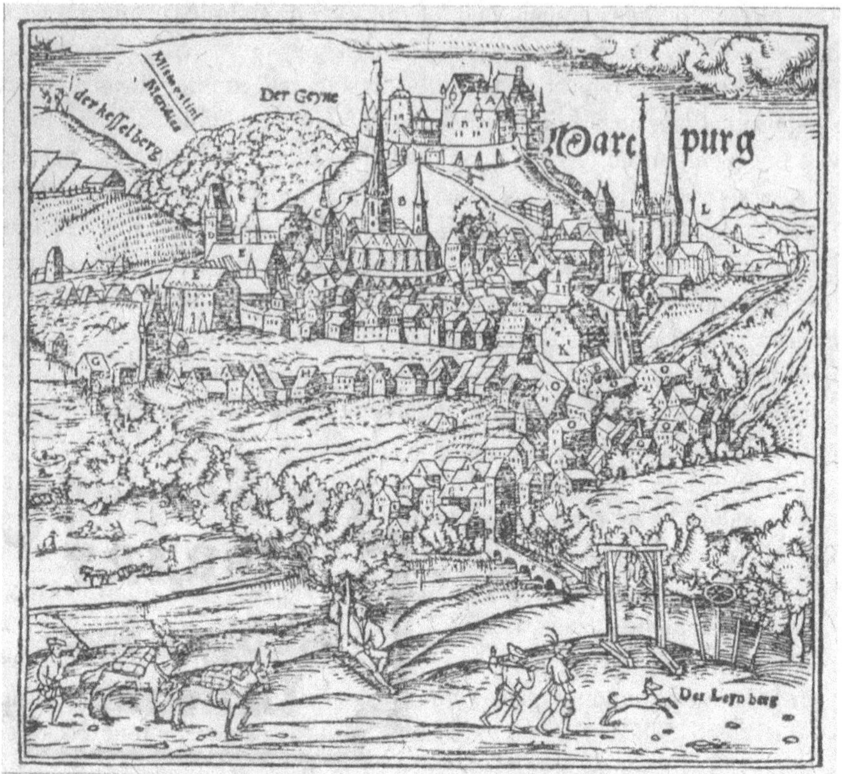

FIGURE 14 Marburg

After the sixteenth century, as the landgraves obtained more control, they removed effective legal autonomy from these local courts except in small matters.[23] With the growth of the administrative state, local self-governance and communal settlement of problems dwindled. By the late seventeenth century, most local courts including the serf court and the *Rügegericht* and the *Brückengericht* (both also in Upper Hesse), as well as local noble jurisdiction held by regional clans like the Dernbach or Riedesel, saw a decline in their traditional freedoms. As princely bureaucracies increasingly supervised the local courts and took appeals from local verdicts, did Germans lose or gain freedom? Was it more just or less just for local affairs to be supervised and ultimately limited by modern, professionally trained regime jurists in the capital towns? Consideration of these questions is threaded through the remainder of this book.

23 Thudichum, *Wettereiba*, p. 49.

FIGURE 15 Before the law (the gates of the Marburg Renthof, that is)

Why were these changes important? Princes' courts, staffed by jurists trained in the modern understanding of European common civil law, applied their newly developing, professional jurisprudence as a kind of check or filter on customary law and customary courts. In effect, the central appellate courts slowly transformed German law from 1500 to 1800. They checked abuse. As we will see in Chapters 4 and 5, they filled in blanks, such as what law should apply in the absence of a specific custom. And they spread modern ideas from legal scholarship. These phenomena have usually been discussed under the heading of the Reception of Roman Law, the influence of ancient and medieval ideas specifically about civil law from ancient Rome on the legal practices of modern polities, for example Germany, over the very long period between about 1200

FIGURE 16 Giessen

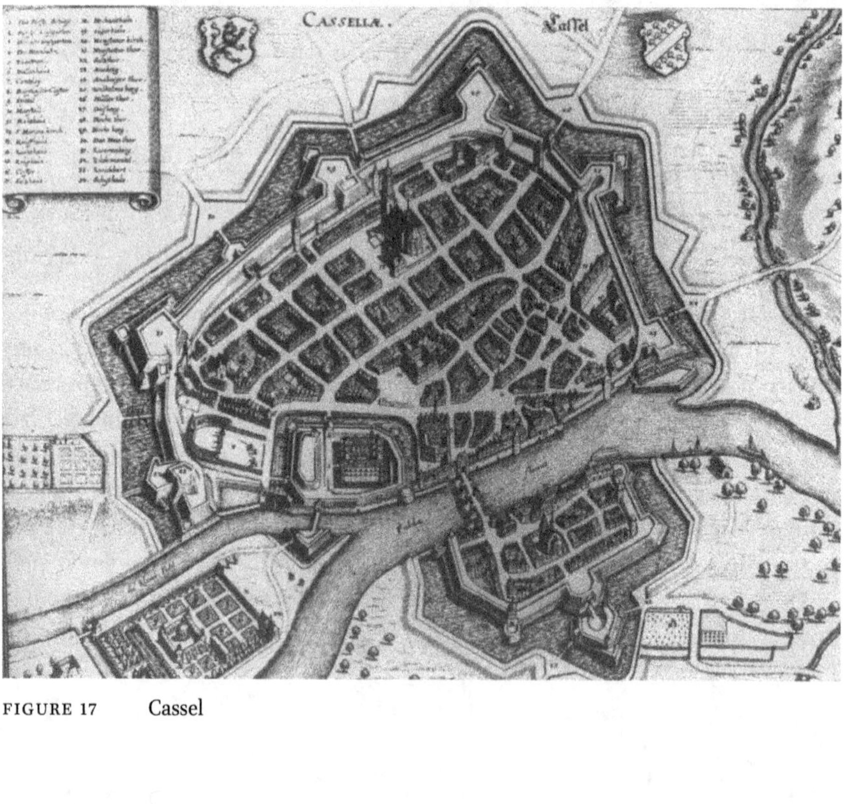

FIGURE 17 Cassel

FIGURE 18 Another view of Cassel from 1596

FIGURE 19 The Renthof in Cassel, where various dues were collected and counted by the central administration. Renovated 1579–1580

Johann Georgen Estors
Fürstl. Hess. geheimten regirungs rates und vicekanzlers
bürgerliche
rechtsgelehrsamkeit
der Teutschen
nach maasgebung der Reichs-abschiede und bewährter
nachrichten auch der regirungs- sodann rechts- und policei-
anbenebst der kammer- imgleichen der stadt- und
landwirtschafts-kunden
ausgefertiget
von Johann Andreen Hofmanne
der rechte öffentlichen lehrern und beisitzern
der juristen facultät

Marburg
verlegt es Immanuel Weldige 1757.

FIGURE 20 A German court – that is, a generic court session as depicted on the title page of Estor's magnum opus *The German Jurisprudence*

and 1800.[24] Among the ideas disseminated, central to this book, were concepts of natural freedom and modern rules about civil liberty.

This point should be made as clearly as possible: lawyers and judges working in courts created, altered, and transmitted ideas in the course of their work. They brought ideas from their studies in university law faculties and from their reading in law libraries. They found practical problems in suits in which they were involved and articulated new interpretations of them. As noted above, they also took jurisdiction over the smaller, formerly free, *sui generis* domains absorbed by princes in the sixteenth and seventeenth centuries. Strictly speaking, this might be thought of not as law-creation but as taking into consideration law that was not previously known to them or incorporated into the centralizing university law-knowledge bodies. But for practical purposes, as the professional institutions of law (courts and universities) were coming to learn about and control the legal activity in small places, from the point of view of the administrative power centers, new law was being created. To describe a legal system in new detail is, practically, to create new knowledge.[25]

As stated above, when courts expanded their activity, their juridical staffs grew and worked to create new professional knowledge. They encompassed the laws and customs of small, previously free domains in the Holy Roman Empire which were folded into the new, larger territorial governments. Appellate court jurisdictions grew not only because they were commanded and funded by ambitious rulers, but also because there was a bottom-up demand for institutions of justice from subject populations – people seeking redress

24 Students from countries like France and the German empire would travel especially to Italian universities, read and learn ancient Roman law as interpreted by modern medieval Italian jurists like Irnerius or Accursius, and then return to practice ether privately or for regimes in their home countries. The net result was the tremendous influence of Roman ideas on public and especially private law in modern polities like the Netherlands, Spain, France, the German imperial government, and the increasingly autonomous German principalities. See Bellomo, *Common Legal Past*; on the several waves or zones of Roman law reception, Osler, *Bibliographica iuridica*; and, for an example of an early reception, Conte, "Modena 1182: The Origins of a New Paradigm of Ownership." See also above, Ch. 1, p. 32, n. 49.

25 See "Truth and Juridical Forms" and "Governmentality" in Michel Foucault, *Power*, ed. James D. Faubion (New York: New Press, 2000); also see António Manuel Hespanha, "Form and Content in Early Modern Legal Books: Bridging the Gap between Material Bibliography and the History of Legal Thought," *Rechtsgeschichte* 12 (2008) and Ben Golder and Peter Fitzpatrick, *Foucault's Law* (Milton Park: Routledge, 2009). French comparison might be made to the *Coutumes de Beauvaisis* of Philippe de Beaumanoir (Philadelphia: University of Pennsylvania Press, Middle Ages Series, 1992).

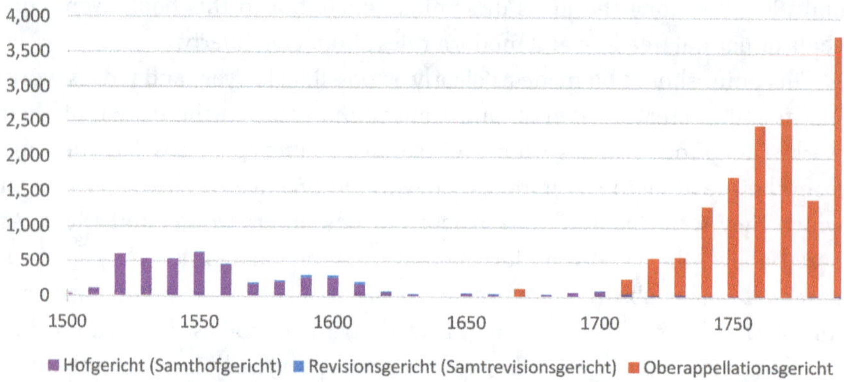

FIGURE 21 Appellate court activity in Hesse and Hesse-Cassel (1500–1800): Total suits decided per decade (estimated)

and aid in disputes with one another and against their lords. Let's look at these specific courts and their changing activity levels over the early modern centuries in the Hessian state and later its largest successor state, Hesse-Cassel.

The development of court jurisdiction varied with the fortunes of individual states. Hesse and later Hesse-Cassel and Hesse-Darmstadt experienced great changes of fortune across the sixteenth through eighteenth centuries, changes reflected in the pattern of Hessian appellate court activity.[26] (See Figure 21.) In the sixteenth century, Landgrave William (r. 1493–1509, Figure 22) established a Princely Court (*Hofgericht*). His son Philipp the Magnanimous (r. 1519–1567, Figure 23) strengthened the Court, which began to hear appeals from local seigneurial and other courts. The Princely Court's busiest period, averaging about 35 suits per year, was 1510–1620, with a high of 62 suits heard one year. Most of these suits were decided by a panel of jurors taken from territorial nobility and the law faculty of the University of Marburg after its founding in 1527.

In 1524 Philipp established the Review Court (*Revisionsgericht*) to take appeals from the Princely Court. The Review Court served as a check on the activity of the regime's own appellate court. The most active period for the Review Court was 1560–1630, when it heard an average of 2–3 suits per year. After 1567, the Review Court was weakened by the division of Hesse into

26 The Hessian states were periodically divided and reconsolidated. What was called Hesse-Cassel after the mid seventeenth century was the legatee of the united Hessian state of the sixteenth century, Hesse-Marburg, as well as numerous smaller polities like Hessian cadet domains and Hanau.

FIGURE 22 Landgrave Wilhelm II of Hesse, who established the Princely Court (Hofgericht). Father of Philipp the Magnanimous

several sub-territorial princely states. Increasing acrimony among the Hessian princes turned to fighting during the Thirty Years War, causing the rise of separate sub-territorial bureaucracies and the almost total breakdown of the functioning of pan-territorial institutions like appellate courts. Tense and hostile peace ensued after 1648 in the territory, with the major rulers in Darmstadt and Cassel signing cooperation agreements which, at least in this area, never amounted to much.

Landgraf Philipp von Hessen.
Nach dem Holzschnitt von Hans Brösamer
zu Erfurt.

FIGURE 23 Portrait of Landgrave Philipp the Magnanimous

In 1730, Hesse-Cassel re-established a supreme appellate court, the Upper Appellate Court (*Oberappellationsgericht*). Throughout its life from 1730 to 1820, this court heard far more appeals than its predecessors and competitors, ranging from a low of about 53 per year to a high at one point of probably 255 per year. The activity of this court burgeoned after 1746, when the territory received a Right of Non-Appeal (*Privilegium de non appellando*) from the empire, effectively preventing appeals to the imperial supreme courts in most matters. In summary, appellate court activity in Hesse-Cassel was characterized by three distinct phases:

1) Expanding territorial appellate supervision in the sixteenth century;
2) A decline of appellate activity across the whole territory from the early to late seventeenth century, associated with the chaos of the Thirty Years' War; and
3) The reestablishment and massive expansion of appellate supervision in the middle of the eighteenth century.

The other, smaller territorial states in the region such as Hesse-Darmstadt and Solms had appellate structures on smaller scales: some supervision of local courts, a first-level appellate regime court, possible review by the princes' own counselors, and occasionally a supreme territorial appellate court.[27]

Courts grew not only because states created them, but also because people wanted their services to sue for damage or injury, to protect their rights and freedoms, or to obtain protection against abusive or venal local seigneurs. We could call this an increased demand for the "use of justice" (*Justiznutzung*), in the modern economics sense of intersecting functions of supply of and demand for a service. People sought and used law courts and comparable modes of obtaining redress for themselves.[28] But how to measure demand, if all we know is that the actual activity rose? Was demand also really rising? I think so, based on the longitudinal change in a substitute demand function, namely the submission of petitions and supplications to the regime chanceries. Supplications and petitions were an old practice in Hesse-Cassel and in almost every European government. Generally, a supplication or petition was a means of seeking relief or clemency outside of the official channels of the estates' diet or a lawsuit. People sent in requests and complaints to the princely regime centers for all sorts of things, including requests for special extraordinary mercy, for relief from onerous fines or tax burdens, or complaints about alleged misbehavior of officials or vacancies such as that of a

27 Generally, regimes sought to expand and to extend their supervision and control of jurisdiction. Larger states like Hesse-Cassel could afford well-staffed courts while smaller dominions like Hesse-Rothenburg, Solms, the condominate Riedesel "republic" or individual local seigneurs could not. Waldeck was about the smallest state in the region that could field a functioning chancery capable of acting as an autonomous bureaucracy. All German regimes were devastated by the Thirty Years' War. Rebuilding in peacetime, all sought once again to extend their supervision of and control over local legal conflicts. On Waldeck, see Gerhard Menk, *Georg Friedrich von Waldeck (1620–1692): Eine Biographische Skizze*, Vol. 3, Waldeckische historische Hefte (Arolsen: Waldeckischer Geschichtsverein, 1992).

28 Armand Maruhn, "'Justiznutzung' und ihre Grenzen wie der Landauer Bürger David Bick 1592 Graf Franz III. von Waldeck herausforderte," *Geschichtsblätter für Waldeck* 94 (2006), p. 58, p. 63.

parish priest. Supplications came "from people of all social standings, including the very poor and the very powerful, from individuals, corporations, and *ad hoc* pressure groups alike."[29] The relationship in principle of the regime and its Chancery to supplications was that "it was the duty of any Christian authority to take note of its subjects' problems and – in line with the Gospels – show mercy whenever it could." Hearing supplications and petitions also had the added benefit to the regime that they brought it information about what was going on at a local level, information originating not from the not-always-trustworthy local nobility but from common country people, priests, and burghers in town. A major part of the daily scheduled work of the central Hessian legal bureaucracy, the Chancery, was devoted to reading through supplications and deciding which ones merited intervention, with elaborate regulations as to how this was to be done. Often supplications were basically of the same substance as appeals from local court proceedings – that is, complaints that there had been some injustice at the local court level. So as the volume of supplications and petitions rose considerably over the sixteenth through eighteenth centuries, we can take this as a reasonable indicator that, the high tide raising all boats, they were probably also making an increased number of formal appeals to the high appellate courts themselves, as well.[30] Hessian authorities were receiving some 1,000 petitions per year in 1600, and at least 4,000 per year by 1787. Indeed in the final decades of the eighteenth century, the ratio of supplications to formal hearings by the *Oberappellationsgericht* was about 10:1. (See Figures 24 and 25 for the Marburg Chancery and a depiction of a court session.)

Supplications and appeals to the Chancery benefited the princely regime by providing it with information as well as with numerous, small opportunities to interpose itself into local affairs. For example, the regime might override the allegedly unjust decisions of hereditary local jurisdictional lords or the regime's own lower-level justice officials, to suppress violence, or to adjudicate disputes over real estate properties or financial relationships. Thus the state gained not only information about local affairs, and good will from subjects

29 Beat Kümin and Andreas Würgler, "Petitions, Gravamina and the Early Modern State: Local Influence on Central Legislation in England and Germany (Hesse)," *Parliaments, Estates & Representation* 17 (1997), pp. 43b–44, citing in part John Theibault, *German Villages in Crisis: Rural Life in Hesse-Kassel and the Thirty Years' War, 1580–1720*, Studies in German Histories (Atlantic Highlands: Brill, 1995), p. 27.

30 "Petitions concerning seigneurial rents and estates … were passed on the to rent chamber. The most important documents, containing matters of principle, reports of serious crimes, or complaints against officials, went directly to the landgrave." See Kümin and Würgler, "Petitions, Gravamina," pp. 44–45, 57–58.

FIGURE 24 A court session in Marburg in 1551

FIGURE 25 Marburg Chancery (*Kanzlei*) building. Built by Landgrave Ludwig IV of Hesse-Marburg

whom it granted appeals or redress, but also ad hoc opportunities to extend its control further out into the common life of Hessian subjects. In this way, state-building was not only a one-way process (center outwards), but a cooperative process between rulers and subjects. Sometimes, changes implemented by the court could alter the situation at the local level actually creating the possibility of new violent conflict – the opposite of greater peace and order. As Robert von Friedeburg puts it:

> The participation of officials was superimposed upon – but did not replace – traditional forms of local conflict … Thus even as the conflict was 'legally justified,' the law itself was 'instrumentalized.'

This dynamic was hardly unique to Hesse, but also played out elsewhere, as in Württemberg and Brandenburg-Prussia as well for instance.[31]

The Chancery often intervened into complaints about injustice or conflicts over dues, especially if the conflict was between a village and an official. These complaints would concern matters of "such prejudice or other serious maleficence" including where "one of our officials or one of the nobles or someone else has oppressed someone among our subjects with violence, or … something of ours has been taken away or alienated by a nobleman, or … an official has embezzled or cheated, or kept back [dues owed to the landgrave]."[32] This litany reflects the landgrave's care both for his domains and for justice: legal

31 Peter Taylor goes so far as to claim that, in general, as state extractions – *Kontribution*, recruitment – increased, *so too* did the levers of power operated by local officials, noble and non-noble alike, through the patron-client distribution of power. Such a "superposition of personal feud through princely officialdom … [probably happened in] all territories in which the territorial lord had already far succeeded in imposing itself against the intermediary estate powers, but did not administer through a financially independent and disciplined officialdom on the village level." Robert von Friedeburg, "Landgemeinde, adlige Herrschaft und frühmoderner Staat in Hessen-Kassel nach dem Dreißigjährigen Krieg: Merzhausen 1646–1672," *Hessisches Jahrbuch für Landesgeschichte* 41 (1991), p. 158 and p. 171m; and Taylor, *Indentured to Liberty*, Chapter 6. For comparisons, see also James Allen Vann, *The Making of a State: Württemberg, 1593–1793* (Ithaca: Cornell University Press, 1984) and Hagen, *Ordinary Prussians*.

32 "Seind aber diese Sachen also gethan, unnd eines solchen praejudicii, daß unserer selbst eigenen resolution darinnen vonnöthen, oder aber sonsten schwere malefiz und andere wichtige sachen vorkommen, oder daß jemand unsere unterthanen von den Beampten, denen von Adell oder andern mit Gewalt untertruckt würdenn, oder das uns von denen vom Adell etwas entzogen, oder von denen Beampten oder andern etwas unterschlagen oder hinterhalten werden wollte …" See Kleinschmid and Apell, *Sammlung*, Vol. 2, Canzley-Ordnung of March 20, 1656, §8.

prejudice, official corruption, official misconduct, fraud, and embezzlement. The typical form of intervention was first to consider the submitted materials, possibly then to establish a local investigatory commission, and, if warranted, for the prince's local magistrate to intervene against a wrongdoer.[33]

The largest Hessian state, Hesse-Cassel, issued a Chancery Order in 1656 that for centuries was referred to as laying the groundwork for legal bureaucracy. The 1656 Order mandated that in matters handled by local courts that were worth more than 20 guldens – roughly the value of a medium-sized peasant farmstead without animals or rents it was owed – a decision might be appealed within ten days.[34] Title IX of Hesse-Cassel's Chancery Order of 1656 specified how this process was to work, including how the complaint (*Libell*) was to be submitted and the proper behavior and "power of attorney" (*Vollmacht*) required for the *procuratores* on either side. Title IV of the Chancery Order concerned disputes between people in different jurisdictions over an estate or real right. The Chancery was tasked to uphold "right and equity."[35]

3 Supply, Demand, Population, and Commercialization

Modeling the development of court activity as a supply and demand of justice is a good way to get at the ultimate causes of all this. A ruler increased the supply of justice because, as everyone knew, that is the right and godly thing for those entrusted with the ruling of society to do. It was also the case that receiving and selectively granting supplications, petitions, and appeals permitted regimes to gain information, undermine the nobility, and keep or extend their control of property relations (especially on the landgrave's own extensive domains). Why did people seek redress and/or justice? No doubt the chief answer is that they believed something was unjust or because they wanted to get something they thought should be theirs or defend themselves against

33 John Theibault, "Community and *Herrschaft* in the Seventeenth-Century German Village," *Journal of Modern History* 64, no. 1 (1992), p. 2.

34 Kleinschmid and Apell, *Sammlung*, Vol. 2, Canzley-Ordnung, Part IX, §§1–5, 25, 27, 46, 49.

35 The Chancery was to investigate, share information about any violations of domain properties among the different parts of the regime, and prosecute the landgrave's rights, but not trespass against "right and amity." "... gezänck und irrthumb zwischen deb Beampten, Landsassen, von Adeel oder von unterthanen, es sey umb Obrigkeit-Folg ... Gericht ... Wildbahn, Jacht, Gehölz oder anders zutrüge ..." (ibid., Vol. 2, Canzley-Ordnung, Part V, §9). "Jedoch keinem gegen Recht und Billigkeit etwas zu entziehen ..." (§10). "Die Rentkammer soll der Regierung [sc. dem Statthalter und Rähten] alle Amts-Gebrechen ... [und] Verschmälerung der Grenzen, Rent- und Zinsen ... anzeigen" (§11).

threat. Powerful exogenous drivers on this demand were population growth and commercialization.

Commercialization may be thought of as a suit of phenomena observed in the seventeenth and eighteenth centuries in Europe:

- increasing division of labor in society, not only in industry but also in agricultural production
- increased production of raw and finished goods for sale at market
- increasing monetization, and transfer of real assets
- mobilization of previously "immobile" wealth through transfer and mortgage (or pledge), creating new means and modes of investment
- debt contracts such as annuities became more sophisticated
- natural resources were exploited with more planning and efficiency for industrial purposes.

For the purposes of this book, the conflicts over property adjudicated in law suits and discussed in theoretical works generally fall under the categories of market sale of goods, real estate transactions, and new means and modes of investment.[36] Put differently, those economic activities associated with commercialization are the activities which provoked jurists to refine ideas about freedom. Capitalism has historically been broadly associated with civil liberty and the spread of ideas about freedom (Smith, Hayek, Friedman), although a tenacious left wing of economic historians has always associated it contrariwise with domination and exploitation instead (Marx or most recently

36 Commercialization or early capitalism in this mold may be thought of as the growing power or dominance of capital (movable, earmarked, investable wealth) in directing society's energies. The growth of dynamic competition, financial markets, commodity markets, and the "acquisitive spirit" (Weber) mark the transition from commercial society to capitalism. Historians generally hold that capitalism was beginning to emerge as early as the sixteenth century in England and the Netherlands, and in France and Germany by the late seventeenth century, becoming more robust in the late eighteenth and early nineteenth centuries. In fairness however the term "capitalism" was already used in eighteenth-century Germany, but meant something more like rentiership. For instance Fürstenau, *Versuch einer Apologie des physiokratischen Systems*, p. 32, mentions that in one contemporary view, "capitalists [*Kapitalisten*] who invest their capital either in foreign lands or in production or trade which is made for foreign lands" are one of the three groups in the "sterile class," according to "economic reason." For the distinction between commercial society and capitalism, see Michael Sonenscher, *Capitalism: The Story Behind the Word* (Princeton, New Jersey: Princeton University Press, 2022), Chapter 1. The foregoing broad synthesis brings together both liberal and Marxist perspectives. Consider for instance North and Thomas, *Rise of the Western World* and Tigar and Levy, *Law and the Rise of Capitalism*.

e.g. Sven Beckert).[37] While I do not go into great depth about these proto-capitalistic phenomena directly, they loom in the background of this book, especially Chapters 6–7, playing roles in policy, court decisions, and local commercial activity.

Population began a long-term growth in England and the Netherlands in the seventeenth century. It stayed steady in Germany and then declined tremendously on account of the Thirty Years' War, but began long-term growth there after the reconstruction following 1648.[38] in continental Europe. Population historically tends to trend upward in post-subsistence societies, absent negative exogenous shocks like war, plague, or famine. Population increase in turn generally causes all institutions to intensify or grow.

4 Universities and Law Faculties

So what did the legal operators in these swelling courts all think and do? We now move to look at the growth in legal training and what was taught and learned in law faculties and adjacent disciplines in the Hessian and Rhine-Main region in the seventeenth and eighteenth centuries, The number of universities and "high schools" (*Hohe Schulen*) which had law faculties grew steadily in the seventeenth and eighteenth centuries, with new faculties being founded and others revived. Regional rulers patronized law faculties in part to create a steady supply of trained professionals who could serve in the growing bureaucracies, especially for taxation, domain administration, and justice. As at least 80% of law students were of non-noble origin, legal training heavily benefited the rising urban classes of artisans, merchants, and professionals, and indirectly disadvantaged the rural nobility. As law faculties expanded, so too did the number of jurists. In the sixteenth, seventeenth, and eighteenth centuries, university matriculation lists, law dissertations, and law suits all increased many times.[39]

---

37 Sven Beckert, *Empire of Cotton: A Global History* (New York: Vintage Books, 2014).

38 See North and Thomas, *Rise of the Western World*, p. 97, p. 103t; W. O. Henderson, "The Genesis of the Industrial Revolution in France and Germany in the 18th Century," *Kyklos* 9 (1956).

39 Part of this may be due to pent-up demand amid university closures during the Thirty Years' War, but the growth after 1648 seems too high to be fully accounted for by that. Matriculation records for the universities and high schools in the region are found in or can be reconstructed from (in alphabetical order by institution name): Gregor Richter, ed., *Die Studentenmatrikel der Adolphsuniversität zu Fulda (1734–1805)* (Fulda:

As a rule, law faculties were closely integrated with the hierarchical structure and patronage of local princely governments, to the point that the Chancellors and Vice Chancellors of regimes were usually law professors. Prior to the Reformation, there was one place where young men could study law in the Hessian and Rhine-Main region: the Mainz high school, itself only founded in 1476. During the heyday of the Reformation, two more were added – the University of Marburg and the Hohe Schule (High School) Herborn. High or upper schools could provide training for licensing to practice law, but only universities could award jurisdoctorates. Thus by 1600, students from the region could study law at three different institutions, Marburg being the most important. Four more were added in the next few decades: the University of Giessen (1607), the High School Hanau (1607), the University of Paderborn (1615), and the University of Rinteln (1621), bringing the total to seven by the end of the Thirty Years' War. After periods of wartime dormancy, the schools in Marburg and Herborn were revived in the decades following the conclusion of peace in 1648. In the early part of the eighteenth century, a new law faculty was added at the Carolinum in Cassel (1709) and the University of Fulda and the State- and Chancery-Academy of Hanau (1733 and 1749) were founded, each with law

---

Fuldaer Actiendruckerei, 1936); Ernst Klewitz and Otfried Praetorius, *Die Matrikel der Universität Gießen* (Giessen: Ricker, 1957); Ernst Ebel Karl Klewitz, *Die Matrikel der Universität Giessen, 1608–1707* (Nendeln/Liechtenstein: Kraus Reprint, 1980): Gottfried Zedler and Hans Sommer, eds., *Die Matrikel der Hohen Schule und des Paedagogiums zu Herborn*, Vol. 5, Veröffentlichungen der Historischen Kommission für Nassau (Wiesbaden: J. F. Bergmann, 1908); Antonius von der Linde, "Matricula studiosorum scholae Herbornensis (1584–1726)," in *Die Nassauer Drucke der koeniglichen Landesbibliothek in Wiesbaden* (Wiesbaden: 1882, 1887); Carl Heiler, "Die Matrikel der Hohen Schule zu Herborn (1725–1817)," in *Nassauische Annalen*, Vol. 55 (Wiesbaden: Verein für Nassauische Altertumskunde und Geschichtsforschung, 1935); Wilhelm Falckenheiner, *Personen und Ortsregister zu der Matrikel und den Annalen der Universität Marburg, 1527–1652* (Marburg: N. G. Elwert, 1904); Theodor Birt, ed., *Catalogus studiosorum Academiae Marpurgensis cum annalibus coniunctus series recentior annos 1653–1830 complectens* (Marburg: Robert Friedrich, 1903–1914); Josef Freisen, *Die Matrikel der Universität Paderborn: 1614–1844* (Würzburg: Fränk Ges -Dr, 1931); August Woringer, *Die Studenten der Universität zu Rinteln (Academia Ernestina)*, Mitteilungen der Zentralstelle für deutsche Personen- und Familiengeschichte (Nendeln [Liechtenstein]: Kraus Reprint, 1980); Gerhard Schormann, ed., *Rintelner Studenten des 17. und 18. Jahrhunderts*, Schaumburger StudienC Bösendahl, 1981); and generally Gerhard Menk, "Die Hochschul- und Wissenschaftslandschaft zwischen Main und Weser in der frühen Neuzeit," in *Wege der Neuzeit: Festschrift für Heinz Schilling zum 65. Geburtstag*, ed. Stefan Ehrenpreis, Vol. 85, *Historische Forschungen* (Berlin: Duncker & Humblot, 2007).

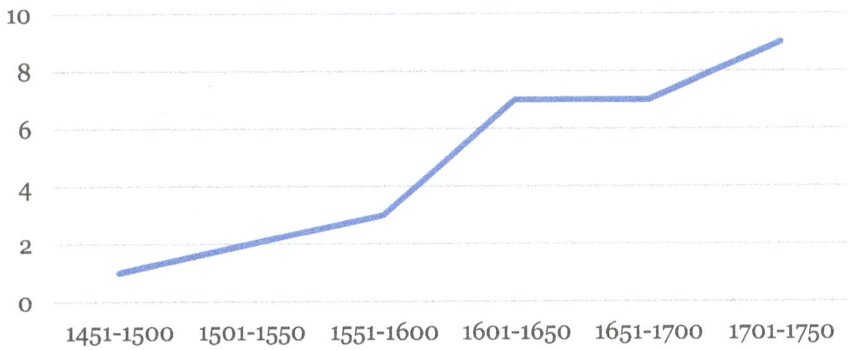

FIGURE 26 High schools and universities in the Hessian and Rhine-Main region, 1450–1750

faculties.[40] Thus the possibilities for legal training increased remarkably over three centuries, from a single institution to ten schools (see Figure 26). Four of these were universities, but the five high schools also provided valuable, respected legal training. Perhaps not coincidentally, the most distinguished early modern proponent of German imperial federalism, Johannes Althusius, taught law at the Herborn high school in the sixteenth century.[41]

Indeed Hesse was filled with institutions of higher learning including legal instruction. Reigning for almost sixty years and becoming increasingly wealthy, the pre-eminent Baroque prince of Hesse, Landgrave Charles (Karl),

---

40 The University of Marburg was founded in 1527, the University of Giessen in 1607, and that of Rinteln in 1621. The Upper School of Herborn was founded in 1584; its first professor of law was Johannes Althusius (1557–1638); matriculation was very low from 1626 to 1685 on account of the war but revived thereafter. In 1618, Landgrave Moritz transformed the Cassel finishing school (Pagenschule and Hofschule) into the Collegium Mauritianum. The remnant of this was refounded as the Collegium Carolinum with a law faculty in 1709. Among the professors there later in the century was Conrad Wilhelm Ledderhose, who wrote about German legal antiquities. The Upper School of Hanau was opened in 1607. One famous jurist, Heinrich Philipp Zaunschliffer, received his license there and subsequently taught there in the early eighteenth century. The University of Fulda (later called the Adolphsuniversität) opened its doors in 1733 and had professors of canon law; it was closed by the French in 1804. The Mainz Hochschule, founded in 1476, also had a law faculty. It too was closed by the French (in 1800). The famous cameralists Johann Joachim Becher (1635–1682) and Johann Friedrich von Pfeiffer (1718–1787) were among its professors. The Philosophical-Theological Academy in Paderborn was founded in 1615 and included professors of canon law.

41 For discussion of the schools in Marburg, Rinteln, and Cassel in the later eighteenth century, see Charles Ingrao, *The Hessian Mercenary State: Ideas, Institutions, and Reform under Frederick II, 1760–1785* (Cambridge: Cambridge University Press, 1987), pp. 75–79.

surrounded himself with high art and learning. Charles established the Collegium Carolinum in Cassel in 1709, which historian Karl Demandt calls "perhaps the first technical university of Germany," since it included an art academy and an institute for natural science as well as a law faculty. Other technical subjects followed quickly in the eighteenth century, including cameralistics and economics. Hesse seems to have been fairly forward-looking as German principalities went in regard to economics.[42] In Hesse-Darmstadt, the University of Giessen added an economics faculty in 1777, under the leadership of the Enlightenment reformer Friedrich Carl von Moser (son of the liberal reformer and constitutionalist Johann Jakob Moser, who had himself founded the above-mentioned Hanau Academy of 1749). The Giessen economics faculty became a center of German physiocratic thinking in the mid eighteenth century amidst the broader German interest in Adam Smith's liberal political economy.[43] One of the most respected German physiocrats, Jakob Mauvillon, had come to Cassel in 1771.[44] So we may well infer that law students picked up pollical economy ideas even while law and economics faculty rubbed elbows and married into one another's family and friend networks.[45]

While there were a number of law schools in the region, Marburg was preeminent. The schools in Giessen and Herborn produced some highly respected jurists, but were not nearly so highly or consistently esteemed as those in Marburg. Hence the Marburg University law faculty is the anchor of the primary sources used in this book: about two thirds of the sources are written by the chairs of law at Marburg from the seventeenth and eighteenth centuries, with many other works by their students, associates, or correspondents. However, as detailed below, other kinds of economic and intellectual relationships branched out from Marburg through employment and patronage.

---

42 Demandt, *Geschichte des Landes Hessen*, p. 229.

43 Kurt Braunreuther, *Studien zur Geschichte der politischen Ökonomie und der Soziologie* (Berlin: Akademie-Verlag, 1978); Diethelm Klippel, "Johann August Schlettwein and the Economics Faculty at the University of Giessen," *History of Political Thought* 15 (1994); Bertram Schefold, "Die Bedeutung des Freihandels in wirtschaftstheoretischen Debatten in Deutschland während des 19. Jahrhunderts" (paper presented at the Völkerrecht und Weltwirtschaft im 19. Jahrhundert, Frankfurt am Main, September 2009); Mack Walker, *Johann Jakob Moser and the Holy Roman Empire of the German Nation* (Chapel Hill: University of North Carolina Press, 1981).

44 Ingrao, *Hessian Mercenary State*, p. 78.

45 A good sense of the interrelatedness of the various faculties at the University of Marburg can be gained by reading the hundreds of their individual mini-biographies in Franz Gundlach, *Catalogus Professorum Academiae Marburgensis: Die Akademischen Lehrer der Philipps-Universität in Marburg von 1527 bis 1910*, Vol. 15, Veröffentlichungen der Historischen Kommission für Hessen und Waldeck (Marburg: N. G. Elwert, 1927).

Of the subjects taught at these law schools, most relevant to the focus of this book was the teaching of Roman law, natural law, and political economy. From its beginning in 1527, the law faculty at the University of Marburg trained men principally in the modern evolved form of ancient Roman law – the *ius commune*. The teaching of Roman law in new universities like Marburg was closely bound up with the reception of Roman law (mentioned earlier) that played out in imperial courts, territorial courts, and universities. As we saw in Chapter 2, the relatively new application of Roman civil law in imperial and princely courts was criticized by humanists and other opponents like Ulrich von Hutten as being un-German and harmful to local, vested interests.[46] Law students would also have likely studied canon law, Roman-German public law, and modern criminal law, all of it adjusted to circumstances of usage in the territory. More detailed canon law and mercantile law were elective specializations pursued by some faculty and students. In the early period covered in this book, the chief intellectual movement in law was the tail end of legal humanism and the late medieval natural law tradition, for instance as represented by the Spanish Scholastics. Legal humanism had been the largely successful program to carefully edit and perform source criticism on classical law, distilling pure texts and isolating later additions. In the sixteenth century, several important humanists taught at the University of Marburg, including Johann Oldendorp, Johannes Goeddaeus, and Hermann Vultejus. Another key influence in jurisprudence was the *usus modernus*, or study of modern legal custom, created by David Mevius and Samuel Stryk. In a vein similar to Mevius, the eighteenth century would also begin to see historical jurisprudence associated with Johann Jakob Moser, Johann Georg Estor, and Justus Möser.[47]

In the eighteenth century, when "the Enlightenment pretended to subject everything to reason,"[48] the most famous names associated with the Law of Reason in the Hessian and Rhine-Main region were Christian Wolff, Johann Georg Estor, and Johann Heinrich Christian von Selchow, the work and/or

46 Wieacker, *History of Private Law*; Bellomo, *Common Legal Past*; James Q. Whitman, "Long Live the Hatred of Roman Law!," *Rechtsgeschichte* 2 (2003).

47 Important for their own accomplishments of the day, these three were also influential on the Historical School of Law. For the later part of this story, see Arno Buschmann, "Estor, Pütter, Hugo – Zur Vorgeschichte der Historischen Rechtsschule," in *Vielfalt und Einheit in der Rechtsgeschichte: Festgabe für Elmar Wadle zum 65. Geburtstag*, ed. Thomas Gergen, Vol. 136, *Annales Universitatis Saraviensis* (Cologne: Heymann, 2004). Many details of the legal-intellectual movements mentioned above can be found in Wieacker, *History of Private Law*.

48 This felicitous phrase comes from Borges, *Selected Non-Fictions*.

influence of all of whom is discussed in the following chapters, along with many other jurists of the age of reason.

Particularly influential on modern natural law was the work of Hugo Grotius, the most influential and esteemed jurist of the age.[49] His epochal *De iure belli ac pacis* (Paris: 1625) exploded across European legal thought, including in German law faculties. Chairs of international law and natural law in the Grotian cast were established at many German universities and his work was widely influential, even in quotidian matters. "Natural law" has long been a term with many meanings. Historians distinguish classical natural law, the product of Aristotelian and Stoic political theory, from modern natural law after Grotius. The most important elements of Grotian natural law for our purposes were that it was expressly individualistic, based on consent, was dressed up in humanistic robes, but was scholastic in structure, abjured divine foundation, was ambivalent about freedom and domination, and could be used to help understand law and government both terrestrial and maritime, and hence was truly global and international in scope.[50]

Besides the innovative works of Grotius and Hobbes, several factors influenced the development of natural law thought in Germany: the move toward teaching and scholarship in the vernacular (especially with Thomasius), as it opened up new sources and subjects; the Protestant turn toward eclecticism and away from the metaphysically uniformitarian method of scholasticism; and the growing influence of economic logic (theories of political economy related to both the Grotian and Hobbesian schools of modern natural law).[51]

The above features of natural law are all so to speak substantive. But natural law was often also a method, more precisely the product of making comparisons between laws or their applications, as one method of resolving conflicts of law. As a genre (works which had "natural law" in the title or used the phrase

---

49 See Brian Tierney, *The Idea of Natural Rights: Studies on Natural Rights, Natural Law, and Church Law, 1150–1625*, Emory University Studies in Law and Religion (Atlanta: Scholars Press, 1997). Chapter XIII, especially pp. 316–326, for Grotuis's rhetorical strategy of using humanistic argumentation to advance novel natural law arguments in Dutch interests.

50 Hugo Grotius, *The Rights of War and Peace*, ed. Jean Barbeyrac (Indianapolis: Liberty Fund, 2005 [orig. 1738, 1712, 1625]). Modern natural law is often described as having two major schools or methods, both appearing in the seventeenth century: that of Hugo Grotius, focusing on humankind's natural sociability, and that of Thomas Hobbes, with its essentially individual self-interested approach. See also Wieacker, *History of Private Law*.

51 Germane here is T. J. Hochstrasser, *Natural Law Theories in the Early Enlightenment*, Vol. 58, Ideas in Context (Cambridge; New York: Cambridge University Press, 2000), which opens up many of these issues and conflicts.

frequently), German natural law writings in the late seventeenth and eighteenth centuries were in T. J. Hochstrasser's sense indeed eclectic.[52] They took sources from all over and were not bound to any method aside from a comparativist / rationalist approach: they compared legal sources and sought to find or provide rational foundations for legal institutions. My jurists readily cited Grotius, less often Pufendorf, occasionally Hobbes. The rationales they worked from sometimes resembled Grotian sociability, other times Hobbesian methodological individualism, and occasionally Aristotelian political science. But as the eighteenth century wears on, there is an increasing concern that law support simple, reliable transactions and an atmosphere of confident financial credit.[53]

Rather than beginning with fanciful imaginary legal scenarios of primitive rural settlement, plentiful natural commons, or chaotic violence (Grotius, Locke, Hobbes), working German natural lawyers sought and found nature and natural law by proceeding from concrete modern lawsuits, black-letter civil law, concrete property rights, and custom.[54] They largely did not play with the higher theory of natural law. And yet these jurists do constantly write of "nature" and "natural law," so I think it is not inappropriate to classify this discourse as one of "natural law," even if it does not fit easily into modern theories.[55]

Nigel Simmonds has argued that in England, natural law is best understood as having grown out of juristic comparison of legal sources. From this comparison, jurists distilled what is common to discussions among them on a given topic, articulated that commonality as a principle, and then speculated about the natural or rational foundation of said principle. I see the same thing happening in German natural law, at least to the extent that it is identifiably tagged

---

52 Ibid.

53 "Contracts must be enforced" was a classic adage. "The will of a man is the soul of a deal." "Contract [*geding*] breaks the law of the land." Investment of capital should not be "sterile" "rentiership," but active and productive. Honor and trust are the basis of sound economy. The law of exchange (Chapter 6 here) is important since it "keeps up credit." See respectively Johann Georg Estor, *Der Teutschen Rechtsgelahrheit*, ed. Johann Andreas Hofmann, Vol. 2 (Marburg; Frankfurt am Main: 1758), §3484, p. 292 and §3491, p. 294.

54 See glossary: black-letter law and natural law.

55 Lest I be misunderstood, I do not mean to disregard modern scholarship about natural law. I mean only to emphasize that in practical jurisprudence, jurists reasoned about "natural" law in regard to specific suits or laws or conflicts of law, rather than in the theoretical realm of Grotius, Hobbes, Pufendorf, Locke, and others, though my German jurists often show at least some familiarity with these more famous authors.

FIGURE 27 Representation of the German Republic (aka the Holy Roman Empire of the German Nation). The art of lawbook frontispieces captures much of the neoclassicism of how Roman law was read into German law especially in the eighteenth century, and conversely how German law was interpreted as equal in sophistication and therefore dignity with ancient Roman law. Devices like this one and that in Figure 28 depict very often Roman ruins or isolated forms in rustic wilderness settings. Note the cracks in the marble and the wilderness encroaching on the representation of majesty

as natural law thinking (e.g. writing about "the nature of dominion" etc.).[56] Over the centuries, up to the present, *natural law* has ossified into something like a universal norm. The notion of natural law, however, has been *used* to

56 Nigel E. Simmonds, "Reason, History and Privilege: Blackstone's Debt to Natural law," *Zeitschrift der Savigny-Stiftung für Rechtsgeschichte. Germanistische Abteilung* 105 (1988).

D. Johann Georg Estor,
Hoch-Fürstl. Hessischen Raths und Profess.
Jur. Ordin. auf der Universität Giessen.

Außerlesene
Kleine
Schrifften,

Erster Band.

DEO ET PROXIMO

Giessen,
bey Johann Philipp Krieger,
1734.

FIGURE 28 Like the representation in Figure 27, here is also a classicizing device, albeit a more modest example (from the title page of a collection of Johann Georg Estor's essays). Roman public magnificence, erudition, and Christianity (in the sacred heart) are brought together. Deo et proximo = "for God and neighbor"

critique existing laws and institutions. That is, natural law can be thought of as a critical approach which regarded law as an objective structure, derived from human nature and the nature of human society. Details of the natural law could be discovered through rational examination of holy texts, history,

CORPUS
JURIS FEUDALIS
GERMANICI,
Das ist:
Sammlung derer
Teütschen Lehen-Rechte
und Gewohnheiten,
Worinnen nicht nur die
allgemeinen Reichs-Lehen-Rechte,
Sondern auch
die in denen Teutschen Provintzien hergebrachte
Jura Feudalia, in ihrer Ordnung, mehrentheils aus
ungedruckten Nachrichten, beygebracht worden;
Nebst einer vollständigen
Bibliotheca Juris Feudalis,
auch
ELENCHO und Register.
Dem Publico zum Besten ans Licht gegeben
von
Johann Christian Lünig.
Franckfurth am Mayn,
Bey Friedrich Lanckischens Erben, 1727.

FIGURE 29 Title page of *Corpus Juris Feudalis* – the "Body of German Feudal Law, i.e. collection of German Feudal Laws and Customs" etc. Compiled by Johann Christian Lünig (Frankfurt: 1727). German law is here given the status equal to the ancient and venerable body of Roman law

worldly civil law of many nations, and custom. For the jurists I study, the primary applications of natural law were to *explain* or *justify* a given custom or statute and to *critique* the actions of magistrates.[57] Indeed, natural lawyers

57 As Raoul C. van Caenegem wryly put it, "Natural law is the eternal refuge of malcontents opposed to the established order." See Raoul C. van Caenegem, "The *Rechtsstaat*

developed strong opinions about the limitations on arbitrary lordly authority, based again on classical and medieval civil law: a ruler might not enrich himself without basis at his subjects' expense, nor act as judge in a suit to which he was a party.[58]

The University of Marburg received "new renown ... when Landgrave Charles hired the philosopher Christian Wolff after his departure from Halle" in 1723. Wolff stayed at Marburg until 1740, which "increased the fame of the *Hochschule*."[59] Wolff was an important German philosopher in his own right, usually considered the greatest between Leibniz and Kant, a disciple of the former and influence on the latter. In addition to his own work on science and philosophical method, Wolff popularized natural law ideas from Grotius and Pufendorf to broader audiences in France, England, and America. In Marburg, he taught one of the most important jurists of the region, Johann Ulrich Cramer.[60]

Hessian universities in the early seventeenth century also started to teach political-economic theories. Cameralism began to be taught in the region in 1727 with the appointment of Johann Hermann Fürstenau as professor of *Cammeralwissenschaften*, about the same time as Frederick William established a chair in cameralistics at the University of Halle.[61] I return to cameralism further in Chapters 4–6, but for the moment it can be understood as a Central European variant of mercantilism prominent in smaller and landlocked states, where regimes focused on maximizing resource extraction and increasing territorial wealth, both physical and in the productive capacities of the

---

in Historical Perspective," in *Legal history: A European Perspective* (London; Rio Grande: Hambledon Press, 1991), p. 194.

58 Ernst Hartwig Kantorowicz, "Kingship under the Impact of Scientific Jurisprudence," in *Twelfth-century Europe and the foundations of modern society*, ed. Marshall Clagett, Gaines Post, and Robert Reynolds (Madison: University of Wisconsin, 1966), p. 93; see *passim* for other examples of how Roman law principles were used by medieval jurists to similar effects; Mack Walker, "Rights and Functions: The Social Categories of Eighteenth-Century German Jurists and Cameralists," *Journal of Modern History* 50, no. 2 (1978), p. 241; Christian Thomasius, praeses, George Rudolph Schlösser, respondans, *De praescriptione regalium ad jura subditorum non pertinente dissertatio juridica* (Halle; Frankfurt am Main: Christoph Salfeld's widow, 1696), Cap. 2, §13; and Gaertner, *Meditationum practicarum*, Chapter 25, pp. 48–49.

59 Demandt, *Geschichte des Landes Hessen*, p. 205.

60 Leonard Krieger, *The Politics of Discretion: Pufendorf and the Acceptance of Natural Law* (Chicago: University of Chicago Press, 1965), pp. 2–3, 257–262.

61 For the prominent role of political economic thinking including especially cameralism in eighteenth-century Hesse-Cassel, see Ingrao, *Hessian Mercenary State*, pp. 1–15 and Taylor, *Indentured to Liberty*, pp. 51–54, 76.

population and economy. Soon after the 1720s, cameralistics was also taught at the University of Frankfurt on the Oder. Rinteln (then part of Hesse) was on the cutting edge,[62] as Fürstenau appears to have been a crucial link between German cameralism and French Physiocracy.[63] These scholars and other professors of law, philosophy and *oeconomia* taught generations of future civil servants in the region around Hesse, men who went on to conceive and implement reform projects.[64] It would not be too much of an exaggeration to say that cameralism was the spirit of the relations between regime and village for most of the eighteenth century and that this was institutionalized through university training beginning in the 1720's.[65]

Cameralism – and political economy theories more broadly – was relevant to the story told here in several ways. Most people who wrote about political economy had training in law, at least in Germany, although a plurality were natural scientists (including veterinarians). And anecdotally it seems that a large number of jurists had significant exposure to political economic thinking in turn. It was at this time that political economy was becoming recognized as a separate field, a process which would not be complete however until the nineteenth century. Not surprisingly, then, cameralism and political economy theories more generally influenced how jurists interpreted and treated property ownership (lordship, dominion), collection of dues and taxes, and views about extractions. Economic theory led jurists to think functionally: What role does money play in the territory, aside from paying for soldiers and palaces? How do different configurations of rules alter how land is used or how money circulates? Is it important that serfs are bonded to a given seigneury, when their role in production and national wealth seems at odds with their legal status? These questions differed from those that jurists were trained as professionals to ask, such as: Who has the right in this case? Does prescription apply here? Mack Walker has argued that functionalist thinking crept into juristic thought and shook up the old, more formalist ways of interpreting cases and laws.[66] We are as likely to find an economic treatise in the eighteenth century

62 In the seventeenth century, Rinteln, located in the *Grafschaft* of Schaumburg, was part of Hesse-Cassel.

63 Keith Tribe, *Governing Economy: The Reformation of German Economic Discourse, 1750–1840* (Cambridge; New York: Cambridge University Press, 1988), pp. 130–131. In the same liberalizing spirit, the regime also revoked the economic privileges of the guilds in 1730.

64 Wolfgang Metz, "Zur Sozialgeschichte des Beamtentums in der Zentralverwaltung der Landgrafschaft Hessen-Kassel bis zum 18. Jahrhundert," *Zeitschrift für Hessische Geschichte* 67 (1959), pp. 145–147; Ingrao, *Hessian Mercenary State*, pp. 1–15.

65 This is Taylor's thesis (see above citation).

66 Walker, "Rights and Functions."

written by a jurist as by a cameralist professor of economics. Four prominent eighteenth-century law professors or lecturers furnish good examples of their profession's activity in political economic theory of the day[67] – Johann Hermann Fürstenau (on physiocracy), Friedrich Wilhelm Strieder (on monopolies), Johann Heinrich Christian von Selchow, and Philipp Peter Guden (the last two each writing both on bills of exchange and on credit). Economic thinking often had significant bearing on governments' programs to collect taxes, to invigorate their economies, and (as cameralism gave way to broader liberal political economy) to create widely circulating forms of money.

After this survey of the learning practices and intellectual leanings of jurists, we now turn to consider where jurists came from, what they actually read, and their relationship to the Enlightenment.

5 Jurists

To better understand the legal profession, it is useful to distinguish the stages of a juristic career. We might call this a *cursus honorum*, in the Roman sense: a typical path of advancement with different stations of achievement, recognition, and authority, and concomitantly different types of law-making activity.

Usually after attending lectures for a few years, new jurists produced a jurisdoctoral dissertation or disputation with a senior professor of law, and then obtained a license to practice law privately. A legal *dissertatio* was the written or oral presentation and defense of a set of theses on a specific disputed question or topic considered worthy of study and clarification. After completing study and taking their license, jurists often worked for a time as *private lawyers*, in the service of private clients or in criminal matters. It was also not uncommon for them to teach as low-level instructors (docents or lecturers) at law schools, early in their careers. After such services, they might enter higher echelons as judges, chaired professors of law, states' attorneys, privy counselors, chancellors, or even presidents or regents of regimes.[68] In all of

67 Some work and ideas of Selchow and Guden work will be discussed in Chapter 6 on bills and money. See respectively Fürstenau, *Versuch einer Apologie des physiokratischen Systems*; Strieder, *Über die Monopolien. Nebst Bemerkungen über die in dieser Materie von dem Herrn Probst und Prälaten Quirl und Herrn Kammerrath Klippstein zum Vorschein gekommene Schriften*; Johann Heinrich Christian von Selchow, *Grundsätze des Wechselrechts: Zum Gebrauch seiner Vorlesungen*, 2nd, improved ed. (Göttingen: Johann Wilhelm Bossigel, 1777); and Philipp Peter Guden, *Vom Wechsel- und römischen Rechte über Schuld-Verschreibungen und ihrem Einflusse auf den Wohlstand der Einwohner* (Göttingen: Johann Christian Dieterich, 1790).

68 In this context, a regime regent was a temporary ruler of a regime, standing in while the proper holder of power was unavailable, as during absence or minority.

FIGURE 30 Johann Georg Estor's seal of 1768 is a great example of the upward mobility of the German bourgeoisie in the eighteenth century. He depicts a quasi-noble coat of arms. He implied in his life writing that his family may have been noble without offering any actual evidence for it

these activities throughout their lives, they interpreted, produced, and reproduced law.

Almost all legal operators came from the bourgeoisie. That is, they were the offspring of town-dwelling families whose members (primarily men) were not agriculturalists or artisans; they tended to earn a salary from a recognized profession or they were merchants, shopkeepers, or otherwise worked primarily with writing and numbers.[69] As in other parts of Europe, bourgeois families in the Hessian and Rhine-Main region followed strategies for social ascent when possible, by accruing wealth, if possible a noble title or notable (*ehrbar*) name (e.g. the Moser von Filseck, the family of Johann Jakob Moser), purchasing a notable residence, and marrying into the aristocracy.

As discussed in the previous section, jurists read and engaged with other subjects than law, typically shared many ideas with other intellectuals of the

69 While somewhat piecemeal, I find that this ideal-typical definition of the bourgeoisie tends to fit most period accounts as well as latter-day e.g. Marxist theory. See for instance Tigar and Levy, *Law and the Rise of Capitalism*.

era. The legal world overlapped considerably with other well-known Enlightenment worlds, notably science and political economy. Jurists, political economists, and state ministers used metaphors from contemporary science, particularly physical mechanics and chemistry, to model society and nature as rational systems. Jurists were also enmeshed in the same urban networks which scholars are now accustomed to describing in the history of science, in cities such as Edinburgh, London, Paris, and Vienna. Closer and more influential to our region were the great northern centers of commerce – Amsterdam, Hamburg, Leipzig, Jena, and Frankfurt am Main. Books and ideas from these centers made their way out to the smaller provincial centers in the Hessian and Rhine-Main region like Cassel, Marburg, and Giessen where jurists like Johann Nikolaus Hertius, Johann Ulrich Cramer, Johann Georg Estor, Leonhard Heinrich Ludwig Georg de Canngiesser, Johann Andreas Hofmann, and Bernhard August Gaertner were active. Among the imperial territories and cities, jurists traveled, especially earlier in their careers, to study or teach at other universities, for example Estor to Jena or Wolff relocating to Marburg. They brought knowledge and ideas with them from place to place, like insects pollinating flowers. In mid-career, working as a professor or for the regime, a jurist might go and study recently discovered documents shedding light on custom or ancient rights. Nearby Frankfurt am Main was a mecca of knowledge, providing books, patronage, and contact with other jurists like Joannes Fichard or Heinrich Christian Senckenberg who were based there at points in their careers. All of the aforementioned figures were eminent jurists in the region between the late sixteenth and late eighteenth centuries, the later ones being students of the earlier ones. Hessian judges incorporated contemporary arguments and issues from Saxony (Chapter 6) and were conversant with European legal conundrums like the problem of allodial landholding (Chapter 4). At the broadest level, as discussed previously, German jurists saw themselves as bearing and interpreting a common European law (*ius commune*), albeit with regional variations. Hence Grotius's discussion of franc fief or sovereignty, Spanish commentary on possessory procedure, or even trade rights of Europeans in far-off New Spain (Mexico) were all part of the German communion of knowledge and practice. Knowledge passed through networks along paths spanning anywhere from a day's ride to a multi-year sojourn, and textual knowledge gathered on such visits was assiduously copied, discussed, and used.

The great name for the intellectual movement in this time was the Enlightenment, and in law one came to speak of the Law of Reason as a synonym for the forward edge of highly rationalistic natural law thinking. Yet most of the texts examined here perhaps do not look like the Enlightenment discourse we

NICOLAI HIERONYMI GVNDLINGII
CONSIL. REGII INTIM. ET ECCLESIAST. IVR. ELOQV. ET
ANTIQVITAT. OLIM PROF. PVBL. ORDIN.

EXERCITATIONES
ACADEMICAE

PRAEFATIONEM
DE
VSV ET PRAESTANTIA NVMISMATVM
IN IVRISPRVDENTIA
PRAEMISIT
IO. GOTTL. HEINECCIVS, IC.
POT. PRVSSOR. REG. A CONSIL. SECRET. IVR. AC PHILOSOPH.
IN ILLVSTR. FRIDERIC. PROF. PVBL. ORDIN. SOCIETAT.
LATIN. IENENS. MEMBR. HONORAR.

HALAE
IN OFFICINA LIBRARIA RENGERIANA
cIɔIɔCCXXXVI.

FIGURE 31 Enlightenment. This is the title page of the *Academic Exercises* (1736) of Nicolaus Hieronymous Gundling, a prominent period jurist. The page's device shows the archetypal Enlightenment symbol: sun shining light through clouds

might expect. They cut rationalistic figures and took for granted that humans come in some sense from a pre-civil or sub-civil stratum of "natural freedom" But they rarely considered questions about whether human beings are naturally solitary or sociable or the consent of the governed. When they sought and found natural freedom, it was not through abstract thinking, but rather through reasoning about conventional, civil laws and obligations, which could occasionally be peeled back to reveal and re-access natural freedom. The closest connection between the writers considered here and the high Enlightenment would be Immanuel Kant, writing decades later than most of the authors considered here. He read and was responding to Christian Wolff, and famously

FIGURE 32 Portrait of Johann Georg Estor as prochancellor in 1757, at the time of writing his magnum opus, *German Jurisprudence*

declared that enlightenment was man's emancipation from self-imposed tutelage. But by and large, the writers in this book do not use or employ the concepts of rationalism, the state of nature, or abstract pre-historical consent, or consider in detail the way that social or political institutions have changed human nature or locked humans into determinate political forms.

Nevertheless, key features of Enlightenment thought can be identified in the jurists' work. They sought *rational foundations* of institutions in order to argue for institutional reforms. Their work was often characterized by belief in historical stadialism or progress: the modern was different from the medieval and the ancient. They believed that, with proper study, experts could shape and improve institutions such as laws, economies, or bureaucracies. The general philosophy of prescription, which became the cornerstone of the German historical school of law, bears considerable resemblance to the evolutionary rationalism of Hume, Ferguson, and Smith. Finally, jurists evinced an abiding interest in freedom, and many demonstrated a longing for greater legal equality. The story of this book, shorn of all qualifiers, sounds a lot like Kant's fundamental definition of Enlightenment: emancipation from conventionally-imposed tutelage.

Apart from what they studied in school, where did jurists acquire the knowledge with which they made law? Jurists in the Hessian and Rhine-Main region were organized into many kinds of networks – social, intellectual, professional, patronage, and kinship. Their networks tended to be closed, in the sociological sense, that is, they exhibited strong internal linkage among contacts within circles or cliques, for example sitting together on governmental councils or faculties.[70] Closure fostered communication of ideas and community of opinion. Major controversies, for example over freedom and serfdom, that flared up on occasion between the early seventeenth and mid- eighteenth centuries, were notable precisely because they deviated from the usual pattern of closure. A good example of this is the controversy over the freedom (in their property) which "colonial settlers" (a kind of feudal tenant) had over their land and its improvements vis-à-vis their landlords.[71]

70 Ronald S. Burt, *Brokerage and Closure: An Introduction to Social Capital* (Oxford: Oxford University Press, 2013).

71 This controversy included, at a minimum, Stephan Sigismund Wlöm, *Vindiciae iuris landsideliae Hassiaci et Solmensis* (Marburg: J. G. Ebersbach's widow, 1740); Johann Ulrich Cramer, "Unvorgreifliche Gedanken von der im Ober-Fuerstenthum Hessen und Solmsischen ueblichen Landsiedeley," in *Opuscula*, Vol. 2 (Marburg: Philipp Casimir Müller, 1740); Christoph Ludwig Hombergk zu Schencklengsfeld, *Offenbahrer Ungrund der so genannten Vindiciarum Juris Landsideliae Hassiaci et Solmsensis* (Marburg: Philipp Casimir Müller, 1741); and Georg Lennep, *Abhandlung von der Leyhe zu Landsiedel-Recht* (Marburg: Philipp Casimir Müllers Erben und Weldige, 1769). Brief modern commentary is supplied in George Thomas Fox, "Studies in the Rural History of Upper Hesse" (Ph.D. thesis, Vanderbilt University, 1976). Another example would be the controversy over the freedom of serfs in labor service claims, instigated by Johann Hermann Stamm, *Tractatus de servitute personali in tres libros distinctus* (Frankfurt am Main: 1625), rekindled

Healthy networks of ideas often exhibit both closure and what is called brokerage, referring to the acquisition of ideas from outside of one's own network. Outside ideas allow for innovation and rejuvenation, but mostly network members talk with one another, strengthening and standardizing their expertise. Some of the ways that brokerage occurred included academic travel and reading out-of-network books. These occasional career events can be thought of as moments of legal-ideational brokerage. Estor was born in Schweinsberg, studied and taught in the Hessian states (Marburg and Giessen), studied in Saxony (Jena), and came back to a distinguished career in Marburg. Cramer was born in Ulm (Swabia), studied, taught, and served in Marburg, and ultimately became a baron and Imperial Chamber Court assessor (judge) in Wetzlar. Selchow was educated and taught in Marburg, served there eminently on the princely privy council, and later became even more renowned in Göttingen.

6 Books

> Books have their fates.
>
> TERRENCE (2nd c. AD)[72]

Jurists also created knowledge through networks involving books: both connections with institutional book collections and citations to earlier sources of law in their own new work.[73] Legal *training* and legal *publishing* were mutually

in Melchior Dethmar Grolmann, *De Operarum Debitarum Mutatione* (Giessen: Eberhard Henrich Lammer, 1734) (with a preface by Estor), and contradicted by Johann Leonhard Hauschild, *Beischriften von Bauern und Frohnen, und zwar von deren urspruenglichen Bedeutung, der Rechtsvermuthung natuerlicher Freyheit wider die Frohnen, und einigen Gewissensbedenken darueber; nebst einer Vorrede von Beschaffenheit der gemeinen Klagen ueber die Justiz* (Dresden: 1744). For modern commentary, see Winfried Schulze, "Die Entwicklung des "teutschen Bauernrechts" in der frühen Neuzeit," *Zeitschrift für Neuere Rechtsgeschichte* 12 (1990).

72 "Pro captu lectoris, habent sua fata libelli"; books have different fates depending on the capacities of their readers. That is, books can and do do different things in different readers' hands. Terrence (Terentianus Maurus), *De Syllabis*.

73 Colin F. Wilder, "TL;DR, or, an experimental application of text analysis and network analysis to the study of historical library collections, in particular the title catalogs of four libraries in the western Holy Roman Empire in the period 1606–1796, accompanied by some methodological speculations and ideas for further research," in *New Technologies in Renaissance and Medieval Studies* (Toronto: 2019).

reinforcing, and linked legal operators' practices and ideas to larger institutions and forces.

Texts were crucial both as sources and as the canvas or subject for current-day interpretive practices. The book trade grew measurably during this time. Texts were key to the institutions which feature in this book's arguments – university teaching, the jurisprudence of law courts, the book trade, and library collections.

We know something about how the circulation and collection of books influenced juristic practice. For example, the Roman civil law of the Digest, later known as the Pandects, was transmitted in parts through late Roman civil law, more or less rediscovered by Irnerius in Italy in the eleventh century, reproduced in commentaries and florilegia, reconstructed more rigorously by humanists like Cujas in the sixteenth century, sought out and studied in prized old collections like the one in Florence later that century, and then bought in new printed editions at great expense by universities and wealthy patrons in the seventeenth and eighteenth centuries. The transmitted text often deviated from the original, and included insertions, deletions, and emendations, and its modern interpretation was heavily influenced by centuries of commentary, but fundamentally this was an incredible story of the persistence of a multi-authored textual masterpiece persisting and evolving through two millennia, generating new ideas each century. As Goethe wrote, Roman law is like a duck on a pond – it dives down, seems to disappear, and then shows up unexpectedly someplace else, again and again. The ongoing interpretation and transmission of highly respected ancient texts like the Digest is crucially helpful for explaining key ideas and institutions in this book, such as Grotius's new system of natural rights, the concept of "modern custom," or the myth of "ancient Germanic freedom."

As book production and sales increased over the sixteenth through eighteenth centuries, more books were becoming available, access to them increased, and their prices declined. And as a result, jurists used more books – a larger number of titles – in constructing their ideas and arguments. More books were produced because the market demand grew.[74] These phenomena were connected, but not identical. While increased juridical institutional activity (in courts and universities) was a contributing cause, the growth of the printing and offering of legal books was also due to growth in population, education, literacy, and interest in certain topics, as well as political events such as the Revolution of 1525. The book trade and the use of books in new modes

74 Bernd Moeller, *Imperial Cities and the Reformation: Three Essays* (Durham: Labyrinth Press, 1972).

of argument expanded across the sixteenth through eighteenth centuries. An account of the growth of law and of juridical ideas and institutions would be incomplete without considering the contribution of the book trade, including published dissertations.

A survey of law library collections in the seventeenth century can be used as a proxy for the demand for certain books or interest in certain subjects. Regardless of the antagonism between Roman civil law and canon law and between Roman civil law and feudal custom, the University of Marburg library and the Marburg Collective High Court's service library in the regime chancery in that town held numerous volumes in canon law, Roman civil law, feudal law, Germanic customary law, foreign Catholic law, Italian urban courts such as Genoa, and so on. These holdings can be interpreted as reflecting the *usus modernus*, an idea which will appear throughout the coming chapters. Referring to "the modern custom," it was the dominant movement in legal theory from the late seventeenth century until the heyday of natural law a century later. Working jurists of the day were concerned to survey, collect, and organize the rich variety of extant sources of law in the world around them (especially the empire, interpreted generously to include the functionally sovereign Italian polities, but also sibling realms outside the empire, like France).

After some decades of recovery from the catastrophic Thirty Years' War, by about 1700 there had been a "dramatic increase in the sheer number of books available, as well as in the velocity and extent of their circulation."[75] As James Sheehan writes about the Leipzig Fair,

> In 1700, the Leipzig Book Fair catalogue listed 978 titles, almost half of which were on theological subjects; by 1780, the number of titles had increased to over 2,600 and the relative importance of religious works had declined significantly. Over this same period, the proportion of books in German to those in Latin changed from about 2:1 to 10:1. By the 1750s there were large bookshops in many cities; at the same time, cash sales replaced the barter system that traditionally limited a bookseller's ability to expand and reinvest his capital.

This increase in the book trade can be ascribed to the improvement in literacy. Around the year 1800, the German reading public was about 5% of the population, "somewhere between 100,000 and 200,000" people.[76]

---

75 James J. Sheehan, *German history, 1770–1866*, Oxford History of Modern Europe (Oxford: Clarendon Press; Oxford University Press, 1989), p. 153t.

76 Ibid., p. 153–154t, 157b.

In our area of interest – law books – the effect of greater literacy, demand, and availability was transformative. New condensations and handbooks of law put law into people's hands, both professionals and laymen. For example, discussing part of the law book market in Frankfurt am Main (a major center of publishing), book historian Peter Weidhaas explains, "By virtue of their clear format and the commentaries that accompanied [handbooks], a broader knowledge of Roman law was facilitated."[77] By the mid eighteenth century, the number of law books had increased tremendously.[78] Works by Hermann Vultejus (professor in Hesse, 1555–1634), Johannes Arnoldus Corvinus (1582–1650), and Arnold Johann Corvinus van Beldern (d. 1680) are good examples of this development. Vultejus compiled the *Iurisprudentia Romana contracta* (abbreviated Roman jurisprudence), which was edited after his death by Johannes Arnoldus Corvinus and Arnold Johann Corvinus van Beldern and published in 1644. Johannes Arnoldus Corvinus published his own *Enchiridium, seu, Institutiones imperiales insertis latioribus materijs, theoricè ac practicè digestae, et explicatae per erotemata* (handbook or imperial institutes with further material inserted and digested for theory and practice) in 1640, *Elementa iuris civilis Additis ... receptarum utriusque iuris regularum partitionibus* (elements of civil law etc.) in 1645, and *Institutiones D. Justiniani S.S. Princ ... accesserunt ex Digestis tituli de verb. signif. et reg. juris*. (institutes of Justinian to which are added titles from the Digests on the meaning of words and rules of law) in 1654. His cousin and erstwhile co-editor Arnold Johann Corvinus van Beldern compiled the *Iurisprudentiae Romanae summarium; seu Codicis Iustinianei methodica enarratio* (summary of Roman jurisprudence or methodical narrative of the Justinian Codex) in 1655. Such summaries and breviaries have been genres of legal writing since at least the time of Justinian (482–565) himself, as jurists perennially seek ways to skim the vast mass of law to obtain what is essential for making their case. But the institutional changes presented here – book production, library growth, court expansion, and law faculty expansion – indicate a kind of institutional acceleration. Old dogs could learn new tricks. (See Figures 5, 33.)

---

77 Peter Weidhaas, *A History of the Frankfurt Book Fair*, trans. Carolyn Gossage and Wendy Wright (Toronto: Dundurn Press, 2007 [orig. 2003]), p. 30. See further ibid. pp. 31–36 for more information on the nascent international book market of the period.

78 There exists no published scholarly estimate as to how large the legal publishing industry was by the mid eighteenth century. From general research, I would estimate that many thousands of dissertations, treatises, and other law collections were published in the eighteenth century. For the growth of legal publishing and legal systems, see my "Property, Possession and Prescription," pp. 1–27 and *passim*.

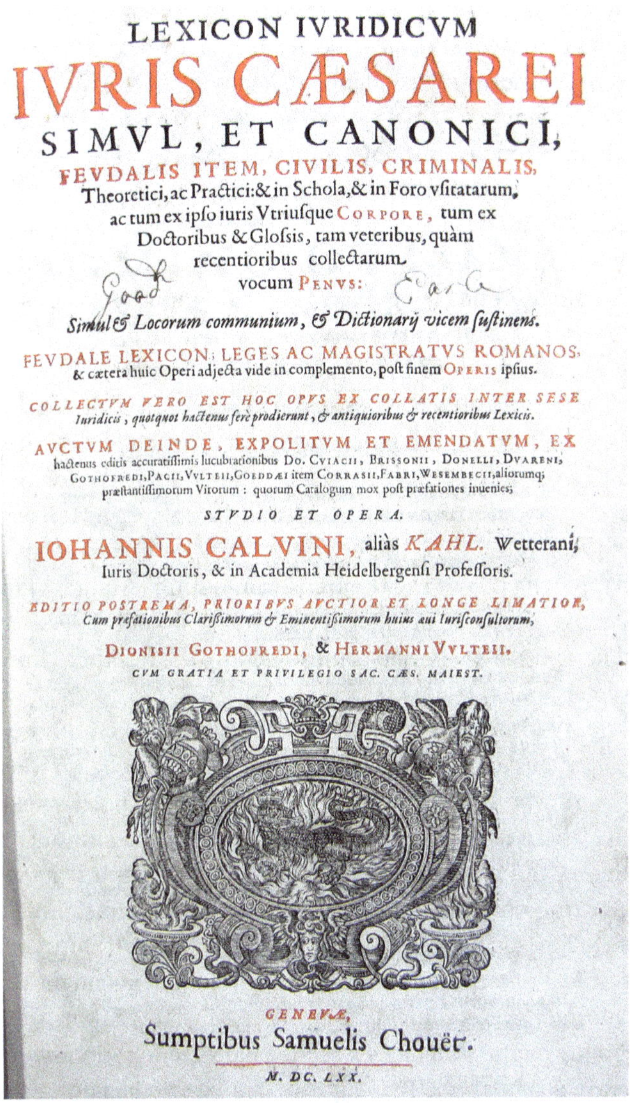

LEXICON IVRIDICVM
IVRIS CÆSAREI
SIMVL, ET CANONICI,
FEVDALIS ITEM, CIVILIS, CRIMINALIS,
Theoretici, ac Practici: & in Schola, & in Foro vſitatarum,
ac tum ex ipſo iuris Vtriuſque CORPORE, tum ex
Doctoribus & Gloſsis, tam veteribus, quàm
recentioribus collectarum
vocum PENVS:
Simul & Locorum communium, & Dictionarij vicem ſuſtinens.
FEVDALE LEXICON; LEGES AC MAGISTRATVS ROMANOS,
& cætera huic Operi adjecta vide in complemento, poſt finem OPERIS ipſius.
COLLECTVM VERO EST HOC OPVS EX COLLATIS INTER SESE
Iuridicis, quotquot hactenus ferè prodierunt, & antiquioribus & recentioribus Lexicis.
AVCTVM DEINDE, EXPOLITVM ET EMENDATVM, EX
hactenus editis accuratiſſimis lucubrationibus Do. CVIACII, BRISSONII, DONELLI, DVARENI,
GOTHOFREDI, PACII, VVLTEII, GOEDDÆI item CORRASII, FABRI, WESEMBECII, aliorumq;
præſtantiſſimorum Virorum: quorum Catalogum mox poſt præfationes inuenies;
STVDIO ET OPERA.
IOHANNIS CALVINI, aliàs KAHL. Wetterani,
Iuris Doctoris, & in Academia Heidelbergenſi Profeſſoris.
EDITIO POSTREMA, PRIORIBVS AVCTIOR ET LONGE LIMATIOR,
Cum præfationibus Clariſſimorum & Eminentiſſimorum huius ævi Iuriſconſultorum,
DIONISII GOTHOFREDI, & HERMANNI VVLTEII.
CVM GRATIA ET PRIVILEGIO SAC. CÆS. MAIEST.
GENEVÆ,
Sumptibus Samuelis Chouët.
M. DC. LXX.

FIGURE 33 Title page of Kahl's *Lexicon*, an influential legal lexicon printed numerous times in the sixteenth though eighteenth centuries

Thinking of knowledge as a network process helps us see other ways that it was produced, line by line as it were. For example, *citation of earlier works* can be thought of (modeled) as a directed, sequential network, whereby authority can be measured by the quantity of citations as well as the relative celebrity of the cited works and cited authors. From around 1500 to 1800, the way that jurists cited authoritative works changed considerably. Early in the period, they mostly cited older works while later in the period they tended to cite more recent work. That is, the *citational horizon* – the distance between author and the source he cites – grew shorter. This change reflected a shift in attention toward recent law and current states of affairs from older ideas and formulations.[79] The lag between arguments and their sources, in practical terms, was getting shorter. The consultation and use of books in sophisticated collections can also be modeled as a network. Practicing jurists such as regime councilors and law professors made use of their organizations' specialized book collections. Court and university libraries tended to collect the important works of respected commentators and humanists as well as the decisions of famous European courts such as those in Jena or Genoa. Such books, published with increasing frequency in this period, were considered to be "sources" of the law. Copies of collections were held in regime chancery libraries and were used and cited by law faculties.[80] Through book distribution and sales and reference libraries, distant, closed networks of knowledge production like the Genoese court, the Leipzig law faculty, and the imperial supreme court became connected even to less happening places like the Hessian and Rhine-Main region. Good collections of books served as hubs of accessible legal knowledge that linked people spread far apart in space and time, providing the resources from which jurists produced arguments.

Finally, network theory also helps to illuminate how jurists co-authored works. Today academic co-authorship generally means an active collaboration between (living) scholars who cooperate in the creation of a scholarly text. In German universities, there typically was a strong element of co-authorship between doctoral advisor and student until at least 1800. In fact, it was not uncommon to see a string of dissertations "presided over" by one professor over several years, each "disputed" by a different student, with titles and body texts almost identical to one another. A teacher and students might co-author a treatise, or a former student might later edit or translate the work of a deceased master. Scholars might – ideally – produce more penetrating scholarship in this way. But it also might be that a junior scholar would gain status by attaching himself to the work of a more celebrated senior peer, who in turn might gain from the labors of students. Standards of originality and authorial responsibility change.[81]

---

79 Bertrand de Jouvenel argued that early modern European jurists generally dressed up legal innovation as recordation, editing, and commentary on existing law. See de Jouvenel, *Power*, p. 209, cited in Bond, *Nemesis*, pp. 19–20 n. 2.

80 Wilder, "TL;DR."

81 On this point, see Fasolt, *The Limits of History*, pp. 94–101.

Jurists were typically well-read, internationally minded, and familiar with ancient letters. They tended to be versed in modern scholarship, including some natural science and often political economy. They produced law in that they learned it, collected and sifted it, taught it, interpreted it, promulgated it, and applied it. They knew one another both in local and far-flung networks that could be social and familial as well as professional. What they did not read themselves, they learned from associates, colleagues, friends, and relations. Notably, by the eighteenth century, common juristic ways of thinking seemed to reflect the rationalism, progressivism, and care for improvement and human emancipation we are accustomed to recognize in Enlightenment thinkers.

• • •

Jurists did not produce or change ideas in the abstract but rather played determinate roles in institutions as judges, lawyers, professors, students, privy councilors, and members of regime staffs. Although dissertations or treatises might sound theoretical or general based on their titles (e.g. *Observationes iuris feudalis*, "Observations on feudal law"),[82] they almost always engaged with real, usually recent suits or controversies and with black-letter law. Case details were primary, followed by judicial or expert interpretation of the case, with theoretical aspects only at the end. Jurists' access to knowledge was itself institutionally channeled, as described above, through the forms of university training, use of library collections, and collegial networks. *Courts and universities can be thought of as agonistic institutions, structured to generate ideational change through competition and reward for innovation in arguments and ideas. Courts, universities, the book trade, and library collections all helped to determine in what ways jurists created, changed, and transmitted legal ideas.* These institutions, in turn, were shaped by broader processes including state competition, increasing commercialization, population growth, and intellectual developments. So while it was jurists and their associates (e.g. lawbook printers) who made law, theirs was a strange kind of agency: They did not necessarily end up producing law according to preconceived plans because they interacted unpredictably with one another and were themselves cogs in larger institutional machinery.

82 Johann Georg Estor, *Observationes iuris feudalis* (Jena: Johann Friedrich Ritter, 1740).

CHAPTER 4

Free Disposition of Estates

In the seventeenth century, Germans gained more freedom to acquire and dispose of real rights, in particular real estate, especially land. This change was driven in part by the efforts of private parties to vindicate their claims to property – their strategies sometimes verged on illegality. This freedom was also expanded by jurists who applied the doctrines of possession and prescription in dubious or difficult lawsuits, preferring the quieting of title to retaining older formalities. Finally, freedom in real rights was expanded at the state level with the Princely Resolutions of 1655, a major constitutional accord in Hesse in the mid-seventeenth century.

Beginning in the late sixteenth century, Germans adopted legal strategies that enabled them to expand private rights to acquire, use, and alienate their property, in defiance of landlords, neighbors, relatives, and social customs. The development of jurisprudence and the constitutional settlement of 1655 together simplified and modernized the law, putting real estate under a more modern, individualistic system governed by simplified Roman civil laws and court procedures which gave priority to recent voluntary transactions among parties, over tradition, custom, or distant feudal authority structures. Both actor-level strategies and state-level policies, laws, and procedures increased people's freedom of action. Sometimes people exercised the freedom to just do as they wished, regardless of what law enforcers might proclaim they should do. Possession and prescription often helped such extra-legal actions ripen into rightfully held rights and freedoms. In other cases, freedom was developed through legal and quasi-legal strategies or new arguments and ideas. Germans gained more freedom to choose both how to use estates and how and to whom to transfer them.

Private parties employed a variety of methods in pursuit of gaining more. Much quasi-legal activity occurred during and after the Thirty Years' War. From the later seventeenth century onward, jurists including judges came to uphold some of this activity in the interests of peace. Most of these methods used by private parties were not new to the mid seventeenth century, some much older. Several were legal fictions which can be traced back to the 1300s. Contemporary examples make the broader point that people used specific strategies for self-empowerment which can help to explain changes at the local level in the mid and late seventeenth century. The impact of the Thirty Years War played a critical role in this expansion of freedom.

 | DOI:10.1163/9789004685178_005

Case studies show how tenants slipped around older, formal, more restrictive rules, which were eventually abolished, to expand their rights. Several examples highlight the activities of less powerful people in society: women, widows, Jews, and less influential members of families. Although some of these strategies could also be used by common, Christian men, their use by marginalized figures is significant and often surprising. People acquired and used allodial or "free and clear" tenure, employed legal fictions to evade restrictions on acquiring or using property, and freely used or alienated family lands. The final sections of this chapter present the laws of prescription and possession in their simplified forms, which allowed people to gain *de facto* rights in the face of custom and feudal law.

The chaos of the Thirty Years' War in the Hessian and Rhine-Main region, as in most of Germany, presented a terrible yet fertile opportunity for common people and for jurists to reconceive law and freedom, as regimes lost institutional knowledge and records disappeared. Common people as well as nobles trespassed and transferred real rights illegally, whether motivated by avarice, need, or older claims of right. States meanwhile sought to restore the orderly collection of taxes and dues in the interest of increasing state wealth and power. Rather than German Freedom writ large, this chapter focuses on rights to real estate, that is, disposal of real rights and the freedom which comes from that.

1 Chaos, Information Loss, and Self-Release

The Thirty Years' War is notoriously complex and can be variously characterized as a great power-struggle between France, factions in the empire, and Sweden or as a Central European religious civil war. It can also be understood as a set of related, smaller and shorter wars of regional or other special character.[1] The first of these was the War over Electoral Palatine (1618–1627), into which the Hessian and Rhine-Main region was drawn in 1621 when the Wetterau was invaded by imperial Field Marshal Spinola. In Hesse-Cassel, Landgrave Moritz was forced by the estates to abdicate in 1627, to be succeeded

1 S. H. Steinberg, *The Thirty Years War and the Conflict for European Hegemony, 1600–1660* (New York: Norton, 1967) and Theodore K. Rabb, *The Thirty Years' War* (University Press of America, 1981) are short, approachable if older works which introduce various basic approaches to understanding the conflict. The most recent and extremely thorough account is Peter H. Wilson, *The Thirty Years War: Europe's Tragedy* (Cambridge: Belknap Press, 2009).

by his son Wilhelm v (b. 1602, r. 1627–1637; married to Amalie-Elizabeth). Wilhelm v was outlawed in 1636 and died in Frisia in exile in 1637. His Lutheran second cousin Georg II (b. 1605, r. 1626–1661) of Hesse-Darmstadt, siding with the Catholic imperial forces, took over significant portions of Upper Hesse. The University of Marburg was united to the University of Giessen (and the Marburg campus closed) between 1625 until the end of the war in 1649. Georg II's Hesse-Darmstadt existed formally at this enlarged size until the conclusion of negotiations at the Westphalian Peace Congress. The Hessian civil war proper was fought from 1645 to 1648 when the forces of Amalie-Elizabeth, regent for her son Wilhelm VI, defeated Hesse-Darmstadt and garnered an advantageous and profitable position at the bargaining table in Osnabrück and Münster.[2]

The fighting in Upper Hesse, the Wetterau, and elsewhere around the region had two consequences we should highlight. First was population displacement. People fled marauding armies. The rapine and pillaging in the Hessian civil war was particularly horrific.[3] (See Figures 34–37.) Second, as a result of the changeovers of rulers, population evacuation, and destruction of local government, there was for all intents and purposes an interregnum, or at least an unsettling of authority. To be sure, the noble leaders and their families were present and powerful at the superlocal, subregional level, for instance the Rau and the Schenck zu Schweinsberg in the villages and towns around Marburg and Giessen. Present too were various figures in the ruling princely house: There were pretenders, temporary rulers, and cadet princes, all claiming various authorities, high feudal lordship, jurisdiction, supremacy over the territorial nobility, and so on. The lesser powers were in conflict with one another and with local officials.[4]

After the War, this profound institutional destabilization left German states like Hesse more vulnerable to challenges to their authority at the local level than they had been for centuries. Regional governments reported of and complained about non-compliance with pre-war directives concerning the control of real estate, as a shadowy world of lost records, transfers without permission, and loss of third-party rights emerged. In some cases this "grey economy" (to

2 On Amalie-Elizabeth, see the great study by Tryntje Helfferich, *The Iron Princess: Amalia Elisabeth and the Thirty Years War* (Cambridge: Harvard University Press, 2013).

3 Hans Heinrich Weber, *Der Hessenkrieg* (Giessen: O. Kindt, 1935); Theibault, *German Villages in Crisis*. More generally on the devastation of the War, see also Kreike, *Scorched Earth: Environmental Warfare as a Crime Against Humanity and Nature*, Chapter 3, pp. 97–136.

4 Friedeburg, "Landgemeinde … Merzhausen, 1646–1672."

FIGURE 34 Ravaging and burning of a German village during Thirty Years' War

FIGURE 35 The miseries of the war

use a modern phrase) seems like simple illegality or the flouting of laws and procedures promulgated by state administrators.

People sought to escape from restrictions on their property rights and other personal activity in a process which could be termed "self-release."[5] They found ways to shake off the obligation to pay dues, perform labor, or seek permissions associated with tenure. Over the years, they created and used strategies to evade the formal restrictions on property use that privileged one social estate or group, such as Christians, feudal vassals, or men, over another, as well as some parts of families over others. In effect, through their own striving, men and women were making themselves more free and equal.

---

5 Self-release is a term from animal control. It is a euphemism for escape.

FIGURE 36 A popular cartoon depicting the monster of war (the Thirty Years' War) consuming men of the population

Thanks to the destruction of the war, information was lost about all types of real tenure. Who rightfully held a certain estate? Under what terms? Who had rights of way or to use water, or rights to hunt or fish? What taxes and dues were owed to whom, and by whom? All of these rights, not just the holding of land, were considered real property – that is, rights appurtenant to real estate. Buy or inherit an estate, and certain rights and obligations probably came with it. With the land, you may have gained a right to hunt or take crops, maybe to enter or exit across a neighbor's land; you may have to pay certain dues, but you may enjoy freedom from certain labor or other dues, even from

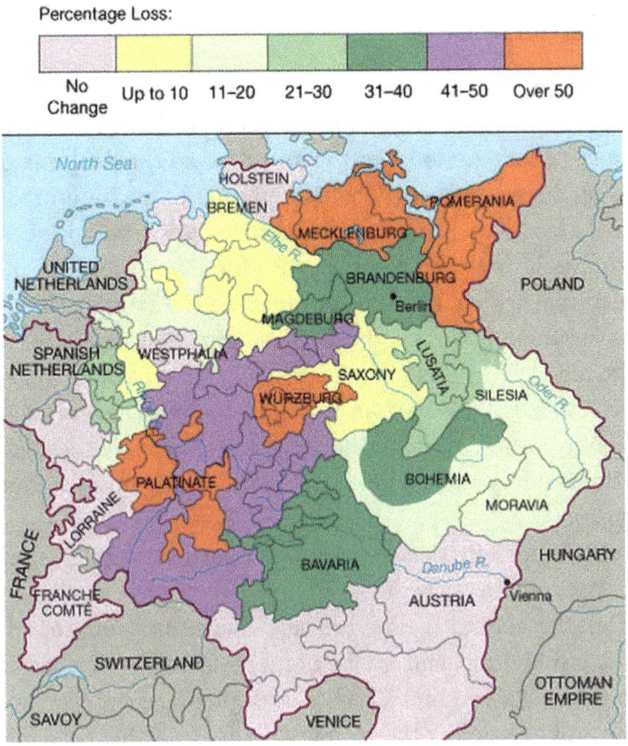

FIGURE 37 Population losses in Germany during the Thirty Years' War

high tax. Such rights and freedoms were similar to and ancestors of modern real estate easements – rights connected to one's own land or to another's land (*iura in re aliena*) which could be held, alienated, leveraged, and litigated over in court. Some of them are strange to modern eyes, such as labor obligations for a tenant or tax immunities connected to a certain estate.

In the post-War period, landlords, tenants, and even the ruler himself alleged illegalities both in transfers of lands and physical spaces such as homes but also in various real rights. These real rights included the collection of fruit, such as field harvest and timbering, as well as the taking of wildlife by hunting, fowling, and fishing. The discussion here interweaves rights in land and real rights such as tax immunities because the source documents I use do so: the jurists who served as regime officials were trained in the civil law (the modern Roman civil law, the *ius commune*), which understood land holding of any sort and the holding of rights appurtenant to land as closely related, to be treated together.

2 Missing Money and Missing Records

In the first decades after the end of the War, the rulers of the two large Hessian landgraviates complained often of non-collection of feudal dues and taxes. In European states of the period, most regimes served the dual role of high feudal lord and public government. That is, the ruler of any non-urban regime (whether called a kingdom, principality, margraviate, or even a princely *respublica*) was very often the high feudal lord of the plurality of estates in the territory and also the formal head of the state government. Here two European constitutional orders confronted one another – those of feudalism and public state law. As feudal high lord, the ruler collected feudal dues, from pennies to chickens to labor service. (In the Hessian example, the prince was feudal lord of an unusually large portion of the territory.) As public head of the state, he held the constitutional duty of collecting taxes for the state administration (mostly foreign defense).

A post-war pattern emerges in Hesse and other German states of non-compliance with directives to raise the dues and taxes which were notionally owed. In Hesse Cassel, the central regime officials alleged that improperly low amounts were being submitted, and similar non-compliance was reported in other locales like Schmalkalden and Cleves. In essence, the nobility was in rebellion – significantly restricting the regimes' ability to gather information and enforce their will. Regime sources tell us about several categories of alleged illegality.

3 Tithe Conversion and Disposal

In 1649, soon after the conclusion of the peace treaties ending the War, the landgravine Amalie Elisabeth issued a decree reminding her cherished subjects that *Vermalterung* could not be undertaken to defraud the owners of tithes.[6] Tithe of course was the traditional, compulsory contribution by farmers of a portion of their current production yield, for instance wheat or seed for future planting. Originally a contribution to the parish church, over the centuries the claim to a given tithe had transferred from the church to any number of other parties, including prince, secular feudal landlords, towns cor-

6 On Amalie-Elizabeth, see Helfferich, *The Iron Princess: Amalia Elisabeth and the Thirty Years War*.

porate, or other well-to-do common farmers. *Vermalterung* can be broadly thought of as tithe conversion – that is, alienating the right to collect tithe and, thereby implicitly, the right to sell it and realize monetary gain from it. The right to collect tithe was something thus like a perpetual annuity with a fixed rate but varying yield.[7] There is evidence in Hesse alone of frustration from the regime toward farmers and local officials over alleged *Vermalterung*, which the government claimed was being done without permission in the commission of fraud – defrauding the landgravial government of some of its tithe revenue. The activity is also attested vaguely in France at an earlier date.[8] It should be noted that in itself the practice was just a (potentially licit) agricultural contract. *Vermalterung* was advantageous to landlords in receiving cash instead of kind and saved on the expense of collecting, transporting and storing huge amounts of grain. Gregory Pedlow writes that,

> To avoid the considerable costs of supervising the amount of grain harvested, collecting the necessary percentage of tithe, and transporting and storing this grain, many landlords worked out agreements with local villagers to sell them the tithe in return for a fixed amount of cash or grain. This process ... usually took place before the harvest ... In effect the landlord was leasing the tithe to the peasants.

People who bought the grain from the landlord were often able to get it at a discount by colluding not to bid the price up.[9] The prince would become unhappy if such activity were being done without his knowledge since that usually betokened people making a deal to partially cut him out.

7 The word *Vermalterung* derives from *Malter*, a "dry measure of cereals or other produce, varying in size by region." See Preussischen Akademie der Wissenschaften, Deutsche Akademie der Wissenschaften zu Berlin, and Heidelberger Akademie der Wissenschaften, *Deutsches Rechtswörterbuch* (Weimar: H. Böhlaus Nachfolger, 1914) (DRW). The DRW has *maltern* as to "rent out a *Maltergut*," the same source defining the latter as "a piece of land whose rent is measured and paid in *Malter*," the latter meaning simply a fixed though unspecified measure of dry weight. *Vermalterung* is treated at Hans Lerch, *Hessische Agrargeschichte des 17. und 18. Jahrhunderts* (Hersfeld: H. Ott, 1926), pp. 65–66. The earliest juristic discussion of *Vermalterung* I have seen is Laurentius Kirchovius, ed., *Consilia sive Responsa praestantissimorum Germaniae* (Frankfurt am Main: 1605), Tomus 4, Consilium 30 by Nicol. Everhard of Ingolstadt, pp. 146–150, on *venditio decimarum*, but the practice is reported in other language going back before the onset of the Protestant Reformation.

8 Tigar and Levy, *Law and the Rise of Capitalism.*

9 Gregory W. Pedlow, *The Survival of the Hessian Nobility, 1770–1870* (Princeton: Princeton University Press, 1988), p. 117m.

FIGURE 38 Landgravine Amalia-Elizabeth of Hesse-Cassel

Amalie's husband Landgrave Wilhelm v had issued a similar edict in 1633.[10] (See Figures 38–40 for portraits and family tree of the landgravial house discussed here.) In Amalie-Elizabeth's decree of 1649, issued some sixteen months before the end of her 13-year reign, when her son was almost ready to assume authority, Amalie Elisabeth called the practices "disorders and dishon-

10 See Penalty-Prohibition of July 1, 1633, and Princely Announcement: concerning how the lordly tithe is to be raised and managed, and other matters, July 21, 1634, both in Kleinschmid and Apell, *Sammlung*, Vol. 2, respectively p. 65–66, p. 145. For *Vermalterung* in the lands of the former abbey of Fritzlar, incorporated into Hesse-Cassel after 1648, see StAMa 17 e: Lgrl. Hess. Reg. Kassel Ortsrepos. Fritzlar 5 and StAMa 17 e: Lgrl. Hess. Reg. Kassel Ortsreposituren Wolfhagen 221.

FIGURE 39 Landgrave Wilhelm v of Hesse-Cassel, unlucky in war, survived by his wife Amalia-Elizabeth and son Wilhelm vi

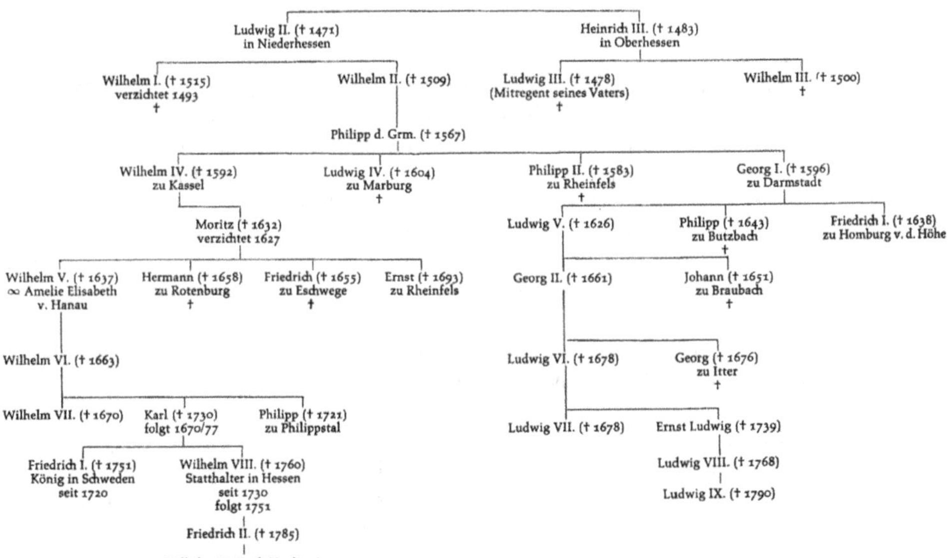

FIGURE 40 Family tree of Landgraves of Hessen

esty which grew up during the War."[11] Evidence suggests that the landgravine knew something about who the culprits were.[12] She complained that both she and other holders of tithes had thus been "maliciously defrauded" of "a very great [amount]" of their due tithes.[13] Holders of the widely scattered tithes included not only the landgrave and various nobles but also other entities like village corporations and wealthy non-noble people. The decree detailed several methods of tithe evasion. One way was for "willful miscreants" (*muthwilligen ubertrettern*) to make agreements to regulate in effect how much was tithed. A second technique involved shifting around the name of the landholder. A third was to move harvest "out of one field into another" in order "to make them tithe-free." Sometimes peasants secretly sold or exported their produce, especially outside of the region or state, to evade tithes.[14]

Another strategy was for tithe-holders and tithe-owers simply "to make agreements to their advantage ... to only pay [in effect] one part out of eleven or out of twenty ...," that is, to sneakily contribute a smaller fraction of their produce than they were supposed to. Such an arrangement might reflect typical shifts in the salable value of such dues. Gregory Pedlow describes the leasing of the tithe in the eighteenth and nineteenth centuries as a normal practice in Hesse, apparently without dint of illegality.[15] Rather, *Vermalterung* had by then become a useful, practical arrangement between (most often) the village corporation and the *Grundherr*.[16]

---

11 "solche beim Kriegk eingerißene Unordtnungen unndt betrieglichkeiten ..." See "Verordnung, Wie es mit der Vermalterung des Herrschaftlichen Zehndens, wie nicht weniger in Ansehung des Aufzehlens und somit zu halten sey," July 2, 1649, in ibid., Vol. 2, p. 145.

12 She enumerated them as "einige Gemeindte in Stätten oder Dörffern oder auch eine gewiße rotte und einzele Persohnen." The Cassel regime must have known roughly who or at least where the culprits were, since they knew of the problem both through reports and "by our accounting." See ibid., Vol. 2, p. 145.

13 "ein sehr grosses ... arglistig betrogen worden seindt ... uns und unserem geliebten Sohn ..." See ibid., Vol. 2, p. 144.

14 "... oder von einem Acker auf den Andern, oder aus einem Felde in das Ander"; "oder auch aus den huffen ezliche Lander zu Erbäckern"; "zehentfrey zu machen" See ibid., Vol. 2, p. 144.

15 Pedlow, *Survival of the Hessian Nobility*.

16 "[A]uch bürger undt bauren zue ihrem Vortheil etwe sich zu vergleichen unterstünden, ahn etlichen orthen wider das herkommen, das Elfte, oder 20. bundt zu sammeln, auch von Neun gebunden nichts zu geben ..." See Kleinschmid and Apell, *Sammlung*, Vol. 2, p. 144. Tithes in Hesse-Cassel typically ranged from one ninth (11%) to one twenty-second (4.5%), so such an arrangement might reflect typical shifts in the salable value of such dues.

Tithe leasing became further complicated when a tithe-owner hired someone else to collect the tithe for him, creating a potential for agency-risk problems. For instance, when a tithe was owned by a corporate entity such as a town, the entity might be forced to hire teamsters, who in turn could "lease the tithes for almost nothing, or … let them spoil in the field."[17] The landgravine Amalie Elisabeth called upon officials to watch out for these evasive strategies and renewed the high penalty set by her late husband in 1633 – a 100 gulden fine per incident.[18] Officials were not only negligent in collecting tithes but also had apparently embezzled dues from landgravial domain lands in previous decades. Before Wilhelm V's reign, earlier princes of Hesse had repeatedly issued edicts (about every twelve years on average) tackling not only officials' embezzlement but also such problems as their alienation of domain possessions (e.g. wood) or making illegal liens against landgravial fiefs.[19]

Tithe avoidance in and of itself did not expand property rights or freedom, nor did the other allegedly illegal activities which are to be considered next. But coupled with the regime's loss of information and weakening control over transfer of real rights through ordinary, bilateral contracts, sales, and encumbrance, people were gaining more *de facto* freedom to use and dispose of their own resources and control their own affairs. And as I will argue in the final section of this chapter, possessory and prescription procedure would come to secure such freedom after the mid seventeenth century.

4 Methods of Self-Release: The Claim of Allodial Property

Now we turn to more direct strategies employed by various parties to circumvent restrictions on their use and disposal of land and land-related (real) rights. Our first example of this will showcase a legal strategy used by family members including widows and their families of origin to strengthen their control of estates. One means of doing this, explored below, involved sale and subsequent enfiefment to another party. Family land holdings could be complicated, especially among larger, wealthier families who were united and organized over several branches and kept records of who held what and how.

17 "… die Zehnten um gar geringes zu vermaltern … oder dieselbe im Felde verderben zu lassen …" Ibid., Vol. 2, p. 144.

18 "Nun hette zwar jedes Orts Beambten inhrer Schüldigkeith nach gebühret, hiruff fleissig Acht zu geben, damit zue gefehrung Ffgl. unndt jegen [= gegen] das herkommen nichts eingeführet werden möge …" Ibid., Vol. 2, p. 144.

19 For instance in 1574, 1587, 1629, 1637, and 1640, in ibid., Vols. 1 and 2 passim.

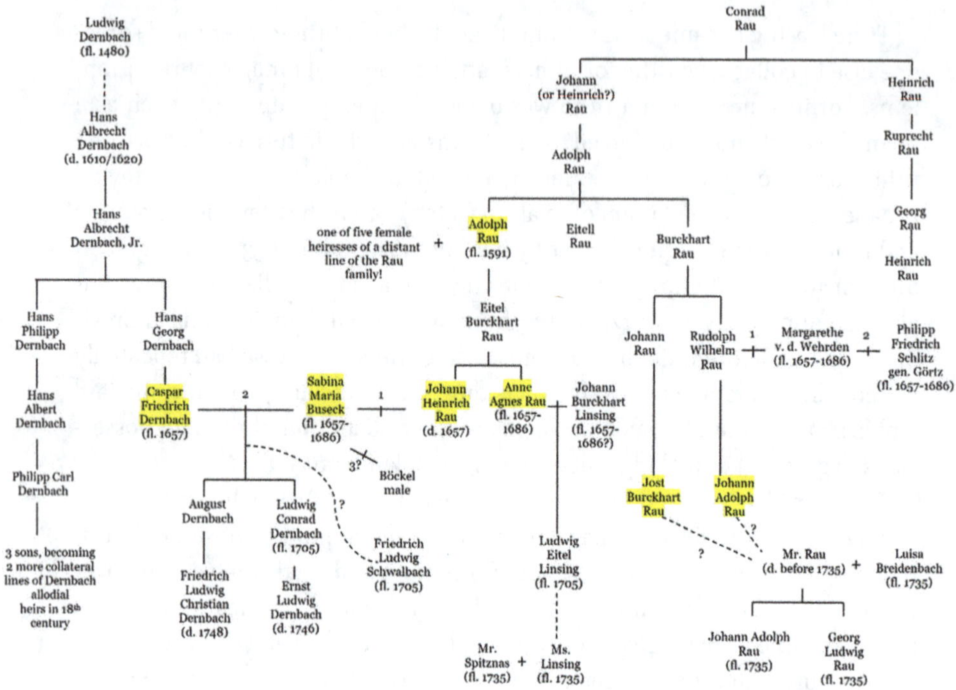

FIGURE 41 Family tree of the Rau, Dernbach, and Linsing families, 1480–1748. Highlighted names are people discussed in this book

A salient example from the mid seventeenth century indicates a family strategy for evading feudal tenure. The example comes from the noble families of the Rau, Buseck, and Dernbach in the Lahn valley between Marburg and Frankfurt am Main.

The story concerns a dispute between on the one hand Sabina Maria Rau (*née* Buseck) and Anne Agnes Rau, and on the other hand their second cousins Jost Burckhardt Rau and Johann Adolph Rau. Sabina Maria had married Johann Heinrich Rau. After Johann Heinrich's death in 1657, she and her sister-in-law Anne Agnes had taken or retained possession of the main Rau estate in Holzhausen. Their cousins sued, but in 1682 the Hessian High Appeals Court vindicated their claim to hold the estate and rights in allod, against the claim of the cousins. Allod, which is considered in greater depth further on, can be thought of as functionally equivalent to fee-simple modern ownership.[20] (See family tree, Figure 41.)

After the death of a husband, a surviving widow typically continued to occupy (i.e. inhabit and use) the real estate they had enjoyed together. What

20 Tigar and Levy, *Law and the Rise of Capitalism*, p. 180.

happened in the Rau case was common. Certainly it was redacted as a formulaic case and pondered over by jurists. The decedent's agnatic kin sued the widow for possession, arguing that the real estate was a fief and therefore would pass to them as male heirs. In inheritance law, *agnatic* means tracing a path of relationships only through male kin, in contrast to *cognatic*, which means tracing any path of blood or legal kindred relationships, through either male or female relatives. In the present case, the *agnatic* kin sued Sabina Maria Rau and Anne Agnes Rau to validate their possession of the estates because they feared for the security of their long-term claim to the estate. And if the women could get their possession recognized by the landgravial chancery, then it could be upheld in subsequent conflicts and legally sold or encumbered (e.g. mortgaged). The cousins identified themselves as the "feudal heirs," showing their claim to the estates was as fief-holders. If the widow lost the suit, the real estate was said to have been fief, and it continued down the feudal road in perpetuity, until this happened again. If she won, the real estate was recognized as allod.

The dispute was over whether the land and rights were held as a fief or as allod. As far as we can reconstruct, all parties understood that, in this context, a feudal tenure would have meant agnatic inheritance, meaning that a widow would have had only life-use (see below) and could not rent out the land and rights, much less bequeath anything to other parties. At her death, land and rights would pass to agnatic family members. If the land was accepted as being held as allod, however, it was, at least notionally, completely under the control of the holder, with no dues on it nor other feudal controls. Germans and German courts in the eighteenth century recognized that holding in allod (*eigen*, literally "own land," "one's own") carried tremendous freedom of disposition – even against the wishes of a strong territorial ruler, king or emperor (unlike in France or England).

A widow often but not always enjoyed life use (*Widem*) of an estate after her husband's death. *Widem* expired with the death of the widow and she was not legally permitted to alienate the estate. In this case, Sabina Maria Rau had *Widem*, but sought more. Her distant "feudal" in-laws did not dispute her possession but rather disputed her claim that the nature of her tenure gave her full (allodial) disposition over the estate. She, her new husband, and her sister-in-law Anne Agnes were able to not only keep possession of the estate but also to give it out in fief to one Hans Heinrich as a manager (*Meier*). So the allodial heirs were themselves giving the estate out in fief. The feudal heirs' only legal position could be that Sabina Maria had only *Widem*, and could not alienate, mortgage, subinfeudate (as she did with Hans Heinrich), and so on.[21]

In 1591, Anne Agnes's grandfather Adolph Rau had apparently bought, with a written bill of sale, real estate from his wife's four sisters. Those five women were members of a distant line of the same family, which became extinct shortly thereafter. Sixty years later, the grandchildren and distant cousins, Jost Burckhardt Rau and Johann Adolph Rau, claimed that the real estate was actually a fief, and therefore that the "sale" was just a transfer of fief from one line of the family to another. As such, the fief should pass to them by feudal succession through male descent – this kind of fief could pass only through sons and brothers.

Anne Agnes and Sabina Marie wanted to solidify their claim to the real estate of their (respectively) late husband and kinsman Johann Heinrich, so they gave their power of attorney (*Vollmacht*) to Sabina Maria's new husband, Caspar Friedrich Dernbach. The women, Dernbach, and their lawyer produced an "instrument of taking possession" (*Instrumentum apprehensionis*) dated June 8, 1657, documenting their actions: Dernbach

> went forth into the tree nursery by the house, broke a branch from [sc. one of] the trees, slashed clods of soil from the earth, as far as the free estate that belonged to the late Johan Henrich Rau had extended. [Sc. Dernbach] in this way took these things into his possession.[22]

Over at the mill, Dernbach

> pulled a nail [*stäne*] out of the mill door post, and similarly took a stone from the river that drives the mill ... He went up to the mill wheel, made it stop, then let it go again. He said that by this he had taken possession of everything and all rights involved in the milling. Saying this ... Dernbach

21 Other examples of feudal-allodial lawsuits in the same territory are presented at Johann Heinrich Christian von Selchow, ed., *Rechtsfälle enthaltend Gutachten und Entscheidungen vorzüglich aus dem teutschen Staats- und Privatrecht*, Vol. 1 (Lemgo: Meyer, 1782), Chapter 8 and Chapter 24 and *ibid.*, Vol. 4 (Lemgo: Meyer, 1785), Chapter 124, "Decisio Von Verjähren jährlicher Renten. Nach Paderborn im October 1784," p. 115t.

22 "fort in der Baumgartten ahm Haus, brach Zinkem od: ast vor der Baümen ... stach Schollem aus der Erde so weit zu dem adelich freyen Ritterguth gehörig, und Junker Johan Henrich Rau ... zuständig gewesen nd in seinem leben eingehabt und besessen wolte ... selbiger gleicher gestalt hiermit in besitzt genommen haben." The present discussion of the Rau and Dernbach is based on the *Instrumentum apprehensionis* of June 8, 1657, and related documents found in StAMa 340 Rau Paket 54 e.

> went to the ... meadow. He sliced a clump of turf out of the ground and handed it to me and said that by this token, he took into his possession [*ergreiffen*] this and all other things which his late brother-in-law possessed. From there, he went to the fields in Mardorf and slashed clods of dirt out of these, too, and gave them to me.[23]

As Dernbach rode around Holzhausen, the notary and witnesses rushed after him. Dernbach made the traditional symbolic forms of taking possession. He visited "the house and grounds [*Haus, Hof*], forests, fields, meadows, gardens, tithes, mills, brewery ... and, in sum, everything that the late *Junker* possessed."[24] The allodial party would subsequently argue that these activities were symbolic forms of taking possession from ancient "Germanic tradition." Thus they were invoking supposedly high authority of ancient customary law to cement their claim of an alternative form of tenure (allodial rather than feudal), during a period of legal confusion characterized by a weakening of former state oversight.

5 Models of Allod

Allod is an ambiguous concept in legal history. It was not exclusive to Central Europe but was also applied and studied in England and France and in early North American jurisprudence. The concept of allodial holding in early modern Germany grew out of earlier concepts of *proprietas* (Latin) and *Eigen* (German). These two terms were common in the earlier middle ages and had a plain, though not perfectly clear meaning of undivided, simple local ownership. An eighteenth-century phrase for allod was (*freies*) *Erbe und Eigen* ("free inheritance and own [ground]"), for instance as used by the local baronial Hessian family, the Schenck zu Schweinsberg, whose extensive local holdings were called the *Schenkisch' Eigen*. This corresponded to the kind of lordship

23 "ferner hieb er stäne aus der Mühlen thür Posten, in gleichen nahm er steins aus dem Gewasser so die Mühle treibet ... über weilte mihr selbige stürtzete auch daß Mühle Raht [i.e. Rad] zu, zog er wiederumb auf, und lies daß wasser wieder auf das Mühlen Rath laufen, und sagte darbey daß er gleichengestalt wolte solches alles mit dem Mahlwerck wassergang und allem andern gerechtigkeit in Possess dardurch und darmit genommen haben." See ibid. pp. 15–16.

24 See *Instrumentum apprehensionis* of June 8, 1657 (Staatsarchiv Marburg, Bestand 340 Rau Paket 54 e), pp. 7–8.

called suzerainty in other contexts.[25] From roughly the fourteenth through eighteenth centuries, this was the meaning of allod used with slight variations, some emphasizing waste land that had been cleared and settled.[26] The thirteenth century saw the development of the theory of divided dominion. This theory distinguished "direct ownership" and "use ownership" (*dominium directum* and *dominum utile*). Divided dominion was constructed out of Roman concepts (*dominium, utilis*) and became the basis of the feudal lordship structure of lord and tenant, as it was practiced in Germany right up to the early nineteenth century, albeit much adumbrated in the final centuries.[27] Allod survived into this period, literally adjacent to feudal tenures, with both forms scattered wildly throughout the empire (and France as well).[28] And so allod

25 Suzerainty seems more to have been used in English and French contexts and meant "immediate personal possession of the land" which "combined in one person or institution the roles of owner and landlord, chief military defender, and lawgiver." Still suzerainty could be quite quotidian: "The impact of this hierarchy of feudal dues and services on property law was formidable. If A rented the house of B, who was suzerain of the place, and B in turn held of C, the death of B without heirs put C into B's place; henceforth, he would receive the whole of the rent paid by A …" Tigar characterizes hard-to-eradicate local pockets of power ("the kind that continued to plague French kings") as "local suzerainties." See Tigar and Levy, *Law and the Rise of Capitalism*, pp. 44, 138, 203.

26 Land cleared from waste such as forest was sometimes called *Rodung*.

27 Allod is the name for what was basically pre-feudal freeholding among the large population of the Franks around the time of Charlemagne. Allod in this account was holding derived from group immigration, occupation, or conquest, which was divided up among members of the group and was not as such subject to special taxes, dues, or other impositions by the leader (prince, *primus inter pares*, king, etc.). In time as feudal tenure over semi-free denizens began, whether *colonii*, serfs, or favored servants like *ministeriales* and knights, the older, allodial form of property became relatively less common both as a matter of proportion in the population and apparently in geographical expanse. Over nine centuries it became increasingly uncommon, but was still known and written about in Germany, especially in the south (Franconia). For similar developments in France and England a century earlier, see Tigar and Levy, *Law and the Rise of Capitalism*, p. 196b and Jan de Vries, *The Economy of Europe in an Age of Crisis, 1600–1750* (Cambridge: Cambridge University Press, 1976), p. 45.

28 Gustaf Klemens Schmelzeisen, "Eigen und Erbe," in *Deutsches Privatrecht*, Vol. 22, *Schaeffers Grundriss des Rechts und der Wirtschaft* (Leipzig: Schaeffer-Verlag; E. L. Hirschfeld, 1935). *Eigen* was one of the early translations of *proprietas*. But *proprietas* was a minor property rights term in Roman law compared with dominion and possession. The Burgundians made *proprietas* the opposite of use (*nützen*). In glossaries of the period, *eigan* was also the translation for *praedium* (an estate), but this word, like similarly *fundus*, might refer to any of several things in actual usage, and hence had multiple Latin synonyms and German translations. *Eigan* also used to translate *patrimonium* and other words associated with the family estate. Gerhard Köbler, "Eigen und Eigentum," *Zeitschrift der Savigny-Stiftung für Rechtsgeschichte. Germanistische Abteilung*. 95 (1978), p. 10, 25.

came to be understood as the complementary opposite of feudal tenure. In feudal tenure the king or territorial ruler held feudal overlordship over the vassal's tenure. Allod, by contrast, was understood to be free and absolute. The allodial holder held it of no one.[29] In medieval Austria, allod was often derived from clearance and colonization, since a person who cleared and settled on wild, untamed land could correctly claim that it had never been subject to feudal dues.[30] The same would appear to have been true in parts in the Rhineland as well at least, where allods "grew up in the wild."[31] Later, the great allodial holders transformed themselves into feudal lords, as in the case of Catzenelnbogen, which later became part of the Hessian landgraviate.[32] A comparable development of territorial supremacy over small allodial holders took place in France, but ended in 1667 with the effective abolition of allodial tenure by Louis XIV.[33]

German jurists in the seventeenth and eighteenth centuries sometimes spoke of land which was functionally allodial as being held "free and clear" (*frei, loß und ledig*): Not only was it not held in fief from any landlord whatsoever, but there was no servitude or collateral lien on it (as from a mortgage); and it was not governed by any set of real rules (such as inheritance rules like

Folker Reichert, *Landesherrschaft, Adel und Vogtei: Zur Vorgeschichte des spaetmittelalterlichen Staendestaates im Herzogtum Oesterreich*, Vol. 23, Beihefte zum Archiv für Kulturgeschichte (Cologne; Vienna: 1985), p. 239 n. 102 corroborates *Eigen* as a translation of *praedium*.

29 Hans Thieme, "Landsiedel," in *Handwörterbuch zur deutschen Rechtsgeschichte*, Vol. 2 (Berlin: E. Schmidt, 1978), pp. 1571–1572.

30 There appears to have been, at least superficially, a similarity between the medieval conditions which gave rise to allodial holding and the conditions toward that end of the Thirty Years' War – a high relative level of chaos, with many lands wild and seemingly uninhabited. In both contexts, there might well have been indigenous inhabitants who were pushed aside by new settlers.

31 "Aside from these royal counties, however, were autonomous [*eigenrechtliche*] counties, immunities that grew up in the wild, mostly from clearances (allodial or landlordly counties)." Bruno Gebhardt, *Handbuch der deutschen Geschichte*, ed. Herbert Grundmann, 8th ed. (Stuttgart: Union Deutsche Verlagsgesellschaft, 1954 [orig. 1891]), p. 631. For Austria, see Reichert, *Landesherrschaft, Adel und Vogtei: Zur Vorgeschichte des spaetmittelalterlichen Staendestaates im Herzogtum Oesterreich*, p. 245.

32 For example, the counts of Catzenelnbogen held land around Cologne in allod. August Heldmann, "Die cölnische Stadt Rhens am Rhein in hessischer Pfandschaft," *Zeitschrift des Vereins für hessische Geschichte und Landeskunde* 31 (1896), p. 3 and Henry Sumner Maine, *Ancient Law* (Dorset Press, 1986 [orig. 1861]), p. 191.

33 Tyler Lange, "Property Rights," in *Cambridge History of Rights, Volume 2: The Middle Ages* (forthcoming).

primogeniture or impartibility).[34] And yet this is ambiguous. For example, if Sabina Mara let out a real right which she held in allod, to Hans Heinrich, the holding would be divided and he would be in possession. Such a sub-tenant would have means of converting possession into effective property by successfully converting (alienating) it or encumbering it, for instance by giving it as collateral pledge, since these activities gave a third party an immediate, seemingly first-order, recorded interest in it.

Though allodial holding was indefeasible from above, it was vulnerable from below, by just the same means: For subinfeudating, renting, or subleasing an allod to a tenant made the allodial holder vulnerable, should the tenant use the same strategy that the allodial heirs themselves did here. The relationship between allod and family inheritance rules is also unclear in current research. Allod was long associated with family-clan holdings, meaning that a family-clan controlled certain estates. This could be rather humble, as in a village. If there were customary rules governing who could inherit or control the estates, was that allod? Older general legal historians like Henry Sumner Maine said yes, allod included family lands whose control and inheritance could be governed by enforceable rules, without it ceasing to be allod, even though such rules contradicted free disposition including free testation.

We may wonder whether allod was truly a clear and determinate legal category, though contemporaries clearly thought they knew what they were talking about. What was disputed in the seventeenth and eighteenth centuries were questions like, *Whether* a given estate was itself allod? *How* and *whether* something could become allod? And *what* this meant for what an allodial owner (lord, *dominus*) could do. Also controversial was *how* fief rules interacted with allod rules.

But the category itself and its basic outlines were *not* controversial. Consider for instance a remark by the Prussian jurist Johann Gottlieb Heineccius (1681–1741), who was celebrated and respected in his day. Prussian by origin, Heineccius comes onto the radar of Hessian-area jurisprudence not only because he became well-known and respected throughout the empire, but also because he was in fact offered a government position in Marburg in 1740 right before his death, though he declined it. In 1737, Heineccius penned a

34 Hugo Grotius and Jean Barbeyrac debated what it could mean to hold a tenement free and clear of obligations. For instance, could a "sovereign" (one who held *maiestas*) hold his power in fief from another party? See Grotius, *Rights of War and Peace* I.3.§23, pp. 332–334, and Barbeyrac's notes thereto. Very insightful on encumbrance, servitude and free and clear tenure is Barry Nicholas, *An Introduction to Roman law* (Oxford: Clarendon Press, 1962), pp. 116, 133.

long opinion concerning the question of succession of allodial heirs to a fief. The dispute he examined concerned "the succession of allodial heirs to a fief which had become extinct in the male line, based on a previous agreement that the free disposition of it be left to them." The object of dispute was the free knightly estate of Frensdorf in Bamberg. Heineccius argued that a fief might essentially become allod if it were sold from one agnate to another, that is, purely through male relations. By this reasoning, Adolph Rau in 1591 had become a genuine purchaser of an estate; it had not simply passed from one fief-holder to another. Heineccius argued from the Lombard law that "when one agnate sells a paternal fief to another agnate, and renunciation has followed for the intervening price, then this is rather more a sale than a simple renunciation." Heineccius added to that a similar conclusion reached by Klock, that "in this case, the purchased fief takes on the nature of allod."[35]

In Holzhausen, the challenge faced by the sisters-in-law was to hold on to the estates they and Dernbach possessed. To do so, they employed the practical strategy to turn around and enfief a third party with the estate – the manager (*Meier*) Hans Heinrich mentioned earlier.[36] Someone else thus came into possession of the estate, albeit on a strict contractual basis. This created a further wall for the feudal claimants or anyone else to get past before potentially overcoming the women's rights claims. It could be thought of as a kind of firewall. Notably, the *Meierei* contract stated clearly that Heinrich was not to let the estate (*Hof*) out, in any mode (rental, feudal, colonial-settlement, etc.) to anyone – whether a common tenant, another Rau party, or the Hessian regime. Had the cousins Jost Burckhardt and Johann Adolph continued their suit somehow (they did not), they would have had to turn first to Hans Heinrich, since he became possessor of the estate in fief, and prove that he was in wrongful possession. But a proper contract existed among discrete parties, involving consideration and conveyance, so the feudal cousins' position would have been untenable. Here what moves underneath everything is not so much *right* in any great heavenly sense, so much as *strategic position and advantage.*

---

35 See Johann Gottlieb Heineccius, *Consilia decisiones et responsa iuris ex schedis paternis*, ed. Johann Christian Gottlieb Heineccius, Vol. 1 (Bratislava: Johann Jacob Kornius, 1744) Responsum 23, pp. 263–278; this collection was edited and prepared by Heineccius's son after the father's death.

36 It was Anne Agnes alone who enfiefed Heinrich as *Meier* or *Hofmann* (estate-manager) with a considerable portion of the estate, for a term of six years. Heinrich contracted to make payments to Anne Agnes, in addition to a number of other obligations that he undertook to fulfill annually in the contract, such as delivery of produce, or a *Möth* of rye here, a sheep there. See the *Leyhebrief* of November 1, 1683 (StAMa 340 Rau Paket 04 k2).

We do not know how frequently enfiefment was used as a strategy for solidifying allodial tenure. But we know of examples which used the same principles. There is an early example of it, provided a century earlier by August Heldman, nearby in Cologne and Catzenelnbogen on the Rhine. In the thirteenth century, the counts of Catzenelnbogen held land in allod in the municipal area around Cologne, just down the Rhine from their county seat. In 1285 Count William of Catzenelnbogen (roughly the great, great, great, great, great, great, great, great grandfather of our William VI of Hesse-Cassel) gave it out in fief for 400 marks to the town of Cologne. Thereby that count buttressed his family's rule by transforming himself into a feudal lord over tenants.[37] Transfer from one holder is described in law through the metaphor of links in a chain, the "chain of possession." As additional transfers are made from one holder (*tenans*, tenant) to another, each an additional chain link, it grows that much harder for the prior holder or tenant to successfully claim he had wrongfully lost possession. However it was that the counts had come to control and claim those lands before 1295, they had become titular feudal lords of them thereafter. Any controversy about lordship and title would have to begin downstream, literally and figuratively, with the Cologne burghers, rather than the counts.[38]

Returning to the case at hand, in 1686 Anne Agnes and Sabina Marie further made a compact between themselves to reinforce their claim to the estates in Holzhausen. Both of them subsequently got married (Sabina Maria remarried), so the importance of this reinforcement may have been to create a durable claim to the estate for themselves and their children, keeping the estate away from stepchildren. One of these stepchildren (Dernbach's son by a previous marriage) would in fact come to sue his first stepcousins (first cousins through his father's remarriage) as well as the feudal heir claimants, the next generation of whom resumed their suit in the early eighteenth century.

The Rau example and other period examples and related scholarship thus help us reconstruct the role of allod in family strategy and striving for power and freedom. By claiming allod, in seemingly disadvantageous situations people of both sexes could then create a novel barrier against other, supposedly

37 Heldmann, "Die cölnische Stadt Rhens am Rhein in hessischer Pfandschaft," p. 3. For the family tree of the rulers of Hesse, see Demandt, *Geschichte des Landes Hessen*.

38 As I have reconstructed the allodial strategy, one might wonder why it would behoove Count William to have given the land out in fief – would he not fear to lose control over it? But of course, farmland needs farmers to farm it – probably an early meaning of *nulle terre sans seigneur*. The Count probably had little to fear from the town and could vindicate his claim to be its lord.

prior claims through selling, encumbering, and enfiefment. This enabled them to take hold of, or strengthen their hold on, an estate and put rival claimant heirs, creditors, or princely tax collectors in the difficult position of pressing claims tied to land against persons who were not in possession of that land. *Hence the allodial strategy was key to realizing one of the greatest freedoms of all of this period*, that of being able to turn immobile assets into cash through strategies of secure sale or rental.

6 Circumventing Requirements through Legal Fictions

As the feudal-allodial contrast illustrates, law and custom might restrict how real estate and real rights were used or alienated. In the Rau examples, we saw parties fighting to vindicate their claims about how real rights (*realia*) were acquired and how the mode of acquisition governed inheritance. Control of real estate was also often restricted in terms of what *kind* of person could hold the tenure at all. This section examines two such restrictions and how people found ways to evade them, thereby gaining freedom and power.

One such restraint was religious. As a rule, Jews were considered legally unfit to hold fiefs or other forms of tenure, because they were unable (or unwilling) to take the specifically Christian oath required for tenancy – literally to take an oath on the Bible that they would uphold the duties of the tenure, including performance of any labor or payment of dues. Hence Jewish tenants, or their Christian lawyers, adopted a legal fiction to work around this requirement – oath substitution, whereby a Christian would take the oath in place of the Jewish tenant-to-be. In this way real estate could be freely transferred in circumvention of a traditional restriction. It is not clear whether the Christian oath-taker would actually be considered the liable party in case of default, but oath substitution was considered sufficient to complete in a legally binding way the sale or enfiefment. Oath substitution was an old practice in several countries, with a well-documented example in Germany from 1760 involving the Jew Levi Aaron Marr of Schmalkalden. In purchasing a house, Marr had paid the sale tax (*Laudemium*) and apparently had contrived to have a substitute (*provassal*) take the oath of vassalage for him, since as a Jew, everyone seems to have agreed, he could not "take the oath of fealty in his soul" that he would perform the fief duties (*praestanda*) "with the help of God and His son Jesus Christ." Someone later objected to the sale – as a rule Jews were usually prohibited from having anything but simple rental tenure in real estate. But the two officials who examined the purchase and the conflict arising from it had not found anything amiss about it; one of them noted that something like the contemporary Prussian law probably applied, which permitted such a substitution.[39]

Another version of oath substitution involved women rather than non-Christians. Although feudal law and rules varied widely, some feudal law specified that fiefs might *not* pass through cognate (female) relations; this was the basis of the Rau feudal heirs' legal position. As we saw above, Sabina Marie and Anne Agnes did not dispute that agnatic transfer was the rule but rather disputed that the estates were governed by feudal rules at all. In other instances a fief might indeed pass through cognate relations. And some fiefs could be held by women in their own names as widows or through proper inheritance or simply through actual enfiefment. This variety is part of the magic – and madness – of German legal history.

Feudal tenure (fief) generally gave better rights, and hence more control and freedom, than *Widem* (widow's life use of her marital estate). As discussed earlier, feudal tenure by default often permitted subinfeudation and transfer after the payment of a customary fee to the feudal lord above (count, landlord, prince). Widow's use permitted none of these things, and widow's estates under *Widem* were carefully watched by heirs-in-waiting.

In the fief scenario of agnatic transfer only, jurists devised another legal fiction similar to the oath substitution mentioned above to circumvent the restriction: "manning the fief" (*Vermannung*). Consider the common case of widows. Recall that in some circumstances, the widow of a deceased vassal (or notional vassal such as Johann Rau, above) might have to fight her deceased husband's agnatic kin to retain control of the fief. Johann Adam Kopp, writing in 1739, described one work-around, dating from at least the fourteenth century. Formally, a woman, whether single, married, or widowed, might be enfiefed with an estate and fictively perform the "fief-service" (*Lehen-Dienst*) associated with it. All of the above rights, duties and prerogatives might come to a woman and post-War jurists still held that she might legally meet the obligations of manly performance by nominating a man to serve as a legal stand-in for the fief. The man would be essentially a fictive tenant, whose role was understood as performing military or other manly service attached to the fief (e.g. heavy labor or an administrative office).

Did "manning" a fief actually increase women's freedom and power in the seventeenth and eighteenth centuries? In some cases, almost certainly. In earlier periods, women needed to take recourse to this legal fiction because they

39 Conrad Wilhelm Ledderhose, ed., *Kleine Schriften* (Marburg: Neue akademische Buchhandlung, 1787–1795), Vol. 2, pp. 303–308.

were very often excluded from obtaining or holding fiefs in their own right. Over the centuries, personal fief service such as labor, military, or administrative duty had often disappeared or been commuted on a given estate. By the mid eighteenth century, fief service for non-peasant vassals had sometimes been commuted into monetary value, sometimes called scutage (*scutagium*). But jurists tend to be formalists. Agnate-only fief transfer rules were the most common and one of the most enduring features of feudal tenure, even long after military service had just turned into scutage. Manning the fief, like Jewish oath-substitution, could make a real difference, as the evidence of several cases from earlier centuries reveals.

In 1739, Kopp produced several examples of manning fiefs. For instance, Emperor Wenceslaus enfiefed the widow Elizabeth of Meissen with estates in Leissnig in 1389. Her brother Margrave Jost of Moravia was to be her guardian in the holding of the fief.[40] Kopp also provided examples of widow's estate which extended past the lifespan of the widow in question. The co-heir lords (*Ganerben*) of Heusenstamm sold a fief to their sister Judta in 1314, formally to be manned by her husband Johann von Bickenbach. Confusingly, the representative of the Heusenstamm co-heirs was also named Johann and the letter was written in both Johanns' voices:

> I, Johann, son of Conrad, a knight of Heusenstamm, make it herewith known that with the consent and knowledge of my co-heirs, I have sold [an unspecified estate] to Johann von Bickenbach and his Lady Judte, his lawful wife ... Further, I, Johann von Bickenbach, acknowledge that I am the husband of the said Judta von Heusenstamm, until a king will come to the land.[41] I, the said Johann and my co-heirs von Heusenstamm also say the same, that we will ask the lord king that he give the fief to the said Johann von Bickenbach and Jutte his wedded woman in proper widowing-use (*Widem*), and also to their heirs, if that happen. The said Johann will be man for the fief.[42]

---

40 See Johann Adam Kopp, *Auserlesene proben des teutschen lehen-rechts, zu desto mehrerer erläuternung derer bey denen teutschen lehn-hofen befindlichen rechten, gewohnheiten und herkommen* (Marburg: Philipp Casimir Müller, 1739), Part IV, §7, pp. 160–161.

41 The mention of a king is an indication of the imperial interregnum between 1378 and 1455.

42 "Ich Johann der etwan was Herrn Conrads Sone eins Ritters von Heusenstamm, thun kunt ... das ich mit Willen und mit Verhengnüsse meiner Gan-Erben ... han verkauft Johann von Bickenbach unnd Frawen Judten, seiner ehlichen Wirtin ... Auch das Ich Johann von Bickenbach mich des erkennen, das ich Mann bin der vorgnanten [sc. Judte]

The husband Johann von Bickenbach is man *for* the fief but not the new fief-holder; the fief-holder strictly is his wife, the co-heir sellers' sister Judta von Heusenstamm. This was one example, albeit a striking one, of the variation in what could be called a *Widem* in the period and place. Judta was given secure possession of the *Widem*, passable to her man and to their heirs. Other examples come from Halberstadt, Cologne, and Hanau (a small county nestled among the Hessian states) through the late sixteenth century.[43] Although we do not know how late *Vermannung* remained in use, it was used in the century before our post-war period of interest. Similar to the allodial strategy, manning the fief was another tool people used to circumvent older formalities and give themselves more freedom of action with real property.

7 Retraction Law

People's ability to sell off what were considered family lands was also limited by customary law. This gave rise to other forms of circumvention. The colloquial names of such customary restrictions were *Abtrieb* ("drive off") and *Näherrecht* ("the right of those closest" or of "neighbors"), but jurists called it *ius retractus* or *Retraktsrecht*, best translated as retraction law or family reversion. Customary retraction law had been recorded and studied by jurists trained in the *ius commune* by the thirteenth century and was still common in the eighteenth century, although as we will see it was being challenged in our period by changing ideas, adverse practices, and state policies.[44] Retraction law provided a resolution to the same problem which the strategies of widows and allodial parties aimed to solve, namely, Did the terms of a person's real holding permit him or her to sell, rent out, or mortgage that right?

The Hessian states had taken an interest in retraction law by 1497 at the latest, when Wilhelm II ordered a survey of practices related to retraction law

von Heusenstamm also lang bis das ein König kommet zu Lande, des sprechen auch ich, der vorgnante Johann und meine Gan-Erben von Heusenstam, das Wir sollen unnsern Herrn den König bitten, das Er den vorgnanten Johann von Bickenbach unnd Jutten seiner ehlichen Wirtin, leith zu rechtem Wideme unnd iren Erben, wann das geschicht, so soll der vorgnant Johann seiner Mannschaft abe sein ..." See Kopp, *Auserlesene proben des teutschen lehen-rechts*, Part v, §9, pp. 224–225; ellipses in original. Kopp calls the above "quite a remarkable document."

43 Ibid., Part v, §8, pp. 221–223.

44 For retraction law, see entries in Zedler's *Universal-Lexicon* and, for modern scholarship, e.g. Hans Planitz, *Deutsches Privatrecht*, 3rd ed. (1948), pp. 44, 96. Tigar & Levy discuss retraction law in the coutumes of Philippe de Beaumanoir for Beauvais (France) at Tigar and Levy, *Law and the Rise of Capitalism*, p. 144.

and marital property.[45] The Collective High Court issued a set of rules and procedures in 1524, §7 of which set it that "in case of a closed deal at chancery … those who claim *Retraktsrecht* have 6 weeks and 3 days to claim their right." Otherwise, so long as "a public auction (either forced or voluntary) has been held … no *Retraktsrecht* will be permitted."[46] In 1572, Wilhelm IV's government had ordered investigation of customs around marital property, inheritance, and retraction law. The reasons stated for this and other investigations previous and later on were complaints of ill-defined "roguery" (*Zank*).[47] We can see not only that regimes spent time and energy thinking, complaining, and learning about these laws, but also that they spent their resources investigating local practices. Moreover, the configuration of retraction and marital property rules remained a major concern of jurists over the centuries: The 1572 survey was published not once but twice in the eighteenth century by two leading area jurists – Senckenberg printing the original Latin version (in 1735) and Estor the original German (in 1749).[48]

It seems that over the course of the sixteenth and seventeenth centuries, jurists developed a clear jurisprudence of retraction law, albeit with expectable local variation. The law constructed what might be called today a right of first refusal to purchase rights or ownership in family real estates: A family member who wanted to sell such rights was required first to offer the rights, either at a traditional or anciently fixed (low) rate or (sometimes) at the same rate as had been offered by an outsider, to other members of the family clan exclusively. Usage varied, but in all versions the first party entitled to buy was "anyone who would have inherited the realty at the death of the seller."[49] It was not a matter of who – insider or outsider – made a higher offer; the family member apparently usually had the right to pay less or to pay the traditional assessed value of the estate. This kept the price of real rights artificially low since it prevented outsiders (noble, common, or bourgeois) from buying up local parcels and rights. Hence incumbent tenants were deprived of their foremost means of realize liquid capital gain from the appreciation of real estate or from eagerness of well-off parties to invest in land. As we shall see further

45 "Stadt- und Landesbrauch des Oberfürstenthums Marburg," p. 50.

46 Ledderhose, *Kleine Schriften*, Vol. 3, p. 292.

47 "Stadt- und Landesbrauch des Oberfürstenthums Marburg," p. 3.

48 Heinrich Christian Senckenberg, "Juridicas Consuetudines Principatus Hassiae Sec. XVI auctoritate publica collectas / Extractus der Statt und Lands Gebrauch im Ober Fürstenthum Hessen die Erb und Anfälle zwischen zwey Ehegemaechten, wie auch den Neherkauf betreffend," in *Selecta iuris et historiarum*, Vol. 3 (Frankfurt am Main: Johann Friedrich Fleischer, 1735); "Stadt- und Landesbrauch des Oberfürstenthums Marburg."

49 Polley, "Retraktsrecht und Weinkauf im Hochstift Fulda," pp. 241–242.

below, sometimes public sale at auction was held to nullify any *ex post facto* exercise of retraction, on the reasoning that potential in-family buyers had had their chance.

The positive interpretation of this law, where it applied, was that it kept strong the "family-land bond" and hence the family as an organized community.[50] Such customs were common at every level, from poor families in villages to great noble and princely clans such as the extended Riedesel clan (which held tightly together, calling itself a "republic").[51]

The most complete sources for customary law in the region which we still have show the prominence of retraction law. Four of these sources were the Solms Territorial Law (1571), the Catzenelnbogen Territorial Law (1572), the Marburg law survey (1572), and the Nassau-Catzenelnbogen ordinance (1616).[52] The local juries and the regime jurists who empaneled them to record their knowledge indicate that rules of retraction were both very important for local affairs and respected by central legal bureaucracies.[53] To be sure, there was variation in German customary law in the premodern period. In case of a sale, relatives had anywhere from three weeks to a year after closing to make an intervening offer.[54] In Solms, retraction was valid against rental or gift but not sale, while in Catzenelnbogen and Marburg it also applied against sale.[55]

The Solms law was drafted by Johannes Fichard of Frankfurt am Main. He included family reversion law in the Solms law. But family reversion law was not included in the other law code which Fichard drafted seven years later for nearby Frankfurt, a code which was equally famous and important.[56] One scholar argues that, in the 1570s, reversion law was (still) too popular in

50 Jane Whittle, "Individualism and the Family-Land Bond: A Reassessment of Land Transfer Patterns among the English Peasantry c. 1270–1580," *Past and Present* 160 (1998).

51 Karl Sigmar von Galéra, *Vom Reich zum Rheinbund, 1713–1806*, Vol. 5, Die Riedesel zu Eisenach: Geschichte des Geschlechts der Riedesel Freiherrn zu Eisenach, Erbmarschälle zu Hessen (Neustadt an der Aisch: Degner, 1961), pp. 12, 20, 22, 142–145.

52 Polley, "Retraktsrecht und Weinkauf im Hochstift Fulda," p. 248. The first and second of these were extremely influential all around the region and even in other neighboring areas.

53 "Stadt- und Landesbrauch des Oberfürstenthums Marburg," pp. 3–5; Gerhard Welkoborsky, "Das Solmser Landrecht," *Archiv für hessische Geschichte und Altertumskunde* 30 (1967–1970), p. 63b.

54 "Stadt- und Landesbrauch des Oberfürstenthums Marburg," p. 25, 30–31, 50, 67–68.

55 Welkoborsky, "Solmser Landrecht," pp. 23–24.

56 See Joannes Fichard, *Der Statt Francken furt am Mayn ernewerte Reformation* (Frankfurt am Main: Sigismund Feyerabend; Georg Raben, 1578). The Solmser *Landrecht* has been printed as "Solmser Landrecht," in *Landrechte des 16. Jahrhunderts*, ed. Wolfgang Kunkel, Vol. 1,2, *Quellen zur Neueren Privatrechtsgeschichte Deutschlands* (Weimar: Hermann Böhlaus Nachfolger, 1938 [orig. 1571]).

the countryside to abolish.[57] By contrast, in the commercial environments of towns and cities, even small ones, simple, alienable tenure (burgage, *Burgrecht*) tenure was common and popular since it was more suited to the mobile, dynamic, and cash-oriented urban economy.[58] By the 1730s however, retraction law was becoming unpopular or at least more contested in rural settings, for instance in Fulda. In the Solms law, if *Retraktsrecht* was exercised, the thwarted outside buyer was entitled, for his trouble, to not only his money back of course but 5% of the money from the new sale to the inside buyer.[59] To prevent fraud, the parties to the transfer had to swear an oath that they were not engaging in "treacherous manipulations." Apparently the exerciser of the law also had to pay the *Weinkauf* money (essentially the closing cost) in wine. Thus in Solms, retraction law both protected the interests of the extended family and served the rule of canon law that contracts must be honored (*pacta sunt servanda*).[60]

Like other non-urban bodies of law, the Rheingauer *Landbrauch* also regulated retraction law. The Rheingau was the region bordered by Mainz and the Palatinate, Frauenstein and Budenheim. The *Landbrauch* was issued in 1643 and valid until 1719, when it was replaced. The "principle of free alienability" was almost complete in the Rheingauer *Landbrauch*, with the exception of the right of *Abtrieb*, that is, to invoke retraction and unwind a sale.[61]

Like primogeniture, retraction law was a strategy that increased family power and stability. It concentrated real holdings into fewer hands and made family holdings harder to alienate. Take the case of the imperial knighthood. Since the knights' imperial immediate status rested on familial holding of lands and rights, usually with rule over a number of common people, serfs, or both, it was crucial to the knights' continuing status and collective existence that they be able, as family lineages, to retain those lands and rights. For this reason, the emperor gave them a right of retraction in 1609.[62] This protection against investment and improvement through alienation caused them to grow

57 Welkoborsky, "Solmser Landrecht," p. 23.

58 Brauneder, "Burgrecht." Over the centuries, explains W. J. Ashley, "economic pressure" led to the creation of "the tenure known as *bourgage* (French), *burgage* (English), *Leihe zu Burgrecht* (German) …" See W. J. Ashley, "The Beginnings of Town Life in the Middle Ages," *Quarterly Journal of Economics* 10, no. 4 (1896), pp. 392–393.

59 Welkoborsky, "Solmser Landrecht," p. 25.

60 Ibid., p. 25. For the rule, see Tigar and Levy, *Law and the Rise of Capitalism*, p. 145.

61 Walter Alberti, "Ueber den Inhalt des Rheingauer Landbrauchs" (Inaugural dissertation, 1913), p. 96.

62 See Dietmar Willoweit, *Deutsche Verfassungsgeschichte: Vom Frankenreich bis zur Wiedervereinigung Deutschlands: ein Studienbuch*, 5th, expanded ed. (Munich: C. H. Beck, 2005), pp. 221 ff.

poor and contributed to their decline: They proudly and defensively clung to their estates and rights and would not and could not profit by selling, mortgaging, or renting them out. By contrast, in the unrestricted and healthy British real estate market, as depicted by Adam Smith, rural landholders slowly sell their lands to rising urban merchants, who improve the land, invest, and innovate.[63] Still, the German knights' right of retraction also had a positive effect for the empire, in that it supported their independence and the independence of other small powers in the empire, especially bishoprics and abbeys.[64] In this way, retraction played a role in the slow growth of the idea of inalienable rights.[65] This was a source of the confederate strength of the Empire – that is, the way the Empire remained a constitutional, monarchical confederation – at the time that France, England, and other countries were becoming strong monarchies.

Princely houses and regional noble families were not the only entities to use the legal tool of retraction law to protect or fortify family holdings and autonomy against the inroads of urban buyers, their lawyers, and regime chanceries increasingly oriented toward simpler, more individualistic and commercially-oriented real estate rules.[66] One of the clauses in the agreement between Sabina Maria Rau (later, in her third marriage, Boeckel) and Anne Agnes Linsing (*née* Rau) was that they specified a mutual right of retraction between themselves – not trusting to the common civil law (*ius commune*) to ensure that right. I suggest they took this step because the chancery had ordered them to prove the allodiality of their holdings. The unwind threshold in their agreement was set for one year and a day, the longest term for an unwind in the customary retraction law. The dispute in this case between feudal and allodial heirs, or their heirs and substitute claimants in turn, lasted until at least 1712, when the feudal heir party appears to have relented and sought to buy out the

---

63 Adam Smith, *An Inquiry into the Nature and Causes of the Wealth of Nations* (New York: Modern Library, 1965 [orig. 1776]), Bk. III Chs. 2–4, esp. pp. 367–368, 382, 391–395; Tigar and Levy, *Law and the Rise of Capitalism*, p. 134.

64 This "seemingly hopelessly antiquated picture of authority performed a specific contribution for political balance of power in the empire. For one thing, many spiritual princes came from the circles of the imperial knighthood. For another, these ancient lordships offered protection and refuge [*Schutz und Bleibe*] to those whose culture resisted the egalitarianization of the early modern state: the Jews, who were expelled from many of the great territories. The "freedom" of the Old Empire is almost unthinkable without these free spaces, which imperial knights and imperial cities offered." Willoweit, *Deutsche Verfassungsgeschichte*, p. 218.

65 Wilder, "Property, Possession and Prescription," Chapter 8, pp. 377–378.

66 Tigar and Levy, *Law and the Rise of Capitalism*, pp. 42, 46–47, 50–51, 107–108, 125, 144–145, 150, 178, 180.

Boeckel and Linsing allodial heirs of that generation. The manuscripts suggest that the exercisers of *Retraktsrecht* had some control over the price they would have to pay. But by then, Sabina Maria's son or step-son Ludwig Conrad Dernbach was arguing that he had a "tacit mortgage" in the Holzhausen estates because of improvements that he had invested in.[67] In other words, the very strategy that the sisters-in-law had employed in 1666 was being challenged by an agnatic relation on the basis of retraction law: he claimed that since the compact of 1666 was made between the women while his father (Caspar Friedrich Dernbach, whom we met earlier) was married to Sabina Maria, he inherited the right of first refusal from Sabina Maria through his father. He asserted this claim to the Hessian chancery until at least 1712. Although we do not know the outcome, we do know from the sources that his claim was taken seriously – and that one could make such an argument based on existing law and jurisprudence.

With regard to freedom, retraction law was a two-edged sword. On one hand, it was a restrictive device used by families to secure their rights, and as such it strengthened family power at the expense of individual freedom. One could argue that it increased the freedom of the family as a collective entity. And yet a well-to-do family was typically ruled as a miniature oligarchy, so family autonomy usually meant the subordination of less powerful family members. This same point can also be made about the families of imperial knights. On the other hand, one meaning of German freedom in the eighteenth century was certainly pluralistic federalism (Chapter 2). Retraction law helped to secure the pluralistic federalist structure by supporting families in retaining their property and power, as shown by the knights but also many other noble families of medium size, such as the "Riedesel republic." Weighing against the retention of this small-group collective freedom[68] was the consequence that individuals within the group *ceteris paribus* had weaker property rights – it was more difficult for them to sell their portion of the estate – and therefore less individual freedom.

Although most cases of retraction law involved family, some cases involved a claim of retraction by other members of the village community.[69] In 1725,

67 "Documents pertaining to Linsing-Dernbach-Schwalbach contest over Boeckel inheritance, dating to Linsing-Boeckel agreement of 1666, over estates in Holzhausen," StAMa 340 Rau – Pk08a01–a22.

68 Historians and economists have sometimes praised primogeniture laws, arguing that they preserve family structure by maintaining farms of a sufficient size to support a family livelihood. (But where do the later-born siblings go?)

69 In small, static, rural communities, there is a relatively high level of inter-relatedness. As a consequence, extended family approximated community.

retraction law was abolished for community use in Hesse-Cassel, though retained for family clan rights. That is, after 1725, people could no longer call on retraction law to try to win back real rights held collectively which had been alienated to third parties.[70] Later in 1778, a court decision for a suit in Witzenhausen ruled that

> If a public auction (either forced or voluntary) has been held, then no *Retraktsrecht* will be permitted. But in case of a closed deal at chancery, the prescription of the *Samthofgerichts-Ordnung* of 1524 §27 shall apply, such that those who claim *Retraktsrecht* have 6 weeks and 3 days to claim their right.[71]

Public sale was already in the sixteenth century a condition that in some cases invalidated retraction right. It seems to have become more common in the late seventeenth century and especially the eighteenth century to consider retraction right invalid if a sale were made openly or publicly solemnized afterward.

Rainer Polley has argued that by the eighteenth century retraction law in Fulda had "became sometimes a hateful threat to one's existence." Fuldan subjects protested against it to the bishop. To these protestors, if a real transaction was publicly sealed at a licensed tavern through a drink together among the parties (the custom of *Weinschenk*), that should suffice. It was, they averred, an old institution based on trust. Two customs were in conflict: *Weinschenk* against retraction law, *Weinschenk* representing belief in final, voluntary renunciation and retraction law representing a lingering equitable right of kin or community members to later assert the right to purchase alienated family property. Did one custom constitute a greater freedom than the other? It appears that the Fuldan villagers thought that free alienation, with a toast and witnesses, was the better kind of freedom than that of the family or community that wished to retain its power or autonomy.

After 1765, the Fuldan regime regulated and restricted retraction law: if it could be proven that someone with the right of retraction had been asked if he objected before the closing and declined to exercise his retraction right, then he therewith had implicitly waived the right. As in the case of prescription (to be discussed in the final section of the chapter), this rule relied on a naturalistic argument about implicit consent. Fulda may have refrained from

70 Kleinschmid and Apell, *Sammlung*, Vol. III, p. 962, edict of February 26, 1725.

71 Ledderhose, *Kleine Schriften*, Vol. 3, p. 292. The *Samthofgerichts-Ordnung* of 1524 is printed in Kleinschmid and Apell, *Sammlung*, Vol. I, p. 47.

abolishing retraction law entirely because it derived revenue from the custom. When a fief was transferred, the episcopal regime collected a sales tax set at 7% of the sale price. If someone later exercised retraction right, the later buyer had to pay both his own 7% fee and make good the disappointed buyer's 7%, for a total of 14% tax on top of the sales price. Thus the exercise of a retraction right meant that the regime collected 14% property sales tax rather than 7%. Because these taxes made up a significant portion of the prince-bishop's revenue, it was thus not in the prince's interest to abolish the law of retraction. Lending further credence to this argument, the regime did restrict retraction right on estates which were not part of the princely fief system, in which buyers did not have to pay this fief-transfer tax. When the occupying French set up a military administration in Fulda in 1793, they abolished retraction law. Hesse under the revolutionary Confederation of the Rhine did the same. Retraction law had been abolished everywhere in Germany by 1850.[72] Its disappearance meant the end of one pillar of German freedom but the strengthening of another, the relative decline of freedom as pluralistic group and family autonomy and the growth of individual civil liberty.

8 Accepting the Results of Free Activity after the War

As I have said at the outset, scholarship on the Enlightenment and the history of natural rights theory has largely told the story of freedom as the story of the ideas of natural freedom, and that in turn through natural law, specifically in the writings of Hugo Grotius, Thomas Hobbes, and John Locke, with its greatest and most rapid development and application during the Glorious Revolution, the American Revolution, and the French Revolution. In the above sections of this chapter, I have tried to show how freedoms were created through strategic practices (e.g. allodial strategy) and juristic connivance (e.g. fictions through substitution). These ideas, practices, and tools were part of post-War jurisprudence. In the second half of this chapter, I argue that free disposition of estates was also strengthened in the post-War period through the way legal operators came to use two ancient Roman legal concepts – possession and prescription.

After the war and the attendant changes in property relations, jurists operationalized prescription and possession in new ways. Prescription was understood as a naturalistic *process* by which laws and rights are born, change, and

72 Polley, "Retraktsrecht und Weinkauf im Hochstift Fulda," pp. 250–255.

die through the mechanism of peaceful, consensual activity. A right (*ius*), such as a property right, is born, changes, maybe is transferred, and passes away. Possession indicates the *rightful holding* of something even without formal right (formal title, as we might say today). Despite distinct antique definitions, and separate conceptual histories, possession and prescription *functioned similarly* and were based on *similar thinking* about the relationship between consent and right.[73]

While possession and prescription were ancient concepts from Roman civil law, they had been extended in the middle ages and afterward, and their widespread use in European courts had led both to alterations in the doctrines and to simplification of procedure and structure.[74] It will be useful briefly to step, for a moment, back out to the broader narrative of legal history which has been sketched partially already in Chapter 1 and Chapter 3. There we encountered the dominant legal movement in the empire at this time, the *usus modernus*, or "[study of the] custom of today." The *usus modernus* conferred on existing "bodies" (*corpora*) of law such as merchant law or feudal law a dignity nominally equal to that of ancient Roman civil law. This led jurists to work to resolve legal conflicts which they found abounding around them – between different bodies of law (civil, canon, mercantile, feudal, and customary) as well as between black-letter civil law and ever-changing natural law theory. Sometimes the conflict was between what one generally took to be the applicable law in a given situation and what the documents or witnesses actually attested. Or what to do when there was simply a conflict of claims, neither of which was based on very strong evidence? For instance, a landlord claimed a certain right (say to relief or a certain rent) but local jurors insisted that the actual concrete order of who held what and on what terms was something else entirely. To help resolve such confusing conflicts, the twin related doctrines of possession and prescription had been developed. Possession was in effect a way of legitimating and dealing with rightful holding of a right without regard as such to the formality of ownership or other modes of holding such as detention or bailment.[75] Similarly prescription gave the sheen of right to an

---

73 Specialists will understand that this is a simplification for present purposes of the definitions of prescription and possession. The law of prescription and the law of possession were not considered identical. See Nicholas, *Introduction to Roman law*, pp. 108–130 for a more detailed account of the two concepts in ancient law. According to Nicholas, prescription was the "original civil mode" (for the ancient Romans) of acquiring possession; see ibid, pp. 116–118.

74 Friedrich Carl von Savigny, *Das Recht des Besitzes. Eine civilistische Abhandlung* (Giessen: Heyer, 1803).

75 See glossary: detention.

existing concrete order of holding, control, or exercise; Grotius had provided a naturalistic account of prescription in 1625, used for two centuries afterward by German and other jurists, which explained why rights so acquired (or lost) through prescription were rightful and natural. In effect, these doctrines blessed a presently existing, peaceful order of who had what, regardless of the strength of title. Generally possession and prescription validated any existing orders of property (of who had what) prejudicially against the older, formal order.[76] States of conflict did not produce clear right (*ius*) or law but rather imperiled it, in as much as parties' claims of right contradicted one another (or were even in violent conflict). The goal of the doctrines of possession and prescription was to quiet title – that is, to create a legal status across the entire territory in which there was a presumption of the validity of existing title to real rights. Nether social estate nor the object of property claims limited the validity of applying prescription or possession, with some marginal exceptions.[77]

The Thirty Years' War had wrought terrible chaos and confusion on German lands, Hesse among the more so during its fratricidal civil war in the last phase of the overall conflict. For all of the terrible loss of life and destruction of structures and investment, however, the War also created an opportunity for a radical reset of government and society in many places. As discussed above, of particular relevance here is that rulers lost their knowledge and ability to coordinate local affairs, and during the interregnum, nobles and common people took over management of their own affairs, at least when they were not fighting.

---

76 As the etymology of *praejudicium* ("previous before the court") suggests, the term meant that a certain action or piece of evidence would enjoy first consideration, often such that if certain simple, formal criteria were met, other actions or defenses were prohibited and the matter would be decided summarily.

77 Social estate did not matter to the process of prescription, which could usually be enjoyed by both men and women, lords and serfs, householders and dependents. It also did not matter what the legal object of the prescription was, whether it was a house, an easement, a local tax, an imperial tax, or the right to receive performance of some labor. "All people who are subject to the burden of paying tributes regularly can prescribe immunity. These include *illustres* like princes, dukes, counts, and barons, but also subjects like farmers, rustics, or nobles." So too, merchants, vassals, emphyteutic farmers, as well as fictive persons like monasteries, cities, corporations, or colleges could also prescribe immunity. See Friedrich Philippi, praeses, Christian Henricus, respondans, *De praescriptione immunitatis â tributis. Von der Verjährung Steuren und anderer Obrigkeitlichen Anlagen-Freyheit* (Wittenberg: Officina Hakiana, 1745 [orig. 1688]), Thesis 40, p. 41tm. This would probably have been the case with Jews, but I do not have an example. I base my inference here on seeing other disputes between Jews or between Jew and gentile where both parties use exactly the same civil law rules of real property, e.g. with urban servitudes and nuisance.

There are two key moments in prescription – the acquisition of a right and the extinction of the claim of right in another party. Acquisitive prescription had to take place slowly and peacefully over a long period of time. That is, one had to occupy and use or exercise a certain space or activity uninterrupted for a period of anywhere between one year and thirty years, in some cases even "time immemorial," which meant that no one could remember it ever not being thus so. Extinction similarly happened over the same long period, as a party failed to exercise a certain right successfully or to occupy an estate over the same period. A shortcut to this slow process happened through contradiction (*contradictio*), known in English as adverse possession. In adverse possession, the party pretending to a right *openly defies* the claim of the other party. If the latter capitulates, either expressly or simply by dropping the pursuit of the claim, then the first party is said to have gained the right the acquisitive prescription with contradiction.[78] Courts in the seventeenth and eighteenth centuries recognized that people could gain property rights and even freedoms through adverse possession. In this way, people gained hunting, fishing, and fowling rights as well as resource collection rights against lords or escaped from service duties. Neighbors gained use of lands or rights to build, enter, or cross through adjacent lots. The well-known dictum that a runaway serf gained his freedom if he lived openly in a town for a year and a day was also an instance of acquisitive prescription with contradiction or adverse possession. Prescription could also create domination, exclusion, or the right to levy dues, so in some cases the *failure or inapplicability* of prescription created freedoms.

Possession was used to connect old practice and current circumstances. Frequently it was the case that one knew the *type* of holding that was supposed to be in place (e.g. holding by feudal tenure, or allod, or colonial settlement tenure, *Landsiedelleiherecht*).[79] And one knew *who actually held* the right or space. But not infrequently the *actual chain of transfer* from the initiation of the former to the actuality of the latter was mysterious. People could merely assert a claim or produce some single corroborating (though hardly conclusive) legal document.[80] Earlier in this chapter the relationship between free use of land in allod was related to successful keeping of possession and strategic manipulation of it. Further, many of the examples mentioned above of

78 Ibid., Thesis 24, pp. 22m–23t. See glossary: adverse possession.

79 Wilder, "Property, Possession and Prescription," pp. 187–213.

80 "'Any pen will do to recount anything whatsoever', observed a German nobleman during a lawsuit." Tigar and Levy, *Law and the Rise of Capitalism*, p. 35.

prescription also involved possession. Jurists after about the fourteenth century concurred that one could possess incorporeal rights such as the right to hunt. Hence in effect any real right over space could be "possessed" even where formal proof of rightful tenure was lacking.

Both prescription and possession were based on the idea that right was determined not so much by formalities as by accepted practice, an idea familiar to what we today call legal traditionalists (after the manner of Edmund Burke).[81] Rather than formalities, the jurist had to consider what was actually accepted in practice to determine what was right. Sometimes this analysis protected old ways, and sometimes it destroyed them.

Still, the tendency of this practice favored the new over the old, as can be seen by paying attention to the sources legal operators used to construct their authority. Whether connected or not, the shift toward the authority of the present order paralleled the undeniable modernization of legal sources. Jurists' use of sources changed between the sixteenth and eighteenth century, reflecting a predilection for new law over old. Sixteenth-century treatises and expert opinions, still within the broad ambit of legal humanism, focused more on the Roman civil law (the *ius commune*) and medieval commentaries (Accursius being the most esteemed). In the late sixteenth century, German jurists were citing ancient civil law, the occasional commentary, or the works of earlier legal humanists, most of them French. By the later seventeenth century, the construction of jurisprudential authority was rather different. Legal writers of all types wrote more about one another's work than they did about the distant medieval and ancient sources of the law; half of the works cited came from the century preceding to the year of publication and they were increasingly published in German cities and towns. By the eighteenth century, easily 80% of the cited literature had been published within the past half century, often within the past twenty years. To put it in bibliometric terms, the *citational horizon* of authority was contracting or becoming shorter, an accelerating modernization of cited sources. As Chapter 3 argued, these sources were also diversifying to include treatises and old law collections, but also dissertations, custom, collections of decisions of various modern courts, and princely edicts. Works of all these sorts were held in regime chancery libraries and were used and cited by law faculties.[82] These texts were considered themselves to be "sources" of the law. Older law was becoming a "tradition" rather

81 Edmund Burke, *Reflections on the Revolution in France*, ed. J. G. A. Pocock (Indianapolis: Hackett, 1987 [orig. 1790]).

82 Wilder, "TL;DR."

than being a specific set of valid texts from which legal thinking always directly began.[83] Practically speaking, the base was modern. Jurists wove an account of *current* law out of the material of *recent* law, while saying that what they were doing was citing and considering *ancient* law (rather than recent or current law).[84]

9 The Princely Resolutions of 1655

> Now was the time that the knighthood and towns stood asunder. Since the body thus divided itself, we have become slaves and must do what we are told.
>
> *The Cassel Chronicle* (1650)[85]

Possessory procedures featured centrally in one of the major constitutional events in Hessian history between the Protestant Reformation and the Napoleonic period. This constitution, formally known as the Princely Resolutions (1655), went a long way toward resolving the stalemate between ruler and estates. The procedures of interest here governed choice of jurisdiction and the role of documentary evidence in determining right and possession; the procedures were not new but rather were post-medieval extensions of classical possessory procedures. I argue that while they formally governed possession rather than right, nevertheless they functioned to change the distribution of rights and freedoms in Hessian society.

In Hesse, the ruler and the territorial nobility ("the estates") had long struggled over their constitutional relationship, as ruler and estates did in almost every European polity in the early modern period. Historically up through the first decades of the seventeenth century, territorial diets gave the nobility and the towns real influence and communication with the ruler. As Beat Kümin and Andreas Würgler put it, "the estates ... managed to put their own interests on the diets' agenda and to contain absolutist tendencies in the wake of

83 The contrast between an aging tradition and a living, earlier source of authority is the same as that explored by John Pocock in his contrast between "the feudal law" and ancient constitutionalism. See Pocock, *The Ancient Constitution and the Feudal Law* and in the present context my essay "The importance of beginning, over and over: The idea of primitive Germanic law," in *Intersections*, ed. Minou Schraven and Maarten Delbeke, Vol. 25 (Brill, 2011).

84 de Jouvenel, *Power*, p. 209.

85 Karl E. Demandt, "Die hessischen Landstände im Zeitalter des Frühabsolutismus," *Hessisches Jahrbuch für Landesgeschichte* 15 (1965), p. 58.

the Thirty Years War with at least partial success."[86] Members of the nobility supervised local court, town, and village institutions; they either served as, appointed, or heavily influenced most key local job appointments such as judgeships, town and village leadership, and parish appointments. Harmony and negotiation between ruler and nobles began to break down after the early seventeenth century, first over Luther-Calvinist disagreements, then over taxes and absolutist tendencies of the regime. The several reversals of the fortunes of war had changed all that and a generation passed before the ruler of a new, poor, burnt-out, exhausted, but quiet and stable Hesse-Cassel sought to convene the diet and get the state once more organized.

In their ongoing suit against the landgrave in the imperial Aulic Council, the knights' bargaining power was initially very strong, though it was weakened slightly in 1653. In that year their co-plaintiffs in the suit, the Hessian towns, made a separate peace with the Landgrave Wilhelm, and they also lost the support of a powerful ally, Wilhelm's estranged uncle Landgrave Ernst of Hessen-Rheinfels-Rothenburg.[87] The balance of power in the Hessian conflict also shifted because the imperial diet in Regensburg resolved in 1654 that subjects of imperial estates, including local nobility, were required to pay the "Contribution" or military tax to the territorial prince.[88]

86 "The diet ... allowed Hesse's subjects a considerable degree of influence. Those summoned to attend met in advance to condense their demands and complaints into a series of *gravamina* – also known as Desideria or Petita – to be presented to the landgrave. Although this customary practice was not formally recognized until 1764, the estates nevertheless managed to put their own interests on the diets' agenda and to contain absolutist tendencies in the wake of the Thirty Years War with at least partial success. They retained the right to approve taxes and fought an incessant battle against the landgrave's increasing demands to fund the new standing army. The prince thus sought to ease his financial problems by letting parts of his armed forces to his allies ... when they were not needed at home." Kümin and Würgler, "Petitions, Gravamina" p. 41.

87 Demandt, "Die hessischen Landstände," pp. 50, 64–65.

88 See Wilson, *Holy Roman Empire*, pp. 63–70; Andreas Müller, *Der Regensburger Reichstag von 1653/54: eine Studie zur Entwicklung des Alten Reiches nach dem Westfälischen Frieden*, Europäische Hochschulschriften Reihe III, Geschichte und ihre Hilfswissenschaften, (Frankfurt am Main; New York: P. Lang, 1992); Anton Schindling, *Die Anfänge des Immerwährenden Reichstags zu Regensburg: Ständevertretung und Staatskunst nach dem Westfälischen Frieden*, Beiträge zur Sozial- und Verfassungsgeschichte des Alten Reiches (Mainz: P. von Zabern, 1991); Adolf Laufs, ed., *Der jüngste Reichsabschied von 1654: Abschied der Römisch Kaiserlichen Majestät und gemeiner Stände, welcher auf dem Reichstag zu Regensburg im Jahr Christi 1654 aufgerichtet ist*, Vol. 32, Quellen zur neueren Geschichte (Bern: H. Lang, 1975); Gerhard Oestreich, *Geist und Gestalt des frühmodernen Staates. Ausgewählte Aufsätze* (Berlin: Duncker & Humblot, 1969), pp. 290–310 especially pp. 291–292; Demandt, "Die hessischen Landstände," p. 52; and Fritz Redlich, "Contributions in the Thirty Years War," *Economic History Review* 12 (1959–1960), pp. 247–254.

The nobles and the prince met to negotiate in December 1655 in a special open-air diet ("under the free sky," *unterm freien Himmel*, an old tradition). This summit produced the "Princely Resolutions" – a traditional term for a negotiated resolution of prince-estates conflict since the prince agreed to "resolve" the estates' concerns.[89] The negotiation seems to have been balanced, or even slightly to the estates' benefit. The Princely Resolutions were a significant compromise between prince and people. Because of the strong bargaining position the nobles were in,[90] their wishes (and those of the towns) played a real role in ironing out basic issues of constitutional and civil law, matters governing diets, taxation,[91] justice, religion, and the service of common people to the princely government (*corvée* and militia). The Princely Resolutions reflected the princely regime's dissatisfaction with the low level of control it could exercise over local jurisdiction, local real estate transfer activity, and payments of dues and taxes, all due in part to its lack of information.

One section of the Resolutions concerned jurisdiction and legal procedure – "the matter of justice." Which court was to hear the first instance of a dispute, how appeals might work, the priority of types of evidence, and what factual matters would create *praejudicum* in a judgment. A *praejudicium* was something which the court procedure *pre-judged*, setting in motion a chain of procedures before any suit had been brought, witnesses called, or documentary evidence submitted.[92] This resolution, like most of the others, was a victory for the estates rather than the prince. The Resolutions determined

89 The best accounts of the Princely Resolutions generally are Demandt, "Die hessischen Landstände," pp. 53–57; Adolf Lichtner, *Landesheer und Stände in Hessen-Cassel, 1797–1821* (Göttingen: Vandenhoeck & Ruprecht, 1913), pp. 1–12 and Armand Maruhn, "Duale Staatsbildung contra ständisches Landesbewusstsein. 1655 als Epochenjahr der hessischen Landesgeschichte," *Zeitschrift für Hessische Geschichte* 109 (2004).

90 Although the nobles had lost the support of Landgrave Ernst and the towns, they were effectively on strike, paralyzing the government. Princes yearned to build expensive baroque palaces, endow institutions, patronize the arts, and direct massive standing armies. Indeed, Wilhelm's brother-in-law, the Great Elector of Brandenburg-Prussia, was a paragon of such German princely activity.

91 The estates extracted a concession from Wilhelm that they would not be compelled to levy taxes on subjects outside of normal dietary procedure except in cases of extreme emergency. Demandt, "Die hessischen Landstände," p. 56; F. L. Carsten, *Princes and Parliaments in Germany, From the 15th to the 18th Century* (Oxford: Clarendon Press, 1959), pp. 181–184; Kleinschmid and Apell, *Sammlung*, Vol. 2, p. 243, Title v; *Landtagsabschiede* of July 5, 1656, November 9, 1658, and January 19, 1666; Demandt, "Die hessischen Landstände," pp. 54–55; Günter Hollenberg, "Landstände und Militär in Hessen-Kassel," ibid.34 (1984), pp. 103–104.

92 For instance, possession of something was prejudicial, in that it entailed that any lawsuit over title or rightful or wrongful possession of the thing would begin with the advantage

which courts had competence in disputes between landgrave and nobles. The landgrave acknowledged that nobles had the right to choose between the older, princely appellate court (*Hofgericht*) and Chancery.[93] The *Hofgericht* represented, or was thought to represent, the older noble and more traditional interests of the region The Chancery was the more bureaucratic organization staffed by bourgeois jurists and other professionals who were looked down on by the old noble families.[94] Moreover Chancery members (*Kanzlisten*) were dependent on the ruler and were trained not in customary law and custom but in Roman civil law as taught in the universities. As noted in Chapter 2, it was widely believed by both local common people and the territorial nobility that Roman civil law privileged princes and burghers, to the disadvantage of the other people of the *Land* – nobles, common people including the very poor and those with little standing, like serfs. Except for certain kinds of suits (see below), the noble right to use a friendly or at least not unsympathetic court venue of their peers was thus retained.

Aside from status issues of nobles having to plead before common men, something much bigger weighed on the nobility's mind: a struggle over their rights vis-à-vis the prince. Numerous edicts from the Hessian regime in the 1650s claimed that people had been trespassing on rights or had taken over real estate in the uncertain years of the war and its aftermath. Government commands had periodically attacked this problem by trying to get more information about what was actually going on. In the Princely Resolutions, ruler and estates specified the basic legal procedure to be used in conflicts over rights between prince and estates, government and subject, procedures that would remain in place until the Napoleonic era 150 years later.[95]

---

given to the possessing party. The mere fact of possession activated an initial procedure, without regard to documents, witnesses, etc. Merely factual holding with no claim of right is called detention. Sometimes this is referred to as factual possession. The central ambiguity of possession is that it unites fact and right.

93 "The choice of court shall stand to the plaintiff – whether he wants to pursue [an accusation] at the *Hofgericht* or at the Chancery [*die electio fori in potestate actoris, ob er die Sache am Hofgericht, oder bei der Kanzlei ausführen wolle, stehen solle* …]" See Kleinschmid and Apell, *Sammlung*, Vol. 2, pp. 241–242, Title 11, §1. The activity of both courts through the decades was studied in Chapter 3.

94 I have seen numerous examples of (legal disputes concerning) the sale Hessian offices indicating that, while they were for sale, this does not seem to have been as regular and commercialized as it was in France in the same period. Nor is it not clear that purchase of an office conferred tax farming power in the French sense. The real key to entry into the nobility seems primarily to marry a secundogeniture noble child and to purchase a "noble estate" i.e. land with a tax immunity or other typically noble privileges attached to it.

95 Wilder, "Property, Possession and Prescription," pp. 78–101.

The Resolutions set specific new rules for the whole Hessian territory about how litigant and court were to proceed for disputes between prince and subject, that is, disputes in which "the prince was interested." What did a person do, in other words, if he wished to sue the ruler of the territory, his sovereign majesty?

Any suit in which the prince was himself interested had, stated the Prince's Resolutions, to be heard in his chancery. If there was *no praejudicum* in the situation, then the suit would be heard and treated under ordinary chancery rules like other business. A property dispute in which there was no prejudice at all would be one in which neither plaintiff nor defendant had any current or prior exercise of rights in question – a rather small set of occasions. (Expressly excluded was *Austrägal* settlement – essentially, what is today known as alternative dispute resolution, whereby the two sides coordinate the appointment of a mutually satisfactory group of judges to decide the matter and pronounce a binding distribution of the rights in question.[96])

More weighty, and using up much more ink in the Resolutions, were matters in which both the prince was "interested" and there was "great prejudice" (i.e. at least one party already had some existing claim or current or previous possession of the rights or lands).[97] Suits of this nature were also to be heard at the Chancery, as one might expect. Recall that description of the late-war and early post-war situation as a grey economy, in which many transactions and transfers had apparently been made without official approval. The evidence does not make clear whether the alleged perpetrators in these transactions were common people, nobles, or both (though the language of the edicts indicates that the regime thought *mostly of common people*). Here in the Princely Resolutions in the same period was a similar, but not identical problem: The nobility was negotiating with the ruler over how to proceed in situations where one party had an existing claim, or actual possession, but was challenged by the other. And the nobles by and large did not trust the regime's jurists serving in the Chancery. The nobles wanted to secure their position (their property rights, and hence their freedom) against both common subjects and their lord prince. The Resolutions stated that, if possible, a voluntary agreement should

96 For Austrägal courts and *Entstehung der Güter*, see Winfried Noack, *Landgraf Georg I. von Hessen und die Obergrafschaft Katzenelnbogen (1567–1596)* (Darmstadt: Historischer Verein für Hessen, 1966), pp. 57–58; Hermann Keck, *Die Entwicklung des Oberappellationsgerichts zu Kassel* (Cassel: 1906), p. 31; the entries in DRW; and, for famous examples of the use of Austrägal courts, Dietrich Christoph von Rommel, *Geschichte von Hessen* (Kassel: Theodore Fischer, 1853), Vol. 5, p. 109 and Vol. 9, p. 21.

97 Kleinschmid and Apell, *Sammlung*, p. 242, Title II, §2.

be reached.[98] If that did not happen, however, the dispute would have to be resolved through a court decision.

10 Momentary, Ordinary, Summary, and Petitory Possession

Centuries of evolution of Roman civil law and commentary provided a set of distinctions to help order and resolve such problems. Some suits were about what was called momentary possession (*possessorium momentaneum*),[99] a charge brought by a plaintiff who claimed no right to the thing, or at least admitted he had no proof of right. He claimed only that he had been dispossessed by the party he was suing. If either side could show grounds of rightful possession ("*rechtliche praesumptiones fundirt*"), then the Chancery should find in that party's favor. If no right could be produced, the chancery would rule to put the dispossessed party back in possession. Momentary possession was important because sometimes good proof was hard to find, for princes as much as for paupers. The Thirty Years' War killed a third to a half of the population and saw the destruction of many government buildings and great estates where such documents were kept.[100] The various landgraves fought among each other about archived documents from the history of the princely family's possession of estates in the territory. Part of the spoils of war, archives were disputed elements of peace negotiations between rival parts of noble houses. Archival documents, blessed by the *ius archivi* or public authority of the government, held the key to determining who rightly held what.[101] Since so many people had been killed, calling witnesses to attest to the antiquity of one's possession might be impossible. Hence the value of a procedure to recognize momentary possession. If both sides could produce documents and presumptions, then the Chancery should set a hearing date for the two sides to submit

98 "womöglich die Güte vergleichen werden."

99 *Possessorium momentaneum* or momentary possession was a suit to protect possession (*Besitzschutzklage*), a remedy sought when someone having mere detention of a thing was dispossessed of it. The ex-detainer seeks remedy via a *possessorium momentaneum*. The possessory procedures described in this section were not new as such. Jurists trace them back plausibly to ancient Roman *interdicta*. According to Berger, the interdict of momentary possession in classical Roman law was the interdict of force, i.e. against any transfer of possession effected by force. See Adolf Berger, *Encyclopedic Dictionary of Roman Law* (Philadelphia: American Philosophical Society, 1953) and the DRW.

100 Wilder, "Property, Possession and Prescription," pp. 28–101.

101 Randolph C. Head, "Documents, Archives, and Proof around 1700," *Historical Journal* 56, no. 04 (2013).

attestations of witnesses in writing and be ready to have those witnesses be present at the court date. In the meantime, if necessary, the estate or rights under dispute were to be sequestered to prevent use or abuse, alienation, or taking fruits such as crops or wild game.

Similarly in case of dispossession, if both sides adduced the same proof (*auf dergleichen Beweißthumb beziehen*), then the dispute should be resolved as if it were an ordinary possessory suit, here called *possessorium ordinarium* or *possessorium petitorium*.[102] In an ordinary possessory suit, the question at hand was not as such who had possession now or a short time ago, but who had best *title*? Sometimes, as when documentary evidence or testimony was inconclusive or evenly matched, the only way of deciding was to look at who had held actual possession of the thing the longest. Ten years was generally enough to establish solid possession and therewith title. For instance, in a suit at private law decided by the Imperial Supreme Court in 1751, *possessorium ordinarium* involved showing ten years of peaceful possession.[103] Thus in *possessorium ordinarium* or *possessorium petitorium*, the mere fact of being dispossessed would not influence the outcome. A fourth similarly-named possessory remedy was *possessorium summariissimum* (or *possessorium summarium*), "which in contrast to *petitorium* asks only the question of possession in itself [*Besitz an sich*]."[104]

While the bureaucratic public recordation was slowly becoming more standardized over the long term, it was a far cry from what states generally achieve today. Records were eaten by bugs, destroyed in wars and rebellions, rotted, lost, or misplaced; record books themselves might not be registered in any kind of catalog; or there might be dual inconsistent records maintained by squabbling claimants.[105] Hence to practical jurists in the late seventeenth cen-

---

102 *Possessorium petitorium* was "a legal remedy which in contrast to *possessorium* [*momentaneum*] also asks whether it concerns rightful (*rechtlichen*) possession (*possessorium ordinarium*)." This remedy is only brought by a person, not in possession, who wants to take possession. The term *petitorium* has the root *peto* and therefore has the sense of seeking, *pet*itioning. See Eugen Haberkern and Joseph Friedrich Wallach, *Hilfswörterbuch für Historiker; Mittelalter und Neuzeit* (Berlin-Gruenwald: Verlag für Staatswissenschaften und Geschichte, 1935), p. 425.

103 See Johann Ulrich Cramer, "Ob *in Possessorio summarissimo juris venandi* die *a Regali Principis* hergenommene *Exceptio deficientis Titulinur* einige Aufmercksamkeit verdiene, wenn sie andern als Unterthanen oder Landsassen opponiret wird," in *Wetzlarische Nebenstunden*, Vol. 22 (Ulm: Johann Conrad Wohler, 1761), p. 59. See also Haberkern and Wallach, *Hilfswörterbuch für Historiker*, pp. 425, 433.

104 Haberkern and Wallach, *Hilfswörterbuch für Historiker*, p. 425.

105 See the fascinating recent work of Randolph Head on the growth of public archives, beginning with his "Documents, Archives, and Proof around 1700" (cited previously).

tury, prescription came to the rescue; good title was not required in order to prescribe a right.

"Title" (*titulus*) is a period term related to property, but played a different role in property than title does today. Today title is usually understood to signify a firm and unchallenged property right which can vanquish any competing claim to present control over a thing.[106] Pre-modern Latin sources speak of "good title" or "just title" (*justo titulo*). In modern parlance, it is common instead to speak simply of having "title," which implicitly means good or just title. A seemingly odd word for dominion or any other kind of holding, *title* is derived from *titulus*, meaning an inscription, particularly an inscription in a property register. As a practical matter, in early modern Germany good or just title appears to have meant that the holding of a certain thing had been recorded in a title registry (cadaster), a physical book kept by an officer of the governing authority, whether a local seigneur or the territorial government. Generally, having "title" was considered the highest authorization of control – it had been recorded and recognized by public officials. Today we think of title as correlating with ownership (the modern version of dominion), but pre-modern German title registries (cadasters) record other kinds of holding aside from *dominium*, such as possession, fief, and rental. In that era, title meant known, recorded, trusted, presumably rightful holding of real rights of many sorts. One might have title to any number of things – a fief or a rental of land, rights to use a land for hunting or fishing, crossing (way), and so on. A person might record possession for one estate. For another estate, someone might record a right to inhabit or to collect fruit, while for *the identical geographical, physical estate* (*space*) another person might record an easement they held. Title, in this context, was virtually unchallengeable. It was the gold standard for all real possessions, that is, the dominant authority over specific real rights, whether land, fixtures like houses, use rights, freedoms, or other similar things. Even without title, one's deeds or possession or witnesses could provide a strong chance of vindicating his real estate claims. Title was very hard to challenge, so long as you were on the land or exercising the right(s). But if ever title and possession were in conflict, courts leaned strongly toward possession as the claim which should be upheld.

---

106 An interesting modern exception to this is title loan companies in the United States. As in the early modern period, possession and detention (sheer holding, with no right, claim of rights, or prejudice in court) are distinct. The owner might or might not have possession or detention, but the title loan company has a piece of paper, equivalent to a detached bit of a title registration similar to what we are discussing in the seventeenth and eighteenth centuries, which in any court of law will defeat other claims to ownership.

Even in the absence of "just title," the unchallenged exercise of a right permitted a person "acquire title" through prescription.[107] If someone already had title, then he had a clear right. If someone quietly enjoyed a right *de facto* over 40 years, and then claimed it, the 40 years of unchallenged practice transformed the practice into a right that he could rightfully claim – and inscribe that right into the cadaster, formalizing the title.[108] What we today would call having *title* was what obtained when the owner (etc.) of a thing or right writing his information into the book in the presence of an official and witnesses.

And, in mid-seventeenth-century Hesse-Cassel, who controlled or authorized this recordation of title? – the rebelling nobility. Nobles could complain about irregularities of rural recordation and insist that all real transactions had to be notarized, but they could also insist that any conflicts between their own interests and those of the ruler be heard in a different venue than the pro-regime, pro-bourgeois Chancery where the decisions were made by the creatures of the prince.

Even in matters of interest to the prince, if the plaintiff sought to prove title by possession via one of the four possessory remedies above, the Resolutions also affirmed three other options nobles had to seek alternative judgment outside the Chancery. One was an *Austrägal* court, what is today called alternative dispute resolution. The latter option removed any patronage or procedural advantage the prince might have by having a suit heard solely by his own officers. Second, in any case of dispute between prince as high landlord (*dominus directus*) and a vassal (*any* vassal), the vassal had the right to have the conflict heard before a "Fief Court" (*Lehngericht*), which would apply only "common feudal law" and custom.[109] Finally, if any proceeding did not lead to resolution, documents from both sides could be sent to external jurors or law faculty in other parts of the empire for an objective, third-party opinion. This process, called *Aktenversendung*, had been practiced since the sixteenth century ad

107 "With 40 years of prescription, title is unnecessary, but can be acquired through quasi possession over so long a time, even if no other title can be validly shown." See Ferdinand Christoph Harpprecht, praeses, Georg Heinrich Braun, respondans, *Tractatio iuridica de praescriptione immunitatis a collectis* (Tübingen: Johann-Heinrich Reisius, 1683), Cap. 2, §52, pp. 77–78t. See also Philippi and Henricus, *De praescriptione immunitatis â tributis*, Theses 38–39, pp. 35b–40.

108 By the same token, cadastration also limited the prescription of immunity. If someone writes their pretended tenure in a record book, that inscription will strengthen a subsequent claim to right. If someone else writes a contradictory claim in a record book, that contradictory inscription will weaken a subsequent claim to right. See Philippi and Henricus, *De praescriptione immunitatis â tributis*, Thesis 69, p. 71.

109 Kleinschmid and Apell, *Sammlung*, p. 242, Title 11, §5.

hoc, but here the Princely Resolutions formally affirmed the nobility's right to do so.[110]

While possession (*possessio, Besitz*) was then, and remains today, a common and important legal concept, it was unusual to find these four possessory remedies specified in legal codes of the Hessian and Rhine-Main region to detail such procedures, much less in a major constitutional settlement. The remedies were recognized and respected by jurists of the period and were mentioned now and then in period legal treatises but apparently never singled out for detailed study.[111] It is therefore all the more striking that this major constitutional document resolving the prince-estates conflict went into such detail about possessory procedure.

Why then were the clauses about the remedies included in the Princely Resolutions, other than because jurists generally like to have good law to work with? I think the answer is that the remedies clauses indicate the influence of the nobility. It was in nobles' legal and financial interest to inscribe procedures that favored the existing concrete order of property rights in the absence of particular documentary evidence implying impropriety.

Also of great import beyond the immediate context of the ruler-estates conflict was the implication of this constitutional settlement (the Princely Resolutions) for other people down the road. While the Resolutions themselves were a compromise between the ruler and the nobility, each trying to preserve their own interests as much as possible, elements such as the possessory remedies would have benefited, probably unintentionally, *common people* as well. This was because Hessian local and appellate courts would have accepted these procedures as valid law for all litigants, regardless of social estate. Momentary, ordinary, petitionary, or summary possession, invoked by any common Hessian man or woman, was a powerful tool available to all visitors to the prince's courts. When we put this together with the growth of the number of jurists, the expanding activity of courts, and the significance of changes in Chancery, then procedure like those in the Resolutions become

110 Ibid., p. 242, Title II, §4.

111 My sense is that the four possessory remedies were known, recognized, used, and valid, but for whatever reason did make the cut for specialized study. I do not know why this was. Jehan de Malafosse, *L'interdit momentariae possessionis: Contribution à l'histoire de la protection possessoire en droit romain* (anastatica, 1967) seems to be the first focused study. There are also short treatments in two modern law dictionaries: Julius Weiske, Julius Merkel, and Philipp Bopp, eds., *Rechtslexikon für Juristen aller Teutschen Staaten, enthaltend die gesammte Rechtswissenschaft* (Leipzig: O. Wigand, 1839) and Werner Ogris, "Besitz," in *Handwörterbuch zur deutschen Rechtsgeschichte*, ed. Adalbert Erler and Ekkehard Kaufmann, Vol. 1 (Berlin: E. Schmidt, 1971).

even more important.[112] Usually submission of a legal appeal or a petition was done remotely, that is, through an emissary or a lawyer. For most people means were tight so any travel and distant lodging might be too expensive, not to mention dangerous. A common person who did not live within a day of Marburg or Cassel might therefore employ a remote lawyer, perhaps meeting with him once, the lawyer then acting as a corresponding agent. Appellate court activity increased both in the sixteenth century and then again between the late seventeenth century and end of the eighteenth century (see Chapter 3). People spent their money on lawyers because they had reason to believe it could make a difference.

Conceptually, all of this hairsplitting about what to do when, and who was or was not in possession of the estate, and which forum was to be picked might make us wonder, What was actually legal? Recall that in the 1650s, the landgravial government and sometimes the nobility alleged that much illegal activity had transpired with regard to real property: transfer or usurpation of lands and rights without permission or registration, contracts, and evasion of dues, tithes, and labor service. Was this activity illegal? Consider an instance where someone hatches a plan to kick another person off his land and destroy all preexisting title record. The ejected party sues, but the new holder can prove momentary possession. The burden is on the ejected party, but he can show neither possession nor higher title. (This is hypothetical – I have never read of such a planned undertaking.) What could a court do? Witness testimony was a form of evidence. Thus if the former rights-holder could gather several witnesses such as long-term neighbors to attest to the status quo ante, then he would be in a stronger evidentiary position than the new holder and would probably prevail. The illegal activities alleged by the government and nobles were probably mostly of two sorts: (1) consensual transactions between two parties to the disadvantage of absentee landowners, or (2) the occupation of lands and rights such as hunting in a situation where the old owner was dead or long gone, and due to widespread death, absenteeism, and information loss, it was impossible to prove who the rightful tenant was.

The Princely Resolutions bear comparison to other important constitutional settlements occurring in Germany and England at almost exactly

112 Hence in 1785, the Hessian privy councilor Bernhard August Gaertner could write that "All common laws have been received *in subsidium*" in Hesse-Cassel. That is, the imperial common law was completely and entirely applicable as Hessian common law. See Gaertner, *Meditationum practicarum*, p. 2 and Friedrich Wilhelm Strieder, Ludwig Wachler, Karl Wilhelm Justi, and Otto Gerland, eds., *Grundlage zu einer hessischen Gelehrten und Schriftsteller Geschichte, seit der Reformation bis auf gegenwärtige Zeiten* (Cassel; Gotha: J. J. Cramer; Barmeier, 1985), Vol. 4, p. 288.

the same time and in similar circumstances of tense struggle for power between ruler and estates. In 1653 an important compromise had been reached in Brandenburg-Prussia between the Elector and the Junkers. Whereas the Brandenburg Recess of 1653 limited the "process of litigation" for peasants to their local *Gutsherr*'s justice, first and last, the Princely Resolutions in Hesse of 1655 preserved the landgrave's justice for peasants.[113] The Recess however gave the Elector practical autonomy and tax power to build a growing state apparatus. In England, the Tenures Abolition Act of 1660 formally transformed most feudal tenures into free and common socage, essentially fee simple tenure devoid of either feudal dues payments or the need to obtain approval from the feudal lord to change the use or tenure thereof. In contrast, the Hessian settlement in 1655 did *not formally alter "feudal law" as such* but used possessory procedures to *effectively make irrelevant the old formalities in matters of transfer or encumbering fiefs*. Fiefs became tenures governed only by whatever documents could be produced before a court (even then these documents were scarce) or sufficient witnesses who would swear to the conditions of the tenure. If information or documents were lost or local witnesses swore accounts of a new tenure condition, then the court would recognize a different fundamental governing contract. Tenures might still be called fiefs (or other customary tenure forms), but functionally they became whatever a given real estate arrangement created. Under whatever name, the holding of real estate and other real rights largely became more freely usable and alienable, with the consequence that ultimately all Hessian subjects, noble and common, became much more able to freely dispose of real property, regardless of its mode of tenure.

•••

This chapter tells two stories. The first is about the techniques by which people expanded their freedom – what I call self-release or self-emancipation. The second is about how judges and lawyers justified these techniques, validating the expansion of freedom through the jurisprudence of possession and prescription.

In the chaos of the War and its aftermath, people took the initiative to acquire, hold, use, and dispose of real estate and appurtenant rights, such as timbering or immunity from paying certain taxes and dues (to be discussed in

113 Kersten Krüger, *Die Landständische Verfassung*, Vol. 67, Enzyklopädie deutscher Geschichte (Munich: Oldenbourg, 2003), pp. 27–28.

Chapter 5). People gained more freedom to become effective owners of property or rent it to another person (both in the Rau example), to gain sole control over an estate against other relatives, or to evade landlords' prerogative vetoes or interventions.

I see two forces driving this development of free disposition of real esate. One was motivated strategy, pursued presumably in private interest of either family or individual. After historian Andreas Heusler, we could dramatically call this "independently-powered freedom thinking." The extended Rau case study illustrates how widows and cognatic kin might transform an estate into allod, that is, non-feudal tenure held free and clear of other landlords, prince, or extended family. Women and Jews could use legal fictions to circumvent restrictions on what social class of person could hold land, whether an urban lot or a rural fief. Retraction law declined in both popularity and importance between the sixteenth and eighteenth century, thanks again in part to the suits of individual litigants, before its abolition in several places in our region in the second half of the eighteenth century, and everywhere by the mid nineteenth century. Retraction law had disfavored the sale of land to people outside the family, neighborhood, or community, and likewise prevented outsiders from being able to buy and move in. The law's decline represented an increase in people's freedom with regard to property.

The increase of freedom of disposition of real estate was also aided by a second factor, one of jurisprudence (discussed in Sections 8–10 above), the jurisprudence of possession and prescription. Possession and prescription were attractive to jurists because they quieted title to real estate and rights. Use of these concepts privileged the present parties to transactions, implicitly giving them more freedom, at the expense of distant feudal lords, old custom, or other potential claimants. Possession and prescription became the governing rules for control over real estate – in effect, simple ownership (in meaning if not always in name). The 1655 constitutional settlement privileged possession (even in the absence of any documentation or witnesses) over old formalities which might be of dubious validity or at least hard to substantiate. If we are to believe the jurists of that time and later periods, Hessian subjects got a fair hearing in the Chancery *even when they were at suit against the prince himself.*[114] These new possessory procedures were promulgated by the expanding territorial courts. Ironically,

114 For, as Gaertner (mentioned earlier in n. 112) wrote in 1785, "Absent cause, the prince may not take away someone's right simply out of the fullness of his power" because, he explained further on, "in contracts, princes enjoy the law of private persons." See Gaertner, *Meditationum practicarum*, Cap. 25, pp. 48–49 and Cap. 36, pp. 61–62.

procedures which had been sought by the *territorial nobility*, in service of its own interests, would ultimately come to be applied and enforced by courts for the benefit *all common people* as they bought and sold ordinary property.

Why would jurists, who were largely the creatures of state institutions, use doctrines of possession and prescription sometimes to legitimate activities which might originally have been illegal? Jurists, to be sure, benefited from state patronage, making them beholden to princely authority. But local property rights arrangements and real estate dealings were largely beneath the concern of princely authority. Princes were not so concerned about individual real estate or real rights lawsuits as to exert any influence on their bourgeois officers' day-to-day dealings in the chanceries. The many small quasi-legal dealings and conversions undertaken by Hessian subjects and nobles in the seventeenth and eighteenth centuries were passively countenanced by the ruler because they were below his or her level of care. Rulers usually heard important supplications personally (that is, the supplications were presented to them, for their consideration and decision). Although scholarship has not confirmed the extent to which the Hessian ruler sat personally to hear high appeals in civil law matters, he or she did in matters of equity (supplications).[115] However, the Hessian privy counselor Bernhard August Gaertner noted in his treatise on Hessian civil law and procedure that it was standard practice for the prince to recuse himself from adjudicating suits in which he himself held any material interest.[116] (The separation of executive and judiciary functions, so well-known in Anglo-American constitutional prudence, had reached Hesse on about the same schedule, we might say.) Typically, even from the mid seventeenth century onward, a ruler only cared to manage great matters – collection of taxes proper, and dues on princely domains, negotiation between branches of the ruling house, large amounts of money, contracts over transfer of major estates as in noble marriages, significant disputes with the nobility, and war and peace.

115 "Petitions concerning seigneurial rents and estates ... were passed on the to rent chamber. The most important documents, containing matters if principle, reports of serious crimes, or complaints against officials, went directly to the landgrave." See Kümin and Würgler, "Petitions, Gravamina," pp. 57–58.

116 After 1746, the Hessian High Appellate Court was fully separate from both prince and chancery. "After 1746, the court consisted solely of counselors who had been appointed solely to the court and no longer stood in any relationship to the regime. Decisions were prepared and issued by the court on its own – no longer through a privy chancery (sc. serving the prince)." Gaertner, *Meditationum practicarum*, Cap. 25, pp. 48–49 and Keck, *Entwicklung des Oberappellationsgerichts*, pp. 60–61.

Without princely interference, as good Enlightenment thinkers the bourgeois jurists of the regime and universities sought to systematize, rationalize, and ground the developing legal order. To counter chaos, they deployed a simple version of Grotius's modern doctrine of prescription (1625) and used a simplified doctrine of possession to settle problems they encountered in the concrete order of property rights.

The strategies examined in this chapter contributed to the transformation of property in Germany from "a responsible office" into "all-embracing legal power over a tangible object" (to borrow phrases from R. H. Tawney and Karl Renner), or in simple terms from a duty to a property right in the modern sense.[117] Just as ownership changed, so did the relationship between landlord and tenant. All of the illicit transferring discussed above in this chapter probably worked to separate lands, and hence tenants, from the old rights and duties associated with those lands. Old serf tenures were also transformed. If a bourgeois bought a piece of land which was previously held by serfs (Chapter 3), there was no way that he was going to let himself be subject to the serf court.

The developments in this chapter are important for at least two reasons. One is that the broad challenge of this book is to consider evidence for revising the dominant thesis that there was little personal civil liberty in premodern Germany. Another reason though that the theses of this chapter are important in particular, is that they contribute toward our understanding of the growth of commercialization and proto-industry in Germany, although commercialization processes certainly stand in the background of the persons, ideas, and events we have been closely examining. The phase of economic development of the sixteenth through eighteen centuries in northern Europe, characterized by growing commercialization, can be thought of as the pre-industrial phase of capitalism. It was broadly characterized by the strategic reorganization of agricultural real estate and rights in order to increase productivity for sale in local, regional, and international commodity markets. How was free disposition related to commercialization? Free disposition of real estate broadly speaking corresponded to the dissolution of the "family-land bond," the foundation of the pre-modern (pre-capitalist) agricultural European economy. As

117 Of course this process was centuries-long, uneven, and was influenced by more than individual family strategies and windows of opportunity. It is fascinating that, at least in this region of Germany, both configurations of private property – one conception a powerful local office (suzerainty) inconceivable without paternalistic duties, the other conception emphasizing disposal of power at will – coexisted for centuries, albeit in tension with one another. Tigar and Levy discuss suzerainty in ways which help further illuminate this distinction between the two stages or configurations of power in their *Law and the Rise of Capitalism*, pp. 44–45, 138, 196–197.

the family-land bond dissolved, more rural common people held precariously, were underemployed, or became willing to take extra work in proto-industry, as organized by people we could call early capitalist entrepreneurs.[118] (In the aggregate, the labor supply curve shifted to the right.) Consolidation of farmlands made possible agricultural improvement and increased production. Growth in the labor supply meant more hands were available (later) for new urban workshop settings and (later still) the Industrial Revolution could take hold.[119] This process happened later in Germany than in Great Britain, but happen it did. This chapter bears witness to some key points in the process in the Hessian and Rhine-Main region, such as the building of new (unauthorized) mills in the 1640s and 1650s[120] or the enclosure of fields to increase yields in 1738.[121]

The focus of this chapter has been how people worked to gain power and freedom to dispose of real property as they saw fit, for any number of reasons, and how jurists abetted this empowerment or emancipation with the jurisprudence of possession and prescription. I have also suggested that, aside from the inherent significance of this "independently powered freedom thinking" for a new classical liberal metanarrative, these developments also shed light on the

118 As should be clear, free disposition (including free testation and the decline of retraction law) was a mixed bag for common rural folk. It tended to reduce the size of parcels of land more and more below the level a family could raise crops sufficient to live on.

119 de Vries, *Economy of Europe in Age of Crisis*, Chapter 3; Whittle, "Individualism and the Family-Land Bond." I discuss partible inheritance in the Hessian *Hufenedikt* of 1773 at the end of Chapter 6.

120 The regime complained of "dams and other water mill projects" "injurious," since they "hinder the flow of the river." Probably of at least as great a concern was that these had been erected without obtaining a milling concession from the government or other landlord first, so a public revenue had been lost to the fisc. "… sonsten alle und jede den Fluß verhinderde Wercke und Damme und andere dergleichen schädliche Wasser- und Mühlengebaue weggschaft, alles in gehörigen Stand und Wesen gebracht und unterhalten werden mögen" See Kleinschmid and Apell, *Sammlung*, p. 595. The last thorough catastrum had been made in 1585. For comparison, see Moritz's Mühlen-Ordnung of 1615 in ibid. Vol. 1, pp. 530–534. What was more, if a person established peaceful practice of an activity such as running a water mill for ten to twenty years, even without title from the government, it could be almost impossible to force the party later to pay the fee, since it had become established as an independent right.

121 An enclosure example in the Riedesel lands: Karl Galera writes, "In spring 1737 the *Centgraf* suggested that the widely split-up fields and meadows in the Rothenbach in Obermoos, which had been surveyed in the previous summer, be rejoined to one another and rented to 6 skillful persons for 6 years advantageously. The *Condomini* agreed. After the expiration of the rental period on Michaelis in 1738 the project was undertaken." See Galéra, *Vom Reich zum Rheinbund, 1713–1806*, p. 92.

growth of premodern capitalism in Germany. In the next chapter we turn to the other side of real estate, so to speak: rights and obligations appurtenant to it such as dues and taxes – and the freedoms people developed against having to render such payments.

CHAPTER 5

Freedom from Extractions

Between the Thirty Years' War and the mid-eighteenth century, Germans developed rights in another area: freedom from extractions, that is, the rights not to pay certain dues and taxes or perform traditional labors such as the *corvée*. These rights were called freedoms or "immunities." Immunities of this sort have a distant echo in modern law and politics, as in notions of sovereign immunity or language in the US. Constitution about "privileges and immunities." All of these usages have a common genetic basis in European law going back to the middle ages. Such rights had existed for great lords in that earliest period, but they seem to have gone retail in the seventeenth century, at least in the Holy Roman Empire. That is, we see immunities becoming objects of common transactions of real estate and small-party civil lawsuits. This expanded usage of immunities was the result of the expanding territorial court systems.

In the last chapter, we looked at various strategies and legal workarounds people used to gain power and freedom, sometimes in the face of legal disadvantage. There I argued that the wartime chaos, and the regime's needs and weaknesses afterward, created conditions favorable to much new, unauthorized local transfer and encumbering activity of that nature. After the War, the regime in Hesse-Cassel was for a long time unable to catch up with what was owed. It and other governments in the area took decades to reconstruct their previous knowledge of who owed what to whom. The absence of that knowledge hindered the regime's ability to raise the taxes essential to state power. Faced with people's failure to pay taxes or dues or perform services, notable jurists in Hesse and Saxony from the 1680s to the 1740s debated how, when, and why people could legitimately gain freedom from extractions against lords and rulers.

This chapter has a similar legal and political focus as Chapter 4, but a different activity and problem at its core. The political context of both chapters was the War, resumption of peace, and tension with nobility. The legal issue in both chapters was real property rights. In Chapter 4, the core activity was *local transfer*, the problem that princes and other absentee landlords were afraid they were losing control over real estate. In Chapter 5, the core activity is *non-payment of dues and taxes, regimes' anxiety about this, the rise of rights claims from such non-payment, and jurists' reactions to the problem.*

We have already encountered some examples of apparent or alleged evasion of payments, in the example of tithe conversion or *Vermalterung* (Chap-

 | DOI:10.1163/9789004685178_006

ter 4). Conversion of the tithe was just a contractual possibility, perfectly legal, but would be illegal when used as part of fraud against the owners. In Chapter 5, we will hear the Hessian regime worrying and complaining about dues evasion and tax evasion as well. Landlords at other levels also appear to have been concerned. The very same forces that Chapter 4 saw unleashed in terms of local real estate transactional activity should logically have also had the possibility of causing disconnections and disruptions in the collection of payments, as well. Hence we learn about how the Hessian regimes tried to implement or re-implement a large-scale property surveillance program called the Economic State. Finally, the chapter turns once again to the way that jurists dealt with non-payment of dues and taxes, using prescription to determine when and how such non-payment ripened into a rightful freedom not to pay taxes or dues.

1 Noble Trespassing and Evasions

During and after the war, common Hessian people in many instances got away with not paying regular dues or performing services expected by their landlord or ruler. By the time rulers, their servants, and the intelligentsia began to realize the extent of this problem, they were faced with an overwhelming problem – could they turn the clock back?[1] Let us see how those in charge responded to the problem. Most basically, the regimes announced that they detected the problem of trespassing on rights and evasion of payments, and that such illegal activities must stop. The princely government also announced efforts to curb what it alleged was noble trespassing on landgravial domain rights. The 1648 "Princely Announcement" specified that "New *Salbücher* [registries of landholdings] should be drawn up for the Maintenance of Lordly Justice and Jurisdictions / also [matters of] Hunting, Meadows, Groves and Borders, in each Office." Complaining that "many rights of justice and of court … have been lost,"[2] Amalie Elisabeth made this announcement upon

1 A parallel may be drawn to Ludwig Earhardt in West Germany after World War II. See Dietrich Orlow, *A History of Modern Germany: 1871 to Present*, 8th ed. (London; New York: Routledge 2018), p. 248, p. 274.

2 "[A]llerhandt irrungen undt unrichtigkeiten ereugen, und es sich dabey ansehen leßet, daß zum theil aus unwißenheit der Beambten, zum theil auch auß deren nachleßigkeit viele dinge von hochgedachte unsers geliebten Sohns gerecht- unndt gerichtbarkeiten, Jagten, Huden, gehölzen unndt grenzen je zu Handt abgehen und verabseumet werden …" See "Fürstliches Ausschreiben, Daß und wie zu Erhaltung derer Herrschaftlichen Gerecht- und

returning to Cassel and hearing numerous reports of such encroachments from her foresters, hunt masters (*Jägermeister*), and local officials. Orders from the princely Hessian regimes in Cassel and Marburg were also issued in 1568 and in 1682, so again we are looking at a recurrent, long-term problem from the regimes' perspective.[3] (Presuably local common people and nobles felt themselves usually to be doing nothing wrong?)

To address this situation, the landgravine ordered officials in the towns (*Amtsschultheissen*) to make thorough inspections of noble rights and properties to uncover

> what each ... nobleman has ... for jurisdiction (whether civil or criminal), and the same with loan collateral, punishments ... [etc.][4]

Officials were likewise to inquire after the nobleman's claimed hunting rights,[5] pasturage rights, and holdings in local woods.[6] Officials were also to review the *Salbücher*, and then, since these might well not contain all local agreements, "You should also seek out and gather contracts [*Verträge*] which were executed by nobles in your Office, diligently review them, and note down and

---

Gerichtbarkeiten auch Jagden Juden Gehölzen und Grenzen in jedem Amt neue Sal-Bücher errichtet, davon ein Exemplar an die Canzley, das andere an die Rent-Cammer zu Cassel eingesendet, dar dritte aber in dem Amt behalten werden solle," May 31, 1648, in Kleinschmid and Apell, *Sammlung*, Vol. 2, p. 141.

3 In March 1568, Wilhelm IV (Cassel) and Ludwig IV (Marburg) had issued coordinated orders to their treasuries to similar effect. The edict of 1648 resembled these (copying earlier language was and is common in law). In the 1568 program, however, the *Salbuch* instructions were briefer. See ibid., Vol. 1, p. 340, §2. Wilhelm VI's son Karl in turn issued similar orders in his *Rent-Cammer-Ordnung zu Hesse*, dated March 1, 1682. The comparable section of the latter is printed in ibid, Vol. 3, p. 185, §2. Similarity of edicts and rules across related regimes and chanceries was typical and indeed to be expected.

4 "Was ... Jeder ... sitzender vom Adell uf seinem innen habenden Adelichen gütern vor gerichtbarkeit, sowohl civil alß criminal, Item mit angriffen, straffen oder andern derogleichen herbracht habe, oder dessen befügt sey" See ibid., Vol. 2, p. 141. The DRW gives one to understand *Angriffen* as loan collateral in this context.

5 "Ob er Jacht und Jagens gerechtigkeit, nach rotem und schwarzem Wildpreth, oder allein nach haasen und füchsen auch uf was weise und wege, Item ob er mit garnen zustellen oder aber zu laußen zu hetzen oder etwa nur zu schiessen und aufs Wildpreth zu gehen berechtiget seye; Item ahn welchem orten unndt wie weit er solche gerechtigkeit sowohl in Jagen, alß auch im Fischen bißhero ohnstreitig hergebracht und gebrauchet" See ibid., Vol. 2, p. 141.

6 Similar wording to the above citations except: "mit seinem Rindt, Schaff, Schwein [etc.] ... zu hüden ... vermöge Herkommens berechtigt seye ..." and "vor eigen gehölze habe" etc. See ibid., Vol. 2, p. 141.

collect all ... information together" concerning the above spheres of rights.[7] Not only might local noblemen have been assuming rights which belonged to the landgravial domain, but they or others might also have been making deals – apparently written contracts – about these matters. Amalie Elisabeth's edict mentioned contracts (*Verträge*) not once but three times. Clearly these were not just oral agreements but written contracts or accords, since they were to be *collected*. They were likely local forms of fief-letters – subinfeudation – which the princess stated were forbidden. Noble and non-noble tenants appear to have engaged in formal (i.e. written) economic transactions with one another based on the appropriation of rights earlier claimed by the landgraves. Sometimes conflicts went on for centuries, seemingly dying down in the long dark of decades or even centuries before being unexpectedly reignited.[8]

Finally, officials were to create fact-finding local juries. They summoned knowledgeable local witnesses – elders, foresters, shepherds, village officials and others living nearby – to confirm or add to what they had learned.[9] The officials were to write all such information down in their *Salbücher*, copy whatever contracts they had found into the books, and make an index of all bordering noble landholders. They were then to make two extra copies of the *Salbücher* and send one to the Chancery and one to the treasury within about ten weeks of the date of issuance of the announcement.[10]

The irony of this project, and of the projects involving the updating of cadastral information undertaken by Wilhelm VI (examined next), is that the

---

7 "So sollet ihr zugleich nicht allein die bey euwerm Ambt befindliche verträge so mit denen vom Adel gedachtes euwers Ambts vor Alters ufgerichtet worden seindt, ufsuchen unndt bey die hand bringen, dieselbe vleißig durchsehen ..." See ibid., Vol. 2, p. 141.

8 Dietmar Willoweit describes a few legal disputes between landgrave and territorial nobility that spanned the 15th through 18th centuries! For instance, the landgrave claimed Kastenvogtei (administrative protection) over the German Order in Hesse. This conflict began in the sixteenth century in the Reformation, died down under the reign of Wilhelm VI's widow Hedwig-Sophie, and seems to have re-erupted in the eighteenth century. See Willoweit, *Rechtsgrundlagen der Territorialgewalt*, pp. 241–242 and Theodor Niederquell, "Im Kampf um die Reichsunmittelbarkeit: Die Geschichte der Deutschordensballei in Hessen vornehmlich im 16. Jahrhundert," *Hessisches Jahrbuch für Landesgeschichte* 5 (1955) generally.

9 "die Altisten vonn Rath in den Statten, Item die in euwerm Ambt geßene Förstere, sodan die Hirten unndt alle andere alte leute, wie auch Greben unndt Vorsteher in den Dörffen, unnd andere so den Edelleuten am nechsten gesessen unndt wißenschaft davon haben können, vor euch fordern, dieselbe die wahrheit zu sagen, euch ahn Eidts statt angeloben laßen, undt Sie darueff uber die oberwehnte 4. posten fleissig befragen ..." See Kleinschmid and Apell, *Sammlung*, Vol. 2, p. 141.

10 The Announcement was made on May 31, 1648, and the due date was August 11. See ibid., Vol. 2, p. 141.

officials charged with these tasks were clients of the various nobles whose trespassing they were supposed to be inspecting. For while local officials were paid and directed by the prince landgrave, they were also usually enmeshed in multiple other fields of influence, particularly the noble landlord.[11] As Peter Taylor explains,

> The effective administration of patrimonial jurisdiction ... depended heavily upon the lord's [i.e. the *Gerichtsherr*'s] clients, who performed their duties as village officials. These brokers could conceal information about land transfers, conspire to defraud tithe collectors, protect potential draftees from recruitment [into the landgravial mercenary army], and embezzle funds that passed through their hands on their way to the powers of domination [i.e. to prince, landlord, or other lord].[12]

Hessian rulers and the territorial nobility were in conflict from the 1640s until at least 1655, but though probably evidence suggests that the dispute last into the next century several decades later. This conflict undercut the regime's efforts to surveil its territory and collect (what it said was) its dues. Nobles were using legal tools like subinfeudation – but so were commoners.

By the 1650s, knowledge of the tax capital was in shambles, as was collection of tithes, dues, and taxes. On account of both peculiarities in assessment standards and sluggishness of property registration, the reported tax capital was probably only about 25–50% of actual combined assets and income. Less than one half, sometimes far less, than the assessed tax level (the Contribution) was regularly collected.[13]

The regime's effort to produce an updated cadaster of all estates and domains in its territory was needed for several related reasons. One was "tax rectification," meaning the need to assess property values in order to levy the correct level of taxation. A second was domain survey, to discover who tenants were, what their dues were supposed to be, and what the conditions of their tenures were. Third, and related to both, the regime of the new young prince Wilhelm VI presided over a much expanded Hesse-Cassel which now included territories gained in the fortunes of the recent war. In the long view of modern Hessian history, the cadastral project was itself part of a larger, long-term property surveillance program by the Hessian regime. The latter program had

---

11 Friedeburg, "Landgemeinde ... Merzhausen, 1646–1672."

12 Taylor, *Indentured to Liberty*, pp. 133b–134t.

13 Vann, *The Making of a State*, p. 96.

FIGURE 42 Landgrave Wilhelm IV, creator of the *Oeconomic State*

been initiated by Wilhelm IV (Figure 42) in 1567 with a great, whole-territorial, Domesday-like cadaster suggestively entitled *The Economic State*.[14] The latter was a first and famously quite successful effort to gain accurate information

14 Ludwig Zimmermann, ed., *Der Ökonomische Staat Landgraf Wilhelms IV.*, Veröffentlichungen der Historischen Kommission für Hessen und Waldeck; Quellen zur Verwaltungsgeschichte hessischer Territorien (Marburg: Elwert, 1933–1937). It should be immediately noted however that the thoroughness and apparent completeness of the original 1567 project was not again obtained until the late eighteenth century. My findings here echo those of other historians of the region in concluding that wars, chaos, civil conflict, and sheer evasiveness prevented successful updating of the survey project in the intervening two centuries. See Taylor, *Indentured to Liberty*, pp. 26–28, 50–62.

on the people, estates, rights, and other property across the entire, then-united landgraviate. The Economic State project had "created a bureaucracy of non-noble domain managers" to systematically survey the landgraviate, princely domains first, then noble domains. Seventeenth-century Hessian officials described their work here as updating the Economic State. Such projects have of course been common in states going back many centuries, Domesday in England being the earliest post-classical effort on a national scale.

2 Tax Registration, 1651–1654

The Hessian taxation system had been based on the assessment of "tax capital" (*Steuercapital*, combining income and assets or *Vermögen*) since the mid-sixteenth century, so the renewal and correction of this information was crucial to the regime's ability to collect taxes once more and therewith to shore up its material strength or wealth (as measured in cash, properties, goods and the ability to hire soldiers in a standing military force).[15] This was the heart of the cameralist enterprise. Upon his accession, Wilhelm VI ordered the correction of the cadastral information held by his officials, both in his treasury and at the local level by *Amtsschultheissen*. However, the project "came to nothing" just as had the previous one initiated by his father in 1631.[16] On November 1, 1651, Wilhelm issued two almost duplicate announcements, one to the knighthood and one to the *Landschaft*, "that, and how, new Tax-Register should be composed, and the old ones therefore be rectified."[17] These announcements will shortly be examined in some detail, since they are the earliest such in

15 Peter Taylor argues that Hessian domestic administration in the seventeenth and eighteenth centuries applied cameralist thinking about productivity to the administrative project of tax rectification, searching for taxable hidden household assets. See Taylor, *Indentured to Liberty*, p. 71.

16 Günter Hollenberg and Berthold Jäger, eds., *Hessen-Kasselische Landtagsabschiede, 1649–1798*, Vol. 5, Vorgeschichte und Geschichte des Parlamentarismus in Hessen (Marburg: N. G. Elwert, 1989), p. lxiv; Annegret Wenz-Haubfleisch, "'... damit die Landes-Bürden hinfüro mit gleichen Schultern getragen werden.' Ziele und Durchführung der Rektifikation des landschaftlichen Steuerstocks in der Landgrafschaft Hessen-Kassel im 18. Jahrhundert," *Hessisches Jahrbuch für Landesgeschichte* 39 (1989), pp. 152–153.

17 See "Announcement to the Knighthood about Tax Registration," 1651, and "Fürstliches Ausschreiben an die Beamten samt Burgermeister und Rath Daß, auch wie und welchergestalt neue Steuer-Registration formiret, mithin die alten rectificiret werden sollen," November 1, 1651, in Kleinschmid and Apell, *Sammlung*, Vol. 2, pp. 153–154. All cited details are found in both Announcements, unless otherwise specified.

Wilhelm's reign and are representative of the regime's long-term property surveillance program. The landgrave bade his nobles and the officials record all manner of local holdings and employment information, similar to the original survey of 1585. Everything was to be not only listed but assessed in its "correct apparent worth" – its "certain Quantum and Capital" – from piece to piece, according to the quality of each and as it is used."[18] This recording was called an index (*Verzeichnis*) or *Specification*, and was to be written into a book and sent to the landgrave's Commissioners in the treasury within six weeks of the announcement.[19]

The most important category for the purpose of "tax capital" (taxable capital) was properties and improvements to properties, including houses and farmsteads, buildings, mills, gardens, fields, meadows, pastures, forests, groves, ponds, fisheries, livestock and so on. Notably, because

> also many houses stand uninhabited, and many estates lie empty ... these too should be specified and estimated [though uninhabited].[20]

Were they held in fief or in allod? Those doing the recording were to be careful to indicate in which regional office each property fell,[21] probably to ensure that no one's properties escaped taxation and that no one was taxed twice.

Also to be recorded were all kinds of money coupons (rents, dues, interest, tithes), lordly hereditary rights and critical quotidian pasturage rights, liens on properties, and loan repayments. Fungible goods including cash, small goods for sale (*Kramwahren*) and inventory of agricultural stock were to be included in the registration book. The assessing officials were also to make sure that interest on loans was at the legal level, capped at 5% in most cases. The knights and their people were then to discover and record the trades and employments of all people living in the area, how much they earned, and the number of the poor living in the area.

18 "ziemlichen Werth von Stücken zu Stücken, nach eines jeden Guts qualitet"; "eines gewissen Quanti und Capitals" See ibid., Vol. 2, p. 152 and also "Fürstliches Ausschreiben wegen Einsendung richtiger Specificationen der Steuerbaren Güter," October 1652, in ibid., Vol. 2, p. 166, discussed below.

19 The four Commissioners were Obervorsteher of the High Hospital Philip von Scholleyen, Consistorial President Justus Jungman, Privy Councilor David Ludwig Scheffern and Kammerrat Caspar Weiganden. See ibid., Vol. 2, p. 166.

20 Ibid., Vol. 2, p. 152.

21 See "Princely Announcement to the Knighthood that, and how, new Tax-Registration should be composed, and the old ones therefore be rectified," November 1, 1651, in ibid., Vol. 2, p. 152.

FIGURE 43 Landgrave Wilhelm VI the Just of Hesse-Cassel

The knights were first to undertake this project with their own properties, and then summon all their

> administrators, servants who have their own households ... their own vassals ... local [and] inhabitants ... including widows, guardians, minors, Jews and foreigners.

Local judges, landgravial officials, and "heads of villages and elders" were to assist in these efforts. The knights were bidden to conduct this assessment for themselves and then to have it carried out in the villages over which they held jurisdiction. Similarly, villagers and townsmen were instructed to undertake the same project, probably to reinforce the importance and ineluctability of the task. Towns were additionally instructed to summon

> qualified persons from the guilds and craftsmen and people in the villages who understood proper agriculture, each and every individual inhabitant, free or unfree, rich and poor

and other categories, such as widows, minors, etc. The prince admonished the knights and towns to do this diligently.

> Should you find anyone who you suspect has not truthfully recorded everything, inquire him most diligently and if anything comes up, he shall be punished.[22]

It is again striking that Wilhelm was asking his rebellious knights to estimate the worth of all these properties. Not only must such an assessment have been rather arbitrary in the absence of regular and transparent real estate markets – no new criteria had been promulgated since the very irregular ones given in the *Treysischer Anschlag* of 1576 – but why should these knights have cared about accuracy? It seems likely that they would have underestimated their own properties' values and perhaps have supported their vassals by underesti-

---

22 "... so du zu alle deine Verwalter und Diener, so ihre eigene Haushaltung haben, Item alle deine Hintersassen und deren Beywohner, wie auch die Juden und Ausländische mit zuziehen der Greben, Richter, oder Schultheissen und Vorstehernin den Dorffern, wie auch die ältesten, Ackerbaw verständigen erbaren Männer vor dich erforderst ..." "qualificirten Personen, auß den Zünfften unnd Handwercken," and in villages "Ackerbaus verständigen redlichen Männer, alle und jede Einwohner, befreyet oder ohnbefreyet, Reich und arm ..." "da du bey einem oder dem andern einzigen verdacht hettest, daß er nicht alles der gebühr specificiret hette, uff denselben fleissig inquiriren, auch ihn derhalben nach befinden *bestraffen sollest.*" See Kleinschmid and Apell, *Sammlung*, Vol. 2, pp. 152–153.

mating the value of their properties. Perhaps the prince relied on them to act honorably, at least for the sake of not appearing to be cheats if called out. In any event, he likely had little control over these processes.

The "Princely Announcement of July 26, 1652, to Schaumburg Vassals" illustrates a similar situation. The landgrave announced to these vassals that, after the death of their previous lord, Count Otto of Schaumburg and Sternberg, landlordship over them had escheated to himself, and they should therefore formally "seek the confirmation of their fiefs with the Hesse *Lehen-Hof* in Cassel." (Schaumburg is depicted in Figure 3 above; it lies north of the bishopric of Paderborn, north of Hesse-Cassel.) Because the landgraves of Hesse-Cassel had only just assumed direct domain administration over part of Schaumburg, the prince desired these vassals to register their fiefs – in writing, if not in person. As with other cases of fief-registration, the landgrave had opportunity to complain that his vassals in Schaumburg had not registered they were supposed to.[23]

The project was not, in fact, completed in 1651. Over the next few years, palpably irritated announcements issued from the regimes about tardiness, non-compliance, often suggesting that the work had not even been undertaken at all. In October 1652, Chancellor Vultejus issued another, shorter announcement in the prince's name to complain that most of the knights and officials had not yet sent in their specification books.[24] This time lax officials were given six weeks to comply. On July 26, 1653, the regime issued another reminder, complaining that "Although we had hoped that most of our officials and towns would have obeyed, this has not happened." This time the landgrave and chancellor threatened double punishment to recalcitrant officials.[25]

---

23 The county was an old fief of Hesse and had become part of Hesse-Cassel in 1567. Amalie Elisabeth had claimed the escheat of Schaumburg in 1640 after the death of Count Otto. This escheat legitimated her occupation of the county during the War. The powers at Osnabrück in 1648 awarded half of the Schaumburg county lands (an exclave some 20 kilometers north of Hesse-Cassel) to the Hessian landgraves (the House of Brabant). See "Fürstliches Ausschreiben an die Schaumburgischen Lehen-Manne, daß, nach tödtlichem Hintritt Graffen Ottens zu Schaumburg und Sternberg, sie ihre Lehen bey dem Hessischen Lehen-Hofe zu Cassel muthen sollen," July 26, 1652, in ibid., Vol. 2, pp. 161–162.

24 See "Ausschreiben wegen Einsendung richtiger Specificationen der Steuerbahren Güter" of October 1651, in ibid., Vol. 2, p. 166.

25 "Ob wir nun wol verhoffen, gleich wie die meisten von Beampten so wol alß auch den Städten albereits solchen Außschreiben gebührliche folge geleistet, also auch Ihr demselben gleicher gestalt nachgelebt haben würdet, So vernehmen Wir doch daßsolches biß noch nicht geschehen sey" See "Fürstliches Ausschreiben wegen Einsendung der Verfertigenden Steuer-Registration," July 1653, in ibid., Vol. 2, p. 185.

On July 3, 1654, the regime issued yet another announcement indicating that, although it had by then received a number of tax registers, many of them had to be corrected once more. It appears that the project remained substantially unimplemented for decades at least. Updating any records of new ownership (*dominium proprium*) or fief-holding (*dominium utile*) would only have made owners and fief-holders liable to pay more taxes, following forty years in which peasants, towns, and nobles had been assessed high taxes to support wars from which they suffered horribly.

The territorial diet had been paralyzed for decades by the strife between landgrave and knights. Without the cooperation of local lords, the Hessian tax system could not correct itself. The knights accepted the Princely Resolutions of 1655 (Chapter 4) and with things between ruler and estates seemingly settled, the knights accepted the landgrave's tax rectification project, at least in principle. However, in practice many would apparently continue to evade it.[26] Wilhelm's widow Hedwig-Sophie (r. 1663–1670/77 as regent) issued a follow-up announcement in 1668 almost identical to her late husband's. She complained and threatened, and bade that the "Specifications of Taxable Goods" be sent to the head tax collectors within six weeks. Apparently a number of knights and prelates still were non-compliant, thirteen years later.[27] After 1668, rulers tried several times not only to update their registers and/or keep current what they had. The regime of the son of Wilhelm and Hedwig-Sophie, Landgrave Karl, established regular assessment values in 1680 and a commission in 1699 to regulate the registers and keep these current. As Kersten Krüger explains, the commissioners were to

> check on the Specifications which had been sent in, just as had temporarily existed in 1654 and which should advise on tax rectification anew. Nevertheless [the commission] was unable to implement rectification decisively.

Later landgraves Friedrich I, Wilhelm VIII, Friedrich II, and Wilhelm IX achieved qualified success in the decades after 1736. Later success was built on the assessment efforts in the seventeenth century, for all their shortcomings. Indeed they were "the basis for the taxation principles of the eighteenth

26 Krüger, for instance, writes that the compromise "enabled once more regular tax collection and progress in the renewing of the registration." See Krüger, "Entstehung und Ausbau," pp. 113–114.

27 Kleinschmid and Apell, *Sammlung*, Vol. 2, pp. 640–641.

century."[28] The landgraves remained dependent on the local noble officiate structure for tax collection, with all of its little corruptions. Indeed the problem would linger on until at least 1798.[29]

3 The Greying of the Clear Cadastral Picture

After the war, there were many things the regime did not understand, much less control at the local level. We gather this from official, public pronouncements about unofficial land transfers, unrecorded dealings, and transfers of fiefs without approval by the feudal lords or family authorities supposed to have authority over such transactions.

A suggestive modern term for these circumstances is a "grey economy." Used by the modern Peruvian development economist Hernando de Soto, the term describes webs of local property ownership and economic activity in developing countries today. In this paradigm, some economies are "grey" in that they do not rely on formal positive laws or regulation. They are illegible to the state, in the broad sense characterized by James Scott. Though informally regulated through conventions, local customs, and other forms of regulatory and local-lordly authority, de Soto argues that, unbeknownst formally to states, these economies in fact contain massive amounts of wealth hidden from economists (and regulators) who can only see the accounting statements and tax receipts legible to bureaucracies. For instance, in many cases people do not have well-established legal title to valuable assets (houses, land, cars, small businesses), with the result that they are unable to use these assets as collateral to take out loans, thus preventing the ignition of higher-level business activity.[30]

Grey economy seems an apt description for the circumstances noted by voices from the Cassel regime in the decades after the War: nobles whose

---

28 See Krüger, "Entstehung," 113; Hollenberg and Jäger, *Hessen-Kasselische Landtagsabschiede*, Vol. 5, p. lxiii; Strippel, *Währschafts- und Hypothekenbücher Kurhessens*, Marburg 1914 (*Arbeiten zum Handels-, Gewerbe- und Landwirtschaftsrecht* 24), p. 176; and Wenz-Haubfleisch, "Landes-Bürden," pp. 153–158.

29 On the tax issue, see "Princely Resolutions," 1655, in Kleinschmid and Apell, *Sammlung*, Vol. 2, p. 243, Title v; *Landtagsabschiede* of July 5, 1656, November 9, 1658, and January 19, 1666; Demandt, "Die hessischen Landstände," pp. 54–55; and Günter Hollenberg, "Landstände und Militär in Hessen-Kassel," ibid.34 (1984), pp. 103–104.

30 For the hidden revenue angle, see de Soto, *Mystery of Capital*. For bureaucratic legibility and illegibility, see Scott, *Seeing like a State*. The word "grey" here has the same sense as it does in "grey literature" in science publishing and "grey trading" in finance. Greyness in these usages indicates a demimonde, implying hiddenness or criminality.

lands or jurisdictions abutted the landgraves' had allegedly been encroaching on landgravial (or others') rights over the war years, and tithes often did not amount to their customary pre-war levels. As discussed earlier, it appears that *Vermalterung* involved local collusion, usually with other nearby farmers, to reduce the amount of tithe delivered to tithe-holder, whether local seigneur or prince.

Why did the state care so much about recordation of real estate holding, transfers, and encumbering? Basically because in domains which were too large to be known by a corps of official record-keepers acting in concert, it was relatively easy for an estate somewhere to be inherited, sold, rented, etc., thus producing a new tenant or even new owner. If the far-off landlord was not apprised of this, he would lose his chance to approve and/or tax the transaction. He might even lose the estate all together. A chain of transfers might leave no proof nor even living memory of who had held the estate a generation past or what dues he paid or to whom. This lossy triangle (landlord-old tenant-new possessor) appears to have obtained (or at least been anxiously described) regardless whether all parties were commoners or included noble landlord or even prince landlord. It could happen to anyone.

The state's efforts to become recognized and effective arbiter of real estate transactions (claiming authority to grant or withhold approval to them) took a long time to realize, basically most of the three centuries from the Reformation until Napoleon, and maybe longer. Gerhard Oestreich and others have written of the process of *social disciplining* whereby the state became able to enforce a program of order on the conduct of its subjects, whether in religious or financial matters.[31] It should also be noted that states and their client jurists over time have advanced thoughtful justifications for why real estate transactions should be recorded legibly and unequivocally in public knowledge. But in the seventeenth century it seems that *society* was not yet well enough *disciplined* to comply with the princely regime's wishes. Local powers might look favorably upon, say, a new party taking up an abandoned farmstead after the war. But another party or actor might claimed that this possession was wrongful.

Was the state's recordation project the antidote to these nettlesome grey economies? You would think so. Recordation in official register books

31 See e.g. Philip S. Gorski, *The disciplinary revolution: Calvinism and the rise of the state in early modern Europe* (Chicago: University of Chicago Press, 2003); R. Po-chia Hsia, *Social discipline in the Reformation: Central Europe, 1550–1750*, Christianity and society in the modern world. (London; New York: Routledge, 1989); and Gerhard Oestreich, *Neostoicism and the Early Modern State*, ed. Brigitta Oestreich and H. G. Koenigsberger, Cambridge Studies in Early Modern History (Cambridge: Cambridge University Press, 1982).

(cadasters, *Salbücher*) was related to alleged tax avoidance and allegedly illegal transfer activity. Local officials and/or local noblemen were supposed to keep authorized (essentially notarized) records of who held what real rights, not only holding of lands but also real rights such as hunting. (The obverse of such positive rights was positive obligations, e.g. that serfs or common people tenured on a certain estate were obliged to pay a certain level of tithe, render certain dues, or perform a certain amount of labor.) If the register was destroyed and half the area inhabitants killed, or if an estate had somehow changed hands but the new owner/lord was not recorded in the old registry, this would create conflict between the new party and the old landlord (etc.) eventually. Parallels can be drawn between events like these in Germany and changes in tenure in other countries in the same period, including England.[32]

Registration in the book basically meant "title," but it must be born in mind that this merely meant registration of aspects of the property right – an acre where? how large? from whom was it held and on what terms? "Title" was not necessary for tenure or ownership, since "title" meant only the proper recordation rather than a procedurally adequate sufficient transaction making the current holder the rightful holder. Either a transfer contract (deed), or several witnesses, or even unchallenged possession sufficed for good, secure tenure (whether rental, feudal, or even dominion). That is why interested parties (seigneur, prince, neighbor, etc.), who alleged that they were rightfully entitled to certain dues or labor or tithe or other lordly rights, complained about unrecorded holding and transfers. If they could not prove wrongdoing, the present order of real holding of property rights would be considered valid in any court. A new tenure of right could be newly recorded and therefrom obtain the shine of official right. Rightful tenure of the past could be lost and temporarily forgotten, and then overwritten with a new concrete order of property held among other people. Thus there was no easy alignment between the most recent, official, record and what was the actual state of things on the ground recognized by local parties.

The Thirty Years' War was like a great icebreaker, smashing up the old social and legal order. Local life had mutated (changed in unpredictable ways) throughout the *Land* during the war and regimes played a slow game of informational catch-up, in some cases for almost a century. Local property rights and transfers eluded their surveillance. The leasing of tithes, noble trespassing

---

32 The process I describe in seventeenth-century Hesse of loss of old records and creation of new ones seems prefigured in the late medieval creation of copyhold tenure in England. See Tigar pp. 178–180.

on princely rights, the resistance to rectification of tax and domain records, unapproved transfers of estates and rights and other unrecorded dealings, sales of fief without permission – all of these lossy triangles meant that that the regime could not enforce the order it sought; it could not implement the pre-war vision of communal order and prosperity.[33]

This information breakdown had profound consequences. One, which connects to a story of Hessian history better known to Anglophone readers than what we are presenting here, was the inadequate collection of tax revenues. In Hesse-Cassel, this shortfall contributed to the development of the mercenary army, for which the state became well known after about 1700. But our story here focuses on a different consequence, that of quotidian economic activity: With the decrease of supervision, and enforcement at the regional level, *common people and regional noble families were largely left alone to run their own affairs. People married and died; they bought, sold, inherited, and even usurped lands and rights, and generally took advantage of the absence of the traditional supervisory powers in the territory*. As noted last chapter, there were many local powers exerting or trying to exert various authority – noble leaders and their families and various figures in the ruling princely house (pretenders, temporary rulers, cadet princes). *This conflict created a power vacuum which, in combination with local willfulness and juristic inventiveness, permitted the emergence of new forms of personal freedom*. This is not to say that illegality was endorsed by any party involved, nor that illegal activity was (or is usually today) interpreted as freedom. But the grey economic activity (discussed above) and more ambiguous methods of circumventing law created new orders of rights which jurists would come to accept and courts to uphold. These rights were often called freedoms. So freedoms were expanded even when the steps leading to expansion were sometimes rather shady.[34]

---

33 The basic outline sketched here is consistent with Marc Raeff's theses in his "The Well-Ordered Police State and the Development of Modernity in 17th- and 18th-Century Europe: An Attempt at a Comparative Approach," *American Historical Review* 78, no. 3 (1975) and subsequent book *Well-Ordered Police State*. I extend somewhat his thesis through additional focus on property supervision.

34 I would not wish to imply that this was a unidirectional vector toward ever-increasing individual civil liberty, a negative freedom-from-control or freedom-as-non-domination made possible by continuously decreasing state supervision. The most important countervailing force in this context, arising later, was the growing size of the Hessian army. The army originally began as a territorial defensive militia and labor service, growing later into a gigantic standing army which constituted approximately 7% the population. As Peter Taylor has demonstrated, local networks of patronage and clientage were superimposed on to the princely government's drive for tax-capital transparency. This resulted in scouring households for family members to impress into the army. See Taylor, *Indentured to Liberty*, pp. 50–62.

While the rulers and nobility worked to repair and reform systems of tax collection and property registration, jurists were faced with a different challenge. Regimes in Marburg, Cassel, and elsewhere knew that there was considerable underreporting of tax, dues, and other payment obligations. The tricky thing for jurists, especially those employed by regimes seeking to collect taxes, is that just as possession and prescription could settle disputes over land ownership (Chapter 4), so they could also be applied to non-performance of obligations such as rents, tithes, and taxes. All such payments were considered real obligations since they were connected to tenure of land. Furthermore, *the right to collect real obligations could be alienated to another person. And hence also one could gain or hold freedom from paying such rents, tithes, and maybe even taxes.* The juristic desire to quiet title and settle the law on a broad regional or territorial scale, for the sake of the public peace, is typically very strong in Roman-influenced legal systems. Hence jurists like Senckenberg, Estor, and Cramer emphasized prescription, even when doing so helped develop *the legal field of acquiring, through prescription, freedom to not pay taxes or other dues*. In a debate that stretched from about 1680 to 1750, jurists refined the idea of *natural freedom* and, using the concept of prescription, legitimated *ex post facto* ordinary people's unwillingness to accept certain taxes, dues, or labor.

4 New Departures in the 1680s

> It can first be said that we have possessed a negative right and consequently an immunity and there was no one in whose caprice it rested to demand of us that from which we hold ourselves to be free.[35]
>
> J. U. CRAMER (1740)

In the 1680s, jurists tried to resolve the tension between princely sovereignty and prescription of tax freedoms. Tübingen law professor Ferdinand Christoph Harpprecht and his student Georg Heinrich Braun, along with Leipzig law professor Friedrich Philippi and his student Christian Henricus, fashioned what was practically a new law of *immunity* with regard to prescription. Although its consequences were more extensive than previous law in this area, it was

35 Johann Ulrich Cramer, "Kurtze doch überführende Abhandlung von Erlangung einer Immunität durch Verjährung," in *Opuscula, materias gravissimas ex omni iure demonstrativa ratione pertractatas continentia: Antea seorsim edita, iam vero ob raritatem et desiderium virorum doctissimorum collecta*, Vol. 2 (Marburg: Philipp Casimir Müller, 1754 [orig. 1740]) §9, p. 176m.

understood as an extension and elaboration of valid older law. Two features that distinguished this modern law from its predecessors were the prominence it gave to supreme *princely authority* and the role it accorded the theory of *natural freedom*.

The first study, by Harpprecht and Braun, was entitled *Legal treatise on the prescription of immunity from taxes* (1683), and the second, by Philippi and Henricus, *Legal dissertation on the prescription of immunity from tributes* (*and other governmental impositions*) (1688). Apparently the first specialized studies of the prescription of immunity,[36] the two works constructed largely compatible accounts of the phenomenon. Second and third editions of both appeared over the following decades.[37] Moreover, Harpprecht supervised a similar juris-

36 The main sources of the earlier of the two, Harpprecht and Braun (1683), were Aegidius Thomatus, *Tractatvs De Mvneribvs Patrimonialibus, seu Collectis ... Pars Prima* (Mediolani Moschenius, 1557) (itself reprinted 1558, 1559, 1584, 1598, and 1619); Joannes Otto Tabor, *Commentarius ad tit. cod. De metatis & epidemeticis: von Einquartierungen: ad usvm horvm temporvm accommodatus* (Argentorati [Strasbourg]: Johann Philipp Mülbe, 1645); Andreas Gaill, *Practicarum observationum tam ad processum judiciarium, praesertim imperialis Camera, quam causarum decisiones pertinentium. Libri duo. Item de Pace publica et Proscriptis, sive Bannitis Impnis. Libi II. De Pignorationibus liber I. Pn- ICtum D. Andream Gail Agripinatem Caes. Maj. a Consitus etc. Editio II Cum Summariiset Indice* (Coloniae Agrippinae [Cologne]: Apud Joan. Gymnicum, 1580 [orig. 1578]); David Mevius, *Decisiones Super Causis Praecipuis Ad Summum Tribunal Regium Vismariense Delatis: Quibus Praeter priores Decisionum ac rerum indices Accessit Repertorium, Quo Dictae Decisione iuxta ordinem Pandectarum exhibentur*, ed. Johann Jacob von Ryssel, 4th ed. (Frankfurt am Main: 1698); Conrad. von Einsiedel, *Tractatus de iuribus ad imperatoris Romano-Teutonici Maiestatem pertinentibus sive regalibus* (Halle (Saxony): Petrus Faber, 1619); and Wolfgang Adam Lauterbach, *Compendium juris brevissimis verbis, sed amplissimô sensu & allegationibus universam ferè materiam juris exhibens*, ed. Johann Jacob Schütz (Tubingæ: sumptibus Joh. Ceorg. Cottæ: typis Martini Rommeii, 1681), i.e. the famous "Schütz-Lauterbach." None of these nor any of the other sources I can identify in the 168-page dissertation (unusually long for its genre) appears to have been a specialized study of prescription of freedom from extractions. The study by Philipp and Henricus five years later cites a number of the same sources but does not cite that of Harpprecht and Braun. There is no reason to assume this represented a snub rather an oversight from ignorance.

37 See respectively Ferdinand Christoph Harpprecht, praeses, Georg Heinrich Braun, respondans, *Tractatio iur. de praescriptione immunitatis a collectis* (Altdorff: Kohlesius, 1709 [orig. 1683]); Ferdinand Christoph Harpprecht, praeses, Georg Heinrich Braun, respondans, *Disp. de praescriptione immunitatis a collectis* (*Tubinga*: *Bergerus et Cotta*, 1737 [orig. 1683]); Friedrich Philippi, praeses, Christian Henricus, respondans, *Dissertatio Juridica de praescriptione immunitatis a tributis = Von der Verjährung der Steuren und anderer Obrigkeitl. Anlagen Freyheit* 1721 [orig. 1688]); and Philippi and Henricus, *De praescriptione immunitatis â tributis*.

doctoral thesis in 1695, itself also reissued in a second edition after his death.[38] This high rate of reprinting implies significant scholarly and juridical interest in these works.

Harpprecht-Braun and Philipp-Henricus constructed how prescription of such immunity works, bringing together commonly available legal sources in a new way. The basic work and argumentation was the same as what we considered in Chapter 4: Possession and prescription had ancient foundations in Roman law. Grotius had provided a new, naturalistic account of prescription in his 1625 magnum opus. As mentioned earlier, in Grotius's account prescription can be thought of as a kind of recipe for, or set of conditions required for the activation of, a natural process. Possession in good faith was followed by the passage of time, exercise, notoriety, sufferance, contradiction, and tacit acquiescence. Freedom from paying taxes was hardly a novelty in the seventeenth century; it was generally a constitutional feature of the privileged noble and clerical estates in European countries. It was in fact considered part of the pre-modern social contract, we might say. But beginning with Harpprecht-Braun and Philipp-Henricus, freedoms from paying certain taxes, dues, tithes, or other specific extractions came to be considered simply real rights in themselves, abstracted from connection to any *personal estate* such as nobility or clergy. Immunities were still treated expressly as grants of freedom given by a governmental authority, but the granting was said to have been implied rather than to have actually taken place "in real life" as we might say. Such an implicit gaining of immunity could happen through prescription.

While the notion of prescribing such freedoms was built on the ancient Roman civil law, the specific idea of gaining freedoms against the imposition of governmental authority, according to both Harpprecht-Braun and Philipp-Henricus, was distinctly post-classical.[39] For instance, Harpprecht and Braun wrote that

38 See respectively Ferdinand Christoph Harpprecht, praeses, Johann Georg Lupin, respondans, *Tractatio synoptica inauguralis de immunitate a collectis conventionali* (Tübingen: Johann Konrad Eitel & Martin Rommel's widow, 1695) and Ferdinand Christoph Harpprecht, praeses, Johann Georg Lupin, respondans, *Disp. inaug. de immunitate a collectis conventionali* (*Tubinga: Bergerus & Cotta*, 1737 [orig. 1695]).

39 While the concept and term *immunity* derived from classical Roman civil law, in that original context it looked rather different – it was quite particular. The house estate was an immune space within its *termini*; various priests like the vestals were immune; on a grand scale, subject cities or colonies might enjoy this or that immunity. But these immunities were not easily transferable real rights. It was cumbersome to transfer ownership over real estate and, until late in the empire, it had to be done through legal fiction. See Fustel de Coulanges, *The Ancient City: A Study on the Religion, Laws, and Institutions of Greece and Rome*; Nicholas, *Introduction to Roman law*; and references to freedom and immunity in Calvinus, *Lexicon Iuridicum Iuris*, a selective commonplace book of Roman law.

> this question about prescribing immunity from taxes in the empire must be elucidated not from the common law [i.e. the civil law derived narrowly from classical Roman sources] but rather from the statutes and constitutions of our Roman-German Empire.[40]

They understood these freedoms as "negative rights," with the same meaning that term holds today in political theory, that is, "freedom from".[41] The freedoms were also described generally, applicable in theory to most impositions by any level of government, from a customary tax (like *Besthaupt*, on serfs) to a princely regime tax (like the *Contribution*) or obligations to a king or emperor.

In their studies, Harpprecht-Braun and Philipp-Henricus established the requirements for prescription to proceed effectively, akin to a natural process like fermentation. All agreed that *good faith* was required: a person could not claim to have prescribed some right if there was a known lie or misdeed which underlay the present order (recall the discussions of illegality in Chapter 4). If a man knew that he held some land unlawfully, for example by violently dispossessing the previous tenant, then it was generally believed that no amount of time would "ripen" his possession into good title.[42] (It is telling that lawyers use the verb "to ripen" to describe the 'natural' process.) But if the original dispossessor had illegally sold the land to a third party, who was unaware of the injustice, then the third party was a good-faith possessor.[43]

A key question was how much time had to pass for prescription to ripen. In the history of prescription law, going back to the classical Roman civil law, various periods of time were required for different kinds of right to prescribe – sometimes 30 years were required, sometimes 40, sometimes "time immemorial" (meaning that no prior evidence to the contrary exists, either documentary or in living memory). According to Philipp, in matters of *taxation*, one older view was that freedom against such extractions could only be

40 "Sed hanc ipsam Quaestionem de immunitate a Collectis Imperii, contra illud praescribenda, non ex jure Communi; verum ex Legibus et Constitutionibus Imperii nostril Romano-Germanici dilucidandam esse." See Harpprecht and Braun, *Tractatio iuridica de praescriptione immunitatis*, Cap. 4, §3, p. 110.

41 Philipp-Henricus for instance wrote that the dissertation's quarry, immunity, is a negative right. See Philippi and Henricus, *De praescriptione immunitatis â tributis*, Thesis 24, pp. 22m–23t.

42 The problem of title, discussed at greater length in Chapter 4 above, features in both the works of Harpprecht and Philipp, though it featured particularly prominently in the former, where it is treated extensively. See Harpprecht and Braun, *Tractatio iuridica de praescriptione immunitatis*, Cap. 2, §32 (pp. 52–53), §§45–52 (pp. 71–78) and §§61–64 (pp. 87–93).

43 Philippi and Henricus, *De praescriptione immunitatis â tributis*, Theses 38–39, pp. 35b–40.

gained via immemorial prescription. In other words, the only way that a person could rightfully claim to acquire via prescription a freedom against paying a certain tax, was if he had never paid it for as long as anyone could remember or prove. But Philipp rejected this strict formulation of the rule, arguing instead in favor of a rule of 40 years.[44]

In the authors' view, gaining a right of immunity also required what was called *contradiction* over that entire prescriptive period. In prescription law, contradiction corresponds to elements of what is in Anglo-American law called *adverse possession*. The party pretending to the freedom *openly defies* ("contradicts") the demand of the party pretending to be owed the obligation, and the latter then capitulates, either expressly or simply by dropping the pursuit of the obligation at some point without formal announcement. According to Philipp, gaining a freedom to not pay a tax to the territorial government required just such contradiction or adverse possession.[45]

5 The Presumption of Natural Freedom

The idea of natural freedom played an important supporting role in the development of the law of immunity. The scholars who constructed the law of prescription of freedom during this period consistently explained that, beneath the surface of civil law (including civil rights and civil obligations) lay a perdurant substratum of "natural freedom." If a person stood under a civil obligation, such as paying a certain tax or performing certain labor, when that obligation ceased, jurists said that "natural freedom" was "recovered."[46] Philipp and Henricus gave a similar account when explaining part of the legal procedure in lawsuits about immunities. If a person alleges that he is free from paying a certain tax, even if he is the one to sue the lord or prince over the matter, the burden of proof would be on the lordly party – the defendant, the would-be tax collector – because *a person alleging that he is free enjoys "a presumption*

44 Ibid., Thesis 25, p. 24t; Theses 28–31, pp. 27–30.

45 Ibid., Thesis 24, pp. 22m–23t.

46 Harpprecht and Braun, *Tractatio iuridica de praescriptione immunitatis*, Cap. 2, §8, p. 21mb. From a Romanist perspective, this view adopted ancient civil law theories about natural law and natural freedom, although, being practical people, ancient Roman jurists did not develop these ideas extensively, unlike their medieval and modern heirs. And it should be borne in mind that none of these scholars regarded this development of rights as a specific national story, for example of special German rights and laws. When they reasoned about nature, they usually thought of the nature (freedom, consent, etc.) of all human beings.

of natural freedom." Specifically, the plaintiff claiming liberty was interpreted as having "quasi possession" ("like possession," *possessio vel quasi*) of such a freedom. Because this was "like possession," he enjoyed a number of available motions in civil court (called actions) to "protect" his possession.[47]

In the 1683/1688 construction of the law, there were limits to the prescription of freedom. One of these limits was the "case of public necessity." Harpprecht-Braun, Philipp-Henricus and other jurists wrote that prescribed freedoms against taxation could be suspended temporarily in the case of public necessity, usually understood to involve cases of war, public safety, or like peril. For example, Harpprecht & Braun wrote that in cases of war and plague, the validity of immunity is limited.[48] Philipp & Henricus and the leading contemporary scholar of Protestant church law, Justus Henning Böhmer, made similar remarks.[49] This condition may have been a common principle of jurisprudence in that period, a proviso that in times of crisis, normal functioning of expensive rights might be temporarily suspended in order to help the regime deal with the situation.[50] However, such a proviso does not appear in dozens of studies from the period of other legal topics such as debts, indemnity, or servitudes. This discrepancy may be due to what was at stake with freedoms from governmental extractions: revenue. In time of war, it matters little whether the normal process of, say, indemnifying an innocent party

---

47 A person might make possessory (see Chapter 4 above), use, and negatory actions and exceptions. See Philippi and Henricus, *De praescriptione immunitatis â tributis*, Theses 59–66, pp. 62–67, particularly Thesis 66, pp. 66–67. See Berger, *Encyclopedic Dictionary of Roman Law*, pp. 343–344, 593, 637–638 on negatory and possessory actions.

48 Harpprecht and Braun, *Tractatio iuridica de praescriptione immunitatis*, Cap. 4, §§18–19, pp. 138–139, and Cap. 7, §6, p. 164m.

49 Philipp and Henricus write that "The effect of immunity ceases, if the highest and extreme necessity of the republic urges the payment of taxes, since necessity does not have law, but rather laws themselves are subject to it." See Philippi and Henricus, *De praescriptione immunitatis â tributis*, Thesis 70, p. 72t; see also ibid., Thesis 46, p. 51t. Compare Justus Henning Böhmer, *Ius parochiale: ad fundamenta genuina revocatum a spuriis principiis purgatum atque ita adornatum ut ius ecclesiasticum protestantium illustrare et usum modernum libri tertii decretalium quoad praecipuas materias ostendere quest adiecto indice triplici et supplemento novo*, Editio Qvinta Avctior Et Emendatior ed. (Halle: Orphanotrophei, 1738 [orig. 1701]), Sect. 5, cap. 3, §§16–17, pp. 299mb–300t.

50 The principle that ordinary law is suspended in case of emergency dates back at least to the ancient Roman dictatorship. Several of Carl Schmitt's early works focus on this question. See his well-known *Political Theology: Four Chapters on the Concept of Sovereignty*, Studies in Contemporary German Social Thought (Cambridge: MIT Press, 1985 [orig. 1922]). The principle had previously been championed by major writers from Cicero to Machiavelli and Rousseau. The rank of various legal authorities (including matters of public necessity) is also discussed above at Ch. 3, p. 80 including in n. 11 and in Ch. 7, p. 299 including in n. 16.

against eviction from possession is honored. But the regime feels a special urgency to collect every last available *gulden* from the people of the *Land* in order to defeat the Turkish, Anabaptist, Papist, or imperial public enemy.

We might seek a geopolitical explanation for the new arguments about prescription of immunity that emerged in the 1680s. Note that one parameter in the 1680s argued was, against *whom* could prescription be gained? Earlier jurists in the sixteenth century like Andreas Gail had argued that no freedom could be gained through prescription against *imperial* obligations. Gail was a writer of *Kameralistik*, the study of the jurisprudence and procedures of the Imperial Chamber Court, the high appellate court of the empire. It should therefore not be surprising that he argued that prescription could not create rights of freedom against the emperor. That is, freedoms against imperial obligations could not simply be derived from operation of prescription according to the civil law, but rather could only arise through express law creation – grants, imperial statutes (*leges*) or judgments (*constitutiones*).[51] But after the Peace of Passau (1552), the imperial estates became more powerful and independent. The Thirty Years' War was in part a conflict between emperor and princes over the strength of imperial authority. Harpprecht & Braun and Philipp & Henricus were writing a few decades after the conclusion of peace in 1648, generally regarded by historians as marking the ascendance of princely authority at the expense of imperial authority. Their views would seem to reflect the emergent new status quo, in which rights could prescribe against the emperor; jurists, who were the creatures of universities patronized by princes, legitimized this view. The general need to quiet title after the disruptions of the War and, more urgently, the desire of princes to legitimate their authority against the emperor drove writers like Philipp & Henricus to justify 40-year prescription against imperial law, with or without imperial consent. The twin treatises on prescription of immunity from the 1680s reflect a relative *elevation of princely authority at the expense of imperial authority*. First, against Gail, Philipp & Henricus affirmed the position that that immunity can prescribe against the emperor and empire. Second, both Harpprecht & Braun and Philipp & Henricus place the prince (not the emperor) at the center of this contention of prescription of immunity. Clearly the site of disputation on this matter is not so much *before the emperor* as *before the prince*. This chiasmus reflects the growing importance of princely high courts, located in the regime centers and staffed by regime counselors. These princely courts in the late seventeenth and early eighteenth centuries increasingly gained effective

51 Harpprecht and Braun, *Tractatio iuridica de praescriptione immunitatis*, Cap. 4, §3, p. 110.

sovereign jurisdiction by taking appeals and frequently limiting further appeal to the Imperial Chamber Court or to the Aulic Counsel. Both Harpprecht & Braun and Philipp & Henricus restricted the possibility of prescribing immunity against princely authority – accepting it, but stipulating that it required not only time but also at some point recognition by the prince.

6 The Regalianism of Christian Thomasius

Three decades after the dissertations of the 1680s, the celebrated German jurist Christian Thomasius (Figure 44) took up the doctrine of prescription of freedoms constructed by Harpprecht-Braun and Philipp-Henricus, and asserted that the ability to gain freedom against extractions in this way was strictly limited. While Thomasius affirmed the foundation, value, and most of the parameters of prescription, he denied that prescriptive procedure could validate freedom against *princely* governmental authority. To the contrary, he argued, governmental rights in the major matters, such as the ability to levy taxes, were themselves inalienable and imprescriptible. The government could not alienate its authority to tax nor could it be lost (via an immunity against it gained) through prescription. As no royal right was unimportant, it was improper for any such right to be transferred from ruler to subject.

This dispute over prescription of immunities may seem rather obscure, but it reveals a fault line within the political and legal thought of the era. Was the prince above the law, not subject to the laws to which his subjects were subject? Or did the same law apply to all denizens of the realm, whether serf, common man, seigneur, priest, or prince? The views of the jurists from the 1680s (and later as well) varied. Highly regarded "sovereignty brokers"[52] (as liberal critic Johann Jakob Moser called advocates of the absolutist program) like Jean Bodin and Thomas Hobbes held the former view. Christian Thomasius, a major figure of the early German Enlightenment, regarded the monarch as being on a higher plane than his subjects. Thomasius's view can be thought of as a version of princely absolutism, in a synthesis of European public law and Aristotelian political science. Many jurists, however, favored the opposite position, approaching a kind of universal legal equality, albeit differentiated slightly by social estate, akin to modern constitutionalism: The ruler is bound

52 Johann Jacob Moser, "Von der Landeshoheit derer Teutschen Reichsstände überhaupt," in *Neues Teutsches Staatsrecht* (Frankfurt am Main; Leipzig: 1773), p. 256, quoted at Klippel, "True Concept of Liberty," p. 455.

FIGURE 44 Christian Thomasius

by the same basic law as anyone else, and the same reasoning should apply in interpreting his actions.

Along with Pufendorf and Christian Wolff, Thomasius (1655–1728) is considered to have been one of the "three leaders of the Law of Reason in Germany." Early on, Thomasius was influenced by the Christian Aristotelianism of his father, Jakob Thomasius, the teacher of Leibniz. Thomasius the son rose to become a famous reformer associated with the new University of Halle, which he helped to organize in its early years. Thomasius is considered important not for any major theoretical innovation but for a variety of reforming activities that clearly mark him as an Enlightenment figure. For example, he was the first to lecture in German rather than Latin. He argued against the use of torture in criminal procedure or in the persecution of witchcraft. He also staked out the radical position, based on Lutheran Pietism, that religion should be treated as a purely internal or personal matter. The latter argument had weighty consequences: in implying that the Church was purely "an external force," it undercut the validity of natural law, suggesting that positive law was far more important. At Halle, Thomasius became identified with the Erastian political teachings of that University.[53] Thomasius helped found the University of Halle in 1694 and became primary professor of law there and eventually rector. He also served as privy councilor to the Elector of Brandenburg. In 1696, he supervised a dissertation on how, if at all, subjects could gain immunity rights against princely authority. The student respondent of the dissertation was Georg Rudolph Schlösser.

7 Regalian Rights

Thomasius and Schlösser's dissertation addressed the question of how prescription could create or justify negative freedoms for subjects against their governments. They began by giving an account of governmental authority. Unlike the dissertations from the 1680s, however, they did not frame the question as one of acquiring or losing freedoms. Instead, they construed it as a question of the nature and limits of governmental authority. The public law of European monarchies typically held that there were a fixed set of rights, those associated with the royal authority of kings and emperors as well as those exercised by lower rulers like dukes and counts in the name of their imperial

53 What marked Pufendorf, Hobbes, Leibniz, Thomasius, and Wolff as Enlightenment thinkers was their criticism, vaguely in the name of reason, of religio-political orthodoxy (including that of the Lutheran states in which most of them dwelt and worked). "Links with any particular moral system with religion began to weaken. Rationalists attacked with ... fervor the established religion ... In the struggle for the individual's right to choose his religion, the grand idea of freedom of conscience first matured in Protestant lands ..." These moves would soon undermine the metaphysics of natural law, but that did not become clear until Kant in all likelihood. Wieacker, *History of Private Law*, pp. 239b–240t, p. 251t–252. This variety of contributions from the period has come to be known as eclecticism. See Friedrich Julius Stahl, *Die Kirchenverfassung nach Lehre und Recht der Protestanten* (Erlangen: Bläsing, 1840), p. 33, referred to in Robert Isaac Wilberforce, *A Sketch of the History of Erastianism: together with two sermons on the reality of Church Ordinances, and on the principle of Church Authority* (London: John Murray, 1851), pp. 35–36. On the eclecticism of Thomasius and other figures of the German Enlightenment, see Hochstrasser, *Natural Law Theories in Early Enlightenment*.

or royal lords. These rights were called regalia (*iura regalia*, royal rights).[54] The "major regalia" were usually said to be a monarch's authority to make war, to levy taxes, and to settle conflicts. Thomasius and Schlösser framed the regalian functions of government in the Aristotelian terms Thomasius had grown up with, under his father's teaching. Such functions were "to direct the actions of the citizens; to dispose of the republic's things; and making war and peace with foreigners, in order to achieve the goals of the city [that is, the commonwealth or realm]."[55] The activities of government served the internal and external "ends" of the "city" and its "citizens." Thus, for instance, "certain regalia pertain to the regime of the city or to the society of nations," especially the "right to make war ... take booty, make treaties, and send legates." Similarly, essential functions of government internal to the city were to keep the public peace (including to exercise power over life and death), "to appoint magistrates" and subordinate magistrates, to take final appeal, and to confer great dignities. It was commonly understood among jurists that regalian rights had been acquired by other rulers besides kings and emperors, namely by the numerous German princes such as the margrave of Brandenburg-Prussia or the landgrave of Hesse. These transfers of authority had happened through

54 Civilian, canonist and feudalist clerks employed by the emperors in the thirteenth and fourteenth centuries articulated a theory that "there were certain rights and functions which a kingdom had to exercise if it was to exist and flourish." Over time, the list of "regalian" functions or rights grew considerably, even into the hundreds. Functions attributed to the emperor in the thirteenth and fourteenth centuries include "the power to make universal law, to interpret a law equitably, to wage war, to create new taxes, and to sell property in which he had at least half interest ... Another great privilege ... was that over life and death ... the original sense of the *merum imperium* ["pure command"] ... the power to appoint local territorial rulers, control the ways of communication, the exclusive right to coin, control of the mines and revenues of judicial processes, regulation of loans upon taxes, and the right to command or rebuild a fortress wherever one had existed before ... the ... ability to enforce penalty for *crimen leasae majestatis* ... create notaries, legitimize bastards, and, in the case of the emperor, to sit as a court of appeal in judgment on the sentences of kings." *Merum imperium*, usually left untranslated in scholarship, was the original Roman public law term which denoted the authority of the Roman emperors, which was *de facto* unlimited. Hence *merum imperium* has often been considered the functional equivalent of sovereignty. See Peter N. Riesenberg, *Inalienability of sovereignty in medieval political thought* (New York: Columbia University Press, 1956), pp. 3, 7–8.

55 Thomasius and Schlösser, *De praescriptione regalium*, Cap. 1, §8. It was a mark of political Aristotelianism to speak of "the city" or "the republic" rather than a kingdom, state, society, polity, or other name for a political collectivity. But in the early modern Aristotelian science of politics, any of the common political unit names could be interpreted as a city – a lordship, a kingdom, an empire, a city, or town, even a family clan such as the Riedesel "republic" mentioned in Chapter 4.

"agreements, transactions, wartime occupation, and also by consent of the emperor both express and tacit" beginning in the thirteenth century.[56]

However, there was a key fault line within royal constitutional law. Many writers classified some royal activities as minor (the "minor regalia"). In one account, the minor regalia were those which are not "essential to the supreme power nor natural to it but may be naturally separated from it, or at least communicated to others." They included the power of "creating subaltern magistrates, conferring certain dignities, erecting [trade] fairs, legitimating bastards, granting the privilege of age, coining money, confiscating a criminal's estate and goods, appropriating to himself vacant estates, hunting, levying certain customs, and other things of the same nature."[57]

Thomasius adhered to a position, by his day in the minority among jurists, according to which no distinction could be drawn between major and minor regalia. One good reason for denying a distinction was that the Aristotelian framework of the ends of the city made no place for the twofold classification of major and minor functions of government. No purpose of the city was less important than any other. All governmental activities had to serve the common good.[58]

A consequence of this position was that no governmental activities were "minor" enough that they should be "lost" from rulers or "acquired" by subjects through prescription. Only actual rulers, who ruled a realm with the purpose

56 Ibid., Cap. 1, §12; Cap. 2, §3-§5, §8. Throughout the Holy Roman Empire, territorial *princes* had come to rightfully wield these *royal* rights. This was effected through several great agreements made (under the pressure of circumstances) by the German king – especially the Confoederatio cum principibus ecclesiasticis (1220) and the Statutum in favorem principum (1231/1232). "Between 1212 and 1250, [German interests were] sacrificed by Frederick [II] to the exigencies of control of Italy." "Germany took a road which differentiated its history for centuries to come ... from that of England and France; its destinies passed out of the hands of the monarchy into the control of a princely aristocracy, whose horizons rarely extended beyond the boundaries of their own territories, and whose policy showed scant respect for the common interests and traditions of the German people." As a result, regalian functions came to be exercised not only by emperor and king, but also by the dozens of princes in the imperial estates. See Barraclough, *The Origins of Modern Germany*, p. 237, p. 240. For early modern German political Aristotelianism, see Dreitzel, *Absolutismus und ständische Verfassung in Deutschland*, e.g. pp. 10, 133, 136.

57 These passages come respectively from Hugo Grotius and from his seventeenth-century editor Jean Barbeyrac. See Grotius, *Rights of War and Peace*, Book II, Chapter 4, §13, pp. 502–503 and note.

58 See Thomasius's editorial remarks in his edition of Ulrich Huber, *De Jure civitatis libri tres ... in usum auditorii Thomasiani* (Frankfurt am Main; Leipzig: Zeitler, 1708 [orig. 1694]), Lib. I. Sect. III. Cap. VI. Num. 3. pp. 91–92.

of serving the common good, should exercise any of the rights of rule (the regalia).

One of the major regalia was eminent domain (*dominium eminens*), the idea that the prince is the highest (most eminent) lord of all land and resources in the territory. In this early construction, the prince exercised eminent domain over two classes of things. One was all of the unowned (adespotic or "lord-less") things in the world such as fish, game, fowl, the underground, and other common pool resources. The second was public resources such as transportation networks (roads, rivers) and harbors.[59] However, in character with his enlightenment program to limit vague or unaccountable inherited institutions, Thomasius walled the applicability of eminent domain. Its exercise was restricted by its "final cause," "the city's ends," i.e. the flourishing of the realm's people (certainly not the private enjoyment of the ruler). And so eminent domain was appropriate only "to prevent … disturbances."[60] Thus, said Thomasius, it was licit for a prince to deprive subjects of their property rights (their dominions) only for public utility of the most urgent sort. On this ground, it was uncustomary for the prince to take people's existing private property.[61] Anything which the prince does not have in active control, along the foregoing lines, he has left to the "natural liberty" of subjects. Rather like with the arguments about acquisitive prescription of immunity four decades prior, one almost gets the sense here that Thomasius was doing jurisprudential gymnastics to produce a liberal jurisprudence consistent with Prussian autocracy tempered by the rising ideal of the *Rechtsstaat* (state based on the rule of law).

8 Regalia as Imprescriptible

To be sure, like their contemporaries, Thomasius and his student Schlösser readily accepted the value of prescription. It was, as they acknowledged, a valuable process since it helped to keep social peace:

---

59 "Things which [the jurisconsults] say are left in natural liberty are conceded to subjects when derelicted by the prince … This is most clear in the rights to hunt, fish, fowl, take nice things from sea and rivers, mine metals or salt from private fields, treasure discovered in public places." See Thomasius and Schlösser, *De praescriptione regalium*, Cap. II, §6. For the commons, see ibid. Cap. II, §§2–4. For the language of "*adespota*," see Estor, "Belehnung tilget die *res merae facultatis*."

60 For instance, the prince had the right to impose special tribute or other *vectigalia* if the means from the domains or fisc did not suffice "to suppress threat and protect life and property." See Thomasius and Schlösser, *De praescriptione regalium*, Cap. II, §§7–8.

61 "It is not customary for princes to disturb subjects in their enjoyment of things." See ibid., Cap. II, §12.

> Prescription is … the acquisition of lordship accomplished through long quiet and uninterrupted possession, such that society is not disturbed … The end for which prescription was introduced is this, that the public tranquility and human society may be preserved.[62]

But prescription was appropriate only in some areas. It applied, they argued, within "the civil chain," that is, commerce among subjects at private law.[63] Prescription could govern the holding of various ordinary private rights, including real rights in land or servitude. Fundamentally, however, the authors argued, governmental rights such as declaring war and peace or settling legal disputes were inherently *inalienable* and *imprescriptible*. They could not be permanently transferred to subjects, either by active concession or passively through prescription, since such a transfer would conflict with the ability of the ruler to achieve the ends of the city through the exercise of appropriate powers. Given the role that prescription played in the prior jurisprudence on this topic, to assert this position Thomasius had to deny or at least sharply curtail the applicability of prescription and custom to regalian rights. Thus he argued that the public law of monarchy does not alter over time, and the exercise of regalian rights is a function of legal authority–the passage of time could not ripen possession or practice. As a consequence, princely regalian rights were essentially indefeasible, inalienable, and "by … nature imprescriptible."[64]

> Subjects are obliged to turn over to its rightful possessor a thing they possess, even after time immemorial. Here is manifest not the power of time, but the power of broad laws [*legum latarum*] over a possession of which there does not even exist memory. The prince has not bound himself by these laws, in order that a right come to exist thus for his subjects, since he makes laws for others, not for himself.[65]

This is a striking and concise articulation of the legal theory of absolutism, according to which the monarch is *absolutus*, that is, "released" from the law. Several senses of the terms law (*lex*) and right (*ius*) are employed here. Rulers rule by what is sometimes called public law, similar to what is today called a constitution, the fundamental "law" of a political collectivity. It differs in kind

62 Ibid., Cap. 1, §4.

63 The "chain" in question would appear to be the metaphor of the "chain of possession." In the metaphor, possessors are like so many links in a chain.

64 Thomasius and Schlösser, *De praescriptione regalium*, Cap. 1, §13; Cap. 3, §2, §7, §11. At ibid., Cap. 3, §18, the authors buttress the point that "passage of time does not right a wrong" – i.e. the wrongful exercise of or resistance to governmental authority.

65 Ibid., Cap. 3, §7.

from the laws which govern what individual legal subjects are allowed to do, such as criminal law or the law of contracts, and from private rights such as property rights (*iura*).

Today we are accustomed to say that even political officers such as a state president are themselves "subject" to the same law as everyone else. But in early modern constitutional monarchies, one would not say that the ruler was subject to the ordinary civil law; as the authors wrote above, "he makes laws for others, not for himself." The public law which constituted the ruler's authority, including the ruler's concomitant regalian rights, could never, they argued, be extinguished or abolished through mere prescriptive processes.

Moreover, neither in the common civil law nor in the "law of all peoples" (*ius gentium*) could subjects gain rights against the ruler, either tacitly or through active alienation. As a consequence, lawsuits by subjects making rights claims against governmental burdens were also improper. It followed from Thomasius's princely-supremacist argument that *no immunities, including freedoms from common burdens like taxes or labor service against governmental authority, could be gained by subjects of the realm.* No immunity could arise independent of the prince's express arrangement. As a consequence, the authors averred, all special grants of right from a ruler – that is, all privileges and immunities – are weak, being revocable at the ruler's pleasure.[66]

To be sure, regalian functions could be exercised by people other than the prince or his authorized magistrates. But this was only a matter of deputization, a temporary lending of authority. Deputization could never ripen into title.[67] The concession of regalian rights is not permanent,

> even to a person to whom it has come by prescription. For the public good, regalia which have been conceded can always be revoked, no different than the way a *precarium* is revocable at any time.

Neither the technical process of prescription nor any kind of claims of custom could ever detract from the ruler's authority. It was imprescriptible and only alienable through explicit, authorized transfer to other proper rulers, such as emperor to prince.[68]

The Thomasius-Schlösser dissertation reveals a tension in the legal theory of the period. The earlier work of Harpprecht-Braun and Philipp-Henricus

66 Ibid., Cap. 3, §§4–6, §15, §16.

67 "Even if detained by subject for a time, [the major regalia] remain annexed to the highest majesty and revocable at will." See ibid., Cap. 3, §2-§3.

68 Ibid., Cap. 3, §9, §10, §15. A *precarium* is something which one grants precariously, at will, and is at will revocable, such as granting someone permission to cross your land.

sought to stabilize the concrete order of vested rights and interests in society in the decades after the Thirty Years' War by applying Grotius's natural law of prescription to ordinary civil rights of freedom against rulers' levies. They asserted that prescription could obtain against local seigneurs and against the far-away emperor. They vouchsafed more security to the rights of princes themselves, the important middlemen in the federated structure of governing authority in the empire, holding that freedoms against the prince could obtain through prescription if recognized at some point by the ruler himself. However, Thomasius and Schlösser used the paradigm of Aristotelian political science to curtail the applicability of prescription to princes' authority, arguing that the ends of government required that all governmental functions, including imposing levies on subjects, must remain permanently and inalienably in the hands of rulers, always at their disposal. No rights of freedom against such impositions could ever implicitly arise through prescription and were in any event always revocable, in the name of the common good.

9 Too Machiavellian?

For Thomasius, it was never a question whether the territorial civil law could constrain the prince. And Thomasius was hardly alone in this view of monarchical authority over a territory or realm. As mentioned earlier, there were many "sovereignty brokers" before, during, and after the period we are considering. A near contemporary of Thomasius, Justus Henning Böhmer (mentioned earlier), was one of them. Böhmer presented the Lutheran position that the prince simply had certain competencies, which gave him unlimited authority, over any law in the realm within that domain, such as "competency over sacred things," i.e. the supervision of religion.[69]

But others disagreed. One was a fellow Saxon, Carl Ferdinand Hommel, "sometime public lecturer on feudal law and the *Institutes* in Leipzig, as well as member of the law faculty and the High Princely Court [*Oberhofgericht*] in Leipzig."[70] Another prominent critic was Johann Cramer, the Hessian jurist who eventually became a judge at the Imperial Chamber Court. We met Cramer (Figure 45) first as the author of the decision about natural free-

69 Foremost among them, the prince must protect the realm and care for sacred things. However, Böhmer was ambiguous about freedom of conscience and the free internal jurisdiction of Protestant churches.

70 Carl Ferdinand Hommel, *Akademische Reden über Herrn Joh. Jacob Mascovs Buch De Iure Feudorum in Imperio Romano Germanico* (Frankfurt *am Main*: 1758), Cap. IX, p. 290.

dom discussed at the beginning of Chapter 1. Cramer joined the debate about the acquisition of freedoms through prescription in 1740. In his essay on the "Acquisition of an Immunity through Prescription,"[71] Cramer initially staked out a clear position against Thomasius, reaffirming the position of Harpprecht, Braun, Philippi, and Henricus that the ruler's authority and rights could be circumscribed through prescription, even in the high matters of taxation, "the sinews of power." Subsequently, Cramer took a more centrist position. In a later version of the writing to be examined here, he added a new concluding section in which he affirmed that major regalia were imprescriptible, a middle ground between the arguments of the 1680s jurists and the more recent ones of Thomasius.

"Acquisition of an Immunity through Prescription" was published when Cramer became a Court Counselor (*Hofrat*) and republished while he was a member of the Imperial Chamber Court. The essay opened by stating that considerable dissent had arisen in the past several decades over whether, via prescription, subjects could acquire freedom against taxes or labor service owed to an ordinary lord or to the territorial government. Cramer offered a sharp rejoinder to Thomasius (who had died twelve years earlier):

> There is a crazy notion among many subjects that, just because they have never borne or known about or been subjected to or paid a certain burden, they should thereby be free of it. Many jurists say, contrariwise, that no one can actually gain freedom against public burdens through prescription. [Sc. The latter is the view held by] ... the jurists who agree with Thomasius, that there can be no prescription against the prince. And while not all [sc. jurists] cultivate this Machiavellianism [*Machiavellismum*], still there are many who do not concede that immunity can be acquired, even where burdens have been imposed, the subjects refused, and the lord let it go. This division among jurists has the not small consequence, especially in matters of taxation and other burdens, of encouraging many expensive lawsuits.[72]

---

71 Johann Ulrich Cramer, *Kurtze doch überführende Abhandlung von Erlangung einer Immunitaet durch Verjährung: wodurch zugleich die von ihm über Herrn Carl Friederich Neckers, J.P.P. auf der Hohen Schule zu Genff kurtzen und aus denen eigentlichen rechten Quellen hergeleiteten Unterricht in dem Staats-Recht des Heil. Römischen Reichs Teutscher Nation den 22ten April um 10. Uhr anzufangende Lectiones Privatae eröffnet werden* (Marburg: Philipp Casimir Müller, univ. Buchdr., 1740).

72 See Cramer, "Abhandlung von Erlangung einer Immunität durch Verjährung," §1, p. 174mb. There Cramer also refers the reader further to his *Observationes juris universi ex praxi recentiori supremorum imperii tribunalium haustarum* (Wetzlar: Ph. J. Winckler, 1758–1772), Vol. DLII.

FIGURE 45 Johann Ulrich Cramer, well pleased

Articulating his own moderate position, Cramer dedicated himself in the essay to arguing against Thomasius's "Machiavellian" position. In a later essay, Cramer used equally harsh language to describe that view, calling it a "lawless and capricious art of ruling" and writing that it had "no place" in the empire.

> While many more recent jurists, especially Thomasius, let no prescription work against the territorial lord in tax matters, even of time immemorial, so has this new discovery of a wholly lawless and capricious

Joh. Ulr. Freyherrn von Cramer,
Kayserl. und des Reichs=Cammer=Gerichts=Assessoris,
Wetzlarische
Nebenstunden,
worinnen
auserlesene, beym Höchstpreißlichen
Cammergericht entschiedene Rechts=
Händel
zur
Erweiter= und Erläuterung der Deutschen
in Gerichten üblichen Rechts=Gelehrsamkeit
angewendet werden.
Neun und siebenzigster Theil.

POSSUNT SED NON VOLUNT

Ulm, 1768.
Verlegts Johann Conrad Wohler.

FIGURE 46 Title page of Volume 79 of Cramer's *Wetzlarische Nebenstunden*

art of ruling found absolutely no approval in the German empire. Rather it has been fundamentally rejected by Harpprecht and many others.[73]

73 Johann Ulrich Cramer, "Ob geistliche Fürsten immunitatem ab oneribus publicis, in specie Collectis, auch in praejudicium derer übrigen Unterthanen in perpetuum, ohne

Echoing the two-century-old idea of the Free German Empire we considered in Chapter 2, for Cramer the German empire was a realm or state which is lawful and in which capricious rule is unconstitutional – against the fundamental law. The constitutional principle is lawfulness and regularity; to breach it is caprice. Neither Cramer nor any previous jurist had asserted that princely authority waned simply through the passage of years: For his authority to lessen required "first the denial and then the acquiescence of the territorial prince."[74] Nor did jurists think that monarchy as such was the root of capricious rule. The political and legal theory of this period was almost uniformly monarchical (this can even be said in a certain sense of republican polities like cities).[75] Instead, the key issue for Cramer was the extent to which princes could limit their own authority, that is, implicitly or explicitly give up their own authority in certain spheres. That possibility was what Thomasius had rejected and Cramer would now affirm.

Cramer rejected Thomasius's position of imprescriptible princely authority, naming it "lawless" because it had sidestepped the seventeenth-century body of authoritative jurisprudence about prescription. As noted above, Thomasius-Schlösser had argued that princely authority could never be lost or limited through the passage of time, it could not be abandoned, and it could not be given away. Against this position, Cramer argued that princely authority was *not* higher than law. Rather, princes *live by law*.[76] That means that law also is *the condition or ground of princely action*. Hence if a prince gave something away, then by law he no longer owned it.

One might say that Thomasius had tried to put aside part of natural law and Cramer called it back. From the remove of almost three centuries, Cramer's

---

Consens des Capituls, ertheilen können, wann die Exemtion ob bene merita geschiehet?," in *Wetzlarische Nebenstunden*, Vol. 26 (Vols. 25–28 bound in one codex) (Ulm: Johann Conrad Wohler, 1761 [orig. 1757]), §15, p. 21m.

74 Cramer, "Abhandlung von Erlangung einer Immunität durch Verjährung," §15, p. 179; see also the new §20 added in the 1754 edition.

75 Even the urban republicanism/communalism of the towns and cities throughout Europe was usually founded on the ancient-constitutionalist principle that they enjoyed their urban privileges by rightful ancient grant from the German-Roman emperor. The good old law conveniently supported urban liberties. The fact that Rousseau founded his democratic republicanism in the mid eighteenth century on social contract theory, and not on ancient constitutionalism, is what made it so radical – not the fact that it was urban republicanism (that was old hat).

76 Thomasius and Schlösser had in fact quoted the old legal commonplace that "Legibus principes vivunt," "princes live by [or from] laws." See Thomasius and Schlösser, *De praescriptione regalium*, Cap. II, §13. The locus classicus of this idea is Digna Vox in Justinian's Code (1.14.4), in which Emperors Theodosius and Valentinian announced in 429 that "our authority depends on the authority of the law. For greater even than empire is to subject the principate to laws." I thank Constantin Fasolt for this reference.

intervention seems in effect to *re-activate the earlier doctrine constructed by Harpprecht and Philippi*.[77] Philippi had argued that subjects could gain freedom – that is, defensible, negative rights – against princely authority.[78] Cramer not only generally affirmed this position, but specified how and when such immunization happened: if the prince or prince's magistrate knows about the contradiction, and suffers it, then this activates acquisitive prescription:

> What concerns particularly immunity from taxes [*Collectis*], it is clear to see that one can *not* generally say that immunity from taxes can be acquired *without* first the denial and then the acquiescence of the territorial prince. Rather, this requirement must always be present, anytime one is aware that something had in the past ever been taxable. Obviously this is not required if there is no such knowledge, or, in things that are taxable, one was in fact never taxed on it before.[79]

In general, adverse possession is required to gain any kind of guarantee of freedom against a tax, unless there is no trace of it in the past, either in general or at least for the person pretending to the freedom.[80]

Perhaps to show the limitation of this framework, in the second edition of his essay, published in 1754 when he was a judge in the Imperial Chamber Court, Cramer added three new sections, including the following:

> It should be clear that the non-exercise of regalian rights alone does not put subjects in possession of a freedom from associated burdens. For it rests in the arbitrary will of the territorial lord, to use or to not use a regalian right, and as a consequence, to demand those burdens from subjects …[81]

---

77 This is an instance of legal change through voice-supersession, or one voice of authority superseding another. See Wilder, "Teaching Old Dogs New Tricks," pp. 14–16.

78 Philippi and Henricus, *De praescriptione immunitatis â tributis*, Thesis 24, pp. 22m–23t; ibid., Thesis 41, p. 42t.

79 Cramer, "Abhandlung von Erlangung einer Immunität durch Verjährung," §15, p. 179t.

80 Immunity against service to a lord, Cramer argued, generally could be gained through simple prescription – that is, peaceful exercise. But if service was standing – that is, ongoing – then an obliged party obviously could not simply desist and claim prescription. For standing service, a *contradiction* (resistance to a claim) was necessary, followed by acquiescence by the lord. See ibid., §11, pp. 176–177; this is moreover the thesis of §16, which contains one of the text's three long excerpts.

81 Ibid., §18, p. 192. The original version (1740) contains a different version of §18, essentially just an afterward about how the lectures were published rather than a substantive argument.

In other words, quiet possession was insufficient, since princely regalia were "perpetual rights"[82] which might be exercised only occasionally. But Cramer also argued that contradiction and acquiescence do suffice to prescribe immunity against princely regalia. In summary, he circumscribed *subjects' freedom* by making princely authority imprescriptible by pure lapse of time, but he also circumscribed *princely authority* by affirming that it could be blocked through either alienation or adverse possession. Cramer thus linked this seemingly unremarkable topic of the prescription of taxes and rights to questions of sovereignty and constitutional prudence at the highest level. This echoed the English construction of law's supremacy over unlimited princely authority begun by Edward Coke a century earlier.[83]

•••

Much of the jurisprudence from the seventeenth and eighteenth centuries – *not* that which has been examined here – took what we may call the old-fashioned approach to immunities, namely interpreting them as "noble." And to be sure, in other writings some of the jurists whose work is discussed in this book did engage with the conception of immunity as "noble" (where noble, free, and immune are almost synonymous).[84] In that view, part of what could be called the pre-modern social contract, the nobility and clergy enjoyed tax immunities connected to their real estate holdings because of the special role that these social groups played in society: Nobles fought to protect society and the clergy administered the sacred.[85] The activities and jurisprudence

82 Ibid., §20, p. 202m.

83 For Coke and the rule of law in England, see Berman, *Law and Revolution II*, pp. 238–240.

84 An example of considering immunities as noble estates, even amid transfer of estates on a real estate market in the eighteenth century, is Johann Ulrich Cramer, "Ob ein Landes-Herr Immunitatem ab oneribus publicis, in specie Collectis, auch in praejudicium der übrigen Unterthanen ertheilen könne, wenn die Exemtion ob bene merita geschieht?," in *Wetzlarische Nebenstunden*, Vol. 24 (Ulm: Johann Conrad Wohler, 1761).

85 Otto Brunner offered a nuanced historical critique of this premodern social contract. According to Brunner, the basic functionalism of the multi-estate pre-modern social contract view was correct enough. But in reality there were additional parties (ruler and towns), who appeared in various configurations and guises, with historically contingent causality, and governed by actual contracts like Magna Charta. Such actual contracts specified exact rights and duties often well outside of the ideal type of the premodern social contract. These actual contracts often were created as grand bargains between conflicting parties, in effect marking the change from an old order and set of arrangements to a new order with new arrangements. The notion of a simple triptych of three estates was a pleasant picture created by kings, especially French ones, to publicly advertise a story of

examined in this chapter strike quite a different chord, however. The jurisprudence discussed here omits any consideration of the special roles of nobility or clergy, or indeed any role assumed to be played by the holder of immunity-bearing real estate.

Instead, the relevant context for the new immunity jurisprudence was the Thirty Years' War. During the period from 1648 to 1786, people developed greater freedom from extractions – most notably in the form of new freedoms from taxation. The chaos and loss of information triggered by the Thirty Years' War resulted in a period of legal and political uncertainty. Common subjects exploited this uncertainty to ignore the demands of their landlords and rulers. The regimes in Marburg and Cassel complained about non-payment of dues and taxes, but levies did not improve until the resolution of the ruler-estates conflict in 1655 with the Princely Resolutions. Similarly, update work on the Economic State project did not really commence in earnest until much later. Meanwhile, people allegedly avoiding their payment obligations eventually sold or mortgaged their estates to others, or died and the estates were inherited. Through such quotidian, natural processes, new ideas about what was or was not owed on an estate arose. This led to conflicts between *lords* claiming they were owed dues or taxes or services and *possessors of estates or exercisers of activities or claimants of freedoms*. These conflicts made their way into the courts. Jurists were charged not only with the task of ruling on the specific cases in their dockets but also with the challenge of developing broader resolutions to the types of legal challenge these conflicts represented. In Hesse and in other regions around this time, courts struggled with how to respond to both the volume and complexity of these challenges. On the one hand, common subjects were probably sometimes breaking the law by arrogating new rights. On the other, the sheer number of these actions, and frequent lack of legal evidence to contest their actions, made it difficult, if not impossible, to enforce previously existing law. During the period from about 1680 to 1750, jurists sought to address the problem using legal concepts, especially the doctrine of prescription, to establish a clear legal framework for resolving suits in order to decrease the need for future litigation related to extractions. The use of prescription to resolve this problem represented the use of a legal fiction to justify the existing order and minimize destabilizing

three, stable elements who each served its role in a greater harmony, implicitly under the rule of their king above them. See Otto Brunner, "Feudalism: The History of a Concept," in *Lordship and Community in Medieval Europe: Selected Readings*, ed. Fredric L. Cheyette (New York: Holt Rinehart and Winston, 1968 [orig. 1956]). I take the term *premodern social contract* from Constantin Fasolt.

legal and political conflict. Jurists focused on the fact that immunity was a real right, appertaining to real estate, under private civil law. As such, it was governed by the well-developed jurisprudence of imperial common law (*ius commune*) as well as by the theories of natural freedom and supreme princely or territorial authority. In prescription theory, the prescriptive acquisition of a freedom in civil law was treated, through a legal fiction, as an implicit grant of that freedom on the part of the ruler against whom the freedom was enjoyed. The freedom so prescriptively acquired was interpreted as the re-emergence of a person's natural freedom. We could say that all seven of the writers behind the works discussed above shared a basic liberal jurisprudence, in that they all held that natural freedom slept beneath civil law including the concrete order of property rights. A person claiming a civil liberty to not have to pay something or perform a certain onerous activity hence enjoyed a presumption of natural liberty. However, Thomasius sought to curtail this form of freedom against princely government by arguing that European public law (part of the *ius commune*) and Aristotelian political science set strict limits on where and how prescription could curtain princely authority when the public good was at stake. The 1680s authors spoke of prescribing freedoms, while Thomasius refocused the debate on the imprescriptibility of rulers' authority (regalia). This conflict of frames reflects an underlying disagreement over the limits of a ruler's lawful authority and its relationship to ordinary civil law. Cramer's liberalism flashed here in his rhetorically describing Thomasius's position as Machiavellian, since it did not recognize lawful limits on rulers' authority.[86]

86 Recall that it was also Cramer who wrote or at least anthologized the imperial chamber court decision which was used as the opening vignette in Chapter 1, in which monopoly licensing claims are criticized (indeed ridiculed) for extending too far into individual natural freedom.

CHAPTER 6

Free Use of Paper Money

> Merchants act on the basis of equity and goodness.
>
> DAVID MEVIUS (Lübeck, 1642)[1]

•••

> Money is coined liberty.
>
> FYODOR DOSTOYEVSKY (St. Petersburg, 1860)[2]

This chapter puts in place the final kind of freedom which Germans gained in the late seventeenth and eighteenth centuries, something I call the free use of paper money. *Paper money* is a loose term denoting anything that acts like money but is made of paper rather than precious metal (or other non-paper material). *Money* is today usually said to have three functions: to serve as a medium of exchange, a store of value, and a unit of account. It might be more abstractly and succinctly defined as a means "to move economic value across time and space."[3] Like the free disposition of estates and freedom from extractions, the free use of paper money was not entirely new in the seventeenth century, but rather had old roots. It is tricky to speak of exactly when

1 "Inter mercatores ex aequo et bono agitur." See David Mevius, *Commentarii in jus lubecense libri quinque*, 4th ed. (Frankfurt am Main; Leipzig: Joachim Wildius & Johannes Heinrich Richter, 1700 [orig. 1642]), p. 900, number 3, quoted in Carl Eduard Morstadt, *Commentar über das Handelsrecht Deutschlands und Frankreichs*, Vol. 1 (Heidelberg: Verlag von Julius Groos, 1849), p. 156. Mevius repeated variations on this principle in several places; compare p. 594, *summaria*, number 10, and p. 596, number 10.

2 Quoted in Glyn Davies, *A History of Money: From Ancient Times to the Present Day*, 3rd, revised ed. (Cardiff: University of Wales Press; Julian Hodge Bank Limited, 1994), p. 656.

3 For the history of money, see John F. Chown, *A History of Money: From AD 800* (London; New York: Routledge, 1994); Saifedean Ammous, *The Bitcoin Standard: The Decentralized Alternative to Central Banking* (Hoboken, New Jersey: John Wiley & Sons, Inc, 2018), Chapters 1–3, especially pp. 1–31, is especially clear on the functional determinants of sound (hard) money in contrast to easy money. The quotation comes from ibid., Chapter 1, p. 1.

 | DOI:10.1163/9789004685178_007

paper money was invented or how to measure its growth, because it had been used by small merchant communities in Europe since perhaps the thirteenth century, but not by the majority of people until the late eighteenth or early nineteenth centuries. Also like the free disposition of estates and freedom from extractions, the freedom offered by paper money was increasingly valued and sought after, and spread to become ever more widely held. Also like other freedoms, this freedom was spread through several quite different means operating simultaneously – state policy, the jurisprudence of myriad semi-independent but networked legal operators, and the anarchic, self-interested activity of numerous ordinary people. And this freedom, like all the others discussed in different levels of detail in this book, contributed to Germans' sense of their freedom by the time of Kant and the late Enlightenment.

More specifically, this chapter tells a German part of the broader story of the growth of paper money in the early modern period, in the form of the *bill of exchange*.[4] The complex structure of bills will be explained further below, but in a nutshell they can be thought of as functioning like circulating promissory notes or IOUs, transferable from one person to another. The making, use, and settling of bills was governed by a body of law called the *law of exchange* (*Wechselrecht, ius cambialis*), where "exchange" refers not to the fact that the paper instrument itself changed hands so much as that it originally involved

4 A very detailed but still accessible source on the law of exchange at its high point, and in its rich complexity, comes from the Marburg Privy Councilor, Vice Chancellor, and Professor of Law, Johann Heinrich Christian von Selchow (r. 1782–1795), although he produced the lectures at the height of his previous posting as extraordinary professor of law at the University of Göttingen. See his *Grundsätze des Wechselrechts* (op. cit.). Very helpful in this are lecture notes to Selchow, published by a student in his course on the law of exchange in Göttingen, Heinrich Gottfried Wilhelm Daniels, much later after the end of the Napoleonic period and in the new era of legal positivism in Germany. Daniels's account integrates Selchow's overview with the Prussian General Territorial Law of 1794 and the French code de commerce of 1807. See Heinrich Gottfried Wilhelm Daniels, *Grundsätze des Wechselrechts: Nach Herrn von Selchow, mit besonderer Rücksicht auf das Allgemeine preußische Landrecht und das französische Handelsgesetzbuch* (Cologne: Bachem, 1827). Selchow himself said (see his §11) that the best sources in his own day on the law of exchange were Johannes Christophorus Franck, *Institutiones iuris cambialis: ex legibus cambialibus diversum gentium indole negociationis moribus campsorum ac iure communi nova methodo collectae … L.* 1 (Halle: Novum Bibliopolium, 1721), Johann Gottlieb Siegel's introduction to his own co-edited source volume, *Corpus juris cambialis, das ist: Vollständiges Sammlung derer auf den vornehmsten Handels-Plätzen auch anderer Orte in Europa üblichen allerneuesten Wechsel-Ordungen (etc.)* (Leipzig: Johann Samuel Heinsius, 1742–1757), Theil II, pp. 371 ff., and Johann Gottlieb Heineccius, *Elementa iuris cambialis: commoda auditoribus methodo adornata* (Amsterdam: Iansonius Waesberg, 1742).

the exchanging[5] of an amount of one currency into another amount of a second currency; bills were originally used in long-distance, cross-border trade around Europe and the Levant. The law of exchange was said to be a part of the *law merchant* (merchant law, *lex mercatorum*), a set of practices used by merchants in their dealings including privileges they often enjoyed given them by local rulers who encouraged their activities.

Once again, recovery after the Thirty Years' War is the real starting point of this story. Prior to the early seventeenth century, the law of exchange was used only by merchant communities in trading hubs such as Antwerp, Amsterdam, Paris, London, Hamburg, Florence, and Genoa. This list should be extended to the numerous other cities where long-distance merchants lived or visited, keeping in touch with one another along trade and communication routes. The more important point is that in this way the law of exchange was restricted spatially and demographically to a tiny portion of the European (and German) population. Wartime refugees from the Netherlands brought new rules around the use of bills to England and Germany in the early seventeenth century. After the Thirty Years' War, the imperial diet adopted the law of exchange in order to help the settlement of wartime debts. In the coming decades, numerous cities and states around the empire and in Europe more broadly adopted the law of exchange, some slowly, some quickly, spurred by the belief that doing so would aid economic development. Hesse adopted the law of exchange piecemeal in 1721 and then tinkered with its application over the following half century. As in Chapter 4, we again see a pattern of state actors initially trying to restore an old order fallen away in the War, and then over the following century shifting toward subtle legal innovations, often cloaked in the fictions of legal traditionalism, to recognize and legitimate new transfers and uses of property in commerce, with an eye to economic growth and state power.

State fiscal interests played an important part in these developments as did a great concern for stability and security of credit. Despite the persistence of ideas about the proper role and position of social estates[6] (such as Christians, Jews, merchants, women, and farmers), the class concerns of the regime declined through the mid eighteenth century. As with their treatment of legal tools for real estate (Chapter 4), regimes began to be more interested in economic growth of territorial wealth than in class restrictions. This shift reflected the influence of new economic theory on policymakers and jurists. Beyond

---

5 "Exchange" translates German *Wechsel* and Latin *cambium* < *cambiare*, to exchange, barter, or change money.

6 See glossary.

natural resources and agricultural production, policy-makers and rulers understood that the wealth of nations also required commercial activity. That meant merchants and markets. Which meant pluralism and a general liberalization of rules about who could engage in trade. Or, perhaps states backed into liberalization more accidentally. Hesse-Cassel pursued cameralist surveillance of domains and estates for the sake of collecting dues and taxes. Accepting the equivalent of copyhold tenure[7] and the broad application of simplified rules of possession and prescription legitimated the burgeoning mutations of the grey economy, which were proving too complex and dynamic for ponderous, unreliable state surveys to keep up with much less correct.

And so it was that the extension of the law of exchange, meaning the use of bills in commercial activities and investment, brought with it a new and different kind of freedom to people who had not enjoyed it before, especially professionals, women, other non-merchant members of the intelligentsia, then the bourgeoise more broadly, and eventually more or less everyone in society. It would not be too much to say that, as law merchant was broadly adopted into the territorial constitution of states like Brandenburg-Prussia, Hesse-Cassel, or Hesse-Darmstadt, a more general conception of legal subjecthood was emerging. The generic legal person was someone (man or woman) mentally competent and not under the domination of another person or power in society.

Through all of this, there is an interesting philosophical ambiguity – did freedom lead to the growth of money and markets? Or was money a sort of fertilizer (cause) of freedom?[8] Or is money more like an expression or measure of freedom?[9] The theoretical connection between capitalism and freedom has

---

7 See above Ch. 5, p. 195 n. 32 for the copyhold comparison and Ch. 4, p. 175 for a comparison with the English Tenures Abolition Act.

8 Historians, anthropologists, economists, and political scientists have advanced a variety of arguments about what dynamics the advent of money brings about when it is adopted. For example, one strain associated with the Left, found recently in David Graeber's work, argues that money makes hierarchical obligations fungible and leads invariably to debt peonage and debt slavery. Montesquieu argued that the advent of paper money made it much harder for rulers to confiscate their subjects' monetary wealth and thus reduced some of the harshness of regimes' rapacity. I discuss the latter argument below at Ch. 6, p. 287.

9 As Georg Simmel wrote, "Money, as an intermediate link between man and thing, enables man to have … an abstract existence, a freedom from direct concern with things and from a direct relationship to them, without which our inner nature would not have the same chances of development." See his *The Philosophy of Money* (London; New York: Routledge, 1978 [orig. 1900]), p. 474.

been drawn by both left and right political theorists of the twentieth century.[10] It certainly seems that the general use of money in relatively free markets for goods and services is unthinkable without at least a significant sphere of civil liberty to transact or not to transact, and to bargain over prices and conditions. All of this of course on its own has nothing to do with many other kinds of freedom people might want to enjoy, or other important rights (such as the franchise or protection against police oppression) or associated political goods like peace, justice, openness, responsible government, or written constitutions. We are getting far ahead of 1648 or even of 1804, but the connection between money and freedom is present in this chapter and remains mysterious and thought-provoking.

1 Paper Money, Bills of Exchange, and Political Economic Ideas

Bills of exchange played a big role in the growth of paper money, itself a recent chapter in the long history of currency. Hard money – coins of precious metal – has been freely circulating for perhaps 2,500 years. Paper has been used in the West as an instrument to hold and transmit monetary value for perhaps 700 years. While not inherently valuable for their material composition, paper instruments had the novel virtue of being more secure and less difficult and expensive to use than precious metal. The use of paper instruments, from notes to bills, demand deposits, national debt bonds, or shares of companies, came to different parts of Europe and its colonies at different times in the period from about 1300 to 1800. Since about 1700, paper instruments have become ever more liquid, that is to say, easily and securely transferable, as merchants and policymakers refined the rules governing them. In the nineteenth century, European governments began to issue permanently circulating "bank notes" from national banks, redeemable on demand – the first appearance of paper money. What historian Glyn Davies writes about the history of money and bills in England is roughly true also for Germany, albeit the latter running 30–50 years later: Bills of exchange were, Davies writes, an "early

10 Karl Popper, *The Open Society and its Enemies* (London: Routledge, 1945); Milton Friedman, *Capitalism and Freedom* (Chicago: University of Chicago Press, 1962). Consider also the political ideals of the *Open Society* Foundation of today. A scholar whose work connects freedom, property, and economic growth is Douglass North; see for instance his "The Paradox of the West," in *The Origins of Modern Freedom in the West*, ed. Richard W. Davis (Stanford: Stanford University Press, 1995), which argues that the reason European courts developed from protecting property to also protecting people is that economic growth in the long run is tied to personal freedom.

form of credit." By the mid to late eighteenth century, all over Europe including in Germany, bills had come to "perform three functions – they transmit funds, they provide credit, and they supply holders with a most convenient and highly liquid reserve …" That is, bills functioned as both a medium of exchange and a means of storing value. By the late eighteenth century, "bills were also used as currency in London, and even more so in parts of Lancashire and Yorkshire, until banknotes and cheques took their place" in the nineteenth century."[11] It is not clear to me, and it is outside the scope of this book, when bills came similarly to be actually used on an everyday basis like currency in Germany. This chapter chronicles the beginning stages of that phenomenon, but its culmination probably took place during or after the Napoleonic Wars or the Restoration.

A bill was a form of credit, but it was not secured credit in the sense of pledged collateral (like a pawn or mortgage). In a secured debt, the creditor has possession of the collateral against which the loan is secured. In case of default, the possession converts to ownership. The defaulting debtor has no free space of play to try to evade conveying the collateral since the creditor already holds it. Alternatively, sometimes a creditor could be given possession of fruits or revenues deriving from fruits (e.g. crops) deriving from the debtor's property, to service the outstanding debt principal. Unsecured lending was more risky to the lender since he did not take possession of collateral and therefore could not easily obtain ownership of an asset against default on the loan. In most places, a debtor could not be arrested for failing to honor a paper debt note such as a promissory note. Therefore, in case of default on a promissory note (an unsecured loan), the creditor was left really just with a claim, valid yes, but one which he could not use as the basis of effective legal action against the debtor to recover his loan principal. Suretyship (where the borrower has someone stand surety for him, in effect offering his own back-up guarantee the loan would be repaid if the debtor defaulted) was developed as an improvement on unsecured lending and was sometimes called a form of security. But suretyship had the flaw that it merely assigned the same uncollectable debt problem to an additional party. The security of a bill was akin to that of suretyship in that default of payment triggered a legal mechanism which would ensure that the creditor received payment. But where suretyship was usually toothless, the law of exchange was not: Summary procedure and

11 The Bank of England issued notes in the early eighteenth century, as did smaller private English banks. Davies, *A history of money*, p. 172, p. 339; Chown, *History of Money*, Chapters 15–18.

strict liability gave the creditor more advantages than other forms of credit. The prospect of arrest and detention of property acted like a pledge. Summary procedure made it hard for the debtor to slip out of the situation. Bills' speed, certainty, and sharp power of arrest made them "rigorous."

Changes in the usage of bills of exchange across Europe were partially informed by ideas about political economy which circulated through professional, bureaucratic, and other intellectual networks (Chapters 1, 3). The concept of political economy was arguably born in the sixteenth century but matured in the seventeenth and eighteenth centuries; the best-known schools of political-economic thought in the period were bullionism, mercantilism, cameralism, physiocracy, and liberalism. A currency-oriented program, bullionism was concerned with the nation's aggregate amount of precious metal. Mercantilism shared bullionism's focus on the importance of the metropole acquiring wealth but understood this might also take the form of intangibles like trade opportunities, colonies, plantations, and other new, value-producing operations. Cameralism is usually thought of as the territorial, non-colonialist version of mercantilism, again concerned with the growth of resources but more focused on natural resources, land-based commodity production, and applied science. Physiocracy focused on domestic agriculture and domestic trade, seeking to use state power to create laws optimal for the production and circulation of valuable resources. Liberalism (liberal political economy) was associated early on with David Hume and Adam Smith. Like the physiocrats, liberal political economists believed that circulation of money, goods, and services, domestically and across borders and oceans, was governed by grand natural laws, only just coming to be recognized, whose refinement could lead to progress and prosperity. Smith called this notional system of law "the system of natural liberty."[12]

The changes underway in eighteenth-century Germany moved, albeit haltingly, toward the liberal model in which many actors produced and sold more things freely, with circulating free currency, to the benefit of whole societies (both the average person and the collectivity). By the 1760s and 1770s, new physiocratic and liberal economic ideas were in the air, blowing eastward from France and Scotland, and quickly became popular in Germany. Adam Smith's *Wealth of Nations* was published in German translation in Leipzig the very

12 This paragraph summarizes presentations in Tigar and Levy, *Law and the Rise of Capitalism*; Chown, *History of Money*; Small, *The Cameralists*; Raeff, *Well-Ordered Police State*; and Landes, *Wealth and Poverty of Nations*. Specialists will recognize that my presentation here is simplified, highlighting some salient features of each school.

year it was published in Edinburgh.[13] In the span of centuries, the liberal political economists – the followers of Smith – were to become triumphant, with their vision of societies internally free to produce, offer, buy, and consume as individuals saw fit, with little restrictive licensing. But too often unrecognized is how the also-rans in this contest (mercantilists and cameralists) were also highly influential in the growth of the economies of nation-states.[14] In the German states, the contest was between cameralists and liberals, with cameralism predominating until the French Revolution.

Despite their distinctions, the five schools of thought shared family resemblances. All were concerned with the maximization of resource production (e.g., agriculture) and extraction (e.g., mining). Most were concerned to improve the terms of trade, though the liberals argued that international trade, like all exchange, found its "natural level" and that free production and exchange would benefit societies more than forced extraction and trade wars.[15] All schools assumed something like "free trade," at least for domestic and regional product markets, the carry trade, and properly licensed and taxed international merchants. Political economists generally advocated for extensive civil liberty of the sort explored in this book, because they assumed that the important activities of producing, extracting, selling, buying, lending,

13 Diethelm Klippel, "Der Einfluß der Physiokraten auf die Entwicklung der liberalen politischen Theorie in Deutschland," *Der Staat* 23 (1984); Braun, "Economic Theory and Policy in Germany, 1750–1800"; Heiner Klemme, ed., *Reception of the Scottish Enlightenment in Germany: Six Significant Translations, 1755–1782* (Bristol: Thoemmes, 2000); Adam Smith, *Untersuchung der Natur und Ursachen von Nationalreichthümern*, trans. Johann Friedrich Schiller (Leipzig: Weidmanns Erben und Reich, 1776).

14 Adam Smith is commonly misunderstood to have been an advocate of "laissez faire" when in fact he advocated certain useful regulations of economic activity as well as social welfare provisions to ameliorate problems caused by the division of labor. Modern development economists have also argued that protectionist provisions for the home economy are necessary to help a country jump-start industrial development, after which liberal trade policies are beneficial. See for instance Ha-Joon Chang, *Kicking Away the Ladder: Development Strategy in Historical Perspective* (London: Anthem, 2002). For Smith, see his *The Theory of Moral Sentiments*, ed. D. D. Raphael and A. L. Macfie (Indianapolis: Liberty Classics, 1982 [orig. 1759]) and for instance Fonna Forman-Barzilai, *Adam Smith and the Circles of Sympathy: Cosmopolitanism and Moral Theory*, Vol. 96, Ideas in Context (Cambridge: Cambridge University Press, 2011).

15 David Hume, "Of the Balance of Trade," in *Essays, moral, political, and literary*, ed. Thomas Hill Green, Thomas Hodge Grose, and Eugene F. Miller (Indianapolis: Liberty Fund, 1987 [orig. 1777, 1752]); Istvan Hont, "The 'Rich Country, Poor Country' Debate," in *Wealth and Virtue: The Shaping of Political Economy in the Scottish Enlightenment*, ed. Istvan Hont and Michael Ignatieff (Cambridge University Press, 1983).

borrowing, investing, and improving were undertaken by many different merchants, professionals, landowners, miners, and adventurers, as well as rulers and old elites. To undertake these activities, these diverse economic actors needed the "presumption of natural freedom" to buy and sell land, leverage it, and offer and accept free pricing on goods and services – and the ability to use good money.[16] The generally shared goals of political economists were to increase economic production, healthy public credit, efficient disposition of labor, and active and free circulation of money within an economy. Among the German and broader European intelligentsia, many believed in sometimes conflicting liberal and mercantilist ideas while largely sharing this conception of how to invigorate economic production.

That bills of exchange had benefits beyond their use to merchants began to be perceived by political economists in the second half of the eighteenth century at the latest. Those who wrote about law throughout our period often talked about how law affected commerce. In 1790, Philipp Peter Guden praised the economic efficacy of the law of exchange. The "Law of exchange for drawn [*trassirte*] bills of exchange brings advantage to every *Land* and in no regard any damages."[17]

In 1777, Johann Heinrich Christian von Selchow in his lectures on the law of exchange said that bills created a "security" for creditors, a security which was "necessary in order to keep credit up [*den Credit aufrecht zu halten*]."[18] Earlier still in 1748, Montesquieu had argued that bills made commerce more safe and reliable, and that commerce softened social *mores*.[19] Paper money had come under great suspicion in Europe after the bursting of the Mississippi Company scheme in 1719–1720 (and the similar related events in Britain's South Sea Bubble). Policymakers and thinkers became cautious about the danger

16 This account must be understood as intentionally generalized. Some bullionists believed in free trade as did some mercantilists. Mercantilists and cameralists sought to enrich societies, primarily with an eye toward increasing the supply of valuable physical resources in the society, especially bullion and resources such as ore, timber, or other produce. Sometimes, less restrictive trade regulation was a means toward this increase, to be sure, but so were domination and forced extraction. The aim of mercantilist and cameralist programs was to enrich and empower monarchs and elites. Adam Smith thought that British management of trade within its maritime empire was beneficial.

17 Guden, *Vom Wechsel- und römischen Rechte*, Vorbericht, page v; Div. I, Cap. II, §7, p. 25; and epitome of Div. I, Cap. III, §13.

18 Selchow, *Grundsätze des Wechselrechts*, §4, p. 9, citing Johann Marquard, *Tractaus politico-juridicus de iure mercarorum et commerciorum singulari etc* (Frankfurt am Main: 1662).

19 Montesquieu, *The Spirit of the Laws*, Book 21, Chapter 20, p. 389.

of speculation in bills, but after 1720 no one could un-see the incredible role that paper was irresistibly playing in the growth of liquidity and economic development. Already in the late 1600s, regulators and their interlocutors were considering how to refine the rules of bills and other paper instruments in order to promote the growth of national and state wealth. To the many individuals interested in political economy, it seemed modern, expedient, and advantageous to permit more and more people to use merchant rules involving bills.

Did ruling elites and professionals care about civil liberty as a civil right to be enjoyed because freedom helps human beings to flourish? In some instances it seems so, based on remarks by German physiocrats and jurists who espoused such liberal or Aristotelian ideas. However, expediency regarding the growth of wealth in a territorial economy seems to have been the overriding purpose. According to many jurists and other writers, the expansion of commercial freedom would serve the goals of increasing investment, production, circulation, wealth, and state power.[20]

2 Evolution of the Law of Exchange in Europe

Bills had four parties, unlike a promissory note, which had two. (See Figure 47.) A person wishing to use a bill as a medium of exchange to buy goods or services first (Figure 47: upper left) pays money to the maker of the bill (Figure 47: lower left). The first party, called the remitter, sends or remits the bill to the party from whom he is obtaining the goods or services. The seller of goods is the remittee. He delivers the goods or performs the services. The remittee then presents the bill to the fourth party, called the acceptor and payor since he is supposed to accept the bill and pay its face value to the remittee. At this point, the remitter has paid for the goods and the remittee has received money for them, but the parties doing the respective receiving and paying are

20 This argument has affinities with the research program into the history of governmentality and neoliberalism initiated by Michel Foucault. See Graham Burchell, Colin Gordon, and Peter Miller, eds., *The Foucault Effect: Studies in Governmentality: With Two Lectures by and an Interview with Michel Foucault* (Chicago: University of Chicago Press, 1991). As John O'Neill has written, Foucault did not see "history … as the story of individual freedom, even though western political history is only intelligible as its invention. What intervenes is the logic of the institutions that bring together rationality, individualism and freedom in the large-scale disciplinary enterprises of capitalism, bureaucracy and the modern therapeutic state." John O'Neill, "The Disciplinary Society: From Weber to Foucault," *The British Journal of Sociology* 37, no. 1 (1986), p. 43.

Pays out cash for bill to bill maker (is ***numerans***). **Remits** bill to seller (is **deliverer**, **remitter**, ***remittans***, ***dator***). **Buyer** of goods or services.

Seller of goods or services. **Receives** remitted bill (is **remittee**). **Presents** bill to acceptor (***praesentans***). **Receives payment** from payor (is **payee**). Also called ***cambsarius***. If he is the same person as the lender, then he is the *remittans*, q.v. If he is not also the lender, but is simply the payee, then he is simply called the **bearer** or **holder of the instrument**, the ***Briefinhaber***.

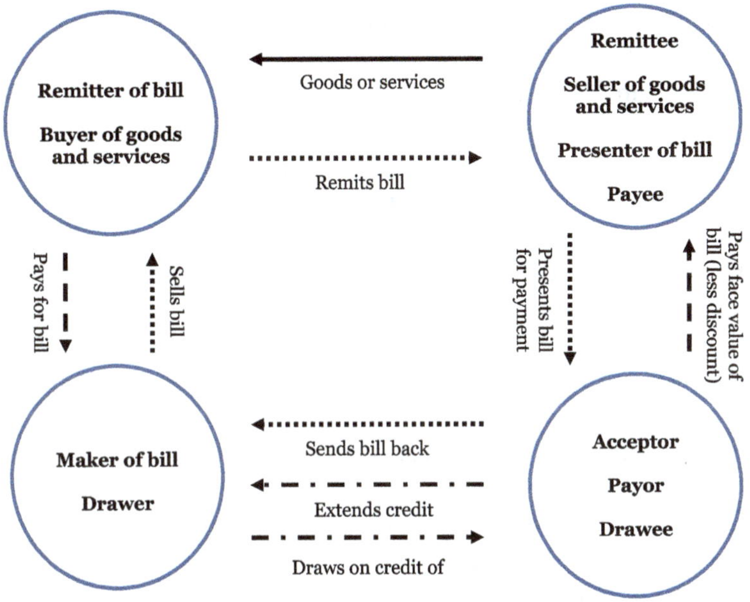

Draws on acceptor's credit (is **drawer**, ***trassans***). **Makes bill** in the first place and **sells it** to buyer of goods (is **bill maker**, ***Aussteller***, ***cambsans***, ***campsor***, ***cambist***, ***Wechselgeber***). **Takes the money** of the buyer of goods (is **taker**, ***prenditore***). Often a **merchant banker**.

Accepts bill from presenter (is ***acceptans***). **Pays** presenter (is **payor**, ***Geldausgeber***). **Extends credit** to drawer (is **drawee**, ***trassatus***, **creditor**). Often a **merchant banker**.

Ideal type of the bill of exchange in the eighteenth century: This diagram should be read in clockwise fashion, beginning with the upper left. That person is a buyer of goods and services. He begins by buying the bill from the drawer (lower left). The buyer then remits the bill to the seller of goods and services (upper right) and takes delivery of product. The seller then presents the bill to his banker (lower right, the accepter of the bill or *acceptans*) for payment and the latter pays him. So now buyer has paid and seller has been paid, albeit not by one another. Acceptor is now out money, so he sends the bill to the drawer. At the end of this cycle, one element is left undiagrammed: the drawer finally owes the face value of the bill to the drawee, since the drawer has received cash payment for some amount (usually face value less discount) and the drawee or creditor has paid out some amount (probably slightly less than the former) to the seller of goods or services. *Sources*: Selchow (1777), Neal (1990), de Roover (1942).

FIGURE 47 How bills work

not the original buyer and seller, but rather merchant bankers, specialists in the making and accepting of bills.[21]

21 The best overview of this structure in English is Raymond A. de Roover, "What is Dry Exchange?," in *Business, Banking, and Economic Thought in Late Medieval and Early Modern Europe*, ed. Julius Kirshner (Chicago: University of Chicago Press, 1976 [orig. 1944]). The terminology of acceptance is still found in the modern *banker's acceptances*.

It should be stressed that there were variations on this tetradic structure. For instance, sometimes it was used within a single region with no difference in currency, as between Marburg and Frankfurt (a couple days' ride). Or a bill could be used purely as a vehicle for lending at interest, with no function for the purchasing of distant goods. This was called dry exchange and was viewed as chiefly a cover for usurious lending. Sometimes bills were used in a further structure of re-exchange, whereby the paid-out money was in effect sent back to the original deliverer via a second bill which traveled in the reverse direction. As we shall see, there were other variations and uses of bills. Despite the complexity of the four-part structure, bills became popular because they were so *compact* compared to sending large amounts of currency and were therefore easier and cheaper to transport. They also reduced security costs because they were not attractive targets of robbery (being worthless to anyone except the original four parties).[22]

In his magnum opus, *German Jurisprudence* (1758–1767; Figure 48), Johann Georg Estor constructed an edifice of notionally Germanic law, two central features of which were consent and (honoring) obligations. Some Germanistic jurists imagined that German law had invented a native German version of seemingly every important legal concept or institution, much as English lawyers for centuries imagined English law to have grown up largely uninfluenced by continental civil law. Estor was hardly one to imagine such a closed legal biome, as his work in other areas of law attests.[23] Estor was the pioneer of the "Germanistic" account of the origins of the law of exchange: He thought the German version of the strict liability in exchange law derived from native German practices of hostage-taking. He in turn interpreted letters of exchange and IOUs (*chirographia*) also as Germanic legal institutions. He thought they derived from an original Germanic form of guaranty instrument which bore a person's seal.[24]

In the early seventeenth century, Flemish emigres to cities like Hamburg and Frankfurt am Main brought to their new homes the Dutch practice of

22 North and Thomas, *Rise of the Western World*, p. 54.

23 For instance in his *Opusculum de abusu rerum merae facultatis in foro Germanico praesertim feudali*, 2nd expanded and corrected ed. (Jena: Johann Friedrich Ritter, 1744), Estor carefully set forth the doctrine of pure abilities, which was by any account a doctrine thoroughly grounded in and developed out of classical Roman civil and natural law, canon law, medieval theology, and modern Grotian natural law. Estor then systematically considered which such "abilities" were consistent with or also native to German law as he constructed it.

24 See Estor, *Der Teutschen Rechtsgelahrheit*, Chapter 4; Chapter 6; Chapter 31, §3698; Chapter 33, §3709; Chapter 36, §3738–3741; and Chapter 37, §3748, p. 386. See Lutz Sedatis, *Über den Ursprung der Wechselstrenge: Eine historischdogmatische Untersuchung der Lehre vom rigor cambialis* (Duncker & Humblot, 1967).

Johann Georgen Estors
der
Teutschen
rechtsgelahrheit
dritter teil
ausgefertiget
von Johann Andreen Hofmanne
doctorn und ordentlichen lehrer der rechte auch dermaligen dechante der löblichen juristen-facultaet und zeitigen Pro-Rectorn in der Fürstl. Heßischen Universitaet zu Marburg.

Frankfurt am Maine,
bei Johann Gottlieb Garben 1767.

FIGURE 48 Title page of the final volume of Estor's *German Jurisprudence* (1767), a compendium of imperial and Hessian territorial civil law and procedure and early work in historical school of law

endorsing bills, similar to today's practice of endorsing checks: The third party to the bill, rather than presenting it to the fourth party (the banker), would instead sign it over to a new person – a substitute third party, usually known as the *bearer*, who would pay the original third party a sum of money for it. Substituting in a new third party (or if you prefer, a fifth party) via endorsement was dubbed "negotiability."[25] The amount paid would be a fraction of

25 For examples of the latter usage, calling endorsable bills "bills to bearer," see Dave de Ruysscher, "Innovating Financial Law in Early Modern Europe: Transfers of Commercial

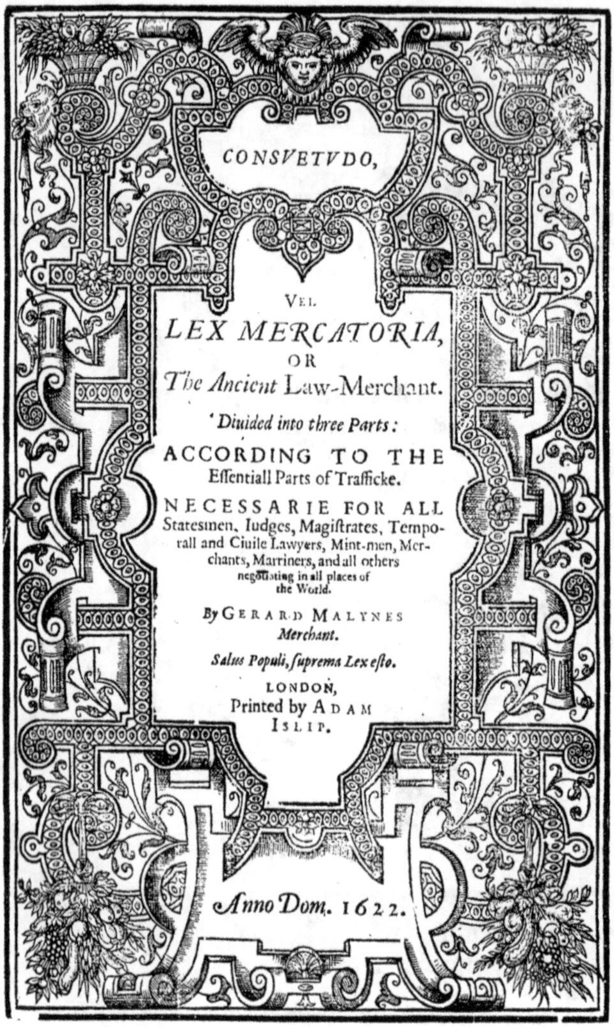

CONSVETVDO,

VEL

LEX MERCATORIA,

OR

The Ancient Law-Merchant.

Diuided into three Parts:

ACCORDING TO THE Effentiall Parts of Trafficke.

NECESSARIE FOR ALL Statesmen, Iudges, Magiftrates, Tempo-rall and Ciuile Lawyers, Mint-men, Mer-chants, Marriners, and all others negotiating in all places of the World.

By GERARD MALYNES Merchant.

Salus Populi, fuprema Lex efto.

LONDON, Printed by ADAM ISLIP.

Anno Dom. 1622.

FIGURE 49 Title page of Gerard Malynes, *Consuetudo vel Lex mercatoria* (1622), one of the best known treatments of law merchant in the period

the face value of the bill – the fraction approached par (face value) as the bill approached its due date. This practice of paying a variable fraction in exchange for an endorsed bill was called *discounting* in that the sale price of the bill was

Paper and Recourse Liability in Legislation and *Ius Commune* (Sixteenth to Eighteenth Centuries)," *European Review of Private Law* 19, no. 5 (2011). Raymond de Roover wrote that negotiability was invented in Florence no later than 1519; see de Roover, "New Interpretations of the History of Banking," pp. 219–220t.

a "discount" from its full face value. When the term date was further off, the discount was higher, and so the amount one would pay for the bill was less, since the bill could not be presented for cash until term. The closer a bill was to term when sold, the less time one would have to sit on it and not earn any money from it, so the discount was less. Thus as term approached, discount decreased, and the market value or discounted price of a bill approached its face value or par value. Discounting was more broadly the easiest way to build fees into the handling of bills. In the example given here, both the acceptor / drawee and the original maker / drawer – i.e. the two parties who were not actually using the bill as a medium of exchange in a transaction for goods and services – had to be compensated for their time and acceptance of risk. Any time a person paid money in exchange for a bill, he probably paid at a discount off the bill's face value, therewith making a small fee for each handling of a bill.

3 The Political Economy of German States after 1648

Like their counterparts in other countries, German jurists and statesmen regularly asserted the state's sovereign authority to regulate commerce and particularly to take measures to encourage production and trade. The way that German jurists and statesmen viewed this authority in the second half of the seventeenth century can be seen in a dissertation supervised by Johann Niklaus Hertius, *Dissertatio de superioritate territoriali* (1682). Professor of law and eventually chancellor in Giessen, Hertius was an important figure in law and politics, a theorist of sovereignty and a pioneer in the rigorous study of German customary law. Giessen was one of the two administrative capitals of the second largest Hessian state, Hesse-Darmstadt, and Hertius, in achievement and range, resembled Estor a half century later.

The *Dissertatio*, co-produced with Hertius's student Joannes Conradus Fabricius, was a study of "territorial supremacy." For jurists in the service of post-Westphalian German princes, this meant the sovereignty (*maiestas*) of German princes (as well as German republican regimes like Frankfurt). From the thirteenth century onward, explained Hertius and Fabricius, territorial governments operated a number of policy levers over money and commerce. For instance, rulers had long seen the value in holding the right to mint their own coinage. This allowed them when possible to create liquidity and the means to pay their debts, as well as putting them in a position to periodically debase coinage either to extend their own means or to attack a neighbor's economy.[26] Rulers were also concerned with trade. Since trade is necessary "to live life well" (wrote the authors, quoting Grotius), under ordinary circumstances it was inappropriate for the ruler to prohibit or restrict trade for reasons outside of the common public interest. Rulers could not be "arbitrary" in their regulation of imports and exports.[27] Jurists (like Hertius) who served government and guided policy believed increasingly that merchants and markets preferred predictability (more than other groups do).[28] As Michael Tigar puts it, bourgeois lawyers

> served the interests of commerce by helping to fashion a legal system favorable to it. The crown was beginning to see the value of acting predictably, according to a certain rationality which came to be expressed in a system of rules and maxims, for predictability is essential to commerce.

Specifically, rulers and their servants wanted to excite native commercial activity, to attract merchant sellers, and generally to create favorable terms of international trade for parties within their own lands. Hence regimes licensed local markets and fairs (*nundinis minus solennibus, Jahrmärkte*).[29] Common people were granted the formal permission (franchise) to hold regular markets in order to foster commerce, favor protected market environments, and prevent unsupervised dealings.[30] This grant often accompanied the granting or assertion of other municipal privileges, such as limited self-government or control of local jurisdiction. According to Hertius, since trade was necessary for good human life, princes could not "prohibit [their] subjects from going to a market elsewhere," nor was any

---

26 See Charles P. Kindleberger, "The Economic Crisis of 1619 to 1623," *Journal of Economic History* 51, no. 1 (1991) for a treatment of the latter phenomenon by small German polities during the early phase of the Thirty Years' War.

27 Hertius's Latin suggests he was using the language of "pure abilities" and contending that arbitrary attenuation of trade should not be considered a "pure ability" of princes: "Cura importandorum vel exportandorum non est in mero imperantium arbitrio." See Joannes Nicolaus Hertius, praeses, Joannes Conradus Fabricius, respondans, *Dissertatio de superioritate territoriali* (Giessen: Karger, 1682), §XIII, p. 19m; Hugo Grotius, *De jure belli ac pacis*, ed. Jean Barbeyrac (Cambridge; London: John W. Parker, 1853 [orig. 1622, 1712]), Book II, Chapter 2, §XIX. For pure abilities, see Wilder, "Property, Possession and Prescription," Chapter 8, pp. 386–387, 393–402, 406–423.

28 Tigar and Levy, *Law and the Rise of Capitalism*, p. 125.

29 Hertius and Fabricius, *Dissertatio de superioritate territoriali*, §XII–XIII, pp. 16–20.

30 Tigar and Levy, *Law and the Rise of Capitalism*, pp. 46–47, 139.

> neighboring imperial state, if it has imperial authority to hold a market … impeded from holding a market, even on the same day.[31]

Writing in 1682, in the era of growing territorial supremacy and independence among states of the empire, the authors also argued that the right of staple (*Staffel-Gerechtigkeit, jus stapulae*) was justified. Staple was the right to force traveling merchants to offer their goods for sale wherever they passed through. To keep this less cumbersome, though, by old tradition the right of staple was formally limited to "the great republics," meaning the older and larger commercial centers. [32] These included both imperial free cities like Bremen, Speyer, and Frankfurt am Main as well as those like Ingolstadt, Magdeburg, and Passau, which were subject to the authority of territorial princes.

Princes and the legal operators around them interpreted all of this as "free trade." In what sense was this trade free? The answer seems to be in somewhat the same sense as I have entitled this chapter the "free use of paper money." Governments interpreted freedom in trade as being, yes, more or less what modern readers would think of as unregulated international commerce with no fixed prices and no tariffs. But the more complex issue was how the inside and the outside of a territory were free – what kind of laws inside best and most attractively conduced to the territory and its ruler profiting from free trade? Hence *free trade* meant the construction of sophisticated, positive regulation to create or maintain good (beneficial) conditions of trade in a given territory or jurisdiction.[33] Such law slowly developed within a given system of political and juridical authority and a concrete legal order of rights and privileges.

In the period of relative tranquility and growth in the empire after peace was negotiated in 1648, there was growing opulence among the aristocracy,

---

31 "The only exception to this is if the prince can show that he has an easement of this norm in public law." The full original passage reads: "et privilegium mundinarum hebdomadalium olim auctoritate Caesarea obtento vicinum statum Imp. non impediri, quo minus nundinas similes eodem die instituat, subditosque suos, quo minus ad alias mercatum eant, prohibeat … nisi a privilegiato doceatur servitus juris publici … Sic etiam immunes, dum mercaturam exercent, oneribus illius fiunt obnoxii …" See Gaertner, *Meditationum practicarum*, Cap. 33, pp. 58–59.

32 Hertius and Fabricius, *Dissertatio de superioritate territoriali*, §XIII, p. 20t. The right of staple meant variously the right to prohibit certain imports or to force traveling merchants to offer their wares for sale within the jurisdiction as a condition for transporting them through.

33 Consider for instance Gerard Malynes, *The Maintenance of Free Trade*, Reprints of Economic Classics (New York: A. M. Kelley, 1971 [orig. 1622]).

a rising bourgeoisie, and booms in patronage and defense spending. Reconstruction after 1648, writes Horst Dreitzel, "led to a kind of economic miracle [*Wirtschaftswunder*] for nobles and princes" whose high point was "the period of Baroque princely power in the decades of the transition from seventeenth to the eighteenth centuries." Baroque courts flourished and were centers of patronage of arts and learning. University foundations boomed and governmental administration of justice grew (Chapter 3). The political-military side saw the growth of expensive new fortifications and of large, powerful standing armies. France was the Continental heavyweight, followed by Vienna and numerous smaller powers such as the dozens of waxing German principalities with their courts, universities, armies, and bureaucracies.

But for all of the opulence of the aristocracy, older, static ideas about political economy were beginning to give way, as I have said above, to new ideas about how production could be dynamically increased, valuable resources harvested, and products and specie made to circulate in a manner favorable to one's own country (free trade again). These new ideas and energies were associated with the bourgeoisie, new money, and new ways of making money.[34] It was a period of economic modernization and "revealed a growing divergence of interests in society through the rise of the urban classes": Both rulers and urban classes wanted economic reform in order to increase wealth-creating opportunities. But rulers were less interested in reforms of autocratic governmental practices more generally, while the appetite of the

34 I do not wish to put too much pressure on the identification and agency of the bourgeoisie. I have long struggled with the ambiguity of the latter term and am sympathetic to Sara Maza's approach in her *The Myth of the French Bourgeoisie: An Essay in the Social Imaginary, 1750–1850* (Cambridge: Harvard University Press, 2005). I do tend to think that Marxist historians overstate and reify the closure, agency, and purposive action of the "bourgeoisie," owing to that school's broad caste duty of interpreting events as conforming to Karl Marx's simple historical drama of intentionalistic and solidaristic class conflict. All that said, I find that, if one reads it against the grain slightly, Marxist historiography about "the bourgeoisie" is often thought-provoking and even apt. The bourgeoisie was not an actually-existing international class with set ideas and plans which acted ruthlessly in its own self-interest, in the way that a corporation is legally taken to be a person in modern commercial law. Ministers, lords, religious, sovereign rulers, and many other individuals (of every social estate, completely beyond the officially proto-bourgeois estate of male Christian urban merchants) occasionally wrote or acted like bourgeois or like capitalists. Their actions over time created legal conditions congenial to merchants and commerce, not because they really were somehow already bourgeois, but because the bourgeois legal-political ideal as it was being developed by European thinkers in the seventeenth and eighteenth centuries was intellectually attractive to them. In the eighteenth century, people found the bourgeois ideal increasingly attractive, built it in reality, added to it, practiced it, and enjoyed its privileges.

bourgeoisie for thorough-going reform was far greater.[35] The greater freedoms around real estate and against tax impositions explored in Chapters 4–5 exemplify this, even as regimes tried to modernize their tax bureaucracies. More broadly, rulers were under pressure to "make comprehensive reforms" in the areas of agricultural and financial regulation, import and export rules, and taxation.[36] Here, we are going to see specifically how regimes including law courts extended the use of mercantile law throughout their territories, in Germany as in other European countries including England at this time.[37]

The use of bills presumably came to German trading centers like the Hanse towns, Leipzig, and Frankfurt am Main by way of long-distance traders, probably originally Italian. Although there is no evidence that any law of exchange was formally used in the Hanse towns before 1600, it is attested soon after the turn of the century:

> Hamburg like Amsterdam saw a lively trade in bills, initially with the devastation [*Trümmern*] in Antwerp at the end of the sixteenth century. This made it possible for proper Law of exchange to be introduced in Hamburg in 1603 and Amsterdam in 1601. But Hamburg did not have fairs or privileged money changers [*Campsores, Münzbürger*]; rather, trade in bills was permitted freely to all burghers from early on.[38]

Trade in bills grew lively in the next few decades. In Frankfurt, by contrast, bills were used for centuries before the refugees from Antwerp settled there in the seventeenth century.[39] Before that time, according to Hans-Peter Ullman, Frankfurt lacked a "money trade," that is, professional specialization in the handling of such tools or speculation in their future value. Bills were only used for the carry and product trade – that is, instruments used purely in

35 Walker, *Johann Jakob Moser*, pp. 200–204.

36 Dreitzel, *Absolutismus und ständische Verfassung in Deutschland*, p. 15, For a comparative treatment of several European societies in "pursuit of Albion" in the eighteenth century, see Landes, *Wealth and Poverty of Nations*, Chapter 16.

37 For England, see Tigar and Levy, *Law and the Rise of Capitalism*, p. 50; for the bourgeois character or characterization of mercantile law, see ibid., pp. 51, 145.

38 Georg Friedrich von Martens, *Versuch einer historischen Entwickelung des wahren Ursprungs des Wechselrechts* (Göttingen: Johann Christian Dieterich, 1797), p. 64.

39 A bearer document is attested from 1372 and a letter of "exchange" from 1396, though the latter may have been a simple letter of credit (*Eigenwechsel*), not one *drawn* on a local banker. There is ambiguous evidence of negotiability – or at least some kind of simple, formal transfer of debt obligation through signature on a note – in Frankfurt in the fifteenth century.

the pursuance of specific trading activities and neither intended nor expected to circulate on their own as a form of liquidity (money).[40] There was probably discount (in order to include fees to make bill acceptance work) but not endorsement and hence negotiability – no broader circulation of bills outside of actual, discrete business transactions. Bills used only in the carry trade and product trade and not in a money trade were more like a really good kind of contract, rather than being truly a kind of paper money.

Fleming emigrants in the seventeenth century brought the practice of endorsement with them to Frankfurt. It appears that endorsement was a practices in merchant communities, Flemish and later others, well before it was recognized by actual civil governments e.g. the Frankfurt senate, the city of Antwerp, or the city of Genoa.[41] Probably the main reason the negotiability was suspect to many was that, up to that point, bills of exchange had been interpreted as loan contracts. The transfer of the credit on a loan debt to a new party was done by an additional, complicated legal contract called an *assignment*, basically a contract to assign the debt from one debt instrument to another debt instrument. Though assignment was cumbersome, it was a trusted, known, ancient element of the European common law. Observers were wary of potential recording hazard – the less that formal recorded or witnessed procedure is required for a money transfer, the more it encourages frivolous activity and fraud.[42] It was not until mid-century that governments in the Low Countries or Italy gave endorsement full legal sanction. Later in the seventeenth century German cities reversed their policies, recognizing and enforcing endorsability – Frankfurt did so in 1666. Indeed although endorsement had been *developed* by the Flemish over a century before, it was only fully *accepted legally* in Antwerp and other Low Country towns in 1630. Once

40 According to Hans-Peter Ullmann, in the seventeenth century, "the trade in bills of exchange [*Wechselhandel*] became a separate branch of business [and] along with the carrying trade [*Commissions- und Speditionshandel*]." The former "became one of the main activities of 'merchant bankers' resident in Frankfurt." See Alexander Dietz, *Frankfurter Handelsgeschichte*, Reprint ed. (Glashütten im Taunus: D. Auvermann, 1970 [orig. 1910–1925]), Band 3, pp. 197, 201, 203, 207 and Hans-Peter Ullmann, "Der Frankfurter Kapitalmarkt um 1800: Entstehung, Struktur und Wirken einer modernen Finanzierungsinstitution," *Vierteljahrschrift für Sozial- und Wirtschaftsgeschichte* 77 (1990), pp. 76–77.

41 In Frankfurt am Main, "initially endorsement was prohibited, but all the same it was used in trade."

42 Jürgen Schneider, "Hat das Indossament zum Niedergang der Wechselmessen beigetragen?," in *Geldumlauf, Währungssysteme und Zahlungsverkehr in Nordwesteuropa 1300–1800: Beiträge zur Geldgeschichte der späten Hansezeit*, ed. Michael North (Cologne: Böhlau, 1989), p. 186mb.

again, like we saw in Chapter 4, juristic theory and statute sometimes lagged behind actual accepted rules of practice or the concrete order of existing rights and interests.[43]

4 Adoption of the Law of Exchange Throughout the Empire

While a few German commercial republics like Hamburg and Nuremberg codified law merchant in the early seventeenth century (1603 and 1621 respectively), a rush of ambitious states like Brandenburg Prussia and other commercial urban republics like Frankfurt am Main did so later, including law of exchange into their ordinary civil law. The Imperial Diet did so as well in its Recess of 1654.[44] Breslau adopted the law of exchange in 1672, Leipzig in 1682, Brunswick in 1686, Danzig in 1700, Naumburg and Magdeburg in 1703, and many other places in the empire, not to mention England and France.[45]

---

43 See de Ruysscher, "Innovating Financial Law in Early Modern Europe," pp. 505–510 and Amend-Traut, *Wechselverbindlichkeiten vor dem Reichskammergericht*, pp. 19, 267–269.

44 Martens, *Entwickelung des wahren Ursprungs des Wechselrechts*, p. 76. The law of exchange was first promulgated in black-letter law in 1654 in the "Youngest Imperial Recess," a kind of omnibus law of the Diet (or parliament) of the Holy Roman Empire. This was the major meeting of the great parliament (called the Diet) of the empire shortly after the prolonged peace negotiations at Munster and Osnabrück finally settled all terms concluding the War. The Diet's decisions and resolutions were recorded in its "recesses," a term referring to the record of its actions when a given meeting of the diet concluded (recessed). The 1654 Recess was its "Youngest" or most recent because, when it convened the next time in 1663, it never recessed again but sat continuously until abolition of the empire itself in 1806.

45 Jean Baptiste Colbert, minister of finance to Louis XIV, issued his Ordonnance du Commerce in 1673. Colbert also introduced generalized rules of trade in bills for the same reasons. The English case of the adoption of exchange law centers on Gerard Malynes, English by ancestry, raised in Antwerp, and returned to England where he had his career as policy advisor and mint master. Before about 1650, endorsement of bills was not recognized in England; bills could only be transferred via assignment. Malynes is famously associated with advocating for the adoption of what he and his party implied was a settled part of the continental civil law tradition (*lex mercatoria*). "After 1650 the introduction of the doctrine of negotiability, the emergence of domestic bills, and the creation of a discount market for commercial paper" all became "instrumental in dissociating credit from exchange." Contrary however to the goals of Malynes and his party, the English royal courts of common law gained jurisdiction over merchant legal disputes, including settling bills of exchange. See Raymond A. de Roover, *Money, banking and credit in mediaeval Bruges: Italian merchant bankers, lombards and money-changers* (Cambridge: Mediaeval Academy of America, 1948), p. 265, de Roover, "What is Dry Exchange?," p. 194rt, and Mary Elizabeth Basile, Jane Fair Bestor, Daniel R. Coquillette, and Charles Donahue, Jr., eds., *Lex Mercatoria and Legal Pluralism* (Cambridge: Ames Foundation, 1998), pp. 143–144.

The Diet's adoption was particularly momentous because it signaled the applicability and recognition of obligations from bills for a vast swath of Central Europe (notwithstanding imperial federalism). The Diet underscored the importance of the law of exchange for the settlement of war debts, that is, for public finance. As we shall see, in the following century, however, laws, court decisions, and treatises justified expanding the law of exchange for other, ordinary reasons of state and economy. The Diet Recess in 1654 was oriented not toward improvement through innovation, but rather toward restoration and recovery. The Diet acted to counter the chaos and uncertainty of three decades of war, even though the post-1648 ordering of estates reflected a formal transformation of the relationship between German princes and the imperial government. Order had to be restored. Roads had to be repaired and made safe for common people and traveling merchants alike. Financially, massive debts had to be settled, debts which had been taken out both with and without pledged collateral. Indeed, as Marc Raeff has argued broadly, the policies of many German governments of the late seventeenth and early eighteenth centuries at times buttressed or restored the legal status quo, at other times innovated.[46]

Immediate imperial polities like Hesse-Cassel, Hesse-Darmstadt, Saxony or Frankfurt could and would still create their own law. But the Diet's adoption meant that, if there were no applicable, contravening local law, the supreme courts of the empire would apply law merchant to settle disputes over the making, negotiating, and settling of bills and notes. As mentioned earlier, local and territorial law usually would prevail against imperial law, unless the emperor's rights were at issue. Also, the law would have directly applied to all imperial estates – that is, princes, counts, and other immediate estates (all lordships held directly of the emperor). The imperial adoption was significant because the supreme courts would now have guidance in how to settle inter-territorial disputes about bills. The 1654 Recess emphasized that summary execution was to apply at "trade fairs and in other situations."[47]

Given the felt and stated importance of the law of exchange especially for acute problems of public finance, it is at first particularly surprising to learn that in Antwerp, Hamburg, Frankfurt am Main, and a few other places, bills of exchange were used long before there was law about them on the books of the ruling government, in the case of Hamburg centuries before. After all, the widely accepted historical narrative is that bills played an outsized role

46 Raeff, "Well-Ordered Police State"; Raeff, *Well-Ordered Police State.*

47 See Reichsabschied of 1654, in Johann Jacob Schmauss and Heinrich Christian Senckenberg, eds., *Neue und vollständigere Sammlung der Reichsabschiede* (Frankfurt am Main: Ernst August Koch, 1747), Vol. 3, pp. 640 ff., §107.

in the development of European trade and, by extension, international trade in the age of exploration.[48] And German cities like Frankfurt, Hamburg, and Nuremberg were already major trading hubs by this time, and only growing busier. Why then so little legislation about so significant a piece of contemporary financial technology? I contend that the procedures for using bills were not seen to have required codification in the "great republics" like Frankfurt am Main, Leipzig, Naumburg, and Strasbourg, where merchants enjoyed special imperial privileges according to which they could hold "great fairs." These privileges excluded regional lords around those cities from licensing fairs themselves.[49] Traveling foreign merchants came to the great fairs and generally ignored the comparatively unimportant weekly, monthly, and annual markets in lesser towns like Marburg. The law of exchange was no organized body of law (*jus* or *corpus iuris*), much less specific statutes (*leges*), but rather a set of in-group practices, legally enforceable through special privileges, among trusted members within networks, many of whom were itinerant foreigners. These "franchise" privileges as they were called in English, granted to itinerant merchant communities by local governments, included immunity from local jurisdiction which enabled them to settle matters themselves.[50] Hence when merchants congregated at the annual fair in Frankfurt, for example, they already practiced customary law merchant with its rules of exchange.

The law of exchange only came to be regarded as having the dignity and force of a legal source upon scrutiny by eager jurists of the *usus modernus* beginning in the period ca. 1642–1662, when Mevius (see Figure 50) published his extensive commentary on Lubeck law including law of exchange

48 North and Thomas, *Rise of the Western World*; Larry Neal, *The Rise of Financial Capitalism: International Capital Markets in the Age of Reason* (Cambridge: Cambridge University Press, 1990), Chapter 1.

49 Hertius and Fabricius, *Dissertatio de superioritate territoriali*, §XIII, p. 20t.

50 Albrecht Cordes, "The search for a medieval *Lex mercatoria*," in *From lex mercatoria to commercial law*, ed. Vito Piergiovanni, *Comparative Studies in Continental and Anglo-American Legal History* (Berlin: Duncker & Humblot, 2005). Such jurisdictional immunity was essentially the same as that discussed by jurists, as in Chapter 5. Sheilagh Ogilvie's magisterial *Institutions and European Trade* (Cambridge: Cambridge University Press, 2011) contains many examples of how merchants procured such privileges from rulers. For example, she writes on p. 167: "[The] interaction between rulers and guilds was … complicated. Rulers did not *open up* trade in such a way that it could rise to the efficient level. Rather, they *segmented* trade by granting specific commercial 'privileges' to identifiable interest-groups in return for specific streams of payments and services. Relations between rulers and merchant guilds were governed … by 'the age-old notion of an exchange, of a privilege being granted in return for a fiscal benefit to the state.'"

and Johann Marquard published his *Tractaus politico-juridicus de iure mercarorum* (political-judicial treatise on law merchant) in Frankfurt am Main. These works marked the beginning of learned (i.e. university-trained) legal commentary on law merchant.

Before that point, most jurists would have treated law merchant as a foreign law they were not competent to apply, and merchants who themselves regularly used the law of exchange would not have sought or needed the services of typical jurists. Jurists as such were trained in, and creatures of and users of, the European common law (*ius commune*), not law merchant. And merchants as such had assembled over centuries in law merchant a somewhat eclectic set of ideas and rules from various legal sources, in particular canon law. It is no surprise that the two seemed foreign to one another before the work of Marquard and Mevius. In the decades after 1662, we see a merging of the two legal communities (merchant law and learned civil law).[51] We shall soon examine how, as testimony to this merging, regimes and courts extended the coverage of their civil laws and court jurisdictions to include disputes over bills.

51 Marquard's *usus modernus* study of law merchant was a civil-law-inspiried examination of what was, to jurists with his background, essentially a well-known, important, and seemingly alien (non-Roman) "body" of law. See Karl Otto Scherner, "Zum Sonderrecht der Kaufleute bei Johann Marquard," in *Usus modernus pandectarum: Römisches Recht, Deutsches Recht und Naturrecht in der Frühen Neuzeit; Klaus Luig zum 70. Geburtstag*, ed. Hans-Peter Haferkamp and Tilman Repgen (Cologne: Böhlau, 2007), pp. 199–200 and Vito Piergiovanni, "Genoese Civil Rota and mercantile customary law," in *From lex mercatoria to commercial law, Comparative Studies in Continental and Anglo-American Legal History* (Berlin: Duncker & Humblot, 2005), building on Heinz Mohnhaupt, "'Jura mercatorum' durch Privilegien: Zur Entwicklung des Handelsrechts bei Johann Marquard (1610–1737)," in *Wege europaeischer Rechtsgeschichte*, ed. Gerhard Köbler (1987). The major publication of the "body" of the law of exchange in Germany in the eighteenth century was Siegel and Ubl, *Corpus juris cambialis*. In the late twentieth century, a debate among legal historians raged as to whether states or merchants should be credited as the originators of law merchant. The latter view was represented in works like Richard Epstein, "Reflections on the Historical Origins and Economic Structure of the Law Merchant," *Chicago Journal of International Law* 5, no. 1 (2004) and Peter T. Leeson, "One more time with feeling: the law merchant, arbitration, and international trade," *Indian Journal of Economics and Business* special issue (2007). This debate reflects a larger debate over how much credit to give state agency and non-state actors in the creation of successful, complex institutions in Western history, other examples of which include banking and stock markets.

FIGURE 50 David Mevius, important early figure in the *usus modernus* and not coincidentally one of the first great figures to collect and systematize law merchant as a German legal development, through the customs of the town of Lübeck

5 Summary Procedure and Strict Liability ("Rigor")

By the end of the seventeenth century, in Germany and other countries like England, two further features of bills had emerged, which have persisted in the law of exchange ever since: *strict liability* and *summary procedure*. These have universally been interpreted as conferring advantages for the users of bills and as having positive external reputational and economic consequences as well. Summary procedure was how disputes over bills were handled. Strict liability meant the simplicity, rigidity, and reliability of the sanction for not honoring a bill through proper payment. Together strict liability and summary procedure were said to create a particular strength, which specialists called the "rigor"

(*rigor, Strenge*) of the law of exchange.[52] When jurists and publicists argued for the adoption of the law of exchange, they invariably gave this "rigor" as the most important quality of bills and their governance. By reducing the costs of litigation and insurance, these two features of bills increased security and reduced risk and litigation costs, and therefore generally reduced transaction costs.[53]

Here is how the great Marburg law professor, privy counselor, and vice chancellor von Selchow explained these two features of bills to his students:

> Suits arising out of exchange instruments [*aus Wechseln*] are tried summarily [*summarisch behandelt*] ... Lawsuits are ... very brief, since this is advantageous to trade [*dem Handel daraus zu erhaltenden Vortheile*]. One often tries to shorten proceedings by using a judge-arbiter [*Schiedsrichter*] or [suits] ... are brought to a trade or business court or, where there is none such, to an ordinary court [*ordentlichen Gerichte*, i.e. a regular civil court run by the territorial regime] ... Sometimes [suits are argued] without lawyers ... No objections or extenuating circumstances such as fraud ... or that the money was not paid out in the first place (*exceptio non numeratae pecuniae*) are considered, but rather only, 'Is the instrument yours?' [... *der Beklagte den Wechselbrief für den seinigen erkannt hat* ...] ... The Judgment is executed upon personal arrest [*Das Urtheil wird vollstreckt und auf Personal-Arrest erkannt*]. As soon as the defendant should admit the instrument for his, speedy [*schleunige*] execution is ordered, without regard to person [*ohne Ansehen der Person* –

52 The term "rigor" is usually said to date from the jurist Heineccius (writing in 1723), though the routine application of summary procedure and personal arrest to the law of exchange can be clearly traced as far back as decisions of the Genoese Civil Rota in the sixteenth century. See Sedatis, *Über den Ursprung der Wechselstrenge*, pp. 10–14 and originally Heineccius, *Elementa iuris cambialis*, Cap. I, §IX, p. 3.

53 The following paragraphs are based generally on Simona Cerutti, "Law Merchants: a Model for an Egalitarian Society in 18th Century Europe" (paper presented at the Conference on Political History: Recent Trends in International Perspective, Bielefeld, December 10–12, 2009) (on Savoy); Estor, *Der Teutschen Rechtsgelahrheit* (see specific citations above); Heineccius, *Elementa iuris cambialis*; Piergiovanni, "Genoese Civil Rota"; Sedatis, *Über den Ursprung der Wechselstrenge*; and Johann Ludwig Uhl, ed., *Franckfurtische Wechsel-Responsa: welche von hiesiger hochlöbl. Juristen-Facultät von Zeit zu Zeit auf Begehren sind ausgestellet und ertheilet worden* (Franckfurt an der Oder: Johann Christian Kleyb, 1749), Responsum 8, pp. 8–10. Other more specific citations also follow below here. Sedatis's is the most recent specialized, book-length study of the development of the law of exchange in Germany, though there have been specialized articles published since then.

> i.e. personal social estate or sc. other personal privileges or freedoms). A personal arrest is also ordered. Appeal of the judicial decision [where permitted] does not suspend the execution.[54]

Summary procedure (*beschleunigtes Verfahren, parata executio*) is a civil law term referring to an expedited, simplified adjudicatory practice. This is the same kind of procedure we encountered in Chapter 4 in the context of possession – a special, abbreviated procedure which the court would unswervingly apply when certain criteria were met. In the law of exchange, summary procedure would be used if the person to whom a bill was presented (who should be the acceptor and payor) refused to pay the bill upon presentation. In this context, summary procedure entailed that only a few reasons were accepted as valid defenses (*exceptiones*); the suit had to be decided within a very short period of time (for instance, three days); and no countersuit by the defendant was permitted during the proceedings. These were typical of the law of exchange elsewhere, as well.[55] As a rule of thumb, summary procedure works to the advantage of the plaintiff in a suit.

If the court found for the plaintiff, then it would order the defendant acceptor to pay the face value of the bill within a short time, usually a few days to a week. Selchow and many sources speak cooly of personal arrest as a sanction for default on a bill in widespread use in the eighteenth century. *Arrest*, in German as in English, means the use of authorized legal force to detain a person. Generally speaking, arrest was used in Germany in this period. In some cases it referred not to detention of person but seizing of mobile capital (chattels).[56] Hence with summary procedure backed by strict liability able to produce seizure of the debtor's person and/or goods until payment was made, the bearer of a bill could be confident that he could collect what was owed to him within a matter of days (outside of panics).[57]

---

54 Selchow, *Grundsätze des Wechselrechts*, §§105–112, citing various sources special to these topics, but also Georg Melchior von Ludolff, *Observationum forensium continuatio* [*Obs. 111–240*] (Wetzlar: *Nicolaus Ludovicus Wincklerus*, 1732), P. II, obs. 179, p. 442 and Jakob Friedrich Ludovici, *Einleitung zum Wechsel-Process* (Halle: Wäysenhaus, 1713) c. 9. §2.

55 In Savoy in this period, summary procedure [also] entailed that little or no documentary evidence was accepted, but instead evidence was taken through a small number of testimonials about facts, under oath.

56 For an earlier English example of confiscation, see Tigar and Levy, *Law and the Rise of Capitalism*, p. 85.

57 In panics, chains of credit including those involving bills collapse because declining liquidity leads ineluctably toward insolvency. For Dutch, English, French, and German

It is hard to reconstruct exactly where and under what circumstances arrest was used in the Hessian and Rhine-Main region over money matters (as opposed to violence). It must be made clear that arbitrary arrest (without grounds, evidence, or a specific broken law) was loudly and prominently forbidden in important territorial law codes in sixteenth-century Germany[58] with language about arrest and bodily constraint such as legal historians expect mostly to find only in pre-modern English law. It appears that personal arrest was not used for bills in Frankfurt until sometime between 1662 and 1739.[59] In 1670 in Frankfurt an der Oder (in Brandenburg-Prussia), arrest was an accepted sanction for default on payment of bill debt at the fair. As of 1758, the Hessian territories did not permit personal arrest for default of payment on a bill of exchange. But apparently Hesse-Cassel, Hanau, Frankfurt am Main, Saxony and Nuremberg did permit *imprisonment* for *debt* in some cases (meaning I suppose not bills but ordinary debt in some scenarios – unclear). Selchow taught generally that arrest for default on bills was readily used in 1777. An eminent modern historian of the imperial supreme court says that summary

examples, see Charles P. Kindleberger, *Manias, panics, and crashes: a history of financial crises* (New York: Basic Books, 1978); Charles P. Kindleberger, *A Financial History of Western Europe* (London: 1984); Kindleberger, "Economic Crisis of 1619"; and Neal, *Rise of Financial Capitalism.*

58 There is evidence that strong protections against arbitrary seizure of person and property existed from at least the end of the sixteenth century onward, and that these protections were based on concepts of nature and equity already operational in Hessian jurisprudence by 1535 at latest. The regime permitted arrest only in case of contumacy or when flight was a present danger. The influential Catzenelnbogen Territorial Law (1572) prohibited arrest, stating, "we repeat the … reformation of Our Lord Father [Philipp the Magnanimous] of 1535 and have earnestly forbidden all arrest and seizure, both of persons and of estates." For arrest was "against nature and equity." The law proceeded to hedge a little on this, however, stating that regime officers might seize a person in a few, specified scenarios: contumacy, flight risk, and other emergencies. See Kleinschmidt, "Katzenelnbogen Landesordnung," Vom Arrestiren und Kümmern, pp. 557–559.

59 Publishing a "short practical guidebook" on exchange in Frankfurt am Main in 1662, Johann Theodor Sprenger emphasized that the law of exchange gave the presenter of a bill high priority over other creditors as well as the assurance of summary execution. Sprenger called this "the favorability of bills of exchange." Note that he mentioned merely priority, not arrest. Johann Theodor Sprenger, *Kurtze Wechszel-Practick auss den vornemsten Wechsel Scriptis* (Frankfurt am Main: Fickwirht, 1662), §18, p. 91. Several laws, including the exchange rules (*Wechsel-Ordnungen*) of 1739 in Frankfurt am Main, provided for similar imprisonment in case of default. Amend-Traut, *Wechselverbindlichkeiten vor dem Reichskammergericht*, p. 316.

procedure and personal arrest were (generally, she implies) used in German into the nineteenth century.[60]

I think the way to resolve this is that there were at least two ambiguities. One was that arrest might be a custom observed and enforced among merchants but not until sometime later adopted into the broader civil law of the state's jurisdiction. So in effect it was probably often at work in trade fairs and other merchant community events in many places in the seventeenth century but not widely recognized by outsiders. And generally, arrest was understood to be appropriate when flight was a risk – as for foreigners, persons not embedded within trusted local networks, or traveling salesmen (our merchants). The other ambiguity is that sometimes arrest was on the books but was not actually employed by magistrates.[61] According to many sources, by the late eighteenth century, arrest was on the decline, in disfavor, or even outlawed in many parts of the realm, including states in the Hessian and Rhine-Main region. The Imperial Chamber Court would late criticize the sanction of personal arrest, reasoning that Roman civil law prohibited debt imprisonment.[62] Political economists of the time (e.g. Guden, Martens) were sensitive to issues both of efficacy and of equity.

6 Regional Finance in the Seventeenth Century

We learned earlier how princely governments in Cassel and Marburg after the War sought to rebuild their administrative networks for collecting domain revenues and taxes, organizing the corvee, and supervising rural officials of the princely government (for example village officials and judges). The Marburg

60 Arrest remained in use into the nineteenth century. Historian of the imperial supreme court Anja Amend-Traut writes, "the formal rigor of exchange remained an essential component of the use of bills until into the nineteenth century. This meant that any person capable of using a bill had not only to agree to summary procedure, but also above all else be willing to accept personal arrest." "Demgegenüber galt die formelle Wechselstrenge bis in das 19. Jahrhundert hinein also wesentlicher Bestandteil der Wechselfähigkeit. Das bedeutete, dass sich jede wechselfähige Person nicht nur seinem schnellen Gerichtsverfahren unterziehen musste, sondern vor allem, dass bei Unterliegen des Schuldners die Forderung durch Personalarrest vollstreckt werden konnte." Amend-Traut, *Wechselverbindlichkeiten vor dem Reichskammergericht*, p. 315t.

61 For example, Georg Friedrich von Martens (1797) wrote that, while personal arrest was on the books, as we might say, it was not commonly used by courts unless there was a significant flight risk (as at trade fairs). See Martens, *Entwickelung des wahren Ursprungs des Wechselrechts*, p. 79.

62 Amend-Traut, *Wechselverbindlichkeiten vor dem Reichskammergericht*, pp. 315b–316t.

government also worked hard to reestablish the authority of princely courts to supervise local and appellate procedures and the conduct of lawyers.

In the midst of the Hessian states lay old, free, and rich Frankfurt am Main, a regional as well as continental entrepôt. Several overlapping fields of activity involving local product trade and capital markets were implicated in the development of the bills to be examined here.[63] Trade in produce and craft product around the region naturally centered on Frankfurt. The original capital market (Weber's "traditional" economic activity) was the carry trade in which merchant networks bought and sold products across various distances, in many different currencies, with all the risks of travel, transaction, and change of prices and rates (including arbitrage risk). Another, later echelon of capital market saw further development in the sixteenth century – the business of borrowing and lending moneys in large amounts not tied to specific commodity sales.

The fact that bills were used for carry trade in Frankfurt, and later on a rudimentary money market emerged there using "dry" bills, meant that negotiable instruments also became more common with regional actors such as merchants in nearby Marburg or Cassel and regional magnates such as princes and nobles. Average farmers or artisans living in villages frequently used simple debt notes (chits or IOUs) in the seventeenth century. However, their well-to-do neighbors began using negotiable instruments in the late 1600s. Regardless of station, the poor and the rich, villagers and burghers, were all implicated in local economies that included the circulation of coin and land, and it became more frequent in the period from around 1650 to 1750 to conduct high-value transactions with bills rather than with debt notes.

Before the widespread introduction of the law of exchange in the region, the financial regulations which affected most people concerned lending and borrowing. As we would expect, much of the applicable law was a synthesis of imperial common law (the *ius commune*) and custom. Law suits involving financial security and studies of financial law often concerned practices like suretyship, giving a pledge or pawn in collateral against a loan, and official corruption in local government[64] – but regulators were particularly concerned with interest rates. From the mid seventeenth century onward, the princely regimes in Marburg and Darmstadt issued regulations and reminders limit-

---

63 Ullmann, "Der Frankfurter Kapitalmarkt um 1800," p. 76.

64 See for instance the "Reformation und Ordnung" of Louis III of Hesse-Marburg of July 13, 1573, parts of which are printed in Kleinschmid and Apell, *Sammlung*, Vol. 1, p. 141, p. 436, p. 685.

ing interest on cash loans to 5%.[65]As might be expected, legal regulation of loan interest employed the concept of usury, lending at what were considered abusive rates, usually by Jews to Christians.

Anti-usury laws, including those specifically naming Jewish lenders or dealers, should be seen as an effort to preserve the dominant Christian socioeconomic order, specifically by setting limits on interest rates Jews were permitted to charge. Most local policymakers of the day tended to hold the conservative interpretation of lending at interest, namely that it was permissible at the just price, but only as a means to enable the production and marketing of goods, not a money-making activity in itself.[66] Hence princes, privy councils, and territorial diets renewed or re-announced traditional rates. In 1654, the Youngest Diet Recess had fixed interest at 5% (in some places 6%) for loans made during the Thirty Years' War.[67] Jewish and also apparently Christian merchants and moneylenders were in many places permitted to charge 5–8%. In many places, we are told, the *true* going (and *illegal*) rate of interest was around 15–20%.[68] Furthermore, while Christian merchants and Jews were permitted to lend at interest, secular authorities in most places took a dim view of "common [Christian] people" lending money at interest. Outside

65 I have not taken a measure of the relative frequency of regime activity around interest rates. It could be assessed through study of regulatory activity around matters involving cash use such as suretyship, loan collateral, payment of debts – a broad class of legal-economic issues to be sure – but perhaps excluding commercial issues like import/export regulations, taxes, or mining concessions.

66 A widely held misconception is that in pre-modern European history, loans at interest were prohibited as "usurious" in most Christian polities. On the contrary, merchant Christians and Jews were in most places permitted to charge 5–8% interest on loans. As an example, the influential Catzenelnbogen Territorial Law (1572) stated the rate of 5%. As Walther and Bode wrote, interest is "honest money, which the negotiators look forward to" in an exchange deal, to compensate for "their industry, works, expenses, and risks." See Johannes Walther, praeses, Matthias Bode, respondans, *Dissertatio Iuridica De Cambiis* (Marburg: Chemlinus [Ex Officina Typographica Chemliniana], 1646), Thesis 10, pp. 45–49. Similar views can be found in numerous other sources. In this context for example, see the discussion of usury and just price in bills of exchange at Raymond A. de Roover, "Cardinal Cajetan on '*Cambium*' or Exchange Dealings," in *Philosophy and Humanism. Renaissance Essays in Honor of Paul Oskar Kristeller*, ed. Edward P. Mahoney (New York: Columbia University Press, 1976), p. 6. Short accounts can be found at Berman, *Law and Revolution II*, pp. 161–163, and de Roover, "What is Dry Exchange?," p. 198l.

67 Estor, *Der Teutschen Rechtsgelahrheit*, Chapter 22, §3629, pp. 337–338; see also following Chapter 23, pp. 337–339.

68 Ibid., Chapter 23, §3635 with further reference also to the Juden-Ordnung of Hesse-Cassel of 1749. See also Walther and Bode, *Dissertatio Iuridica De Cambiis*, Theses 6, 8, 10, 16. For the illegal rate, see de Roover, "What is Dry Exchange?," p. 198l.

of a few mercantile hotspots like Hamburg or Frankfurt, the use of bills was restricted to specialist merchants embedded in networks of high trust and good credit, secured by great capital.

The Hesse-Cassel regime's first general regulation of negotiable financial instruments came in the Jewish Ordinance (*Juden-Ordnung*) of 1679, which prohibited discounting. As mentioned earlier, to discount a bill meant that whoever obtained the bill paid the previous holder less than the bill's face value – in the modern idiom, he got the bill at a discount. This might be done when the bill was created (inception) or, alternatively, if and when the bearer sold it at discount to a third party. In financial centers like Amsterdam or Frankfurt am Main, discounting was considered licit since it reflected the changing value of money and commodities in relation to events. But in the more closed market networks of regional commerce, it was usually understood to reflect a scheme to charge illegally high interest on a loan.[69] While the 1679 rule specifically concerned Jews (the *Juden-Ordnung*), it also aimed at practices of collusion between Christians and Jews to evade the limits on interest rates,[70] taking aim at the practice of Jews ceding bills to Christians or, put another way, at Christians buying bills from Jews. At the time in Hesse, Jews could charge 5%, but non-merchant Christians could not charge interest. If a Jew lent money to a Christian, and the parties created a debt note by which the latter or his associate would become payer to the Jew, and then the Jew ceded (i.e. sold) the draft to a second Christian, then in effect the second Christian would have been able to lend money to the first Christian at 5%. In §20 of the Jewish Ordinance, the regime prohibited Jews from ceding drafts to Christians. The use of bills to hide high-rate lending was widely criticized by jurists and lawmakers, despite their growing liberal political economic thinking. The imperial notary Johann Jacob Heydiger called discounted notes "clothing for inequitable usury." Reflecting on the expert legal opinion of another jurist (in Cölln, where he practiced, the old other half of Berlin), he wrote:

69 See Raymond A. de Roover and Lorenz Laubenberger, "Wechsel, Wechselrecht," in *Handwörterbuch zur deutschen Rechtsgeschichte*, ed. Adalbert Erler, Ekkehard Kaufmann, and Wolfgang Stammler, Vol. 5 (Berlin: E. Schmidt, 1998), pp. 1180–1182. For the "Juden-Ordnung" of 1679, see Kleinschmid and Apell, *Sammlung*, Vol. 3, p. 3, p. 129. The ancient Roman *lex Anastasiana* already prohibited discounting of debt assignment in the sixth century. The practice of discounting described here was the ancestor of buying interest-bearing securities such as bonds at fluctuating market rate, thus yielding variable effective interest (the yield) despite a fixed nominal interest rate.

70 See §20 of the Jewish Ordinance.

> It is contrary to … [natural] equity if the bill-giver or others of his people should enjoy what the original drawer of the check has not received from him.[71]

Lawmakers remained concerned about usury and discounting through at least the late eighteenth century, long after they began to encourage the use of bills among growing segments of the population.

7 New Directions in the Eighteenth Century

> Credit is the soul of all commerce, and neither trade and commerce nor artisans … can live without it.
>
> *Instruction concerning Police and Commerce*, Hesse-Cassel (1721)[72]

At the turn of the eighteenth century, as far as we know the only place in the region where the use and enforcement of bills was recognized was in the "great republic" of Frankfurt. Negotiability of bills was not enforceable in the Hessian lands or elsewhere in the region surrounding that city. If a person wanted to "sell" a debt, he had to cede the assignment action to another person in court. But great changes were beginning. This was the age of the "Financial Revolution," the last stage of preindustrial economy in European countries (before the Industrial Revolution ignited later in the century). This era was marked by the tighter integration of markets, for instance in Amsterdam, Paris, London, and Hamburg, and growth in the volume of trade in paper money instruments, both shares in companies and debt. In 1719–1720, new investment schemes in France and England had led respectively to the Mississippi and South Sea Bubbles, which resulted in the collapse of the French currency, widespread loss of investments, and skepticism, anger, and panic about speculation in paper money. Panic had spread to the money markets in Amsterdam and Hamburg as well. The period after 1720 was marked by conservative regulatory reaction against joint stock companies and national banks, even while observers marveled at the power of circulating paper money in creating liquidity and encouraging (potentially) productive investment.

71 See Johann Jacob Heydiger, *Kurze anleitung zu gründlichem verstand des wechselrechts* (Cölln: 1715), p. 123, pp. 139–146. The Catzenelnbogen Territorial Law also described and forbade discounting.

72 Kleinschmid and Apell, *Sammlung*, Vol. 3, p. 867, §17.

This was the setting, then, in which the Hessian regime in Cassel and Marburg changed the course of their financial and monetary policies through an ambitious round of financial regulation. Where many policies in the immediate post-War period were essentially conservative or restorationist, in the eighteenth century the regime would implement financial policies aimed at achieving new ends. These new policies marked a profound change from earlier, more conservative statecraft. Even amidst the fundamentalist revolution of the German Reformation, rulers had promoted the myth of the old order of law and society. But by the late seventeenth century the ruling and intellectual elites were becoming committed to new theories of political economy. They saw the territory as a productive resource, with people, agriculture, and natural resources that could be managed scientifically to increase their productivity. Science and technology should be studied and disseminated. Land should be farmed according to the best modern practices to increase production. To facilitate commerce, precious metals and nascent forms of paper value instruments should circulate, much as blood circulated in the body.[73] Commercial laws themselves should be evaluated by how well they promoted productivity and the accumulation of wealth, and amended to further these ends. These programs reflect the twin schools, mercantilism and cameralism. And while mercantilism and cameralism were primarily focused on elite-managed production and accumulation, they usually shared some of the tenets of the later schools of physiocracy and liberalism – that the free activities of many (though not necessarily all) individuals to produce, offer, buy, consume, borrow, and lend were essential to the growth of wealth.[74]

The first action of the Hessian regime was to patent a lending bank in Cassel that would sell debt notes as well as give out loans against pledged collateral (precious jewels, real estate, etc.). The second policy change was the formal introduction of the law of exchange into Hesse. In 1721, Landgrave Charles in consultation with his "regime, chamber and commercial councilors" established a commission to stimulate commercial activity in the principality. The commission's program was articulated in the "Instruction and Ordinance Concerning Matters of Policy and Commerce" dated August 9, 1721. Section 17 of this instruction was quoted at the top of this section, saying that "credit is the soul of all commerce, and neither trade and commerce nor artisans them-

---

73 John Law, *Money and trade considered: with a proposal for supplying the nation with money* (Edinburgh: Heirs and successors of A. Anderson, 1705).

74 The various schools agreed in general terms but disagreed as to the extent that emancipation and deregulation were important, for example how much elites should still retain power and control, as in monopoly licensing of production, or in how much the lower classes should be emancipated.

selves can live without it. For this reason, the commission had the mandate to "undertake everything that is found to be necessary to maintain [credit], including in any case the introduction of the law of exchange and strong observance of the same."[75]

In 1723, the Hesse-Cassel regime saw fit to formally introduce the law of exchange. True, merchants in Marburg, Cassel, and Darmstadt were doubtless using bills in their business dealings in Frankfurt,[76] which had the law of exchange by the late seventeenth century, and the empire had adopted it in 1654. However, by promulgating the law of exchange at the territorial level, the regime could regulate specific aspects of the law, such as permitting it for some groups and not others, as we will see below. The formal adoption also meant that regime courts (particularly the High Appellate Court) had to use the body of law merchant to interpret any conflicts involving use of bills. In 1723, the prince of the regime issued a brief and direct "Gracious Resolution":

> We have resolved [...] that the law of exchange shall be valid in our lands, for both Jews and for Christians, and summary execution of it shall be imposed and followed.

Thus the use of bills was seemingly extended to all legal subjects, but discounting bills as a vehicle for high interest lending was still prohibited.[77]

8 Variations on the Theme

We should now pause the historical narrative for a moment to observe that, despite the unity and seeming determinacy of the nominative phrase, "law of

---

75 See "Instruction und Verordnung das Policey- und Commercien-Wesen betreffend" of August 9, 1721, in Kleinschmid and Apell, *Sammlung*, Vol. 3, pp. 865–869. For the authorization of the commission itself, see ibid., Vol. 3, p. 865: "We have [...] given this commission [...] authority [to] take in hand the establishment and maintenance of good policy and the improvement of the useful arts, manufacturing and crafts, and the growth of commerce."

76 For relatively local use of bills around the Hessian and Rhine-Main region, see Estor, *Der Teutschen Rechtsgelahrheit*, §3756, p. 388 (also discussed below).

77 See "Gnädigste Resolution / Wechsel-Ordnung" of 1723 in Kleinschmid and Apell, *Sammlung*, Vol. 3, p. 905 f. The ambiguous language read: "Whereas our regime must attend to such matters [summary execution], and in cases that arise, [we must] adjudicate and dispose of such exchange matters, to this end we thus alter and arrange §19 and §20 of the Jewish Ordinance [*auch zu dem ende die §§19. und 20. der juden Ordnung dahin ändern und einrichten zu laßen*]." It is not clear whether the 1723 language abolished parts or all of §19 or §20 of the 1679 ordinance.

exchange" (*ius cambialis*, *Wechselrecht*), the actual regulations and parameters of this law were somewhat in flux. That is, rules varied by context, polity, and interpreter, just like other bodies of law e.g. "customary law". A term might sound fixed and determinate but actually mean a variety of things. There were many forms of debt; bills of exchange were used in a variety of ways.

The formal distinction between bills and notes, while useful heuristically, seems to belie the muddiness of actual practice in the late seventeenth and early eighteenth centuries. This reflects not just the famous heterogeneity of legal forms among the hundreds of independent German jurisdictions, from Breslau to Hesse-Cassel, but also the different legal forms in any given place. In addition, terminology varied. Among the many vehicles for debt and credit were IOUs (simple chits, promissory notes, *chirographia*), informal quotidian carrying debt (e.g., a bar tab), and short-term merchant carrying debt (in a ledger). There were bills of exchange and debt that had to be serviced in the form of annuities and deeds of rental. There was pledge, in which pledged collateral could be simply left in the hands of the pledge-creditor and the debt would functionally be a sale after a certain period. There were forms of guarantee such as suretyship. Debts could be secured, through collateral or additional guaranty, or unsecured. Some forms of debt were regulated, either through custom, through the *ius commune*, or via new black-letter civil law. Some debts were open and registered or formally recorded with government offices, some were "grey" (done off the books). Sometimes parties made up their own additional conditions, which were sometimes recognized and enforceable by police authorities, sometimes rejected in one jurisdiction or the other or both.[78]

Bills also differed in kind and did not always operate according to the precise rules we read about. (Or as T. S. Elliot would later write, "Between the idea and the reality falls the shadow.") Actors *sought to turn one kind of instrument into another*. For, it seems, financial instruments were more malleable than has been previously noticed by later scholars. And indeed, this is in keeping with the interpretation of local real estate transfer activity and arrogation of rights and freedoms in Chapters 4 and 5. Among bills' formal features, several seem

78 For the variety of quotidian forms of debt, see Estor, *Der Teutschen Rechtsgelahrheit*, Chapter 28, §3674–3677, pp. 357–358, Chapter 29, §3683, p. 361. For comparison, historians of France have also recently revised their view of the commercialization of French society in the same period and similarly found widespread use of many forms of debt and inchoate paper money there as well. See Francesca Trivellato, "Credit, Honor, and the Early Modern French Legend of the Jewish Invention of Bills of Exchange," *The Journal of Modern History* 84, no. 2 (2012), pp. 291–292 and the further literature cited there in n. 6.

to have often been ignored or used only when convenient for one or another party: the formal genre marks of a bill (dates, parties' names, identification of the instrument as a *letter of exchange*), the rule that bills were restricted to merchants, and the feature that bills involved an exchange in different currencies between two different (i.e. foreign) territories. For example, in his study of German jurisprudence from 1758, Estor gave an example of a bill in which the two "foreign" territories across which the bill to be used were Marburg and Frankfurt am Main, which lie only 90 km apart – just a few days travel![79] Underlying the formal terminological simplicity and constancy of bills was heterogeneity, muddiness, and improvisation.

Hence when jurisprudence and case law specific to German governments outside the great trading cities begin to appear in the 1720s, we find jurists confronting this diversity and trying to sort out conflicting practices. In some cases, parties to a debt note or the assignment of a debt note could legally add rider language to the instrument specifying that the note or assignment was to be treated like a bill if dispute arose. Several jurisdictions had statutes permitting parties to add language to notes stating that they must be interpreted in the same way as bills in case of dispute – in other words, they must enjoy the "rigor of the law of exchange." As an example, the Breslau law merchant of 1716 provided that assignment of a note to a third party, if spelled out in the note, had to be treated with the same rigor as endorsement of a bill. By contrast, the Leipzig law (1682) did not permit a non-bill to be treated like a bill with the full "rigor."

In 1758 Estor wrote that, in some locales, makers of notes included special clauses to the effect that the creditor "shall proceed with or without right" or "shall make himself get paid," or that "this assignment be so good as a rightful [bill of] exchange, or shall have the force of a [bill of] exchange ..." According to Estor, such clauses had the effect of a *mandatum sine clausula*" – it simply had to be obeyed.[80] These provisions specified that disputes over such a bill had to be settled with summary execution rather than ordinary litigation procedures.[81]

Johann Gottlieb Heineccius, the well-known law professor in Halle whom we met in Chapter 4 (depicted in Figure 51), penned an expert legal opinion

79 Estor, *Der Teutschen Rechtsgelahrheit*, §3756, p. 388.

80 Ibid., §3700. A *mandatum sine clausula* was a court order or injunction which had to be obeyed without fail. No objection or stay could be made *ex ante*.

81 A modern analogy would be the way that many contracts Americans have to enter into today include clauses stipulating that disputes over the contract will not be settled in ordinary civil court but instead through binding arbitration.

FIGURE 51 Johann Gottlieb Heineccius

or *consilium* involving bills in 1719. In it he treated this problem of the difference between a bill and an assigned debt note. Dispute had arisen between businessmen in the two jurisdictions just mentioned, Leipzig and Breslau. A Leipziger man named "GO" in the source had assigned a debt note of 800 dollars (*Taler*) to another man "CB," after which CB assigned it to the order of a third man "JGW."[82] For reasons not given, GO told his merchant partner "DG"

82 In law casebooks and in governmental edicts in seventeenth- and eighteenth-century Germany it was common to give such abbreviations. This served both to protect the pri-

(the *assignatus*) not to pay the note if presented; CB disappeared or died, and JGW sued GO for the value. According to Heineccius, the assignment *would* have been treated like a bill *except* for two things which caused JGW's suit to fail: First, the assignment was made in Leipzig, so it was governed by Leipzig law. Second, GO had added a clause to the assignment contract stipulating that the assignment was to be treated as a bill if and only if it was actually "accepted" by the merchant DG – which it had not been. Although much about the case is unknown to us, what is clear is that JGW could make a reasonable and plausible but finally insufficient argument for treating a debt assignment as having been endorsed over to him properly. The original creditor GO as well as the jurisconsult Heineccius recognized that such an act could have happened (though it did not) – because it would have been within the scope of ordinary legal financial activities.[83]

The above case illustrates how actors on the ground changed things according to their own, contingent purposes, leaving jurists like Heineccius and the Hessian judges (to be discussed below) to sort things out when required. All this variation and improvisation was not viewed as inappropriate. It was, rather, "the modern custom" or the "Germanic jurisprudence," according to the experts. The *usus modernus* as "the study of modern custom" meant to take stock of existing law and practice, study it, and give it the status of an autonomously body of law.

Perhaps the first attempt to construct a system or body of customary law was an influential work by Hertius, the influential professor and chancellor in Giessen whose work on sovereignty and commercial policy was discussed earlier. One of his earliest works was a 1684 study of German legal proverbs (*paroemia*). One example of a proverb of financial law, for instance, was "he who accepts, pays" – quoted in Italian, the language of the famous Genoese merchants. He to whom a bill is presented – who "accepts" it – must pay. "This Italian proverb only is used among German merchants, as though

vacy of litigants and to strip away unnecessary details (what are called in English law the *dicta*) in order to focus on the holdings or rules illustrated by a case. Abbreviation also had the effect of hiding the social estate of the parties, so that rules were traced out of decisions with reference not to the types of people involved, but to their property rights and their actions.

83 The opinion was written and used in 1719, but only published for broader academic consumption in an anthology of Heineccius's writings after his death. See Johann Gottlieb Heineccius, "XXII. Consilium nack L. an G. H … 1719 … ex nuda assignatione nec cambialiter nec exsequutiue agi potest," in *Vermischte Anmerckungen und rechtliche Gutachten* (Berlin: Johannes Andreas Rüdiger, 1742 [orig. 1719]), pp. 322–330.

received [*donatum*] in our commonwealth ... One is to pay, without exception, as is demonstrated ... in the testimonials of many merchants, as well as the responses of jurists in Strasbourg and Leipzig ..." The custom (*usum*), Hertius explains, was adopted in Germany in order to expedite free exchanges among traveling merchants.[84] Several proverbs were specifically concerned with assignment of debt. Hertius and, later, Georg Tobias Pistorius also examined the maxim that "assignment is good payment," to which there was a variant proverb that assignment was instead *not* good payment. Yes, assignment was a way of transferring credit to someone and therewith settling a debt, but in the more widely held view, it was "not good payment" in that it could not readily produce money, only credit. What was worse, ordinary debts were already hard enough to collect among settled populations; it was even more challenging to force payment of a debt in communities of itinerant foreign merchants.[85] (Hence the value of strict liability in bills.)

This brief discussion of plurality, improvisation, and assimilation of the law of exchange indicate some ways that legal operators actually viewed and applied merchant law, sometimes in ways which clearly differed from the ideal type as generally taught in textbooks like that of Selchow later in the eighteenth century. Legal operators knew that law merchant was sometimes ambiguous, and they interpreted mercantile ideas as an ongoing legal-commercial reality of which they were professionally challenged to make sense. As they saw it, there might be separate sources or bodies of law (civil, canon, mercantile, customary), but henceforth all had to be reconciled into the "territorial constitution" of any given realm or *Land*. Like the ground-level actors and jurists we observed in Chapter 4, here we also see variations in debt, in understandings of bills, in rules about who could use them, and in how and how widely they were used.

---

84 "Proverbio Italico heic locus non fuisset datus, nisi inter mercatores Germanos in usum venisset, civitate nostra quasi donatum ... Nimirum ex usu mercatorum, qui cambium simplicter acceptavit, sine exceptione solvere obstrictus est, ut multorum mercatorum testimoniis demonstravit ... Idque receptum ob necessarium peregrinantium & liberiorem expeditioremque commerciorum usum." Johann Nikolaus Hertius, "De Paroemiis Juris Germanicis Libri Tres," in *Commentationum atque opusculorum de selectis et rarioribus ex jurisprudentia universali, publica, feudali et Romana, nec non historia Germanica, argumentis tomi tres*, Vol. 3 (Frankfurt am Main: Johannes Davidus Zunnerus, 1716 [orig. 1700]), book I, proverb XXIIX, "He who accepts, pays," p. 437.

85 See ibid., book I, proverb XCVI, "Anweissung ist keine Zahlung," I, pp. 554–558 and Georg Tobias Pistorius, *Thesaurus paroemiarum Germanico-iuridicarum: Teutsch-Juristischer Sprichwörter-Schatz*, expanded and corrected ed. (Leipzig: J. C. Muller, 1716), century 2, proverb XXXI, pp. 170–172, "Anweisung ist gute bezahlung."

FIGURE 52 Wilhelm VIII of Hesse-Cassel with the Order of the White Eagle. Wilhelm VIII was the de facto ruler (regent) of Hesse-Cassel responsible for the Contract Ordinance of 1732

9 Reconciling Conflicting Law, 1732–1749

The Cassel regime issued extensive new commercial regulations in 1732, called the Contract Ordinance. This was a modernization program undertaken by the administration of a new regent (Statthalter), Wilhelm VIII (r. 1730-, as landgrave 1751–1760; see Figure 52). Among other things, the Contract Ordinance specified which subjects were permitted to make and negotiate bills. This wider circle, which included "persons of distinction, scholars [*Gelehrte*], merchants, Jews, and townsmen or farmers engaged in trade," were to enjoy the use of the high-stakes rules of summary procedure, execution, and arrest. But "other persons" were excluded from using bills – "especially farm hands or day-laborers who do not run a business."[86] Given this extension, it would seem that the anxiety of the years 1720–1723 about too many people getting involved in the use of paper money may have been wearing off by 1732.

It seems unlikely that this rule really had any substantial disempowering effect on field hands and day-laborers, since such individuals would have made vanishingly few bills. Why then are they mentioned? The default answer of older jurisprudence is that it was to protect the weak, simple, and incompetent from becoming prey to fraud or getting involved in risky commercial activities they did not understand. By the same token, such estate restrictions were also understood to protect counterparties as well from getting involved with potentially unreliable people.

The Hesse-Cassel law of bills after 1723 was vague in some regards. People could and did use bills to transfer large sums of money. Jewish-Christian bill acceptance and negotiation at discount were still illegal. However this must have been a grey area of law, since bills throughout Europe were commonly discounted at unpublicized levels in order to serve as loans at actual (usurious, rather than legal) levels of interest. Further, common law merchant made no distinction in any of its variants (that I know of) to the religious estate of its users; the only personal estate that was ever important for law merchant was whether a person was a member of a community which was privileged to enjoy law merchant. The 1723 rule seemingly allowed virtually all Hessian subjects to use the law merchant, but that of 1732 restricted those of low social estate from doing so. The 1732 rule expressed this estate limitation not only in terms of occupation but also in terms of jurisdiction: People in the big towns and anyone who otherwise enjoyed the prince's direct jurisdiction were permitted to use law merchant, while (by implication) those who were subject to rural seigniorial jurisdictions were not.

---

86 "und sonderlich Acker- oder Handwercksleute, so keinen Handel treiben." See "Contracten-Ordnung" of January 9, 1732, in C. F. Kulenkamp, ed., *Neue Sammlung der Landes-Ordnungen, Ausschreiben und anderer allgemeinen Verfügungen* [*etc.*] (Cassel: Hof- und Waisenhaus-Buchdruckerei, 1828), Vol. 1, p. 312, §11. The sense in which "other persons" were effectively excluded was that, while they were able to make bills, they would not enjoy the law of exchange, in particular summary execution. Bills made by such people would "receive no more than common recognition," i.e. even if they were called "bills" (*Wechselbriefe*), princely courts would consider them to be simple debt notes or IOUs.

New Jewish ordinances in 1739 and 1749 renewed the prohibitions on discounting and ceding bills from 1679, although the Jewish Ordinance of 1749 increased the level of interest Jews were permitted to charge from 5% to a range of 6–8%. Notably, §22 of the 1749 Jewish Ordinance concluded ominously that

> the maker of a bill must in each case acknowledge that he has received the face value of the bill [*Valuta*] in cash. If he can subsequently prove that he was pressured [*induciret*] to say this, and that he did not receive the face value in cash but in goods, then the debt shall be confiscated from the treacherous Jew and he shall be driven from the land with flogging.[87]

The Jewish Ordinances of 1679, 1739 and 1749 all point to collusive relations involving inter-religious evasion of the regime's prohibitions against Christians lending money at interest. Since "merchants" generally enjoyed waivers from such prohibitions, by virtue of being members of merchant guilds in Cassel and Marburg, the 1679, 1739 and 1749 prohibitions were meant to regulate life for common Christians and Jews living in the villages in Lower and Upper Hesse in the vicinity of these two towns within their local trade networks. In other words, quite aside from the second-class status under which Jews lived in this German principality (see Figure 53), by intervals the regime also sought to prevent people of a certain class or status – the majority of farmers or rural artisans – from either engaging in high-interest lending or indeed any use of bills.

Several reasons were cited for the shifting regulation of lending and Christian-Jewish financial relations. The idea that a bill should not be sold (much less discounted) reflected the old qualm that money is not itself a *good* which can be sold and that a bill or note is just a record of an underlying value (debt contract), not a value itself. Regime and courts insisted that lending interest rates had to be capped at "reasonable" levels (the customary rate

---

87 "[J]edoch muß jedesmahl der Aussteller des Wechsels wenigstens bekennen, daß er die Valuta an baarem Geld empfangen habe, und wann er hiernächst beweisen kan, daß er hierzu induciret worden, und von dem Juden die Valuta nicht baar, sondern ganz oder zum theil in Waaren erhalten, so soll gegen selbigen mit der Confiscation der Schuld, in so weit dieselbe richtig befunden werden möchte, verfahren, und überdem der betrügerische Jude noch darzu mit Staupenschlägen aus dem Lande gejaget werden." See Kleinschmid and Apell, *Sammlung*, Vol. 4, p. 1016, §22 and Ingrao, *Hessian Mercenary State*, pp. 93–94.

FIGURE 53 Woodcut cartoon depicting a German farmer and Jewish moneylender

of 5–8%, not subject to short-term fluctuations) and that, in all events, lending at interest must be restricted to Jews and to privileged Christian merchants.[88]

Given the above considerations, the Jewish Ordinances (on interest and usury) seem to have pointed in several, conflicting policy directions. The edicts of 1721 and 1723 normalizing the use of bills can be seen as liberal, and that of 1732 as again somewhat restrictive or conservative. Why? Perhaps they reflected the views of liberal and conservative factions within government:

88 Information about interest rates is regrettably spotty.

some wanted to buttress the older Christian socioeconomic order of estates, while others wanted to liberalize commercial activity and encourage more pluralistic production and consumption.

The messiness around which social estates enjoyed the privilege of exchange also makes it difficult to interpret what the actual rules were. I think there are two important, underlying phenomena, which together point to a new, broader conclusion. One underlying phenomenon is that there existed an almost universal belief that different groups or estates could and should be subject to different rules, appropriate to their nature as Christians, Jews, farmers, burghers, merchants, soldiers, religious, nobles, serfs, minors, criminals, the insane, etc. Here was the profound social and legal inegalitarianism of the Old Regime. The other underlying phenomenon is that these estates overlapped with one another which led to inconsistent interpretations. Consider the following dilemmas:

> If a person whose estate was protected by retraction law (Chapter 4) accepted but refused to pay a bill, could the estate be encumbered? This problem lay behind the exclusion of nobles sometimes from using bills proper.
>
> Could Christian merchants sell bills to other Christian merchants at usurious rates? (No.)
>
> If a professional owned a productive farm, was he a professional or was he a farmer? If he former, he enjoyed the use of bills, if the latter, not. (See below.)

The conclusion I will draw from this conflict of laws is that jurisprudence around bill use would help the emergence of a unitary legal subject, what we might call a generic legal person. The essential characteristic of this new legal subject, for purposes of applying the law of exchange, was that he or she not be under the domination of another (what Phillip Pettit terms *non-domination*[89]). Such a person had control over his (or *her*) estate, mental competence, freedom from the physical restriction of another's authority, and was of the age of reason (not a minor). Let us call these the freedom criteria for using bills. These freedom criteria implied the exclusion of a variety of different social estates. One was soldiers. The jurist and publisher Samuel

89 Pettit, *Republicanism: A Theory of Freedom and Government*, Part I, pp. 17–128.

Grünhut reported in 1903 that Austria still (in 1903) excluded from the Law of Exchange those "active and retired officers and the male population of the fighting estates" (*die Mannschaft des streitbaren Standes*, presumably meaning those eligible for military service or conscription), not including reservists.[90] More fundamentally, in 1625 Grotius had explained that "mercenaries" are under an "imperfect form of slavery," presumably because they are under army discipline and must obey their superior officers.[91] So were people locked in disciplinary institutions such as the insane or persons under arrest, since these did not have freedom of their own body or choices at law.[92] In the late eighteenth century, Selchow taught in his lectures that religious and certain state officials and were excluded. Domestic women under the authority of a head of household were excluded from using bills, although women generally were legally permitted to do so. Jurists called the former condition *Frauenzimmer* (literally "a woman's or women's quarters" within a home).[93] This seems to have meant, by euphemistic association, something like a domestic woman under some form of guardianship or supervision, even in the sense of a wife who was more or less under the control or tutelage of her husband. The term also seems sometimes to refer to the maid staff of a household. The contradiction between women's general privilege but the restriction of *Frauenzimmer* is another example of the clash between legal rules mentioned above. But *Frauenzimmer* was not

> enjoyed by all, for instance not affecting businesswomen. By virtue of the manly trade they pursue, [businesswomen] do not enjoy this womanly right.[94]

---

90 Carl Samuel Grünhut, *Grundriss des wechselrechts*, 2nd, improved ed., Grundriss des österreichischen Rechts (Leipzig: Duncker & Humblot, 1903), p. 3t.

91 Grotius, *De jure belli ac pacis*, Lib. II, Cap. V, XXX, p. 337.

92 Wilhelm Endemann, *Studien in der romanisch-kanonistischen wirthschafts- und rechtslehre bis gegen ende des siebenzehnten jahrhunderts* (Berlin: J. Guttentag; D. Collin, 1874–1883), pp. 186–187m. For arrest, see Selchow, *Grundsätze des Wechselrechts*, §20, p. 23.

93 Selchow, *Grundsätze des Wechselrechts*, §21, p. 24 and Grünhut, *Grundriss des wechselrechts*, p. 3t state that in some places the condition of *Frauenzimmer* was held to constitute grounds for exclusion from the use of bills.

94 "… und zumahl die Kauf = und Handelsfrauen nicht trifft, als welche wegen des männlichen Gewerbes, welches sie treiben, in Handelssachen, sich dieser weiblichen Gerechtigkeit am wenigsten zu erfreuen haben." See Selchow, *Grundsätze des Wechselrechts* §21 pointing further toworks by Beck, Rebhan and Manzel, and most eminently Jakob Friedrich Ludovici, praeses, Christoph Carl Bruckmüller, respondans, *De muliere cambiante* (Halle: C. Henckel, 1734) on businesswomen. We encounter Ludovici again further below; he was another major Hessian jurist.

Rulers (on the advice of their jurist privy counselors) were concerned to restrict the use of bills for both moral and practical reasons. Morally, it was thought that some classes of people needed to be taken special care of, to be kept under tutelage, e.g., minors and unmarried women. Practically speaking, the use of bills also involved great risk. A poor subsistence farmer might have been forbidden from using bills because, if he could not settle a bill, he stood to lose the only livelihood he had, namely whatever patch of land nourished him.

Jurists thought that "field workers and manual laborers who do not engage in commerce" basically excluded themselves from market activity, in the sense of using cash or credit for exchanges of non-subsistence goods and services. If such persons ever had debt, it only had the validity of a "common recognition (handwritten note)."[95] Some states carried this principle further than others. For instance, in Saxony and Brandenburg-Prussia, "small burghers" who "do not practice trade or any job which requires great outlays, or rent estates" were also excluded.[96] Again, the reasoning behind the exclusion here was implicitly that such persons had no need for high-stakes paper money since their affairs were small. Again, such paternalism justified the legal inegalitarianism of the Old Regime but actually protected remitter and remittee of bill alike, for the reasons given earlier.

The patented lending bank in Cassel encouraged the widespread use and purchase of debt notes by segments of the population. However, the Cassel bank would not take bills or notes as collateral for loans, so it was not itself yet in the discounting business.[97] The 1723 liberalization of financial law in Hesse was a response to increased demand for circulation of bills and notes. The cap on interest rates was raised in 1749 for similar reasons.

Before 1732, under the old regime in Hesse, the society of estates had been treated as a static collection of resources from which to squeeze as much as possible. In 1732, the regime of the new regent Wilhelm VIII moved to unlock the economic potential of plurality, of multiple productive and commercial agencies. Although the rules of 1721, 1723, and 1732 seem liberalizing, a more parsimonious explanation would be that they were guided by the prevalent political economy ideas of mercantilism and cameralism.[98] Mercantilists and cameralists from Veit Ludwig von Seckendorff to Joseph von

95 To this point, Estor cites an order of 1732 in Hesse-Cassel and two from Brandenburg of 1722 and 1724. See Estor, *Der Teutschen Rechtsgelahrheit*, §3786–3787.

96 Ibid., §3786.

97 I am indebted to Daniel Menning of the Universität Tübingen for pointing this out to me.

98 Physiocratic and liberal theories of political economy did not begin to circulate widely until slightly later.

Sonnenfels already conceived of a territorial or regional economy as including a domestic market for the offering and purchasing of produce and commodities. They understood this as a dynamic resource which had to be unlocked, after which it could be encouraged and strengthened. It was well known that the more sophisticated actors in domestic markets, particularly in and around large commercial centers like Frankfurt or Hamburg, wished to engage in the transfer and use of paper money and debt notes. They were concerned about farmers' productivity, not their function helping to circulate cash in the economy. But bills helped accelerate marketization. Marketization meant at least three things: The proportion of transactions involving cash for provisioning daily needs (food, clothing, and tools of livelihood – capital stock) grew, replacing self-production (subsistence) and barter. Further, prices for goods, services, and real estate changed and were perceived as changeable. Finally, where traditional economies tended typically to involve a fixed set of actors from the community or close connections, marketization meant that local economic networks became less closed, with outsiders increasingly linked to them.[99] More circulating cash meant more state revenue to be collected through levies such as *accisia/ungeldt* and *licentia*.[100]

10 Market, Social Estate, and Civil Law, 1750–1759

Sometimes we catch a glimpse of details about what individual actors themselves thought and did, as it were below the level of jurisprudence. The following example about high-level real estate investment shows actors thinking about the dwindling world of subsistence agriculture – and the old laws which separated old agricultural identities from modern investment opportunities.

Bills not only greased the wheels of everyday commerce in commodities but were also the vehicle by which magnates and rulers financed territorial growth, security, and warfare. Bills were sometimes used to borrow or to transfer large amounts of capital for broader political or entrepreneurial purposes, a process that did not fit the traditional formula of the trading arrangement typically described by historians of bills. Across the seventeenth and eighteenth centuries, the Hessian landgraves in Darmstadt and Cassel borrowed

---

99 Burt, *Brokerage and Closure*; John Frederick Padgett and Walter W. Powell, eds., *The Emergence of Organizations and Markets* (Princeton: Princeton University Press, 2012).

100 Johann Andreas Hofmann, praeses, Johann Wilhelm Dietmar, respondans, *De immunitatibus castrensibus aliisque libertatibus praecipue in Hassia* (Marburg: Universität Marburg, 1780), §19, pp. 50–52.

money from bankers in Frankfurt for purposes such as raising armies (in the Schmalkaldic War and Thirty Years' War) and piecemeal territorial expansion. Similarly, princes of Hesse used bills and the similar instrument of the "*Sola-Wechsel*" to buy offices and to invest their riches in industrial operations. In 1725, Landgrave Ernst Ludwig of Hesse-Darmstadt and one Jakob Bernus raised 900,000 guldens via the subscription of 100 backers in Frankfurt to establish an alchemical gold-foundry (*Goldmacherei*) in Seeheim, an office of the county of Erbach just southeast of Darmstadt in the Hessian Odenwald. The loan was executed through a species of bill of exchange called a *Sola-Wechsel*. The leveraging of assets in a bill can be illustrated in turn when the same prince borrowed 100,000 guldens by putting up the office of Nidda as collateral in 1708. Princes flush with cash also used bills of exchange, of course; this was how Landgrave Frederick II in Cassel invested the 10 million *Taler* of revenue which he had generated when he contracted to send Hessian troops to support British troops in colonial North America in 1775–1776.[101]

Although it is underappreciated, the ruling classes and the bourgeoisie of the period lived in a cash and credit economy, in some ways similar to ours. Market exchange was omnipresent and there were, at least after a fashion, markets then as now in the transfer of units of power themselves e.g. great lordships. Below the level of the principality, it is not much of an exaggeration to say that government itself was a *transferable real estate*. In a sense, capital was power and power was capital.[102] To move such great things around, magnates used *bills* rather than traditional secured forms of credit because bills could serve as clear, short-term loans governed by simple rules.[103] (It seems

101 See Eckhart G. Franz, "Der Finanzplatz Frankfurt und die Hof- und Staatsfinanzen der Hessischen Fürstenstaaten," *Blätter für Deutsche Landesgeschichte* 125 (1989), pp. 52–55. The venture itself went about as well as one might imagine: The foundry failed to produce, the prince defaulted, and Bernus took his case to the Aulic Council of the Empire, unsuccessfully seeking payment of "more than 19 tons of gold" (*eine Forderung von mehr als 19 Tonnen Goldes*). This would seem to be an improbably large quantity of gold. The gold amount is mentioned at ibid., p. 54 n. 36, quoting a document from the Hessisches Staatsarchiv Darmstadt.

102 This phrasing intentionally alludes to Jonathan Nitzan and Shimshon Bichler, *Capital as Power: A Study of Order and Creorder*, RIPE Series in Global Political Economy (London: Routledge, 2009), although the authors mean something different by it. I do mean that institutional authority structures (dominions, powers) were fungible although very illiquid and sticky and were like capital in that they could be invested in producing certain political and economic output. Nitzan and Bichler mean very loosely the same thing, albeit in the context of modern western economies and financial regulatory structures.

103 Tigar and Levy, *Law and the Rise of Capitalism*, pp. 42, 46–51, 107–108, 125, 145, 151, 174.

unlikely that princes would have been arrested by a merchant court in case of default!)

Even prosperous rural farmers and other entrepreneurs used bills of exchange when possible, as illustrated by a lawsuit which began in 1750 in Hesse-Cassel and was conclusively decided in 1759. The suit and the ultimate court decision marked a new turn in exchange-law jurisprudence for the region, a turn which was to have great significance for the future by effectively eliminating the exclusion of farmers from exchange law, subjecting them to modern financial liability.

In 1748 in Rothenburg (Hesse), an official of the princely government known to us as "S" had leased one of the large commercial farms in the township of Eschwege, owned by the cadet prince, Landgrave Carl Constantin. The prince of Hesse-Rothenburg had about one hundred such large farms, and this practice of leasing them out to entrepreneurial farmers for commercial profit was common. The lease term was rental for nine years. Constantin (Karl Konstantin) was a cadet prince of Hesse who ruled the Rothenburg Quart in northeastern Hesse-Cassel between Eschwege and Marburg. (See above Figure 3.) He had supervision of local administration through his chancery in Rothenburg, but suits of high value and those involving noblemen were heard directly by the high courts of the super-jurisdiction of Hesse-Cassel, of which the Landgraviate of Hesse-Rothenburg was a quasi-autonomous sub-principality.[104] In 1750, as lessee, S ceded this lease to two men, a local town leader named "L" and a miller named "M."[105] Eschwege, where the farm in question lay, was the center of the eponymous administrative district in the Rothenburg Quart or region.

L and M made a new rental contract directly with the landgrave. This was to be accompanied by M paying S a sum of 1,000 Reichstaler as a buy-out of S's rights as lessee. L and M were further to pay the landgrave another 1,000 Reichstaler. L and M made a bill of exchange (*Wechselbrief*; *ein tausend Rthlr.*

---

104 See Arthur Kleinschmidt, "Prinz Karl Konstantin von Hessen-Rothenburg," *Zeitschrift des Vereins für hessische Geschichte* 35 (1901). In 1850, there were 101 large estates which were the *Meiereien* or *Vorwerke* in Electoral Hesse (the successor state of Hesse-Cassel) alone. The prince let them out as term-leases "to entrepreneurs normally of non-peasant background." These hundred farm estates made up some 2.3% of the territory's arable land. See Lerch, *Hessische Agrargeschichte*, pp. 13–17; George Thomas Fox, "Land Tenure, Feudalism and the State in Eighteenth-Century Hesse," in *Themes in Rural History of the Western World*, ed. Richard Herr, *The Henry A. Wallace Series on Agricutural History and Rural Studies* (Ames: Iowa State University Press, 1993), p. 133.

105 See Leonhard Heinrich Ludwig Georg de Canngiesser, ed., *Collectionis notabiliorum decisionum Supremi Tribunalis apellationum Hasso-Cassellani* (Cassel: Johann Martin Lüdicke; Bernhard Christian Duysing, 1768–1771), Vol. 1, pp. 190–191 (Decisio 50).

Wechselschuld) out to S for 1,000 Reichstaler, payable in two years.[106] Later that year, M successfully sued to annul his debt to S, based on his claim that he held an earlier, still outstanding credit against S. Defeated in court by M, S sued M's partner L for the 1,000 Reichstaler; the first court ordered L to pay; L appealed to the Hessian High Appeals Court, which confirmed the order for him to pay S the 1,000 Reichstaler.

L had made several arguments. First, L argued that S was suing over a debt note rather than a bill. A bill was summarily executable, so if the debt took the form of a bill, L would have been liable to pay immediately and subject to arrest and seizure. Note that we see here again the tactical advantage parties recognized in creating a debt via a bill rather than a weaker form of paper instrument like a promissory note. If the debt were just in the form of a debt note, however, L could put off paying S much longer. If L could convince the court that the issue at law was a debt for which he was a surety, rather than being a payer on a bill, then S's claim would have a lower priority against L's assets, and S could not force immediate payment.

L also argued that "he was no more a businessman than is any farmer who sells his crops."[107] As (putatively) a mere farmer, he cited the rules which excluded farmers from using bills. Hence any agreement of whatsoever name L entered into had "no more than common priority" against other debts. By this means, L could escape from paying S or delay the payment for some time. It may seem strange that L, a "Schulz" or town leader, who had bought a lease on a production farm for the large sum of 1,000 Reichstaler, would say that he was just a farmer, not a businessman. But these terms (*Bauer, Bürger, Kaufmann*) were well-worn social categories that resonated with people's worldview. What after all is a farmer if not one who farms? Perhaps he really did see himself as a farmer, different in social estate from burghers and merchants like one saw in bigger towns and cities.

The High Appellate Court rejected L's argument that he was not a businessman. The Court's president Leonhard Heinrich Ludwig Georg de Canngiesser (1716–1772, Figure 54) wrote that "burghers and farmers [*Bürger und Bauer*] who do business are excluded from the [...] rule" that farmers cannot make out bills.[108] The court found that the town leader fit the description of a busi-

106 Ibid., Vol. 1, p. 190, p. 191.

107 "Appellant zu behaupten vermeynet, daß er so wenig ein *commercium* tribe, wie ein anderer Bauer, welcher seine Früchte verkaufet etc.." Ibid., Vol. 1, p. 192.

108 "Alldieweilen aber ... commercierende Bürger oder Bauern, welche Handel treiben, von obiger Regel ausgenommen sind, und allerdings *eum ad effectum*, daß Wechselrecht *executive* gegen sie geklagt werden mag, Wechselbrief von sich stellen können." Ibid., Vol. 1, p. 192.

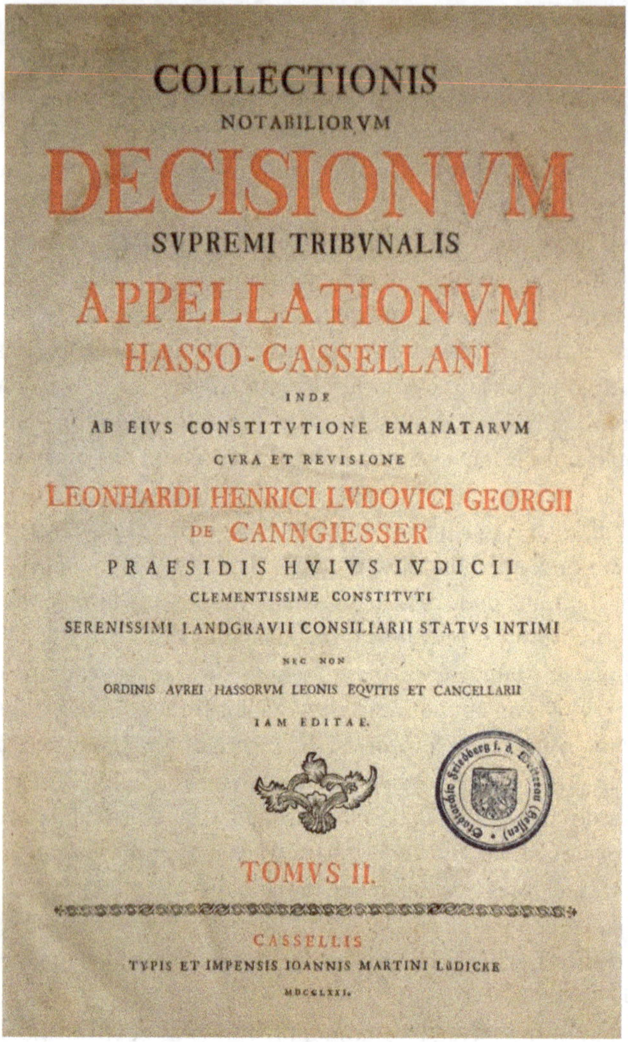

COLLECTIONIS
NOTABILIORVM
DECISIONVM
SVPREMI TRIBVNALIS
APPELLATIONVM
HASSO-CASSELLANI
INDE
AB EIVS CONSTITVTIONE EMANATARVM
CVRA ET REVISIONE
LEONHARDI HENRICI LVDOVICI GEORGII
DE CANNGIESSER
PRAESIDIS HVIVS IVDICII
CLEMENTISSIME CONSTITVTI
SERENISSIMI LANDGRAVII CONSILIARII STATVS INTIMI
NEC NON
ORDINIS AVREI HASSORVM LEONIS EQVITIS ET CANCELLARII
IAM EDITAE.
TOMVS II.
CASSELLIS
TYPIS ET IMPENSIS IOANNIS MARTINI LÜDICKE
MDCCLXXI.

FIGURE 54 Title page of Canngiesser's collection of decisions by the Hessian supreme appellate court

nessman inasmuch as the farm that he and the miller were leasing sold crops at market.

The monetary value of the suit seems to have played no role in the decision. We have no reason to suspect that the court decided as it did because of the large value of what was being disputed. Rather, the value was immaterial and was not to be considered. Instead, the court interpreted matters in terms of social categories. The court's criterion for true "farmers" were those who did not sell any of their produce at market. The rule was qualitative: social estate ended at the marketplace. It drew a broad, clear distinction between people who were competent to create negotiable bills, with all attendant liability, and people who were not. And the court put almost everyone in the former category. The Göttingen jurist Selchow would later cite this lawsuit for its clear formulation of the exclusionary rule for farmers and day-laborers without reference to the face value of the bill in question.[109]

With this decision, an important organ of state authority – the appellate court – seemed to be turning away from law oriented to the society of estates toward a view of a more universal legal subject. If a person got involved in using bills to borrow or lend money, and then the arrangement broke down, he could not arbitrarily claim immunity from financial law (based on his social estate) in order to gain an advantage against other parties. To be fair, this class of farmers (people who do not sell at market or borrow or lend money, presumably ever), as understood by the court, probably did not encompass many people by the mid eighteenth century. It seems rather like the Marxist ideal type of medieval farmers – people not involved in market exchange.

Seeking to defend his interest in not paying 1,000 Reichstaler, L had enunciated two principles. First, suretyship for a debt was different from being party to a *bill*. The court found that this formally did not apply. Second, farmers were excluded from being parties to bills. The court upheld this rule formally, but effectively stripped it of all content by finding that L, as someone who sold crops at market, was a businessman.

The court's reasoning in its holding (*ratio decidendi*) does not say whether there were governmental interests at stake. However, the court's decision was in keeping with the general principle that security of debt contracts must be upheld (*pacta sunt servanda*) and that rules which encourage further commerce are good. The decision was also in keeping with equity, for it would have seemed inequitable to let a rich man wrap himself in the cloak of the poor to escape paying a debt.

109 See Selchow, *Grundsätze des Wechselrechts*, §21. A legal adage has it that "hard cases make bad law." See William S. Holdsworth, *A History of English Law*, ed. Arthur L. Goodhart, Harold Greville Hanbury, and John McDonald Burke, Vol. 9 (London: Methuen, 1924), p. 423. I have found no distribution pattern of decisions indicating a correlation between value of *causa*, any other proxy for social estate, and holding of the court. In other words, I see no pattern of decision bias connected with value or social estate favoring rich or poor.

11 Assignment, Negotiability and Freedom from Equities, 1768

We saw earlier that jurists developed variations in the law of bills. One mutation, unremarked by later historians, was a growing split between two different schools of thought about third-party protections in the enforcement of negotiated bills. One school favored an interpretation which strongly protected third parties; this principle came to be called "freedom from equities" in English law, but did not have a name in the eighteenth century and appears still not to have a name in the civil law jurisprudence in Germany or Europe. The principle was first articulated and applied in 1699 in Leipzig.[110] ('Freedom' in this context means something like insulation.[111])

The presentation below is based on a lawsuit heard and decided by the Hessian High Appellate Court in 1768, in which each of the two litigants justified his arguments using different interpretations or models of how bills worked. One was the more traditional interpretation, common throughout the empire at the time. The other involved freedom from equities, which would later become recognized as "stronger" and would come to predominate in Germany and eventually around the world.

In 1768, the Hessian High Appellate Court decided a case involving the value of a bill of exchange. Here again non-merchants were making and taking bills of exchange. We should now not be surprised at this, given the law of 1732 and the supreme court decision of 1759. In this case, a Hessian sculptor (*Bildhauer*) named Meyer made up a bill with a face value of 400 Reichstaler to the order of an unnamed party. Soon after, this unnamed original bearer ceded the bill to Henrich Müller of Berlin, who thus became the new bearer and payee. Müller presented the bill to Meyer, and Meyer refused to pay.[112]

The two parties offered different interpretations of the law. Müller argued that a bill had to be paid at its face value. The requirement that the face value had to be paid was, all other things being equal, the usual rule. Meyer, as original maker of the bill, claimed that the original bearer (the unnamed

110 Ludovici, *Einleitung zum Wechsel-Process*, §XXXI, p. 185. The earliest mention of "freedom from equities" in Anglo-American law is 1851, although the Google Ngram viewer shows 1892 as the first appearance, Google Books as 1891.

111 It has recently been argued that elements of law merchant, including freedom from equities (in function though not in name), began to appear in English common law in the sixteenth and seventeenth centuries and that the hostility of English common law courts to law merchant before the eighteenth century may have been exaggerated. See James S. Rogers, *The Early History of the Law of Bills and Notes: A Study of the Origins of Anglo-American Commercial Law* (Cambridge: Cambridge University Press, 1995).

112 de Canngiesser, *Collectionis*, Vol. 2, Decisio 266, pp. 457–458.

man who had ceded the bill to Müller) had owed him 250 Reichstaler. Meyer argued that because of that debt, he only owed the unnamed man 150 RT (since 400 – 250 = 150). Thus, according to Meyer, if and when the unnamed man had presented the bill back to Meyer, Meyer would only have had to pay 150 RT. Therefore, the bill was only worth 150 RT, rather than its face value of 400 RT.[113] This kind of argument derived from imperial common law (the *ius commune*, Roman civil law in its modern form) and was called an *exceptio compensationis*. In ordinary commercial litigation (not involving bills), an *exceptio compensationis* was used by a defendant in a lawsuit to block or mitigate the plaintiff's claim by proving that the plaintiff owed the defendant money which should "compensate" or count against the sum sought by the plaintiff. *Exceptio compensationis* was not part of the law of exchange proper as developed in merchant communities (such as those in Antwerp, Amsterdam, or Frankfurt) and was apparently not usually recognized by them, since law merchant was (thought to be) in its essence a distinct, non-Roman procedure intended precisely to avoid the sometimes heavy machinery of the imperial common law!

Müller's suit had two main components. First, by textbook law of exchange, since the face value was 400 RT, he should be paid 400 RT. However, the report of the judges in 1768, our source, reveals that most territorial law courts, such as those in Hesse, did not apply strict law of exchange. Instead, they applied a hybrid of (1) law of exchange and (2) imperial common law, which included *exceptio compensationis*.[114] Seeking to counter the latter, Müller appealed to a fundamental pillar of property law: "no one can alienate something against his will."[115] That is, ownership can only be given up voluntarily. Müller had a claim to 400 RT. Regardless of any other claims or obligations, he said, he would not voluntarily give up (alienate) this right. Other debts or credits might be legitimate but had to be treated separately and could not *implicitly* negate his claim to the 400 RT.

In his defense, Meyer argued that the *exceptio compensationis* should apply here, even in a suit by a third party (Müller), because of another pillar of civil property law: the rule of derivative title or "*nemo dat* rule." Short for "nemo

113 Deducting a previous credit from a new debt in this way was generally supported by courts through an *exceptio compensationis*.

114 A scenario somewhat resembling the 1768 lawsuit, involving excluding possible invalidation of a contract through *exceptio compensationis*, albeit dating from thirteenth-century Grasse (Provence, France), is described at Tigar and Levy, *Law and the Rise of Capitalism*, pp. 172–173.

115 Heineccius, "In quantum princeps antecessoris sui facta confirmare teneatur?," p. 356.

dat quod non habet," this rule is classically formulated in English as holding that "no one can give a better right to something than he himself has."[116] It entails that the quality of a person's title to something derives from the quality of the title of the person from whom he obtained the thing in the first place. Thus, if a person is renting a house, he cannot sell the house to someone, since he has possession of the house only in rental tenure, not as owner (freehold). A husband may not dispose in any way of his wife's dowry (since it is not his), nor may a squatter let out squatted land to someone else in rental. By this logic, the original bearer of the bill only had "title" (claim) to 150 RT against Meyer. Therefore, what the original bearer ceded to Müller was only worth 150 RT. Therefore 150 RT was all Müller could demand of Meyer. The Hessian High Appellate Court accepted Meyer's argument. As the presiding judge Leonhard de Canngiesser wrote, paraphrasing the rule of derivative title, "the ceding party [sc. the giver] can impart to the cessionary [sc. the receiver] no better right than he himself has."[117]

This suit reveals a divide between two different schools of thought and practice in the Holy Roman Empire of the German Nation throughout the eighteenth century. In most of the empire – in imperial courts and in most of the courts of the empire's member states – jurists followed Meyer's position, based on the rule of derivative title. That is because most jurists were basically Romanists and, when in doubt, would apply Roman common law (*ius commune*) rules rather than strong merchant law rules. A bill's face value could not be vindicated indefeasibly. That is, it would sometimes (as in this case) be unjust to give the bearer of a bill its formal face value. The value at presentation depended on the quality of earlier titles, that is, relationships of debt and credit among previous parties to the bill.

But apparently beginning in Leipzig in 1699, the general courts of some cities and territories had begun to apply not imperial common law but in effect strict mercantile law: the law of exchange. This position rejected ordinary civil

116 The *nemo dat* rule is first attested in Ulpian: "Nemo plus iuris ad alium transferre potest quam ipse haberet." See D.15,17,54. It was formulated various ways by medieval commentators and has circulated ever since. It is still operative in modern law codes, albeit with many modifications. Another common form is *nemo plus iuris transferre potest quam ipse habet*. See Henry Campbell Black, *Black's Law Dictionary*, ed. Joseph R. Nolan, 6th ed. (St. Paul: West Publishing Company, 1990 [orig. 1891]), p. 1037 and Peter A. Alces and Harold F. See, *The Commercial Law of Intellectual Property* (New York; Toronto: Little, Brown, 1994), p. 466 f.

117 "[D]er *cedens* kein besseres Recht auf den *cessionarium* bringen kann, als er selbst hat." See de Canngiesser, *Collectionis*, Vol. 2, Decisio 266, n. 6, p. 458; see also Ludovici, *Einleitung zum Wechsel-Process*, §XXXIII, p. 187.

FIGURE 55 Jakob Friedrich Ludovici, whose work is cited in this chapter and in Chapter 2, was a major Saxon and Hessian jurist. His *Einleitung zum Wechsel-Process* (1713) contains the earliest discussion I have found of what I call the Saxon model of freedom from equities, discussing a 1699 law. Ludovici had been full professor of law at the University of Halle, where he was a colleague of Thomasius (see Chapter 5). He later moved to the University of Giessen in Hesse where he also served as privy councilor and vice chancellor, the same positions as Hertius (qv) a decade earlier

law remedies, procedures, or objections (such as the *exceptio compensationis*). Given that the latter position apparently lacks a name in civil law, as an alternative to the very English "freedom from equities" we could also call it the Saxon model. The Saxon model would eventually become the hegemonic international rule governing the value of bills up to the present. Jurists from Ludovici (1713) to Canngiesser (the present opinion, 1768) and Kopp (1796) consistently contrasted the two models, calling the Saxon model the "stronger" of the two.[118]

The Saxon model can be traced at least back to a Special Edict of the government of Electoral Saxony in 1699. According to that edict, the rationale behind the rule was the prevention of fraud. It read,

> Since [the *exceptio compensationis* and other objections] are wrongly misused, even though many people are found who stand in good credit, others verge on bankruptcy, and give out letters of exchange which they owe such and such, but at the same time have taken counter-letters or other debt notes for the same or higher amounts of money, when their letters are presented to a third party, and the counter-letters or counter-debt notes are in hand, and an *exceptio compensationis* is claimed, and thereby nothing can be gotten from the first [i.e. original] holder of the letter of exchange, the holder or presenter gets nothing [*um das seinige gebracht worden*] ...[119]

An insolvent person might issue a bill to one party, but then collusively create a counter-bill with an unethical associate for the same amount or more. Then when the bearer of the bill (or a subsequent holder) presented the bill for payment, the bankrupt fraudster would claim *exceptio compensationis*, delaying payment of the bill's value indefinitely or arguing that the counter-bill had already completely devalued the bill.

Remember that negotiability through endorsement made bills easily transferable. The "rigor" of the law of exchange gave the bearer of a bill confidence that he would be paid the face value at term or transfer it reliably to a new party. These features created the possibility of long chains of possession, with intermediate parties disappearing in the course of ordinary, legitimate business and commerce. Given the potential complexity of commercial relationships, there would frequently be uncertainty about possible debt claims which could be the basis of using an *exceptio compensationis*. Easy transferability was in tension with protecting the rights of the original bill maker, in the scenario which Meyer described. After all, maybe the original bearer (the unnamed

118 In 1796, Kopp could write that, by comparison with new practices elsewhere, in places like Hesse "the law of exchange [*Wechselrecht*] is not strong [...] the debtor can make an *exceptio compensationis*, because the first bearer cannot give better right to the next bearer than he himself has." See Kopp and Wittich, *Handbuch*, Vol. 2, p. 312.

119 Ludovici, *Einleitung zum Wechsel-Process*, §XXXI, p. 186m, quoting a Special Edict in Electoral Saxony of 1699.

man) really did owe him 250 RT, and Meyer really did only expect to have to pay that man 150 RT at term. But no evidence of the debt could be produced. More convoluted scenarios which magnify these hazards can easily be imagined. For bills to be easily transferable and reliable, the civil law protections for the initial parties had to be excluded in favor of present parties. Such was the position of merchants and the business-inclined Saxon court in 1699. Over the following two centuries, most other German governments would come to agree.

The 1768 decision is important for my broader arguments for two reasons. First, the 1768 suit reveals the divide between two different approaches to bills in the eighteenth century in the empire. The older view, held by most governments, sought to integrate the law of exchange in a limited way into their civil law – states' "territorial constitutions". This meant accepting some parts of the law of exchange like negotiability but in other instances retaining civil law rules like *exceptio compensationis*. This position favored original parties to bills and treated bills more like records of an underlying matter (*causa*) such as a loan arrangement. The newer view, the Saxon model or freedom from equities, apparently meant accepting most or all of the rules of mercantile law, that is, the law of exchange. This view favored new parties to bills, assuring them that they could get exactly what the bill said, regardless of what arrangement might have existed between earlier parties. According to this abstract view, a bill was not a record of an underlying arrangement but rather held value and force in its own right. Whoever rightfully held the bill was owed its face value at term, almost like an endorsable modern bank check.

Second, the freedom from equities created by the Saxon model was, I suggest, at least as important as two other, much-vaunted features of bills, namely negotiability and strict liability ("rigor"). Negotiability and strict liability made bills useful and reliable within high-trust, mercantile contexts. But freedom from equities subtly turned the bill into something else: a token of value trusted by parties but detached from personal circumstances and relationships. So did paper become a kind of money – a medium of exchange and a store of value.[120]

Rigorous, negotiable, equity-free instruments could work well among trusting, limited, high-capital networks to which they had previously been confined. But then law merchant rules became available to the general population, a population for which they had not been developed. And this widespread

120 These are two of the three functions conventionally used to define money. The third is that it is a unit of account. See for instance Chown, *History of Money*.

adoption of foreign, mercantile law constituted the entrance of a paper money into wider and wider circles of the population, to accompany coin.

12 Was the Law of Exchange Good for Eighteenth-Century Germans?

Sources throughout the eighteenth century praised the use of bills: Montesquieu said that they reduce rulers' ability to arbitrarily confiscate or embargo wealth as forced loans, since bills could only be transferred voluntarily. German commentators shared the opinion of political economists of every school in other countries that the use of bills brought "advantage ... and in no regard any damages." Several directly attributed to the use of bills the improvement of credit for those using them. Occasionally we encounter a misgiving, as in the remarks by Philipp Peter Guden quoted above (1790). If the acceptor refused to pay, he wrote, he

> can be driven from his estates and taken into arrest and kept there until his debt is paid, when he could just as well have resided on them [his estates] the while.[121]

Since the nineteenth century, economists and economic historians have concurred with and refined the positive assessments, ultimately contending that bills were a new, improved, more efficient economic institution.[122]

But for all of their broad economic-developmental value, how did the wider use of bills affect eighteenth-century Germans? An incident in the 1770s in Hesse may shed a little light on this question. A few years after the Cassel High Appellate Court made its ruling in 1768, a situation unfolded that we might call a natural experiment, that is, an unrelated set of events that may offer a new perspective on the question we are asking. In the early 1770s, the Hessian regime in Cassel responded to a series of bad harvests by trying to ameliorate the economic hardship of numerous smallholder farmers. One such effort was the infamous Farmstead Edict (*Hufenedikt*) of 1773, which prohibited division of rural estates through sale or inheritance and excluded daughters and younger sons from inheritance for this reason. The edict exacerbated rural

121 See the passages cited earlier, as well as Guden, *Vom Wechsel- und römischen Rechte*, Vorbericht, page v; Div. I, Cap. II, §7, p. 25; ibid., epitome of Div. I, Cap. III, §13; and Martens, *Entwickelung des wahren Ursprungs des Wechselrechts*, §21, p. 78.

122 North and Thomas, *Rise of the Western World*, p. 54.

poverty rather than ameliorating it and was abolished after a few years.[123] In another effort, an edict of November 26, 1773, granted a debt moratorium to all "subjects who earn their subsistence from field agriculture." Many farmers owed debts, but the bad harvests reduced sharply the amount of cash they held. Some debts were unsecured and some, like modern American home mortgages, were secured through pledged collateral. The regime perceived that indebted farmers who went into default might stand to lose their pledges (usually real estate, equipment, or livestock), a scenario which would cause mass impoverishment. The moratorium – an automatic forbearance on payments of loan principal – thus was aimed at keeping farmers on their land, able to feed and clothe their households and grow crops. They were only required to pay current interest on debts and to work out schedules for payment of half of back-owed interest during the moratorium.

The form of debt in question was not bills of exchange but simple debt notes, the paper records of debts which recorded both principal and secured collateral if there was any. As discussed earlier, bills of exchange had generally been developed centuries earlier as a sophisticated variant of debt notes. However, debt notes continued to be used and were a reliable means of securing credit, although not quickly convertible into cash like bills were. Despite the flexibility in bill rules, bills fundamentally differed from other kinds of debt in another way not yet mentioned. Unlike bills, some kinds of debt had scheduled (re)payment programs, such as annuities or modern mortgages or institutional loans. Debt notes also continued to be used for most smaller loans because they were easy to create: in most instances, they could be reliably created just like any private-law contract, with signatures, a few witnesses, and some paper and ink. Notaries, lawyers, bankers, or far-away agents were not required.

In the present context, since these debt notes were difficult to transfer via assignment and were viewed as less secure, they had little *present* value during the moratorium, despite having secure *future* value as credit. The holder of an affected debt note in this condition would collect only present interest under the November 1773 edict and nothing more; the note produced only present debt service (i.e., cash) and no current repayment of principal. And one did want to be repaid, of course. Legal operators like Minister Bose in the Cassel government or Judge Canngiesser on the High Appeals Court were concerned that the moratorium was drying up local credit because debt notes

123 For more details on the Farmstead Edict, see Ingrao, *Hessian Mercenary State*, pp. 117–120, 134, 213 f.; Wilder, "Property, Possession and Prescription," pp. 8, 204, 362.

were fairly illiquid. Moreover, during a debt moratorium, if debt notes against a farmer were held by Person 1, the notes would return little cash. If Person 1 in turn owed money to Person 2, then Person 2 was unlikely to be willing to take them in payment of the debt owed him by Person 1, since the notes produced little cash and assignment was costly, tedious, and who wanted to buy small debts against insolvent local farmers, cash-poor under the best circumstances, during a moratorium? Person 1's lack of cash (i.e., liquid transferable value) could render him insolvent, that is, lacking the means to pay his own debts. (In today's terms, a liquidity crisis created a solvency crisis.) To remedy this problem, Bose added a rule to the 1773 moratorium (paragraph 6) which obliged creditors to accept assignment of debt notes on request in lieu of cash or further liens on property. In other words, *the government made debt notes a little more like bills of exchange by making them more easily transferable*. In the above hypothetical example, Person 2 would be obliged to accept the currently non-paying debt notes from Person 1. This rule in effect forced the acceptance of (regrettably bad) debt to create liquidity by forcing the circulation of paper instruments not designed for this purpose.[124]

By 1776, trouble had ensued. Debtors were using paragraph 6 to pay off creditors with illiquid debt notes even when they had cash or real estate on hand. After all, why not pay with your worst assets rather than your best? The general language of the 1773 law seemed to permit this conduct, although it also seemed inequitable. When the Cassel Privy Council asked the High Appeals Court for a clarification, the court explained[125] that paragraph 6 gave this benefit only to a debtor who had "no other means of paying [his creditors] aside from these debt-obligations." In short, paragraph 6 in 1773 had expanded the law of debt notes to give them one of the advantages of bills without as much risk but had created a moral hazard which damaged credit as much as it succored it. The 1776 clarification tightened the application of the benefit so as only to help those debtors who had no other recourse. The clarified rule still spread the possible harm of bad debt to uninvolved third-party creditors but at least restricted the practice to dire cases.

As in the 1768 court decision, the two-step change in the rules in 1773 and 1776 was based on old principles: Contracts must be honored; debts must be

124 "In the case of a creditor who cannot get what is his owing to this moratorium, and who is himself indebted to others, these latter creditors, if they do not wish to wait patiently, shall satisfy themselves by the assignment of debt," i.e. the debt held by their debtor but illiquid during the moratorium. See Verordnung of November 26, 1773, in: Sammlung Fürstlich Hessischer Landes-Ordnungen, Vol. 6, 749, §6. See also Handbuch zur Kenntnis der Hessen-Casselischen Landes-Verfassung, Vol. 2, 313.

125 In an opinion dated October 29, 1776.

paid. It seemed reasonable to require creditors to be satisfied with receipt of illiquid debt in the name of broader circulation of capital. Like the note-issuing bank in Cassel in 1720 and the expansions of the effective use of bills to professionals in 1721 and 1723 and to farmers in 1759, the new rules in 1773 and 1776 further extended the use of paper financial instruments, in this case by making non-bills more like bills rather than by bringing bills themselves to more people.

A moratorium was not the same as *exceptio compensationis*, discussed above. According to *exceptio compensationis* in the imperial model, even if a new creditor was substituted for the original creditor, whatever relationship had existed between the debtor and the original creditor carried over to the new creditor. The 1773 moratorium on the payment of principal and the forced acceptance of debt notes by creditors worked in a different way. It halted repayment of principal, thus lowering the value of debt notes drastically in the indefinite short term. Forced acceptance of bills allowed a creditor of a temporarily valueless note to force a third party to become successor-creditor and accept the non-paying note in satisfaction of another debt. Like freedom from equities, this double regulation in 1773 involved the transfer of obligations among creditors. Then as now, there is a close link between having cash (liquidity) and having means (solvency). If debt collection had been "rigorous" in the moratorium case of 1773/1776, thousands of farming families would have lost their pledged collateral, probably crippling their ability to make a livelihood. They would have been pushed off their lands or disenfranchised into a lower status such as share-cropping.

•••

After the Thirty Years' War, the imperial diet in Regensburg adopted the law of exchange generally, but imperial legal federalism limited imposition of law merchant to jurisdictions in the weaker and smaller territories and to those which did not have explicitly contravening laws. Not until 1723 did the regime of Hesse-Cassel formally introduce the law of exchange, meaning that bills were recognized and enforced in Hessian courts. Edicts and high court decisions in the following few decades show the regime tinkering further with the rules governing bills. By 1771, reported the eminent Hessian jurist Carl Philipp Kopp, the law of exchange was widely applied in Hesse-Cassel and adjudicated through the ordinary regime and appellate court system.[126] In the early period

126 Carl Philipp Kopp, *Ausführliche Nachricht von der ältern und neuern Verfassung der Geistlichen und Civilgerichten in den fürstlich-hessen-casselischen Landen. Anderer oder practischer Theil*, Vol. 2 (Cassel: J. J. Cramer, 1771), Title 22, §341–344, pp. 300–302.

after the end of the Thirty Years' War, policies tended to be restorationist – restore the faltered old status quo ante, or make such reforms as seemed to settle immediate problems. At least in the law of exchange, nothing new was contemplated. Even commercially-minded governments like the senate of Frankfurt am Main were hesitant to adopt new exchange practices like negotiability. France and Britain experimented with large new securities markets in the early eighteenth century, including secondary markets in bonds, promissory notes, and joint stock company securities. The collapse of the bubbles in 1720 in Paris and London and the related events in Amsterdam and Hamburg produced a reaction of caution and distrust toward putting stock in novel tradable financial paper of all sorts for some decades. But states all over Europe, including in the Hessian and Rhine-Main region, slowly resumed adopting the law of exchange, cautiously at first and then energetically, into their territorial constitutions.

One thing which remained conspicuously present despite the expansion of the use of bills by the mid eighteenth century was restrictions on interest in lending. The sources I see for Hesse-Cassel do not make the matter perfectly clear, but it appears that in that territory, it remained forbidden for ordinary people to lend at interest. Christian merchants were permitted to lend at 5%. After 1749, the Jewish limit was raised to 6–8%. The regime apparently saw no reason to liberalize interest rate restrictions any more than that. Dry bills were a legal means used to hide high interest and thus skirt the prohibition (*cediren*; *cessio crediti iudaici in christianum*).[127] So Jews could lend at high rates but Christians could not use either cession or discounted dry bills to get in on the usury as lenders themselves. The regime remained determined to prevent this. I take it to have been an open secret that the aristocracy broadly could and did use usurious bills as needed but public morality required maintaining the customary limit.

The expanding franchise for using bills, if we may call it that, was a symptom of a more general trend in the eighteenth century for social estate to lose some of its importance as a delimiter for rights to engage in certain commercial activities. Our example came from a lawsuit about a litigant who tried to use the customary exclusion of farmers from exchange law, only to be told that since he engaged in marketplace commerce, he could not avail himself of that rule. I expect that we would find the same kind of logic applied to other exclusions as well, such as soldiers or women in patriarchal households, though this

127 Ledderhose, *Kleine Schriften*, p. 319.

remains here only a hypothesis. During this period, we see the emergence of a unitary legal subject, understood as a mentally competent person not under the domination of another person or power in society. This generality was circumscribed in many ways, but emergent it definitely was.[128]

Bills of exchange were in a strange relationship with freedom. Bills were somehow both restrictive and liberating. They created freedom because their rigor empowered people. The development of the law of exchange in the seventeenth and eighteenth centuries was not spurred by any great campaigning for individual civil liberty, but the expansion of bills seems to have helped expand civil liberty all the same.[129] Summary procedure helped make bills a more reliable way of exchanging value, which gave people more economic power. Thus bills created the realistic expectation that force/sanction stood ready to guarantee that future parties in the bill process (3rd, 4th parties, future additional bearers) would honor the bill. Otherwise the taker of the bill has simply been duped by his banker (the bill's maker) and/or the presenter of the bill later would be holding worthless paper if the party to whom he presented it did not honor it. A number of writers and political constituencies beginning in the early twentieth century have regarded the ability to mobilize and exchange value as a major form of freedom.[130] The creation and steady expansion of permission to use such bills constituted a substantially new form of property right, and with it greater civil liberty for ordinary Germans. This freedom was not a classical liberal sort, for instance of the form constructed by Thomas Hobbes or John Locke, yet bills did create freedom: in the form of an artificial social power, which was disposable arbitrarily by individuals in society, and which gave individuals more capability than they would otherwise naturally have to effect their visions and wills.

Perhaps money is a fertilizer for freedom, something which helps freedom grow. Georg Simmel and others have long said that money gives form or expression to our freedom, something which would mean different things to

128 The generic subject I describe resembles the Marxist conception of the emergent bourgeoisie or capitalist, albeit without the latter ideal type's Viking-like levels of ruthlessness, pitilessness, and insatiability.

129 Recall the remark by John O'Neill quoted earlier, to the effect that the great metanarratives of "western political history" are not as such "the story of individual freedom, even though western political history is only intelligible as its invention."

130 This was a theme of many critics of socialism in the twentieth century. An eloquent spokesman for this position was Friedrich Hayek, e.g. in his *Constitution of Liberty* (Chicago: University of Chicago Press, 1960).

different people.[131] On the other hand, freedom also seems to be at the basis of money: Free individuals and group activities seem to have a "natural propensity to truck, barter, and exchange" (Smith) and in the course of these activities they generate credit and debt obligations.[132] People find ways of denominating and settling those credits and debts in tokens, whether cowrie shells, electrum coins, or tobacco warehouse receipts, and eventually merchant communities start to trade and settle those very credit and debt relationships against one another, as with the settlement of bills of exchange after about the fourteenth century. In effect, self-liberating commerce causes the development of money, as Scottish Enlightenment thinkers discovered. Furthermore, civil liberty is unthinkable without transactions and market freedoms, at least to some tangible, meaningful extent.[133] Yet for all this, money is clearly conventional and differently configurable. For instance, its paper mode was the product of technical evolution through trial and error, comparable in unevenness to the slow technical improvement of specie money (coin). The example of the divergent exchange rules of the Saxon school of thought as opposed to the common imperial approach to equities and the conflict between freedom from equities

131 Dostoevsky had written that "Money is coined liberty." Simmel, originator of the memorably-titled "philosophy of money," articulated a Neo-Kantian idea about freedom and creative expression: "Money, as an intermediate link between man and thing, enables man to have ... an abstract existence, a freedom from direct concern with things and from a direct relationship to them, without which our inner nature would not have the same chances of development." John Maynard Keynes wrote that "Lenin is said to have declared that the best way to destroy the Capitalist System was to debauch the currency." The historian of money Glynn Davies summed up the position of Milton Friedman and others when he wrote that "Sound money, in the sense of an optimally adjusted supply, is the foundation both of capitalism and of freedom." See Simmel, *Philosophy of Money*, p. 474 and Davies, *A history of money*, p. 656.

132 For the generation of credit and debt relationships as a cross-historical, global phenomenon, see David Graeber, *Debt: The First 5,000 Years* (Brooklyn: Melville House, 2011). Underground economies demonstrate the same dynamics through negative counterexample. In black markets, goods and services are offered and people illegally adjust prices and currency values to accord with actual supply and demand. The underground economies in the Eastern Bloc countries during the Soviet era seem to confirm this. Great examples of this for Poland are given in Czeslaw Milosz, *The Captive Mind* (New York: Knopf, 1953) and Norman Davies, *Heart of Europe: A Short History of Poland* (New York: Oxford University Press, 1984). For the non-naturalist view of the development of money, see Christine Desan, *Making Money: Coin, Currency, and the Coming of Capitalism* (Oxford: Oxford University Press, 2014).

133 We accept impositions on our market freedoms up to a point without feeling that our civil liberty is majorly curtailed. That's the moral side; for the financial breaking point, see Rosenberg and Birdzell, *How the West Grew Rich*, Chapter 10, pp. 302–209.

and the rights of original parties to bills, discussed above in this chapter, illustrates that thoughtful people could come to different conclusions about the best design for money.

Finally, we should also come back to a famous (perhaps the only famous) remark from this era about bills of exchange. Montesquieu expressed hope that

> One has begun to be cured of Machiavellianism, and one will continue to be cured of it. There must be more moderation in councils. What were formerly called *coups d'état* would at present, apart from their horror, be only imprudences. And, happily, men are in a situation such that, though their passions inspire in them the thought of being wicked, they nevertheless have an interest in not being so.[134]

It is significant that the Imperial Diet adopted the law of exchange in 1654, around the same time as England and a little before France, and that many German principalities and commercial urban republics did likewise not long after. For, as Montesquieu quietly wrote, rulers learned or should learn that the use of bills of exchange to transfer money and effectively store it in short-term debt cycles made it almost impossible to confiscate that wealth, as rulers often wanted to do and felt emboldened to do whenever they thought they could get away with it. King Charles II Stuart expropriated the London goldsmiths, calling it a forced loan. A fait accompli, the depositors were left with nothing but receipts for their vanished property and cries of injustice. With bills this was impossible. Princes could only get money from people who held it in bills by soliciting their consent. In Europe, the hinge or threshold period for this change was roughly the 1650s–1680s. That is, after the time, it became increasingly difficult for regimes to find large stockpiles of specie to seize. Hence princes were generally, and reluctantly, led to better secure the property and freedom of civil subjects. When money hid in paper, forced extraction was impossible. The only way of expropriating wealth stored in bills or other paper money is by violating the civil law of contracts: The ruler cold not force his way into the contractual obligations of the parties to bills, e.g. forcibly making himself the payee of an accepted bill. Why? Because governments had relied, for centuries by this point, on the functioning of their civil law systems and economic systems based on stable, secure property rights. Without these, no wealth to tax and products to buy, including professional armies and gunpowder. With the rise of paper wealth transfer and bank accounts, much of the

134 Montesquieu, *The Spirit of the Laws*, Book 21, Chapter 20, p. 390.

wealth of the well-off in society was just lines in bank ledgers and/or the payor was agent of a foreign banker who was not likely to play ball with a "sovereign" bent on confiscation. A line in a ledger somewhere, inside or outside of a jurisdiction, was impossibly harder to locate and control than was a pile of actual gold.

The significance of this switch from hard money to paper money also lets us see the conversion of tithes (*Vermalterung*) from Chapter 4 in new light as well. To convert the tithe meant to liquidate it as one wanted to, at the most local and immediate level. One found a buyer who would offer cash or credit for it and haul it away. Thus bulky produce disappeared but how would government revenue agents know what, whom, or how much to tax? Coin was already hard enough to levy a tax on if one had no knowledge of persons or amounts, but paper was completely in the wind. The very decrease in princely arbitrariness (autocratic forced extraction of wealth), which Montesquieu described and which seems empirically to have indeed occurred, itself meant an improvement in a classical liberal guarantee of civil liberty – freedom as protection of person from arbitrary distraint.

And yet, in a final seeming paradox, governments clearly sought to promulgate the use of paper money at the same time. For rulers and their advisors had come to believe that paper money increases liquidity, which through increased velocity and reduced transaction costs creates more wealth and stimulates higher production levels.[135] In a word, bills accelerated marketization, leading to economic growth, which meant more potential tax revenue (at least in the places and forms one knew to look for it).

---

135 See Walker, *Johann Jakob Moser*, pp. 202–203 on velocity, transaction costs, and capital in Johann Jakob Moser's synthesis of cameralist and other thinking in the mid eighteenth century.

CHAPTER 7

Conclusion

Germans had long boasted of their freedom, both when considering solely their own realms and when making comparisons with others, although this is not to say they did not admire others' accomplishments and ways of living. A historical puzzle has been what they meant when they spoke by the second half of the eighteenth century of "German freedom." The question may never be finally answerable since there was of course no total and authoritative text and their scattered remarks refer to assorted things which they understood to constitute their freedom. Historians point to features of state and society such as religious toleration, pluralistic federalism, constitutional monarchy, respect for law, and limitations on arbitrary power through courts' upholding of black-letter civil law and property rights. All of these are certainly typical of modern liberal states. But missing in all of this has been what modern readers might expect to find at the center of liberal societies, namely strong and reliable individual civil liberties both negative (freedom from oppression) and positive (heightened capacity to realize one's own free will in life projects). I think that I have at least partially filled this lacuna, showing that

- the growth of property rights in all of their variety, however imperfectly, did strengthen individual civil liberty in a meaningful and appreciable sense
- this was by and large recognized and encouraged in many different quarters of the day for diverse reasons, and
- it was not seen as conflicting with the good order of monarchy, whose basic supremacy in great matters was undisturbed

This book's thematic organization, in Chapters 2–6, has been crafted to illustrate the mechanics of the development both of ideas of freedom and of justiciable civil liberties: Ideas about freedom from diverse sources were transformed through institutions. The most consequential of these institutions, courts, applied said ideas to growing swathes of the population, increasing civil liberties in the use and control over space, freedom from extractions, and the abstraction of real wealth into fungible, secure paper wealth.

1 Property Rights and Freedom in Early Modern Germany

My arguments belong with the work of revisionist historians, in opposition to the unaccountably long-enduring historical narratives which say that Ger-

 | DOI:10.1163/9789004685178_008

man societies and states before the French Revolution were simply or uniformly authoritarian and illiberal. In a way, the revisionist position is not even revisionist – one could rather say that it began life as an original, contemporary discourse in Germany about Germany, a discourse which was developing up until the dissolution of the empire in 1806. Considered this way, Montesquieu, Goethe, and Wilhelm von Humboldt were revisionists before there was a black legend to revise. And from the early twentieth century until today there have been accounts by Peter Blickle, David Blackbourn, Otto Brunner, Bernhard Diestelkamp, Gottfried Dietze, Horst Dippel, Horst Dreitzel, Sean A. Eddie, Geoff Eley, Robert von Friedeburg, William W. Hagen, Erwin Hölzle, Bernd Ulrich Hucker, Diethelm Klippel, Ulrich Meier, Sheilagh C. Ogilvie, Wolfgang Schmale, Alexander Schmidt, Georg Schmidt, Barbara Stollberg-Rilinger, Maiken Umbach, Dietmar Willoweit, and doubtless many others I embarrassingly fail to have noted. This chorus of voices has firmly established a continuing research program exploring the presence of ideas and practices of freedom, tolerance, constitutional balance of powers, and reform of old legal practices in the period between 1600 and 1800. Recent scholarship on the German Enlightenment also contributes to this in characterizing the Enlightenment as sponsoring some liberal or quasi liberal ideas as well, namely pluralism, the "limits of state action" and individual self-improvement. Ordinary Germans always cared about freedom, long fought for it, and often achieved it.[1]

2 Free Disposition of Estates

The expansion and extension of property rights was a powerful engine for the growth of freedom in the period. I have tried to illuminate the actual workings of the legal system, its institutions and practitioners as well as to tease out how property rights actually worked for real people, of all classes, in a range of situations.

Ordinary people gained greater power over their use of real estate and, consequently, greater personal freedom and security for themselves and their families. After the mid seventeen century, rulers in the Hessian and Rhine-Main region gradually lost some of their ability to control transfer of (and sometimes to raise taxes from) many estates throughout their domains. Com-

1 The dynamism and pluralism of the German Enlightenment is emphasized in the work of Georg Schmidt, Frank Grunert, Ian Hunter, T. J. Hochstrasser, and Knud Haakonssen. See bibliography for references to work by the above-mentioned writers used in this book.

mon people used strategies to wrest control from landlords or other interested parties (whether princely, noble, or bourgeois). These included the acquisition of allodial or "free and clear" tenure by widows and oath substitution that enabled Jews and women to evade restrictions on their ability to acquire or use property. The decline and eventual abolition of retraction law allowed people to sell "family property" more easily to those outside the family or community. Rulers tried to counter this tendency, apparently to little avail. Jurists sought to clarify and sharpen the rights of individuals – especially non-dominant classes of people: wives, widows, unmarried women, younger siblings, stepchildren, and joint heirs to estates, that is, people who were not the dominant social category of elder, property-owning, free, Christian men, or social collectivities like families or communities dominated by one or a few such dominant Christian men (noble or common). People gained more freedom against their families, dominant family members, controlling communities, elder siblings, new stepparents, landlords, Christian legal structures, and so on, by becoming effective owners of property.

These practices, some centuries old, others apparently novel, had two sources, different in kind. We may say that one source of them was people's motivation – family or individual strategy, pursued presumably in partisan interest. Another source was the development and application of possession and prescription. I see a proliferation of legal writings about possession and prescription beginning in the second half of the seventeenth century, building theoretically on the new natural law of prescription constructed by Hugo Grotius in 1625.

I see the principles of possession and prescription practically applied to Hessian civil governance in the Princely Resolutions of 1655. That constitutional settlement made universal the principle that peaceful possession, even without good, recorded title, would enjoy legal prejudice, that is (absent proof to the contrary) presumption in favor of current possessor. Possession and prescription were attractive to jurists because they quieted title to real estate and rights. Use of these concepts privileged the present parties to transactions, implicitly giving them more freedom, at the expense of distant feudal lords, old custom, or other potential claimants.

Already here we see the first glimmer of the shape which emerged in greater contrast in Chapter 6, namely the modern, generic subject of civil law. This figure resembles what Marx described as the early bourgeois capitalist, someone who was able to mobilize capital through liquidation or credit, without permission of kin or seigneur, and was even able to enter into cross-border, long-distance financial contracts.

3 Freedom from Extractions

People also gained greater freedoms from paying taxes and dues in the wake of the Thirty Years' War. For some time, the governments of the region were in disarray. The rulers of Hesse-Cassel issued numerous complaints of widespread tax evasion and failure to perform required services. The prince complained about non-payment of taxes (as well as noble trespassing) and both prince and nobility complained about non-payment of dues. Generically we can say that conflicts arose between *lords*, claiming they were owed dues or taxes or services, and *possessors of estates or exercisers of activities or claimants of freedoms*. As mentioned in Chapter 5, we should again here underline the transposability of these roles. Just as a person can today be a husband, son, father, businessman, and a landlord, so could in the early modern context a person have been both noble landlord and a noble tenant (a vassal), a possessor, even a renter, as well as other estate kinds. The key is that the basic two positions of landlord and tenant are not distinct, exclusive groups, but positions in which one might find oneself at one or another time, or at the same time with regard to different arrangements. The conflicts between tenants and lords over extractions made their way into the courts, first in most cases at the local or seigneurial level, and then to the appellate level. Law professors and judges debated how or whether non-payment of dues and non-performance of required actions might *prescribe* into actual *rights* to not pay or not perform – that is, *freedoms*. By the mid eighteenth century jurists seem to have concluded that such freedoms could be acquisitively prescribed, but only against landlords such as local nobility or property owners; freedoms against the princely government could not be permanently gained merely through prescription (as opposed to an express grant). Moreover, jurists consistently said that civil liberties so acquired were actually the re-emergence of a person's natural freedom and that, in conflicts where it was hard to determine who might actually owe what, courts should begin with a "presumption of natural freedom" for those against whom obligation was claimed. The gain of rights and freedoms against local lords or powerful neighbors was very significant in the lives of ordinary people and communities. The view represented by Thomasius, in which princely sovereignty trumped the ability of individuals to essentially gain tax freedoms against their own territorial government, probably prevailed in most polities, as indeed it probably would prevail in most places to this day. But that should not prevent us from noticing how powerful the role of that cornerstone of liberalism, individual consent, was in "German jurisprudence."

4 Freedom and the Use of Money

A third major kind of civil liberty which grew, and which was also very consequential for individuals and for society as a whole, was in the use of paper money, in the form of bills of exchange. The expanding use of bills in German society created new opportunities in two ways. One was that people increasingly used bills to do new things. Another was that new classes of people began using bills. Since their invention half a millennium prior, bills had been used to buy and sell working capital, for instance exotic commodities or finished goods, or agricultural produce. But by the mid eighteenth century, at least in the Hessian and Rhine-Main region, bills were also being used to transfer and leverage real estate, invest, lend, and simply transfer money itself (for whatever unknown reasons). After the Thirty Years' War, the same spurt of institutional restoration which we met earlier in matters of real estate and taxes also drove governments to adopt the law of exchange in the spirit of restoring the "former good old order which had fallen away." The law of exchange, it was understood, could facilitate large-scale and long-distance merchant finance and public (state) finance. And this era was indeed the highest stage of pre-industrial capitalism.[2] Policy makers wanted commerce to be intensified both within princely states as well as across estate jurisdictions throughout the empire. From the late seventeenth century through the mid eighteenth century, states extended the franchise to use bills. This was motivated by political economic ideas about credit, liquidity, and velocity of money, but its political theory rested on the basically liberal ground of modern natural law.[3] Class exclusions on the use of bills deteriorated. Practitioners created variations. Italian and other ideas and ways of thinking about bills and payment were adopted and studied. Debates developed in jurisprudence about how best to configure bills to balance security, utility, and justice.

5 German Freedom

I do not say that liberalization of property law began in the seventeenth century or ended in the eighteenth century, or that Germany was unique in this regard. I do contend, however, that enhanced property rights for ordinary Ger-

2 de Vries, *Economy of Europe in Age of Crisis*, Chapters 4–8.

3 Jerry Z. Muller, "Justus Möser and the Conservative Critique of Early Modern Capitalism," *Central European History* 23 (1990), p. 154.

mans made many people more free and were deeply connected to jurists' thinking about the idea of natural freedom. This is what eighteenth-century intellectuals meant when they spoke of "German freedom" in their time.

We said at the outset in Chapters 1 and 2 that there were a number of loosely defined slogans or stories about freedom popularized in the sixteenth through eighteenth centuries. One was that Germans had, they thought, a national birthright of freedom, based as much in an ethnic anthropology as in their ancient constitution. The Protestant princes and rebels of the sixteenth century rallied to a battle-cry of the Free German Empire, an understanding of the empire as being primarily dedicated to preserving the independence of its hundreds of component counties (including dozens of principalities), baronies, free towns and free villages.

Germans began to realize after the Tacitus reception that they were not simply imperial subjects of an originally all-powerful Roman(-German) emperor. Rather, they came to believe, it was more accurate to see themselves as originally free societies who had been given the mantle of imperial authority for Christmas in 800 AD.

Moreover, as jurists came to investigate the historicity of law, they drew out the "political consequences" of this, as Dietmar Willoweit put it in his study of German constitutional history:

> The history told of original freedom of Germanic tribes and their princes, who gave themselves a common constitution in the Empire out of their own decisions. The original fullness of right of the emperor, from which all feudal law still flowed, was ... recognized to be a fiction. The particular [German imperial] state [e.g. Hesse or Saxony] was discovered to be the primary historical phenomenon ...[4]

The Free German Empire may have begun as a motivated political rallying cry in the early sixteenth century, but when it met the myth of ancient Germanic freedom, historical scholarship, and the jurisprudence of the late seventeenth century, it became *ex post facto* a valid description of Germans' constitutional federal republic. The empire might closer resemble the other permanent confederations of Europe including the Swiss Confederation, the United Provinces, the Polish-Lithuanian monarchical commonwealth, Spain, or after 1707 even the alloyed realms of England and Scotland, rather than the unitary French kingdom with its truly sovereign king. Willoweit again:

4 Willoweit, *Deutsche Verfassungsgeschichte*, p. 203.

> The foundation of the imperial constitution was the 'liberty' of the imperial estates. Contemporaries understood by this freedom (1) the prohibition of an all-encompassing imperial monarchy [sc. thus leaving the individual principalities autonomy in most of their own affairs]; (2) the right to co-existence of the three great confessions; (3) co-determination in imperial matters; and not least (4) the protection of small lords against the power-political ambitions of the greater German states.[5]

I have also suggested that the much earlier, medieval struggle of the Roman church hierarchy during the Investiture Conflict probably provided a kind of model for the claim of independence by later Protestant actors. Like the freedom program of the medieval Roman church organization, the freedom struggle of Protestant principalities was not imagined as one of liberation of individual persons, but rather liberation of princely monarchical states. Individuals found freedom, so thought medieval and early modern statesman alike, through their membership in a free i.e. independent political unit. The medieval church's demand for freedom from the emperor provided a model for how there came into being within the empire other, increasingly independent polities: the secular and ecclesiastical principalities. In retrospect, as noted in Chapter 2, the papal struggle for "freedom of the church" was functionally copied by secular princes (including urban republics) within the empire over the following centuries, leading ultimately to the sixteenth-century conception of the "Free German Empire" – a pluralistic space of small powers. That is the story of the older origins of the mature German freedom studied properly in this book.

One result of the *usus modernus* movement (heyday ca. 1650–1750), which we have encountered from time to time in the previous chapters, was the appearance of serious attempts to construct or reconstruct "German Jurisprudence" or "German Civil Law." In fact, the former was the title of Johann Georg Estor's magnum opus, *Der Teutschen Rechtsgelehrsamkeit* or *Rechtsgelahrheit* (1758–1767). Jurists believed that Roman and German law[6] were of different

5 Ibid., pp. 220–221.

6 A cautionary note: The notion of some kind of authentic "Germanic law" was put to dangerous use by several generations of nationalistic German legal historians (and especially by exaggerators of their ideas) from the late nineteenth century through the Third Reich. Here is a sample, from Jan de Vries: "The Germanics brought not the idea of the state to the European peoples, but rather in contrast the idea of personal freedom. Eighteenth-century philosophers ... celebrated this Germanic mission exuberantly. Montesquieu sang the praises of our forefathers with sincere admiration; Scandinavia was the cradle of freedom. The

historical essences and protected rights differently.[7] Three of the central concepts in Estor's notion of authentic Germanic legal thinking, or *Teutschen Rechtsgelahrheit*, were loyalty, liability, and consent. Admiring Estor's construction, we might nonetheless describe his project unsentimentally as follows: He described as *German*, law which had been created or modified by the *imperial monarchy or various imperial estates*, under heavy influence from *modern Roman civil law and public law* (the *ius commune* of post-medieval Europe), designating it with *German terminology*, and wherever possible interpreting it through the *fundamental legal concepts of loyalty, liability, and consent.* (See in this connection Figures 6, 7, 20, 27–29, 32, and 48.)

Consent strikes me as of crucial importance to this book's task of understanding the relationship between property law and civil liberty. Simply put, the idea of the fundamental, necessary character of free, individual consent underwrites most of the examples and ideas presented in this book. And consent is, not coincidentally, a required building block of the theory of political

---

northern peoples of Europe conquered because they were free people while the people of northern Asia only conquered because they served a lord. When the Goths subjected the Roman empire, they founded monarchy and freedom. / We now know only too well that here lay a very naïve historical falsification. Enlightenment ideas found an echo in the unspoiled morals of primitive peoples. One thought therewith that [Enlightenment ideas] could be proven to be the natural foundations of human society. But still, there was something correct in there. The conception of personal freedom, which could not be reduced to slavish servitude in a highly disciplined state form, is characteristic for the Germanic perception." De Vries then goes on to quote the eminent legal historian Andreas Heusler, who wrote that "the German brought to the part of the world ruled by Rome this new insertion: against the suffocating, withering supremacy of the state, he asserted the freedom of the individual, freedom from paternalism and exploitation; freedom to breathe, free air. The German as bearer of 'independently-powered freedom thinking' – in that there is much truth." Still, our seventeenth- and eighteenth-century jurists did think that they were, in part, discovering and studying authentic Germanic law in some of their investigations. We must try to understand what they thought that they had found. Vries, *Die geistige Welt der Germanen*, pp. 71–72 quoting at the end Heusler, *Germanentum. Vom Lebens- und Formgefühl der alten Germanen*, p. 38.

7 Wieacker, *History of Private Law*, pp. 159–168. See Johann Georg Estor, *Bürgerliche Rechtsgelehrsamkeit der Teutschen*, ed. Johann Andreas Hofmann (Marburg; Frankfurt am Main: Immanuel Weldige, 1758–1767) and thereto Arno Buschmann, "J. G. Estors System der *Bürgerlichen Rechtsgelehrsamkeit der Teutschen*," in *Wirkungen europäischer Rechtskultur*, ed. Gerhard Köbler and Hermann Nehlsen (Munich: 1997). The German historical school of law would grow soon out of these seeds; see Buschmann, "Estor, Pütter, Hugo." I discuss Germanic law and the necessary problem of considering it as a historical category in Wilder, "Property, Possession and Prescription," Chapter 3, pp. 147–148.

liberalism that was being constructed at this time elsewhere.[8] This is not to say that here is proof that German jurists believed in the principle of the consent of the governed of course, although versions of that idea were emerging at just this time in Osnabrück in the work of Justus Möser (who may be compared with Edmund Burke two decades later).[9]

By and large, the writers in this book do not use or employ the concepts of the state of nature or abstract pre-historical consent.[10] But as Estor noted, a fundamental legal proverb – very meaningful for working jurists and admissible at court – was that "choice breaks the law of the land; agreement breaks the law of the land."[11] As Heineccius noted thirty years earlier, "no one can alienate something against his will."[12] The free access of the Christian's individual conscience was the centerpiece of Martin Luther's Protestant conception of Christian freedom, which itself was used to underwrite the most cited concept

8 By the last remark I refer to works like Grotius, *De iure belli ac pacis* (1625), Thomas Hobbes, *Leviathan* (1651) and John Locke's *Second Treatise of Government* (1689). Free, individual consent was the fundamental, necessary cornerstone of the new natural law constructed by Grotius. While German authors in the late seventeenth and eighteenth centuries occasionally read or cited Hobbes, they poured over and often cited Grotius. On consent as a principle of modern natural law with medieval roots, see Francis Oakley, "Legitimation by Consent: The Question of the Medieval Roots," *Viator* 14 (1983) and Tierney, "Hierarchy, Consent." For Grotius, see his *Rights of War and Peace*, Book I, Chapter III, §1, p. 262.

9 Justus Möser's "visions of local virtue" come close at times to articulating the principle of consent of the governed, with a Burkean estates-constitutionalist color. See Justus Möser, *Patriotische Phantasien*, ed. Ludwig Schirmeyer and Werner Kohlschmidt, Sämtliche Werk (Berlin; Oldenburg: Gerhard Stalling Verlag, 1954 [orig. 1775–1786]) and thereto Muller, "Justus Möser." The crucial missing step however between the consent-based political theories of Möser and Burke on the one hand and Anglo-American political liberalism of the same era would seem to be the type of representation that was deemed adequate to transform that consent into political authority. On this, see Hanna Fenichel Pitkin, *The Concept of Representation* (Berkeley: University of California Press, 1967). Some political theorists working in the Geneva Reformed movement like Theodore Beza did draw a link between the canon law principle of consent and the principle of the consent of the governed; see John Witte jr., "Rights, Resistance, and Revolution in the Western Tradition: Early Protestant Foundations," *Law and History Review* 26, no. 3 (2008).

10 They would have said that freedom in a settled society (i.e. not in conditions of noble savagery) was always and only the product of a concession by lordly power. This idea is explored in C. A. Bond's study of Jouvenel. See Bond, *Nemesis*, p. 15.

11 Estor, *Der Teutschen Rechtsgelahrheit*, §3491, p. 294.

12 "… die Verausserungen, so von ihren Vorfahren ohne ihren *Consens* geschehen, zu *confirmiren* nicht gehalten seyn …" Heineccius, "In quantum princeps antecessoris sui facta confirmare teneatur?," pp. 352–353.

of natural freedom among German jurists, namely the "pure abilities" doctrine.[13] Liberal political economy, all the rave in Central Europe whether from a fondness for freedom or states' avarice for taxable national wealth, was clearly understood to involve a large number of free agents in society producing, selling, buying, and distributing through consensual transactions. Consent was at the same time the basis of one class of the hidden evasions and transactions and of the grey economy complained of by regime officials in Chapter 4.[14] Nor was this just a matter of the dark and chaotic days of the interregnum period in the region between 1621 and 1648. Actual lawsuits give the impression that landlordly or even princely consent to alienation or tenant substitution could be a somewhat empty letter; that is, it might be formally required, but in the case of most land, rights or chattel property, parties to a real estate agreement might quietly assume the consent of landlords or other higher powers. We also saw that in the bishopric of Fulda, people were beginning to prefer clear, simple, at-will consent in business affairs over family-solidarity rules by the mid eighteenth century. People wanted to transact by consent, not by custom or within larger family solidarities or other group hierarchies. Free, individual consent was also the basis of jurists' remedial application of possession and prescription, whether to holding lands or exercising rights or freedoms. Possession and prescription were based on similar thinking about the relationship between consent and right. Finally, consent was also the basis of the relationships among the four parties to a bill of exchange. Here it was consent to sale and consent to take on liability in sheer, canon-law simplicity: An old German legal proverb in 1758, echoing medieval canon law, had it that "The will of a man is the soul of a deal."[15] As Michael Levy has pointed out, the emphasis in merchant law on consent and freely declarable, binding choice, was drawn from canon law. By the early eighteenth century consensual contracts and at-will transactions had been completely integrated into ordinary German civil law. These many examples are not just sleight of hand, my clever re-phrasing of ideas about freedom as ideas about consent: They all indicate that people and regimes recognized, sometimes regretfully, that free, individual consent was the basic building block of much of social life

13 Wilder, "Property, Possession and Prescription," Chapter 8.

14 In some contexts this could have very great material and ideological significance. For smuggling as widespread withholding of consent from extractions deemed unjust, see Rosenberg and Birdzell, *How the West Grew Rich*, Chapter 3, pp. 92–96 on in-land trade and maritime commerce of the British North American colonies in this period.

15 "… der wille des menschen die seele eines handels sey," quoted in Estor, *Der Teutschen Rechtsgelahrheit*, §3484, p. 292.

and of the dynamic, self-ordering society in this sublunar world. The only things that consent did not clearly and directly underwrite were sacred orders and public necessity.[16] Surely this consent was part of what Germans in the seventeenth and eighteenth centuries understood as their peculiar national freedom.[17]

And this great idea actually had real feet. Regular, widely accepted procedures were used to test domination and servitude, based on the evidence of what individuals actively or passively consented to. Civil liberty against domination was said to be based on natural freedom, yet tied to one's own control of space (real estate). This meant that civil liberties were substantial and defensible, although they were also partial, diverse, and arbitrary. Rights could be gained and lost not only by the authoritative actions of rulers or through discursive coordination (such as speeches, protests, or voting), but through an older and more direct form of activism: action itself. In response to threat of domination or oppressive rules, people took recourse to what Albert Hirschman called *voice* and *exit*, that is, recurrent contempt, avoidance, noncompliance, denial, resistance, trespassing, and outright adverse possession.[18] The withholding of consent had consequences.

---

16 The rank of various legal authorities in the early modern empire is also discussed above at Ch. 3, p. 80 including in n. 11 and in Ch. 5, p. 202 including in nn. 49–50.

17 The principle of consent ironically even played a central role in the defining tragedy of the German nation with its failed state, according to the old nationalist narrative of the nineteenth and early twentieth centuries. That tragedy, as the nationalist saw it, was one of seller's remorse: Too many of the Roman-German emperor's royal rights (regalia) had been irreversibly transferred to dukes, counts, and towns through among other things "consent of the emperor both express and tacit." The emperor's own free transfer of his royal rights to lesser lords and communities almost fatally crippled the empire and prevented the emergence of a unitary modern German nation state. See Thomasius and Schlösser, *De praescriptione regalium*, Cap. 1, §12 (no pagination).

18 My construction of action as a mode of political change and a source of rights derives from Hannah Arendt, *The Human Condition* (Chicago: University of Chicago Press, 1958). While Arendt tends to focus on great, dramatic events such as revolutions, my focus is on many small actions, the kind of things which you or I in real life might be capable of. The models of voice and exit come from Albert O. Hirschman, *Exit, Voice, and Loyalty: Responses to Decline in Firms, Organizations and States* (Cambridge: Harvard University Press, 1970), who uses it primarily in the context of discontent membership in a failing organization, rather than resistance within a relationship of positional threat. Hirschman might classify the whole list of actions in the body text above as examples of "voice," which basically means resistance, but I think his category of "exit" captures something that is also present in the list: essentially going away and ignoring the putative authority. This would apply as much to runaway serfs as to people not paying taxes or dues or ignoring the demands of public authorities that they comply with certain rules.

I would suggest that the understanding of civil liberty represented in the sources studied here is similar to that set forth in the work of Edmund Burke, in his *Reflections on the Revolution in France* (1790). Burke articulated a conception of freedom reminiscent of certain contemporary ideas from the Scottish Enlightenment and which, long story short, have also been subsequently picked up in strands of modern intellectual conservatism. Against the Revolutionaries, Burke's argument was that important freedoms had evolved slowly in the legal traditions of the kingdoms of France and England. He acknowledged that these freedoms were neither universally enjoyed by all subjects, nor uniform in their character. They had developed through custom. Burke's conception of custom is similar to German jurists' conception of prescription. Like Scots writers Adam Ferguson, David Hume, and Adam Smith, Burke argued that important, beneficial forms of civil liberty were the results of this evolutionary process. The German jurists considered here did not, as far as I have seen, articulate any such bold statements about the flowering of civil liberty or political liberty generally. Indeed, they did not see individual freedom as a goal of the state (and nor did the Scots or Burke). What the German jurists seem to have thought instead was that freedom was a side-product of traditional state goals: peace, safety, certainty, and the security of vested rights and interests, accompanied by a general presumption of natural freedom.[19]

---

19 This German-Scots-Burkean model, if I can venture so doubtful an expression, stands in juxtaposition to modern liberal conceptions of freedom, which have been modeled on post-1800 French and British political institutions and laws. The modern liberal conception assumes that the consent of individuals is the foundation of legitimate authority. In the liberal model drafted by Hobbes and Locke, consenting to the creation of political authority is a one-time-only event, essentially like an imaginary, high-stakes plebiscite. No subsequent action can legitimately detract from the authority of a regime properly founded on that hypothetical originary act, except perhaps the rare event of a popular revolution. Modern liberal conceptions of individual civil liberty are bound up with liberal anthropology – a deeper view that all human relations are or should be somehow discretely founded on voluntary, rational assent. Nothing can be legitimate which is simply received, assumed, or traditional, whether communities, family structures or religious authority. This identification appears with striking clarity in the work of Carl Schmitt, who defined liberalism as a "metaphysics of absolutist individualism," traceable back through the Romantics to Rousseau and before him to skepticism and ultimately the Copernican Revolution, a supposed arc of degeneration spanning roughly 1543–1850. See Michael Hoelzl and Graham Ward, "Introduction," in their edition of Schmitt's book *Dictatorship: From the Origin of the Modern Concept of Sovereignty to Proletarian Class Struggle* (Cambridge; Malden, 2014), p. xv. For an American critique of liberal anthropology, see Patrick J. Deneen, *Why Liberalism Failed* (New Haven: Yale University Press, 2018).

Genuine social and legal inequality notwithstanding, in their own eyes Germans enjoyed real civil liberty because of the soundness, universality, extensiveness, and individuality of their property rights. Their rights were "fundamentally inviolable" by powerful legal protections in state appellate courts and also the twin imperial supreme appellate courts. As Willoweit writes,

> There is a real line of historical development which leads from legal guarantees in late medieval lordship treaties to fundamental inviolability of vested rights, even in the absolutist period and the legal protection mechanisms of the eighteenth century, not least the Aulic Council and the Imperial Chamber Court.[20]

But not only were property rights strong, but their protections and the social capabilities they created were spreading to ever wider circles of the population. It should not thus be surprising that, by 1793 when everyone in Europe was clamoring about freedom, excited (if nervous) about events in France, a prize essay contest held on the theme of civil liberty in the Erfurt Academy elicited the following responses (as reported to us by Georg Schmidt):

> Civil liberty [*burgerliche Freiheit*] is the 'unconstrained enjoyment of rights which I enjoy and avail myself of, if I wish to live my life, as I see things, as a reasoning human being and good citizen and true Christian.'

Some answers also added that even despotic government might foster civil liberty, so long as the despot was a wise and good ruler. Physiocrats added the importance of the protection of property with an aim toward the common good.[21] These pronouncements seem to combine the legal norms and everyday realities which we have reconstructed throughout this book, in other words, German society and law as people already knew it by the mid eighteenth century.

---

20 Willoweit, *Deutsche Verfassungsgeschichte*, p. 239.

21 Schmidt, *Wandel durch Vernunft*, p. 367. Schmidt writes that German intellectuals of the mid eighteenth century tended to prefer (in their words and counsels) sole monarchy of the enlightened ruler. "The enlightened prince should use unfreedom to create freedom and turn the republic into a reality," recommended Kant (pace Schmidt). See ibid., p. 367. I would say, however, that the jurists I read seem to have been closer to the constitutional monarchy or estates constitutionalism of Montesquieu or Justus Möser, who were more pleased with mixed government, than with despotism no matter how good its incumbent's character.

6 The Extension of Positive and Negative Civil Liberties

The expansion of property rights – or in some cases their strengthening – to more and more classes of people during this period moved steadily toward universality. (Of course they did not reach it, in that striking and significant forms of unfreedom, limited right, subordination, and domination remained up to the very end. As they did everywhere and do still.)

Bills made it easier and safer to make long-distance transactions. To use the terminology of modern political theorists, the increased ability to use bills involved gains in both negative freedom and positive freedom. State legislation emancipated people from restrictions on their ability to use bills, thereby increasing people's *negative* civil liberty. Not only had restrictions been removed, but jurists also crafted rules to give people more legal prerogatives, or freedoms, in commerce (as well as attendant liabilities). But focusing simply on the *elimination of restrictions* fails to get at the way in which using bills was *empowering*: By the mid eighteenth century, bills had become a valuable *positive* civil liberty for the ever-widening set of civil subjects who enjoyed the privilege to use them.[22] By the 1760s, the evidence suggests widespread use of bills, by many different kinds of people in society, in commerce around the region. Jurists favored the "rigorous" settlement of bills as a bulwark of credit. All of this rested on freedom at the personal (or at least household) level, legal universalism, uniformity of legal status, freedom of contract, and free disposition of real and other property. People experienced *freedom* through the *mastery and unconstrained use of property*. As noted earlier, many thinkers over the past two centuries have recognized the intimate connection between not just strong property rights and freedom, but even more specifically also the connection between freedom and the ability to use sound money.

Specific social estates and communities including Jews, other religious communities, women, and "the common man" also gained both positive and negative civil liberties of other sorts as well.[23] Oath substitution was a legal fiction which gave women and Jews the ability to enter into male Christian tenure

---

22 For the concept of positive civil liberty, see Horacio Spector, "Four Conceptions of Freedom," *Political Theory* 38 (2010).

23 An example of how other religious community rights were gained is that of Carlshafen (not discussed otherwise in this book). Hesse-Cassel (like Brandenburg-Prussia) granted asylum and privileges to a large community of Huguenot refugees to settle in the new town of Carlshafen (about a day's travel north of Cassel). The large Huguenot merchant community not only benefited from this policy of religious toleration but also was given special trading privileges similar to those of a chartered trading company (or a nineteenth-century corporation). It is likely that the inspiration for the latter policy

arrangements for land or rights. Allodial strategies gave non-dominant classes of people means of taking and keeping control over real property and rights. Like with bills, here people were gaining new legal power and hence new, *positive freedom*. We might say that they were escaping from the oppression of civil structures of domination and therefore we could say that they achieved negative freedom or "freedom as non-domination". But especially in the case of unentitled or under-entitled family members, the very poor, and serfs, we must observe clearly that gaining control over land and rights, however meager (the right to hunt, a garden plot, pasturage in a common) was often the difference between freedom and unfreedom, even sustenance and starvation. For our understanding of the expansion of freedom, these tools and strategies enabled people to escape from the closed structures of domination, namely the solid house or the solid community. If people had the means to live on their own, they were much more likely to escape the arbitrary power of the master of the house or village notables.[24]

It must also be remembered that, at least if we take at face value the complaints of the regimes in Cassel and Marburg after the Thirty Years' War, people of all social estates took the liberty of making their own real arrangements during the long interregnum between 1621 and 1648, and did not thoroughly heed governmental commands to get with the state's programs of supervision and control after that any time soon either. Possessory rules for Hessian appellate courts and the jurisprudence of prescription blessed this new emergent order over the following decades, not only in its concrete orders of who-held-what, but also through the emerging priority of the principle of possession over older principles of real title.

---

decision came from the similar policy in Prussia from around the same time; the ruling Hessian landgrave was the king of Prussia's first cousin. See Robert Bohn, *Karlshafen, Wirtschafts- und Sozialgeschichte der hessischen Planstadt aus der Barockzeit* (Karlshafen, 2000).

24 Writing of the growth of the putting-out system in Zurich in 1634, Jan de Vries states that "in the upland areas near Zurich," a "new society [was] taking shape as a cottage textile industry spread in the region … In the uplands … the expanding employment opportunities of the putting-out industry deemphasized the importance of [inheriting productive farmland, of which there was a strictly limited supply]. Marriage ceased to depend on acquisition of a sufficient holding, and the choice of marriage partners became less influenced by the economic assets they possessed. Not only did upland couples, with ready access to employment, marry earlier (and produce larger families) but … among them the concept of romantic love supplanted the strategic alliance formation that continued to characterize marriage among landed peasants." de Vries, *Economy of Europe in Age of Crisis*, p. 110.

Another way we can understand the expansion of property rights and civil liberties is through the growth of appellate court dockets. As the above examples show, rights and freedoms were gained, formally and informally, through the evolution of specific concepts, tools, and policy. But legal ideas and innovative private law arrangements would not have had much effect without their extension through precedents in the courts.[25] The role played by an expanded appellate court system, its procedures, and innovative remedies, is recognized in French and English history, but less so in German history, and rarely as a means of legal change. Given the increase in appellate court activity and the extension of appellate courts' reach, the new juristic ideas, tools, and policies presented in Chapters 4, 5, and 6 touched the lives of increasing numbers of residents after 1509 and then even more so after 1648 when high appellate jurisdiction was reestablished following the return of peace (Figure 21 in Chapter 3). Increased appellate activity meant more litigants coming into contact with the central regime. When people took their appeals to the central appellate court, they hired professional lawyers to argue on their behalf (a less likely occurrence at the local court run by the local judge or noble landlord). Those professionals, who were educated in the ideas and strategies discussed above, might well have used them in arguing at the appellate level, increasing local awareness of these options when the litigants returned home.

7 Cooperation, Competition, and Conflict

> From the conflict and collision of things the truth might shine forth the more and be brought to light.
>
> AUGUSTINE[26]

A number of ideas have been put forth as influencing the development of civil liberties in our context of study. But I have also argued that key institutions incubated both ideas and practices. These institutions included regime

25 Charles Ingrao makes the interesting point that the president of the Hessian High Appellate Court, Leonhard de Canngiesser, published two large volumes of that court's decisions in 1768 and 1771 in order to make better known the court's jurisprudence, what we may think of as its holdings and ruling precedents. This was an invitation to come appeal appropriate suits to the court, knowing generally how it would rule. See Ingrao, *Hessian Mercenary State*, p. 80, in reference to de Canngiesser, *Collectionis*.

26 "Ut ex conflictu et collisione rerum magis elucesat et erature veritas." I am indebted to John Patrick Delury for this citation.

privy councils, university law faculties, book production and trade, libraries, and especially courts. Institutional expansion, in turn, found its causes in the population growth and the growing ambitions of states.

Two societal-level phenomena may best explain the changes described in this book: the Thirty Years War and the emergence of commercial markets. These two phenomena created new bases for conflict and forced actors to refine rights concepts. Many kinds of conflicts ended up in the courts (including the chanceries, which regularly heard petitions for extraordinary justice and equity). Beginning after the end of the Thirty Years' War, appellate court activity grew steadily and continuously, far outpacing the increase in population.

What kind of conflicts? We have seen an army of them (no pun intended). One particularly consequential kind, I have said, was that between old and new exercisers of real rights after the end of the War. The new tenants were, sources and scholars suggest, usually variously relatives, strangers, newly settled soldiers from disbanded companies, or people who properly bought estates under the belief that the sale was uncontroversial and rightful (naive good-faith purchasers). Legal confusion grew worse when the new tenant in turn subsequently conveyed the land or rights in the intervening period, producing a chain of possession culminating in a third or even later party. Conflicts in this broad category were exacerbated by widespread non-payment of dues and taxes during and after the war, as common folk took advantage of the chaos and erasure of institutional memory caused by the war to flout the law. Between a third and half of the population had been killed or otherwise disappeared, and fire and a civil war in the region had cast to the whirlwind fragile records where were recorded tenant names, spatial specifications, rights, dues and tax amounts, and so on. These problems were not a major cause of the prince-estates conflict in the Hessian territories, but were important enough to have been addressed in the grand bargain which more or less settled the territory's constitutional conflict in 1655. Appellate procedure was firmly, consensually standardized. Property rights were made governable by prescription and simple possession. The effect of this was to remove much of the mumbo-jumbo quality of feudal forms and permit transfer and encumbrance through well-documented consensual transactions among present parties. And it must be borne in mind that the advantageous procedural rules gained by the nobles in 1655 were available for use by common people as well.

There is also evidence that these conflicts over property rights can be understood as on-the-ground examples of the growing pains of emerging commercial markets, such as when tithed wheat was converted into cash, hauled off by teamsters, and paid for through paper money. Litigants disputed the legal parameters of the use of bills of exchange, spurring changes in the law.

What jurists call "conflict of law" is another form of conflict we can see plentiful examples of and which can clearly be seen to generate new ideas and practices. "Conflict of law" means how to resolve situations in which several equally valid rules seem to apply and to produce different rightful results. Was a sale validated by mutual consent or did the absence of landlord cognizance invalidate it? Did a man using a bill to buy a farm enjoy a farmer's legal privilege neutering the bill's rigor, or did selling farm produce rather mean that rules for merchants applied to him? The related legal doctrines of possession and prescription can also be thought of as means of resolving conflicting legal claims. They generally tipped the scale toward legitimating the currently observed order of property rights, even in the absence of formal enactment or proof. Having settled procedures and presumptions for settling conflict of laws tended to create peace, order, and legal certainty.

Sometimes policy changes rather than court decisions drove legal change or innovation. The imperial diet's recess in 1654 as well as the Hessian Contract Ordinance of 1732 widening the legal permission to securely use bills were intended to resolve financial and legal problems with the aim of increasing economic growth and security.

In some cases freedom was expanded when people engaged in innovative practices to make the existing law do something it wasn't originally supposed to do, via legal fictions. If a law didn't do what you needed it to, then let everyone pretend that circumstances were slightly different, so that the law could produce the desired result. Oath substitution fits this description. Manning the fief was an older method of oath substitution. Another example is the way people began to change the forms and uses of bills in the mid eighteenth century, adding rider clauses and using them for short-distance transactions as between Marburg and Frankfurt (unlike the classic story of long-distance trade across Europe).

Conflicts at high levels, with arguments constructed and publicized by high-ranked legal operators such as law professors and states' attorneys, also generated new interpretations of property rights and of civil liberty and/or the collective freedom of corporate groups. Law professor Heinrich Christian Senckenberg personally crafted an interpretation of the emperor's authority to intervene to maintain the balance of power between small states, in particular Hesse-Darmstadt and Solms, the outcome of which meant either the freedom or the oppression of small villages in the Wetterau. Hesse-Darmstadt championed the freedom of the village of Freienseen against Solmsish oppression.[27] In the mid eighteenth century, a number of professors, their students, and non-university jurists debated intensely over the rights and freedoms of a certain kind of land tenant prominent in the Hessian and Rhine-Main region, namely the "colonial settler" (*Landsiedel*). The writers included future imperial court judge Cramer whom we met earlier, Stephan Sigismond Wlöm, and later privy counselor and vice chancellor Georg Lennep, colleague of Johann Heinrich Christian von Selchow and Carl Philipp Kopp.[28] Jurists embroiled themselves, sometimes quite passionately, in testy public arguments about serfdom and freedom.[29]

Scholars have debated the role of property conflicts in generating new law. Marxists have argued that property relations and avarice helped to determine the growth of property law. According to this argument, while the seeds of "property rights absolutism" lay in ancient Roman civil law, legal development was driven in post-Roman Europe by medieval merchants who became the first capitalists and who began slowly, over centuries, shaping the growth of modern property law in order to extract more value from common workers (as well as colonial peoples and slaves).[30] In the past forty years, modern scholars including critical legal theorists, legal realists, and members of the law and society school have advanced comparable arguments outside of the strict

---

27 Senckenberg wrote the major (unsigned) legal argument on behalf of the government of Hesse-Darmstadt in its suit against the county of Solms over legal supremacy over the village of Freienseen (published later in 1744). See Senckenberg, *Unfug des recursus ad comitia*. Born in 1704 in Frankfurt, raised in Giessen and educated at the university there, Senckenberg practiced as an advocate in Frankfurt before entering the service of the Wild- und Rheingraf Karl von Dhaun. Senckenberg became professor of jurisprudence at the new University of Göttingen in 1736, joined the imperial Aulic Council in 1745 and became an imperial baron in 1751. The role of a powerful entity serving as protector or patron of a weak entity against a middle entity is what Jouvenel described as the high-low-middle strategy of power.

28 See to begin with Cramer, "Unvorgreifliche Gedanken"; Wlöm, *Vindiciae iuris landsideliae Hassiaci*; Johann Heinrich Christian von Selchow, "Gutachten über die eigenmächtige Einziehung der Baurengüter, December 1780," in *Rechtsfälle enthaltend Gutachten und Entscheidungen vorzüglich aus dem teutschen Staats- und Privatrecht*, Vol. 1 (Lemgo: Meyer, 1782 [orig. 1780]) and Lennep, *Abhandlung*.

29 Stamm, *Tractatus de servitute personali*; Melchior Dethmar Grolmann, praeses, Otto Heinrich von Schade, respondans, *De operarum debitarum mutatione dissertatio juridica* (Giessen: Joh. Reinh. Vulpius, 1707); and Johann Georg Estor, "Praefatio de praesumtione contra rusticos in causis operarum, harumque redemtione licita," in *De Operarum Debitarum Mutatione*, ed. Melchior Dethmar Grolmann (Giessen: Eberhard Henrich Lammer, 1734).

30 Karl Marx, *Capital: A Critique of Political Economy*, Vol. 1 (Harmondsworth: Penguin Classics, 1976 [orig. 1867]); Tigar and Levy, *Law and the Rise of Capitalism*.

Marxist historical framework. According to the theory of "adversarial legalism," legal development in the present United States results from the self-interest-driven adversarial legal system of American courts.[31] Classical liberal scholars such as Bruno Leoni and John Hasnas have argued similarly that law is the product of the arguments of privately interested parties at dispute, although they see this not as a reason to criticize market actors but rather to forge a less idealistic interpretation of the law itself.[32]

8 The One and the Many

One thing that seems to have happened is that the ideas and activities of many different parties generated new ideas and practices. This may be called a *from-the-ground-up model*. People were inspired by lots of ideas about freedom. Both liberal and to some extent cameralist political economy suggested the value of at least limited economic freedom. Growing post-War population led to increasing demand for the products and services of idea-generative institutions – only too happy to serve their customers – including printers, specialized libraries, privy councils, chanceries, appellate courts, and law faculties. Growing population also spurred commercialization, which meant that people got into conflicts and went to lawyers (or princes to their states attorneys) to help them prevail and get their way. *Partisan interest moves law, operates law, operates through law.* This driver was especially instrumental in the victory of simple commercial rules favoring equality, consent and individual private claimants over custom, feudal law, and solid group structures which subsumed individual voices within their hierarchies. As Tigar wrote, *the bourgeoisie was "[creating] ... a legal order suited to its own development* from 1500 onward ..." (emphasis added). In the region considered here, at least, this happened under the fiction of restoration and integration of feudal types and rules into what was essentially an *emergent bourgeois order*.[33] After all, as a proverb

31 Robert A. Kagan, *Adversarial Legalism: The American Way of Law* (Cambridge: Harvard University Press, 2001).

32 Leoni, *Freedom and the Law*; John Hasnas, "The Myth of the Rule of Law," *Wisconsin Law Review* 199 (1995).

33 The quotation comes from Tigar and Levy, *Law and the Rise of Capitalism*, p. 184; see also ibid. p. 62, 66–67, 125. Tigar of course was only writing about France and England. Marxists have generally been afflicted with the same blind spot about German developments as other historians. Of course this avoids tackling the hard problem for Marxism of the origins of the bourgeoisie. I think this can be answered by saying that the bourgeoisie was

had it in 1622, "times change" (*tempora mutantur*).[34] This all suggests the outline of a classically liberal model for the formation of political theory and its interaction with practice: Practical affairs including conflicts, opportunistic constructions, and innovative commercial-legal structures generated innovative ideas which later got refined into the jurisprudence taught in schools. Said jurisprudence both reinfluenced practice in turn (worked its way back down to the ground) and influenced the formation of higher political theory (worked its way up). Truly "law is the conduit between discourse and practice."[35]

In all, these examples seem to show new ideas emerging from the plural actions of many people and parties. Through their own voluntary activity, people made themselves more free and equal.

But it also seems to be the case that rulers, patronage, and state administration were what created new ideas of freedom and growing civil liberty. This may be called a *top-down model.* German state formation, rather than a tragic failure, was hearty and successful – only at the "imperial estate" level of a Hesse or Saxony, rather than of the German kingdom/empire as a whole. The German king and emperor was never able to extend his writ all the way down to the German subject, as did the English and French monarchs. Instead, the few dozen most powerful German princes each looked more like a small version of the English king, their writ extending by the late eighteenth century all the way down to the serf or individual villager.

Why did rulers extend their power and seek to shape the lives of their subjects? Bertrand de Jouvenel convincingly sketched out a general strategy rulers followed, a kind of high-low-middle configuration.[36] *Rulers nurtured the German bourgeoisie and played to the latter's desire for egalitarian, uniform, universal laws and procedures, entry into government, and some of the prettiness of the robes of office sported by the nobility. Power and patronage strategically empowered common people,* especially burghers (the bourgeois).

---

a dream type, wished into reality by thinkers and actors. What is more – and quite different from Marxist class-conflict historical stadialism – by the late eighteenth century, the nobleman is essentially a special type of bourgeois with slightly greater civil rights and distinctly higher social status (but from which wealthy bourgeois were usually only one generation away). One of course wanted to be all things – wealthy, noble, and free as a burgher.

34 Quoted at Gerard Malynes, *Consuetudo vel Lex mercatoria, or the ancient law merchant*, 3rd ed. (Abingdon; London: Professional Books; T. Basset, 1981 [orig. 1686, 1622]), p. 6.

35 Amalia Kessler, *A Revolution in Commerce: The Parisian Merchant Court and the Rise of Commercial Society in Eighteenth-Century France* (New Haven: Yale University Press, 2007), p. 288.

36 de Jouvenel, *Power*; see also Bond, *Nemesis*.

Administrative law was used to subordinate and control the poor and buttress the authority of households and heads of households. The alliance of ruler + bourgeoisie worked to undermine the independence and power of the territorial nobility (and later other intermediate powers in society including family clans and fellowships, *Genossenschaften*). Rulers also sought to as it were draw serfs and small communities out from the depths of their subjection to noble estates. The most effective way to do this was through princely edicts and supervision of local courts. Hence it was that the territorial government slowly undermined the independence of the Freigericht (free court of) Kaichen, Burg Friedburg (a castle community), Riedesel "republic" (a noble clan), and local serf self-governance around Gladenhausen. By the late eighteenth century, it was only possible for such groups to vindicate their rights claims as parts of the larger legal fabric spun and watched over by the big territorial governments in Cassel, Marburg, and Darmstadt. The decline of dominions like these probably reduced freedom in one sense while increasing it (along with equality) in another. Administration and courts aimed not only at aiding common subjects against local noble lords. Regimes also tended to slowly but steadily make all territorial subjects uniformly subject to the same law for the whole territory.

But it may also be that rulers were not only motivated by the pursuit of power in the sense of supervision and command for its own sake; they also thought that *strengthening individual civil liberty could help grow the material prosperity of a territory*, and therefore increase its taxable wealth. Princes were more often cameralist than physiocratic or liberal, but eighteenth-century policy and jurisprudence, at least as far as I can see in the Hessian and Rhine-Main region, contributed to liberal results. The statesmen of "good policy" viewed societal wealth as a mysterious phenomenon which could be nurtured and which was closely connected with the creative powers of the individual in the (German) Enlightenment.[37] "Seeing like a state," cameralist-trained administrators brought a "spirit of system" to their work of supervising domain administration, taxation, justice, and public order generally.[38] They imposed grids, simplifying older, customary, local, diverse laws and structures. They mapped their domains, collected taxes, and suppressed crime, in the interest of collecting the government's due. They and political economists more generally

37 This refers to the influential thesis of Marc Raeff in his 1975 article and 1983 book, discussed previously. See bibliography for complete reference information.

38 The phrases in this sentence come respectively from Scott, *Seeing like a State* and Smith, *Wealth of Nations*.

advocated for expanding civil liberties of many subjects (though not all),[39] of the sorts explored in this book, because they assumed that the important activities of producing, extracting, selling, buying, lending, borrowing, investing, and improving were undertaken by many different merchants, professionals, landowners, miners, and adventurers, as well as rulers and old elites.

To undertake these activities, diverse economic actors required the "presumption of natural freedom" to buy and sell land, leverage it, and offer and accept free pricing on goods and services – and the ability to use good money.

In all, these examples seem to show new ideas emerging from the patronage and strategic planning of experts and rulers. Through the premium authority of the growing, enlightened state, usually regarding its own interests of revenue and power, people were treated as being more free and equal. And they were encouraged to behave the part.

So which is it, from the bottom up or from the top down? My study supports the idea that conflicts generate new law and, in particular, challenges the common assumption that formal, programmatic or intentionalistic governance structures served as the primary mechanism through which states established freedoms. Instead, custom, innovation, and negotiation in the marketplace played a role in addition to legal scholarship, lawyers' arguments, and judicial decisions. While not denying the importance of legislation, revolutionary changes, and other top-down modifications of formal governance, it was primarily through the conflict-generated creation of new interpretations of law and legal tools – rather than the passage of laws themselves – that early modern German freedoms were extended or even established.[40] Specifically, it was through the efforts of jurists to resolve hotly contested claims to property and commercial rights that personal freedom as well as freedoms for communities and various social estates grew.

These institutions appeared through large-scale political entrepreneurship (creating institutions) as well as small-scale commercial entrepreneurship. Civil liberty grew more robust, broadly speaking, through the many, often conflicting influences of rationalistic, disciplinary institutions, with their myriad actors and ideas, sometimes altruistic, sometimes partisan, each different, all

39 There was, as noted previously, little administrative concern as such for economically marginal people, at least as measured by apparent taxable income potential: unmarried women in families not engaged in trade; the very poor; those marked out as incorrigible, violent criminals; and the sick and insane.

40 I have also written about the historical sociology of legal change in Wilder, "Teaching Old Dogs New Tricks."

these things produced as functions of top-down supply motives and bottom-up demand pressure.[41]

The foundations of civil liberty in early modern Germany thus have to be sought in the institutional spaces between high politics and day-to-day conflicts over property and economic rights. Jurists' struggles to resolve disputes in property and commerce led them to establish a notion of the rule of law and particular spheres of liberty, which served as the foundation of more modern ideas of liberty that emerged in Germany only after the French Revolution.

---

41 John O'Neill's suggestion about a research vector aligned from Max Weber to Michel Foucault seems apt here: "It is not far-fetched to consider Weber an archaeologist of the power man exerts over himself, and thus to see him as a precursor of Foucault's conception of the disciplinary society. In each case, history is not ransacked for its rational essence, even though it is only understood as a process of increasing rationalization. Nor is history seen as the story of individual freedom, even though western political history is only intelligible as its invention. What intervenes is the logic of the institutions that bring together rationality, individualism and freedom in the large-scale disciplinary enterprises of capitalism, bureaucracy and the modern therapeutic state." O'Neill, "The Disciplinary Society: From Weber to Foucault," p. 43. The modern therapeutic state may have to wait for a sequel to the present volume.

Glossary

This glossary is generally based on primary sources used in this book as well as Adolf Berger, *Encyclopedic Dictionary of Roman Law* (Philadelphia: American Philosophical Society, 1953); Manlio Bellomo, *The Common Legal Past of Europe: 1000–1800* (Washington, D.C.: Catholic University of America Press, 1995); Constantin Fasolt, *The Limits of History* (Chicago: University of Chicago Press, 2004); Barry Nicholas, *An Introduction to Roman law* (Oxford: Clarendon Press, 1962); Friedrich Carl von Savigny, *Treatise on Possession*, 6th ed. (London: S. Sweet, 1848 [orig. 1803]); Brian Tierney, *The Idea of Natural Rights: Studies on Natural Rights, Natural Law, and Church Law, 1150–1625* (Atlanta: Scholars Press, 1997); and Franz Wieacker, *A History of Private Law in Europe*, trans. Tony Weir (Oxford: Clarendon Press, 1995 [orig. 1952]).

adverse possession In prescription law, this is the process whereby an active opposition between two parties causes a change in right. One party asserts a right and the second party challenges. If the first party backs down, then the second party is deemed by jurists to have gained or maintained its right (as the case may be). If the second party backs down, then the first gains or maintains its right.

allod Allod was an ambiguous kind of tenure which apparently existed from about the thirteenth through the eighteenth century in European countries. It can be thought of as functionally very similar to fee simple ownership or free and common socage. An allodial holder holds an estate or rights not from any higher lord but only in his or her own name. Allodial holding was not considered to conflict with subjection to a territorial prince, king, or emperor; it is not clear whether it would conflict with being subject to local seigneurial jurisdiction for criminal law or other delicts.

black-letter law I use this phrase occasionally to denote positive law, law actually on the books rather than merely existing as custom. "The books" might be an actual statutory enactment, a written recording of custom, or a legal court decision in which the court determines that certain law applies.

civil law The law of the civil government of a given realm or territory broadly. Civil is from Latin *civilis*, "of the city." From Roman jurisprudence, civil is understood to be the opposite of natural law, family law, divine law, the law of the church (canon law), or the general legal custom of all peoples (*ius gentium*). Civil law usually is understood to include private law and public law. I use the term generally to mean all valid law for a territory. Civil law may be the black-letter law (*qv*) of a regime, or may be valid but unwritten customary law.

civil liberties I use this term to describe freedoms enjoyed by people as part of civil law (*qv*). Occasionally one reads of "civil rights" (*iura civilia*, *Bürgerrechte*) or "civil liberties" (*libertates civiles, burgerliche Freiheiten*), but these were not fixed, technical terms. (*See also ius.*)

common law or imperial common law (*ius commune*) At the risk of misleading those most familiar with English and not continental legal history, I translate *ius commune* frequently as imperial common law, European common law, Roman common law, or the evolved Roman civil law and public law of post-medieval Europe. The highest form of the ancient Roman civil law can be said to have developed with the creation of the Digest or Pandects in 530–533 AD. With the decline of the Western Roman Empire, official transmission of and training in the Roman law fell into disfunction and abeyance, although it survived and influenced local custom around Europe in the form of "Western Roman Vulgar law." The study of the Digest was revived through its rediscovery by Irnerius in the 1070s in Bologna. There began almost continuous study and glossing of, commentary on, and classical philology of the ancient Roman law, through the period with which this book is concerned. Confusingly for us, contemporary writers in the period sometimes wrote "Roman law" when they meant not the civil, private, or public law of antiquity, but instead the modern *ius commune*. The "Roman law" was said to have been "received" in the Holy Roman Empire of the German Nation with the imperial reform of 1495. This adopted the use of the by-then much-evolved ancient Roman law with centuries of glosses (including the standard ordinary gloss of Accursius), commentaries, and significant new knowledge of the earlier sources beneath the Pandects, not to mention medieval additions which were considered legitimate because emitted by Roman(-German) emperors. Broadly speaking, when legal operators in the seventeenth and eighteenth centuries wrote of the *ius commune*, they meant this modern, evolved form of ancient Roman law. They considered it to be common to Europe, although jurists of all nations knew that actual applicable civil law both public and private had diverged greatly in all European polities – English, French, German, Dutch, Italian, etc. So German jurists called the *ius commune* common and European but really meant that it was common across the empire and had a lot in common with the basic law of other countries outside the empire. (*See also* civil law.)

concrete order of law This refers to the actually existing order of vested rights in society, as opposed to the set(s) of rules or norms (laws as *regulae*). Law includes both concrete orders and rules. Concrete orders do not always accord with rules. Compare *ius*.

detention Mere factual holding of a thing without claim or ownership or possession (*qv*). Detention may be lawful (as when you give over a temporary deposit such as your driver's license) or merely factual (as when you find yourself temporarily having custody of something but make no clam that it is yours). Detention is similar to bailment and custody. (*See also* possession.)

dominion *Dominion* is the anglicization of Latin *dominium* (I use the former and the latter interchangeably). *Dominium* can be translated as both lordship and ownership. This entry cannot offer a comprehensive definition of this key term, but a few important things can be stated.

Generally in this book, dominion is over space, not over things as such, though it usually would include implicit governance and disposal of things and sometimes people within that space. The space in question is, in the contexts of this book, usually an estate (*qv*). It is useful to think of the Roman legal Latin *dominium* through its English legal translations *lordship* and *ownership* separately since they help us keep in mind both aspects of dominion. The sense of "lordship" is still felt in elements of modern property law such as the term "landlord" or an owner's right to grant or forbid entry.

Broadly speaking the ownership aspect of dominion meant the classic Roman triptych of the abilities to use, abuse, and dispose of an estate and any fruits, resources, or wild creatures on it. It seems quite clear throughout my sources that one who held dominion could generally also alienate and encumber an estate, within varying limits. Alienation might mean outright sale as well as temporary forms of giving out such as rental or subinfeudation. Encumbrance means to use something as collateral in a debt, in the modern sense of mortgaging a piece of property or giving something in pawn against a loan. The limits on alienation and encumbrance might come either from the customary understanding of what rules governed the property (e.g. family property, fief, etc.) or from a formality of how the estate was acquired in the first place. The rule of derivative title (Chapter 6) usually limited the terms by which an estate could be given out.

Dominion over space usually included the rightful exercise of possible activities or harvest from that space, such as hunting, use of resources, travel across, or agriculture. These rights could be alienated or encumbered (*see above*). Rights could also be inexplicably separated from an estate, as when one person or entity might own a space such as a forest, but another person or entity might be known to have long enjoyed the customary right to e.g. hunt or collect firewood from that forest. In such cases, which were common, jurists used prescription to explain that the existing order, however unpredictable or unformalized, must be the rightful concrete order of law (*qv*) based on prior, willing agreement.

estate The English word "estate" is used in two ways legally, both of which appear frequently in this book. The two ways correspond to different German and Latin terms. One meaning of *estate* is a unitary parcel of land or land and rights, usually held under sole dominion (*qv*). This meaning corresponds to Latin *praedium*, *fundus*, or *patrimonium* and most often to the German *Gut* or *Hof*. (Confusingly, in in Anglo-American law, because of inherited ancient Roman jurisprudence, an estate in this first sense of the term might in practice consist of multiple discontiguous parcels or even be incorporeal. Nevertheless these meanings are rooted firsmly in the concrete sense of *estate* just given.) The other meaning of the English *estate* is a Latin *status* or German *Stand*, meaning a corporate group at public law. This is the meaning in the idea of "estates constitutionalism," wherein "the estates" of a realm work to guard their traditional rights and privileges (as in the knights in Chapter 4). The imperial princes collectively as a corporate estate in the imperial diet were the *Fürstenstand*. *Stand* however could also be used as a sociological or economic descriptor, as in *Mittelstand* (the middle class) or a legal descriptor, as in the estate of women, of nobles, or of merchants. This social or sociolegal meaning of estate is especially important in Chapter 6, whose jurists understood the law of exchange as applying to some estates in the social sense but not as such binding to estates in the sense of real property.

freedom This term and its synonyms and cognates has meant many things to many people. A glossary should be a helpful, practical guide to meaning and is no place for a pandora's box of conceptual history.

It may briefly be said however that modern theorists have distinguished positive and negative freedom, meaning respectively "freedom to" have or enjoy certain things guaranteed, as opposed to "freedom from" impositions, extractions, or oppression. My sources use *freedom* almost universally in a plain, negative sense as a right to perform a certain activity unmolested or impeded, say to travel, to harvest, use, buy, sell (at free prices), or enjoy the security of one's own dominion (on land or in a building). (*See* dominion, estate, and Chapter 4.)

This general usage notwithstanding, freedom in the pre-modern liberal context was not a *universal* standard or concept in the modern, liberal sense of the term. That is, it would not be true that all people possessed freedoms, except in the New Testament sense that salvation through God's grace has freed mankind from the burden of sin. Further, not only was freedom not universally enjoyed, it was also neither plenary nor uniform. It was not *plenary* in the sense that a person might well enjoy legally free use of his estate with all the activities one could do on it, such as building structures or agriculture, but just the same another person might have rights which imposed on that freedom, such as the right to collect firewood on the land, the right to cross it (way), or magistrate's authority to investigate crime. Freedom was finally not *uniform* in that "freedom" was commonly understood to not have any determinate content except its negative structure – most all freedom was "freedom from," but one person might have freedom from extractions on his estate, which another might have a different specific negative freedom, say freedom from the jurisdiction of outside magistrates under certain conditions (freedom of jurisdiction). There were some positive uses of the concept of freedom, as in both the medieval Catholic and the Lutheran concepts of Christian freedom (*see* Chapter 2). The influence of these on the seventeenth- and eighteenth-century idea of German freedom studied in this book remains a topic for subsequent investigation.

ius *Ius* may be translated as both law and right. It also has dual subjective and objective meanings: In the subjective sense, a *ius* is a right, something portable by and enjoyed by one party. In the objective sense, *ius* is law, in both the sense of rule(s) and in the sense of concrete order (*qv*).

natural law "Natural law" (*ius naturale, Naturrecht*) is difficult to define because it has been defined or implicitly used in many different ways. Philosophers usually take nature to be the essence of something and natural law to be a metaphysical (essential) norm or rule. Rules from revealed religion like the Golden Rule were often taken to be examples of natural law. Roman jurists initiated the concept of *ius naturale* in antiquity when they sought to understand what was common to various civil laws, especially the different civil laws of foreign societies into contact with which their legions (and subsequently their merchants) had come. Sometimes natural laws were given in short form as a nominalization: Hence one might speak of self-defense as being *a* natural law, meaning to say that there is a natural law rule, namely the rule that it is OK to use force to preserve one's own life. A major division in the production of natural law theory lies between ancient and medieval natural law on the one hand and modern natural law on the other (although this delineation gets blurry among late medieval and Spanish scholastic authors, ca. 1300–1600). In this view, ancient and high medieval natural law was imagined as an objective, superhuman order: rightful, universal norms and essences of human things which are true everywhere and always, it was supposed. Modern natural law is usually said to have begun with the work of Hugo Grotius, who seemed to use all of the equipment of classical natural law except to say that natural law had a subjective element: It was based on the ideas and will of any given individual person, rather than upon one universal truth for all human creation. To all of this I would add one important element in the present book: Natural law was not only an abstract theorizing. It was often very practical work sifting details of things at dispute, differing claims, conflict of laws, and similar-but-not-quite-the-same customs. A magnificent example of this is Friedrich Carl von Savigny's treatise on possession, *Das Recht des Besitzes* (1803; transl. London: 1848), whose quarry was the nature of possession (*qv*), or as we might say the natural law of possession.

lordship *See* dominion.

ownership *See* dominion.

possession Possession is easy to understand at a basic level but is notoriously difficult as a technical concept of law. It is similar to ownership (*see* dominion) in that it means rightful holding and control over a thing, space (estate, *qv*), or a right connected to that space. It may be best understood informally to mean a rightfulness of holding even in the presence of someone else's proper ownership of a thing. If the owner rents a thing to you, then you are its rightful possessor. (See also discussion of possession in Chapter 4, Sections 8–10, pp. 159–175, as well as in Chapter 5 *passim*.)

prescription Prescription can be understood as a naturalistic process which creates, changes, and/or destroys real rights. Prescription can be thought of as a kind of recipe, a set of events and procedures which, if followed, produce a certain outcome. What was required first was that someone possess an estate or exercise a right in good faith, over a passage of time. If this continued peacefully for a long period, often thirty years, then the person was said to gain the right by prescription. Similarly, one might become rightfully free of a certain obligation or servitude by not living under it or not performing it, unchallenged, for the long period. Likewise, another party's right might be extinguished over that long period if they did not challenge the peaceful possessor's habitation or exercise. A shortcut to this slow process happened through notorious contradiction (*contradictio*), known in English as adverse possession (*qv*). In adverse possession, the party pretending to a right *openly defies* the claim of the other party. If the latter capitulates, either expressly or simply by dropping the pursuit of the claim, then the first party is said to have gained the right the acquisitive prescription with contradiction. (See also discussion of prescription in Chapter 4 *passim* and in Chapter 5, Sections 4–9, pp. 197–218.)

private law Strictly speaking, there are at least three meanings of this term. One is the "law" (the concrete order, *qv*) which *arises from* private transactions. If I rent a house from a landlord, the contract is said to be private law. A second meaning is the rules which are notionally created from private dealings, famously in the law merchant (though this is contested among historians; *see* Chapter 6). A third sense of private law is the rules themselves which regulate the first meaning. These rules might themselves originate not from any private dealings (i.e., between non-state operators), but instead be enacted by state operators. The US Uniform Commercial Code would be an example of the third type of law, as would the Praetorian Edict of ancient Rome.

property rights In this book, there are so many nuances to property that it is almost impossible to give an overall definition or translation of them into the modern notion (in English here) of property rights. Still, the term *property rights* is broadly useful so long as we always ask what it means in a particular context and not bring modern or external assumptions into what law governed any particular kind of property. Property rights in merchant law and bills meant the rules and procedures of the law of exchange. Feudal law or more correctly feudal jurisprudence governed the interpretation of fief rights. Property rights were held over people, in the form of serfdom, which while declining in the eighteenth century still existed. Lordship over serfs and the complementary obligations and legal outlines of serfs' subjection were governed first by the particular terms of tenure on an estate and secondarily by local custom or custom more broadly. Rules governing property rights in small movable objects (money, chattels such as jewelry, clothing, livestock, furniture, vehicles) were different than rules which governed real estate and its rights, or what I sometimes call the control over space. Add to this that there were other relationships which resembled property rights (that is, resembled dominion, *qv*), such as stewardship over public and sacred things and guardianship over persons and churches.

Bibliography

Sources

Beaumanoir, Philippe de Remi. *The Coutumes de Beauvaisis of Philippe de Beaumanoir.* Middle Ages Series. Philadelphia: University of Pennsylvania Press, 1992.

Birt, Theodor, ed. *Catalogus studiosorum Academiae Marpurgensis cum annalibus coniunctus series recentior annos 1653–1830 complectens.* Marburg: Robert Friedrich, 1903–1914.

Böhmer, Justus Henning. *Ius parochiale: ad fundamenta genuina revocatum a spuriis principiis purgatum atque ita adornatum ut ius ecclesiasticum protestantium illustrare et usum modernum libri tertii decretalium quoad praecipuas materias ostendere quest adiecto indice triplici et supplemento novo.* Editio Qvinta Avctior Et Emendatior ed. Halle: Orphanotrophei, 1738. Originally appeared in 1701.

Burke, Edmund. *Reflections on the Revolution in France.* Edited by J. G. A. Pocock. Indianapolis: Hackett, 1987. Originally appeared in 1790.

Calvinus, Johannes. *Lexicon Iuridicum Iuris.* Colonia Allobrogum [Geneva]: Excudebat Matthaeus Berjon, Sumptibus Caldorianae Societatis, 1612.

Cramer, Johann Ulrich. *Kurtze doch überführende Abhandlung von Erlangung einer Immunitaet durch Verjährung: wodurch zugleich die von ihm über Herrn Carl Friederich Neckers, J.P.P. auf der Hohen Schule zu Genff kurtzen und aus denen eigentlichen rechten Quellen hergeleiteten Unterricht in dem Staats-Recht des Heil. Römischen Reichs Teutscher Nation den 22ten April um 10. Uhr anzufangende Lectiones Privatae eröffnet werden.* Marburg: Philipp Casimir Müller, univ. Buchdr., 1740.

Cramer, Johann Ulrich. "Kurtze doch überführende Abhandlung von Erlangung einer Immunität durch Verjährung." In *Opuscula, materias gravissimas ex omni iure demonstrativa ratione pertractatas continentia: Antea seorsim edita, iam vero ob raritatem et desiderium virorum doctissimorum collecta,* Vol. 2, pp. 174–206. Marburg: Philipp Casimir Müller, 1754. Originally appeared in 1740.

Cramer, Johann Ulrich. "Ob das Bann-Recht einer Schenk-Statt dahin sich erstrecken lasse, dass die gebannte Ehren Zechen bey Hochzeiten, oder Kindtauffen zu halten, und dabey an ein gewisses Getraenck, auch an eine determinirte Anzahl der Mensur adstrigiret werden koennen?" In *Wetzlarische Nebenstunden,* Vol. 12, pp. 85–102. Ulm: Johann Conrad Wohler, 1758.

Cramer, Johann Ulrich. "Ob ein Landes-Herr Immunitatem ab oneribus publicis, in specie Collectis, auch in praejudicium der übrigen Unterthanen ertheilen könne, wenn die Exemtion ob bene merita geschieht?" In *Wetzlarische Nebenstunden,* Vol. 24, pp. 78–98. Ulm: Johann Conrad Wohler, 1761.

Cramer, Johann Ulrich. "Ob geistliche Fürsten immunitatem ab oneribus publicis, in specie Collectis, auch in praejudicium derer übrigen Unterthanen in perpetuum, ohne Consens des Capituls, ertheilen können, wann die Exemtion ob bene merita geschiehet?" In *Wetzlarische Nebenstunden*, Vol. 26 (Vols. 25–28 bound in one codex), pp. 1–23. Ulm: Johann Conrad Wohler, 1761. Originally appeared in 1757.

Cramer, Johann Ulrich. "Ob *in Possessorio summarissimo juris venandi* die *a Regali Principis* hergenommene *Exceptio deficientis Titulinur* einige Aufmercksamkeit verdiene, wenn sie andern als Unterthanen oder Landsassen opponiret wird." In *Wetzlarische Nebenstunden*, Vol. 22, pp. 54–63. Ulm: Johann Conrad Wohler, 1761.

Cramer, Johann Ulrich. *Observationes juris universi ex praxi recentiori supremorum imperii tribunalium haustarum*. 6 vols. Wetzlar: Ph. J. Winckler, 1758–1772.

Cramer, Johann Ulrich. "Unvorgreifliche Gedanken von der im Ober-Fuerstenthum Hessen und Solmsischen ueblichen Landsiedeley." In *Opuscula*, Vol. 2, pp. 99–123. Marburg: Philipp Casimir Müller, 1740.

Daniels, Heinrich Gottfried Wilhelm. *Grundsätze des Wechselrechts: Nach Herrn von Selchow, mit besonderer Rücksicht auf das Allgemeine preußische Landrecht und das französische Handelsgesetzbuch*. Cologne: Bachem, 1827.

de Canngiesser, Leonhard Heinrich Ludwig Georg, ed. *Collectionis notabiliorum decisionum Supremi Tribunalis apellationum Hasso-Cassellani*. 2 vols. Cassel: Johann Martin Lüdicke; Bernhard Christian Duysing, 1768–1771.

Emerich, Johann. "Samlung der alten Rechten und Gewohnheiten der Stad Franckenberg." In *Monimenta Hassiaca*, Vol. 2, pp. 669–756, edited by Friedrich Christoph Schmincke. Cassel: Johann Bertram Cramer, 1748. Originally appeared in ca. 1476.

Estor, Johann Georg. "Die belehnung mit einer sache tilget die *res merae facultatis* und werket ein verbithungs-recht." In *Neue Kleine Schriften*, Vol. 4, pp. 84–92. Marburg: Philipp Casimir Müller, 1761.

Estor, Johann Georg. *Observationes iuris feudalis*. Jena: Johann Friedrich Ritter, 1740.

Estor, Johann Georg. *Opusculum de abusu rerum merae facultatis in foro Germanico praesertim feudali*. 2nd expanded and corrected ed. Jena: Johann Friedrich Ritter, 1744.

Estor, Johann Georg. *Bürgerliche Rechtsgelehrsamkeit der Teutschen*. Edited by Johann Andreas Hofmann. 3 vols. Marburg; Frankfurt am Main: Immanuel Weldige, 1758–1767.

Falckenheiner, Wilhelm. *Personen und Ortsregister zu der Matrikel und den Annalen der Universität Marburg, 1527–1652*. Marburg: N. G. Elwert, 1904.

Fibigius, Gothofredus, praeses. Godofredus Scheffer, respondans. *De iure venandi, aucupandi et piscandi ... Von Wildvogel-, Fischfang- und Forst-Rechten, auch wie man und wer sich dessen anzumassen befugt*. Jena: Heller; Steinman, 1756. Original in 1638.

Fichard, Joannes. *Der Statt Franckenfurt am Mayn ernewerte Reformation*. Frankfurt am Main: Sigismund Feyerabend; Georg Raben, 1578.

Franck, Johannes Christophorus. *Institutiones iuris cambialis: ex legibus cambialibus diversum gentium indole negociationis moribus campsorum ac iure communi nova methodo collectae ... L.* 1. Halle: Novum Bibliopolium, 1721.

Freisen, Josef. *Die Matrikel der Universität Paderborn: 1614–1844*. Würzburg: 1931.

Fürstenau, Carl Gottfried. *Versuch einer Apologie des physiokratischen Systems gegen die Einwuerfe im Deutschen Museum 1778. 10. St. und Hannoeverschen Magazin 48–51 St. desselben Jahrs*. Cassel: J. J. Cramer, 1779.

Gaertner, Bernhard August. *Meditationum practicarum ex jure communi et Hassiaco secund. ord. pandectarum specimen primum*. 2 vols. bound together as one codex. Marburg: Johann Christian Krieger jr., 1785.

Gaill, Andreas. *Practicarum observationum tam ad processum judiciarium, praesertim imperialis Camera, quam causarum decisiones pertinentium. Libri duo. Item de Pace publica et Proscriptis, sive Bannitis Impnis. Libi II. De Pignorationibus liber I. Pn- ICtum D. Andream Gail Agripinatem Caes. Maj. a Consitus etc. Editio II Cum Summariiset Indice*. Coloniae Agrippinae [Cologne]: Apud Joan. Gymnicum, 1580. Originally appeared in 1578.

Goethe, Johann Wolfgang von. *Conversations of Goethe with Eckermann and Soret*. Vol. 2. London: Smith, Elder, & Co., 1850.

Grimm, Jacob, ed. *Weisthümer*. 7 vols. Göttingen: Dietrich, 1840–1878.

Grolmann, Melchior Dethmar. *De Operarum Debitarum Mutatione*. Giessen: Eberhard Henrich Lammer, 1734.

Grolmann, Melchior Dethmar, praeses. Otto Heinrich von Schade, respondans. *De operarum debitarum mutatione dissertatio juridica*. Giessen: Joh. Reinh. Vulpius, 1707.

Grotius, Hugo. *De jure belli ac pacis*. Edited by Jean Barbeyrac. 3 vols. Cambridge; London: John W. Parker, 1853. Originally appeared in 1622; edition with Barbeyrac's extensive notes appeared originally in 1712. See next item below for English translation.

Grotius, Hugo. *The Rights of War and Peace*. Edited by Jean Barbeyrac. 3 vols. Indianapolis: Liberty Fund, 2005. This translation of the Barbeyrac edition (*qv*) was first published in 1738.

Guden, Philipp Peter. *Vom Wechsel- und römischen Rechte über Schuld-Verschreibungen und ihrem Einflusse auf den Wohlstand der Einwohner*. Göttingen: Johann Christian Dieterich, 1790.

Gundlach, Franz. *Catalogus Professorum Academiae Marburgensis: Die Akademischen Lehrer der Philipps-Universität in Marburg von 1527 bis 1910*. Veröffentlichungen der Historischen Kommission für Hessen und Waldeck, Vol. 15. Marburg: N. G. Elwert, 1927.

Gundling, Nicolaus Hieronymus. "De iure oppignorati territorii secundum ius gentium et teutonicum." In *Exercitationes academicae*, pp. 31–96. Halle: Johann Gothfriedus Renger, 1736. Originally appeared in 1705.

Harpprecht, Ferdinand Christoph, praeses. Georg Heinrich Braun, respondans. *Disp. de praescriptione immunitatis a collectis. Tubinga: Bergerus et Cotta*, 1737. Original in 1683.

Harpprecht, Ferdinand Christoph, praeses. Georg Heinrich Braun, respondans. *Tractatio iur. de praescriptione immunitatis a collectis*. Altdorff: Kohlesius, 1709. Original in 1683.

Harpprecht, Ferdinand Christoph, praeses. Georg Heinrich Braun, respondans. *Tractatio iuridica de praescriptione immunitatis a collectis*. Tübingen: Johann-Heinrich Reisius, 1683.

Harpprecht, Ferdinand Christoph, praeses. Johann Georg Lupin, respondans. *Disp. inaug. de immunitate a collectis conventionali. Tubinga: Bergerus & Cotta*, 1737. Original in 1695.

Harpprecht, Ferdinand Christoph, praeses. Johann Georg Lupin, respondans. *Tractatio synoptica inauguralis de immunitate a collectis conventionali*. Tübingen: Johann Konrad Eitel & Martin Rommel's widow, 1695.

Hauschild, Johann Leonhard. *Beischriften von Bauern und Frohnen, und zwar von deren urspruenglichen Bedeutung, der Rechtsvermuthung natuerlicher Freyheit wider die Frohnen, und einigen Gewissensbedenken darueber; nebst einer Vorrede von Beschaffenheit der gemeinen Klagen ueber die Justiz*. Dresden, 1744.

Heineccius, Johann Gottlieb. *Elementa iuris cambialis: commoda auditoribus methodo adornata*. Amsterdam: Iansonius Waesberg, 1742.

Heineccius, Johann Gottlieb. "In quantum princeps antecessoris sui facta speciatim circa confirmationem privilegiorum confirmare teneatur? Consilium nach Metropol. an F. von B. (Iul. 1721)." In *Vermischte Anmerckungen und rechtliche Gutachten*, pp. 344–58. Berlin: Johannes Andreas Rüdiger, 1742. Originally appeared in 1721.

Heineccius, Johann Gottlieb. "XXII. Consilium nack L. an G. H … 1719 … ex nuda assignatione nec cambialiter nec exsequutiue agi potest." In *Vermischte Anmerckungen und rechtliche Gutachten*, pp. 322–30. Berlin: Johannes Andreas Rüdiger, 1742. Originally appeared in 1719.

Heineccius, Johann Gottlieb. *Consilia decisiones et responsa iuris ex schedis paternis*. Edited by Johann Christian Gottlieb Heineccius. Vol. 1. Bratislava: Johann Jacob Kornius, 1744.

Hertius, Joannes Nicolaus, praeses. Joannes Conradus Fabricius, respondans. *Dissertatio de superioritate territoriali*. Giessen: Karger, 1682.

Hertius, Johann Nikolaus. "De Paroemiis Juris Germanicis Libri Tres." In *Commentationum atque opusculorum de selectis et rarioribus ex jurisprudentia universali, publica, feudali et Romana, nec non historia Germanica, argumentis tomi tres*, Vol. 3, pp. 382–639. Frankfurt am Main: Johannes Davidus Zunnerus, 1716. Originally appeared in 1700.

Heydiger, Johann Jacob. *Kurze anleitung zu gründlichem verstand des wechselrechts*. Cölln, 1715.

Hobbes, Thomas. *Leviathan; or, The matter, forme & power of a commonwealth, ecclesiastical and civil*. Edited by Michael Oakeshott. Oxford: Blackwell, 1957. Originally appeared in 1651.

Hofmann, Johann Andreas, praeses. Johann Wilhelm Dietmar, respondans. *De immunitatibus castrensibus aliisque libertatibus praecipue in Hassia*. Marburg: Universität Marburg, 1780.

Hombergk zu Schencklengsfeld, Christoph Ludwig. *Offenbahrer Ungrund der so gennanten Vindiciarum Juris Landsideliae Hassiaci et Solmsensis*. Marburg: Philipp Casimir Müller, 1741.

Hommel, Carl Ferdinand. *Akademische Reden über Herrn Joh. Jacob Mascovs Buch De Iure Feudorum in Imperio Romano Germanico*. Frankfurt am Main: 1758.

Hortleder, Friedrich. *Der Römischen Keyser- Und Königlichen Majestete[n], Auch deß Heiligen Römischen Reichs Geistlicher und Weltlicher Stände, Churfürsten, Fürsten ... Handlungen und Außschreiben, Send-Brieffe*. Gotha: Endter, 1645.

Huber, Ulrich. *De Jure civitatis libri tres ... in usum auditorii Thomasiani*. Edited by Christian Thomasius. 4th ed. Frankfurt am Main; Leipzig: Zeitler, 1708. Originally appeared in 1694.

Humboldt, Wilhelm von. *Ideen zu einem Versuch, die Grenzen der Wirksamkeit des Staats zu bestimmen*. Berlin: Deutsche Bibliothek, 1841. Originally appeared in 1792.

Hume, David. “Of the Balance of Trade.” In *Essays, moral, political, and literary*, pp. 308–26, edited by Thomas Hill Green, Thomas Hodge Grose and Eugene F. Miller. Indianapolis: Liberty Fund, 1987. Originally appeared in 1752.

Jenisch, Daniel. *Geist und Charakter des achtzehnten Jahrhunderts: politisch, moralisch, ästhetisch und wissenschaftlich betrachtet*. Berlin: Königliche Preussische Akademie Kunst- und Buchhandlung, 1800.

Kant, Immanuel. “What is Enlightenment?” In *Philosophical Writings*, pp. 263–70, edited by Ernst Behler. New York: Continuum, 1986. Originally appeared in 1784.

Kirchovius, Laurentius, ed. *Consilia sive Responsa praestantissimorum Germaniae*. One volume subdivided into 5 *tomi*. Frankfurt am Main: 1605.

Kleinschmid, Christoph Ludwig, and Christian Gerhard Apell, eds. *Sammlung fürstlich Hessischer Landes-Ordnungen und Ausschreiben etc.* 8 vols. Cassel: Johann Nicolaus Seibert; Johann Martin Lüdicke, 1767–1816.

Kleinschmidt, Johann. “Fuerstlich-Hessische Landesordnung in der obern Grafschaft Katzenelnbogen.” In: *Magazin für die teutschen Rechte und Geschichte*, Vol. 1, pp. 477–684, edited by Johann Heinrich Christian von Selchow. Göttingen: Meyerische Buchhandlung, 1779.

Klewitz, Ernst, and Otfried Praetorius. *Die Matrikel der Universität Gießen*. Giessen: Ricker, 1957.

Kopp, Carl Philipp. *Ausführliche Nachricht von der ältern und neuern Verfassung der Geistlichen und Civilgerichten in den fürstlich-hessen-casselischen Landen. Anderer oder practischer Theil*. Vol. 2. Cassel: J. J. Cramer, 1771.

Kopp, Johann Adam. *Auserlesene proben des teutschen lehen-rechts, zu desto mehrerer erläuternung derer bey denen teutschen lehn-hofen befindlichen rechten, gewohnheiten und herkommen*. Marburg: Philipp Casimir Müller, 1739.

Kopp, Ulrich Friedrich, and Claus Wittich. *Handbuch zur Kenntnis der Hessen-Casselischen Landes-Verfassung und Rechte*. 7 vols. Cassel, 1796–1808.

Kulenkamp, C. F., ed. *Neue Sammlung der Landes-Ordnungen, Ausschreiben und anderer allgemeinen Verfügungen* [*etc.*]. 7 vols. Cassel: Hof- und Waisenhaus-Buchdruckerei, 1828.

Laufs, Adolf, ed. *Der jüngste Reichsabschied von 1654: Abschied der Römisch Kaiserlichen Majestät und gemeiner Stände, welcher auf dem Reichstag zu Regensburg im Jahr Christi 1654 aufgerichtet ist*. Vol. 32, Quellen zur neueren Geschichte. Bern: H. Lang, 1975.

Lauterbach, Wolfgang Adam. *Compendium juris brevissimis verbis, sed amplissimô sensu & allegationibus universam ferè materiam juris exhibens*. Edited by Johann Jacob Schütz. Tubingæ: sumptibus Joh. Ceorg. Cottæ: typis Martini Rommeii, 1681.

Law, John. *Money and trade considered: with a proposal for supplying the nation with money*. Edinburgh: Heirs and successors of A. Anderson, 1705.

Ledderhose, Conrad Wilhelm, ed. *Kleine Schriften*. 5 vols. Marburg: Neue akademische Buchhandlung, 1787–1795.

Lennep, Georg. *Abhandlung von der Leyhe zu Landsiedel-Recht*. Marburg: Philipp Casimir Müllers Erben und Weldige, 1769.

Lenz, Max, ed. *Briefwechsel Landgraf Philipps des Großmüthigen von Hessen mit Bucer*. Vol. 2, Publicationen aus den k. preussischen Staatsarchiven, Vol. 28. Leipzig: K. Archiv-Verwaltung; Verlag von S. Hirzel, 1887.

Linde, Antonius von der. "Matricula studiosorum scholae Herbornensis (1584–1726)." In *Die Nassauer Drucke der koeniglichen Landesbibliothek in Wiesbaden*. Wiesbaden, 1882, 1887.

Ludolff, Georg Melchior von. *Observationum forensium continuatio* [*Obs. 111–240*]. Wetzlar: Nicolaus Ludovicus Wincklerus, 1732.

Ludovici, Jakob Friedrich. *Einleitung zum Wechsel-Process*. Halle: Wäysenhaus, 1713.

Ludovici, Jakob Friedrich, praeses. Christoph Carl Bruckmüller, respondans. *De muliere cambiante*. Halle: C. Henckel, 1734.

Luther, Martin. *Christian Liberty*. Edited by Harold J. Grimm. revised ed. Philadelphia: Fortress Press, 1957. Originally appeared in 1520.

Machiavelli, Niccolò. *Discourses on Livy*. Chicago: University of Chicago Press, 1996.

Machiavelli, Niccolò. *The Prince*. 2nd ed. Chicago: University of Chicago Press, 1998. Originally appeared in 1513.

Malynes, Gerard. *Consuetudo vel Lex mercatoria, or the ancient law merchant*. 3rd ed. 2 vols. Abingdon; London: Professional Books; T. Basset, 1981. Originally appeared in 1622.

Malynes, Gerard. *The Maintenance of Free Trade*. Reprints of Economic Classics. New York: A. M. Kelley, 1971. Originally appeared in 1622.

Marquard, Johann. *Tractaus politico-juridicus de iure mercarorum et commerciorum singulari etc*. Frankfurt am Main: 1662.

Martens, Georg Friedrich von. *Versuch einer historischen Entwickelung des wahren Ursprungs des Wechselrechts*. Göttingen: Johann Christian Dieterich, 1797.

Mevius, David. *Commentarii in jus lubecense libri quinque*. 4th ed. Frankfurt am Main; Leipzig: Joachim Wildius & Johannes Heinrich Richter, 1700. Originally appeared in 1642.

Mevius, David. *Decisiones Super Causis Praecipuis Ad Summum Tribunal Regium Vismariense Delatis: Quibus Praeter priores Decisionum ac rerum indices Accessit Repertorium, Quo Dictae Decisione iuxta ordinem Pandectarum exhibentur*. Edited by Johann Jacob von Ryssel. 4th ed. Frankfurt am Main: 1698.

Montaigne, Michel de. "Of Cannibals." Translated by Donald M. Frame. In *The Complete Essays of Montaigne*, pp. xxiii, 883. Stanford: Stanford University Press, 1957. Originally appeared in 1580.

Montesquieu, Charles le Secondat baron de. *Persian Letters*. 2 vols. London: J. Tonson, 1722. Originally appeared in 1721.

Montesquieu, Charles le Secondat baron de. *The Spirit of the Laws*. Cambridge Texts in the History of Political Thought. Edited by Anne M. Cohler, Basia C. Miller and Harold S. Stone. Cambridge: Cambridge University Press, 1989. Originally appeared in 1748.

Moser, Johann Jacob. "Von der Landeshoheit derer Teutschen Reichsstände überhaupt." In *Neues Teutsches Staatsrecht*. Frankfurt am Main; Leipzig: 1773.

Möser, Justus. *Patriotische Phantasien*. Sämtliche Werk. Edited by Ludwig Schirmeyer and Werner Kohlschmidt. 4 vols. Berlin; Oldenburg: Gerhard Stalling Verlag, 1954. Originally appeared in 1775–1786.

Osler, Douglas J., ed. *Bibliographica iuridica*. 6 vols. Frankfurt am Main: Vittorio Klostermann, 2000–2009.

Philippi, Friedrich, praeses. Christian Henricus, respondans. *De praescriptione immunitatis â tributis. Von der Verjährung Steuren und anderer Obrigkeitlichen Anlagen-Freyheit*. Wittenberg: Officina Hakiana, 1745. Original in 1688.

Philippi, Friedrich, praeses. Christian Henricus, respondans. *Dissertatio Juridica de praescriptione immunitatis a tributis = Von der Verjährung der Steuren und anderer Obrigkeitl. Anlagen Freyheit*. 1721. Original in 1688.

Pistorius, Georg Tobias. *Thesaurus paroemiarum Germanico-iuridicarum: Teutsch-Juristischer Sprichwörter-Schatz*. expanded and corrected ed. Leipzig: J. C. Muller, 1716.

Pufendorf, Samuel. *The Present State of Germany*. Translated by Edmund Bohun. Edited by Michael J. Seidler. Indianapolis: Liberty Fund, 2007. Originally appeared in 1667, 1696.

Repgow, Eike von. *Sachsen-Spiegel oder Das Sächsische Land-Recht in Der Alt-Teutschen, Lateinischen und ietzo gebräuchlichen Hoch-Teutschen Sprache*. Edited by Jakob Friedrich Ludovici. Halle: Wäysenhaus, 1720.

Richter, Gregor, ed. *Die Studentenmatrikel der Adolphsuniversität zu Fulda (1734–1805)*. Fulda: Fuldaer Actiendruckerei, 1936.

Savigny, Friedrich Carl von. *Das Recht des Besitzes. Eine civilistische Abhandlung*. Giessen: Heyer, 1803.

Scheidt, Christian Ludwig, praeses. Johann Rudolph Wendeborn, respondans. *De iure erigendi cauponas et hospitia publica tam in genere quam in specie in terrris Brunsuico Luneburgicis von wirthschaffs-und krug-nahrung*. Göttingen: Typis Hagerianis [Johann Friedrich Hager], 1739.

Schmauss, Johann Jacob, and Heinrich Christian Senckenberg, eds. *Neue und vollständigere Sammlung der Reichsabschiede*. 4 vols. Frankfurt am Main: Ernst August Koch, 1747.

Selchow, Johann Heinrich Christian von. *Grundsätze des Wechselrechts: Zum Gebrauch seiner Vorlesungen*. 2nd, improved ed. Göttingen: Johann Wilhelm Bossigel, 1777.

Selchow, Johann Heinrich Christian von. "Gutachten über die eigenmächtige Einziehung der Baurengüter, December 1780." In *Rechtsfälle enthaltend Gutachten und Entscheidungen vorzüglich aus dem teutschen Staats- und Privatrecht*, Vol. 1, pp. 183–90. Lemgo: Meyer, 1782. Originally appeared in 1780.

Selchow, Johann Heinrich Christian von, ed. *Rechtsfälle enthaltend Gutachten und Entscheidungen vorzüglich aus dem teutschen Staats- und Privatrecht*. 4 vols. Vol. 4. Lemgo: Meyer, 1785.

Senckenberg, Heinrich Christian. "Juridicas Consuetudines Principatus Hassiae Sec. XVI auctoritate publica collectas / Extractus der Statt und Lands Gebrauch im Ober Fürstenthum Hessen die Erb und Anfälle zwischen zwey Ehegemaechten, wie auch den Neherkauf betreffend." In *Selecta iuris et historiarum*, Vol. 3, pp. 267–300. Frankfurt am Main: Johann Friedrich Fleischer, 1735.

Senckenberg, Heinrich Christian, ed. *Selecta iuris et historiarum*. Vol. 3. Frankfurt am Main: Johann Friedrich Fleischer, 1735.

Senckenberg, Heinrich Christian, ed. *Senckenbergische Sammlung von ungedruckt- und raren Schriften. Zu Erläuterung derer Rechte und Geschichten von Teutschland; Vier Theile samt Vorrede und General-Register*. 4 vols. Frankfurt am Main: Johann Friedrich Fleischer, 1751.

Senckenberg, Heinrich Christian. *Unfug des recursus ad comitia in unerheblicher antastung seiner Kayserl. Majestät reservati iuris cognoscendi de suis privilegiis, welcher ab seiten der armen gemeinde Freyenseen gegen des Herrn Grafen zu Solms-Laubach Hoch-Gräfliche Excellence*. Edited by Johann Bernhard Christian Hase. Giessen: Johann Müller, 1744.

Siegel, Johann Gottlieb, and Johann Ludwig Ubl, eds. *Corpus juris cambialis, das ist: Vollständiges Sammlung derer auf den vornehmsten Handels-Plätzen auch anderer Orte in Europa üblichen allerneuesten Wechsel-Ordungen* (etc.). *3 or 4?* vols. Leipzig: Johann Samuel Heinsius, 1742–1757.

Smith, Adam. *An Inquiry into the Nature and Causes of the Wealth of Nations*. New York: Modern Library, 1965. Originally appeared in 1776.

Smith, Adam. *Untersuchung der Natur und Ursachen von Nationalreichthümern*. Translated by Johann Friedrich Schiller. Leipzig: Weidmanns Erben und Reich, 1776.

Smith, Adam. *The Theory of Moral Sentiments*. Edited by D. D. Raphael and A. L. Macfie. Indianapolis: Liberty Classics, 1982. Originally appeared in 1759.

"Solmser Landrecht." In *Landrechte des 16. Jahrhunderts*, Vol. 1,2, pp. 173–254, edited by Wolfgang Kunkel. Quellen zur Neueren Privatrechtsgeschichte Deutschlands. Weimar: Hermann Böhlaus Nachfolger, 1938. Originally appeared in 1571.

Sprenger, Johann Theodor. *Kurtze Wechszel-Practick auss den vornemsten Wechsel Scriptis*. Frankfurt am Main: Fickwirht, 1662.

Stadt- und Landesbrauch des Oberfürstenthums Marburg. Marburg: 1749.

Stamm, Johann Hermann. *Tractatus de servitute personali in tres libros distinctus*. Frankfurt am Main: 1625.

Strieder, Friedrich Wilhelm. *Über die Monopolien. Nebst Bemerkungen über die in dieser Materie von dem Herrn Probst und Prälaten Quirl und Herrn Kammerrath Klippstein zum Vorschein gekommene Schriften*. Hannover: Helwingische Hofbuchhandlung, 1779.

Tabor, Joannes Otto. *Commentarius ad tit. cod. De metatis & epidemeticis: von Einquartierungen: ad usvm horvm temporvm accommodatus*. Argentorati [Strasbourg]: Johann Philipp Mülbe, 1645.

Thomasius, Christian, praeses. George Rudolph Schlösser, respondans. *De praescriptione regalium ad jura subditorum non pertinente dissertatio juridica*. Halle; Frankfurt am Main: Christoph Salfeld's widow, 1696.

Thomatus, Aegidius. *Tractatvs De Mvneribvs Patrimonialibus, seu Collectis ... Pars Prima*. Mediolani: Moschenius, 1557.

Uhl, Johann Ludwig, ed. *Franckfurtische Wechsel-Responsa: welche von hiesiger hochlöbl. Juristen-Facultät von Zeit zu Zeit auf Begehren sind ausgestellet und ertheilet worden*. Franckfurt an der Oder: Johann Christian Kleyb, 1749.

Voltaire. *Philosophical Dictionary*. Harmondsworth, Middlesex: Penguin Classics, 1972. Originally appeared in 1764.

von Einsiedel, Conrad. *Tractatus de iuribus ad imperatoris Romano-Teutonici Maiestatem pertinentibus sive regalibus*. Halle (Saxony): Petrus Faber, 1619.

Vultejus, Hermann. "Vita Hermanni Vulteji ab ipso descripta." In *Auserlesene kleine Schrifften*, Vol. (i.e. Band) 2, pp. 199–244, edited by Johann Georg Estor. Giessen: Johann Philipp Krieger, 1746. Originally appeared in 1735.

Waldschmiedt, Johann Wilhelm, praeses. Christian Fridericus Goy, respondans. *De hominibus propriis Hassiacis. Von Hessischen Leibeigenen*. Marburg: 1716.

Walther, Johannes, praeses. Matthias Bode, respondans. *Dissertatio Iuridica De Cambiis*. Marburg: Chemlinus [Ex Officina Typographica Chemliniana], 1646.

Wesenbeck, Matthaeus. *Tractatus et Responsa, quae vulgo Consilia Juris appellantur*. Colonia Munatiana [Basel]: Episcopius, 1575.

Wlöm, Stephan Sigismund. *Vindiciae iuris landsideliae Hassiaci et Solmensis*. Marburg: J. G. Ebersbach's widow, 1740.

Woringer, August. *Die Studenten der Universität zu Rinteln (Academia Ernestina)*. Mitteilungen der Zentralstelle für deutsche Personen- und Familiengeschichte. Nendeln [Liechtenstein]: Kraus Reprint, 1980.

Zedler, Gottfried, and Hans Sommer, eds. *Die Matrikel der Hohen Schule und des Paedagogiums zu Herborn*. Vol. 5, Veröffentlichungen der Historischen Kommission für Nassau. Wiesbaden: J. F. Bergmann, 1908.

Zimmermann, Ludwig, ed. *Der Ökonomische Staat Landgraf Wilhelms IV*. 3 vols, Veröffentlichungen der Historischen Kommission für Hessen und Waldeck; Quellen zur Verwaltungsgeschichte hessischer Territorien. Marburg: Elwert, 1933–1937. Originally compiled in 1585.

Scholarship

Acton, John Emerich Edward Dalberg. "The History of Freedom in Christianity." In *The History of Freedom and Other Essays*, pp. 30–60, edited by John Neville Figgis and Reginald Vere Laurence. London: Macmillan, 1907.

Alberti, Walter. "Ueber den Inhalt des Rheingauer Landbrauchs." Inaugural dissertation, 1913.

Alces, Peter A., and Harold F. See. *The Commercial Law of Intellectual Property*. New York; Toronto: Little, Brown, 1994.

Amend-Traut, Anja. *Wechselverbindlichkeiten vor dem Reichskammergericht: Praktiziertes Zivilrecht in der Frühen Neuzeit.* Vol. 54, Quellen und Forschungen zur höchsten Gerichtsbarkeit im Alten Reich. Cologne; Weimar; Vienna: Böhlau, 2009.

Ammous, Saifedean. *The Bitcoin Standard: The Decentralized Alternative to Central Banking.* Hoboken, New Jersey: John Wiley & Sons, Inc, 2018.

Anderson, Margaret Lavinia. *Practicing Democracy: Elections and Political Culture in Imperial Germany.* Princeton: Princeton University Press, 2000.

Anderson, Perry. *Passages from antiquity to feudalism.* London: Verso; *Humanities Press; NLB*, 1974.

Arendt, Hannah. *The Human Condition.* Chicago: University of Chicago Press, 1958.

von Aretin, Karl Otmar. *Das Alte Reich, 1648–1806.* 4 vols. Stuttgart: Klett-Cotta, 1993.

Ashley, W. J. "The Beginnings of Town Life in the Middle Ages." *Quarterly Journal of Economics* 10, no. 4 (1896): 359–406.

Backhaus, Jürgen G., ed. *Christian Wolff and Law & Economics: The Heilbronn Symposium.* Hildesheim; New York: Georg Olms, 1998.

Backhaus, Jürgen G. "Otto von Gierke (1841–1921)." In *The Elgar Companion to Law and Economics*, pp. 313–15, edited by Jürgen G. Backhaus. Cheltenham; Northampton: Edward Elgar, 2005.

Baechler, Jean. *The Origins of Capitalism.* New York: St Martin's Press, 1976.

Bainton, Roland. *The Reformation of the Sixteenth Century.* Boston: Beacon Press, 1952.

Barraclough, Geoffrey. *The Origins of Modern Germany.* 2nd ed. New York: Capricorn Books, 1962. Originally appeared in 1946.

Bartsch, Adam von. *The Triumph of the Emperor Maximilian I.* Edited by Hans Burgkmair and Alfred Aspland: Holbein Society, 1875.

Basile, Mary Elizabeth, Jane Fair Bestor, Daniel R. Coquillette, and Charles Donahue, Jr., eds. *Lex Mercatoria and Legal Pluralism.* Cambridge: Ames Foundation, 1998.

Baumann, Anette, Peter Oestmann, Stephan Wendehorst, and Siegrid Westphal, eds. *Prozesspraxis im Alten Reich. Annäherungen – Fallstudien – Statistiken.* Vol. 50, Quellen und Forschungen zur Höchsten Gerichtsbarkeit im Alten Reich. Cologne; Weimar; Vienna, 2005.

Beckert, Sven. *Empire of Cotton: A Global History.* New York: Vintage Books, 2014.

Bellomo, Manlio. *The Common Legal Past of Europe: 1000–1800.* Studies in Medieval and Early Modern Canon Law. Vol. 4. Washington, D.C.: Catholic University of America Press, 1995.

Benoist, Alain de. "The Idea of Empire." In *Democracy and Populism: The Telos Essays*, pp. 13–31, edited by Russell A. Berman and Timothy W. Luke. Candor: Telos Press Publishing, 2018.

Berger, Adolf. *Encyclopedic Dictionary of Roman Law.* Philadelphia: American Philosophical Society, 1953.

Berman, Harold. *Law and Revolution II: The Impact of the Protestant Reformations on the Western Legal Tradition*. Cambridge: Belknap Press, 2003.

Berman, Harold. *Law and Revolution: The Formation of the Western Legal Tradition*. Cambridge: Harvard University Press, 1983.

Black, Henry Campbell. *Black's Law Dictionary*. Edited by Joseph R. Nolan. 6th ed. St. Paul: West Publishing Company, 1990. Originally appeared in 1891.

Blackbourn, David, and Geoff Eley. *The Peculiarities of German History: Bourgeois Society and Politics in 19th Century Germany*. Oxford: Oxford University Press, 1984.

Blaich, Fritz. "Die hessische Antimonopolpolitik unter Landgraf Moritz." *Hessisches Jahrbuch für Landesgeschichte* (1966): 121–46.

Blanning, T. C. W. *Frederick the Great: King of Prussia*. New York: Random House, 2016.

Blaufarb, Rafe. *The Great Demarcation: The French Revolution and the Invention of Modern Property*. Oxford: Oxford University Press, 2016.

Bleicken, Jochen, Werner Conze, Christof Dipper, Horst Günther, Diethelm Klippel, Gerhard May, and Christian Meier. "Freiheit." In *Geschichtliche Grundbegriffe: Historisches Lexikon zur politisch-sozialen Sprache in Deutschland*, Vol. 2, pp. 425–542, edited by Otto Brunner, Werner Conze and Reinhart Koselleck. Stuttgart: E. Klett, 1975.

Blickle, Peter. *Die Revolution von 1525 i.e. Fünfzehnhundertfünfundzwanzig*. Munich; Vienna: Oldenbourg, 1975.

Blickle, Peter. *From the Communal Reformation to the Revolution of the Common Man*. Vol. 65, Studies in Medieval and Reformation Thought. Leiden; Boston: Brill, 1998.

Blickle, Peter. *Kommunalismus: Skizzen einer gesellschaftlichen Organisationsform*. 2 vols. Munich: R. Oldenbourg, 2000.

Blickle, Peter. *The Revolution of 1525: The German Peasants' War from a New Perspective*. Baltimore: Johns Hopkins University Press, 1981. Originally appeared in 1975.

Blickle, Peter. *Von der Leibeigenschaft zu den Menschenrechten: Eine Geschichte der Freiheit in Deutschland*. Munich: Beck, 2003.

Bohn, Robert. *Karlshafen, Wirtschafts- und Sozialgeschichte der hessischen Planstadt aus der Barockzeit*. Karlshafen, 2000.

Bond, C. A. *Nemesis: The Jouvenelian vs. the Liberal Model of Human Orders*. Ellenbrook: Imperium Press, 2019.

Bonney, Richard, ed. *Economic Systems and State Finance*. Oxford: Oxford University Press, 1995.

Borges, Jorge Luis. *Selected Non-Fictions*. Edited by Eliot Weinberger. New York: Viking, 1999.

Bouwsma, William J. "Liberty in the Renaissance and Reformation." In *The Origins of Modern Freedom in the West*, pp. 203–34, edited by Richard W. Davis. Stanford: Stanford University Press, 1995.

Brabant, Artur. *Das Heilige römische Reich teutscher Nation im Kampf mit Friedrich dem Grossen*. Berlin: G. Paetel, 1904.

Brady, Thomas A., Jr. *Turning Swiss: Cities and Empire, 1450–1550*. Cambridge Studies in Early Modern History. Cambridge; New York: Cambridge University Press, 1985.

Braun, Hans-Joachim. "Economic Theory and Policy in Germany, 1750–1800." *Journal of European Economic History* 4 (1975): 301–22.

Brauneder, Wilhelm. "Burgrecht." In *Handwörterbuch zur deutschen Rechtsgeschichte*, Vol. 4, pp. 769–70, edited by Albrecht Cordes and Wolfgang Stammler. Berlin: E. Schmidt, 2004.

Braunreuther, Kurt. *Studien zur Geschichte der politischen Ökonomie und der Soziologie*. Berlin: Akademie-Verlag, 1978.

Brunner, Otto. *Adeliges Landleben und europäischer Geist: Leben und Werk Wolf Helmhards von Hohberg, 1612–1688*. Salzburg: O. Müller, 1949.

Brunner, Otto. *Land and Lordship: Structures of Governance in Medieval Austria*. Philadelphia: University of Pennsylvania Press, 1984. Originally appeared in 1931.

Brunner, Otto. "Feudalism: The History of a Concept." In *Lordship and Community in Medieval Europe: Selected Readings*, pp. 32–61, edited by Fredric L. Cheyette. New York: Holt Rinehart and Winston, 1968. Originally appeared in 1956.

Brunner, Otto. "Johann Joachim Bechers Entwurf einer '*Oeconomia ruralis et domestica*'." In *Festgabe an das Österreichische Staatsarchiv zur Feier des 200-jährigen Bestandes des Haus-, Hof- und Staatsarchives*, pp. 121, edited by Richard Meister, Otto Brunner and Alphons Lhotsky. Vienna: R. M. Rohrer, 1949.

Burchell, Graham, Colin Gordon, and Peter Miller, eds. *The Foucault Effect: Studies in Governmentality: With Two Lectures by and an Interview with Michel Foucault*. Chicago: University of Chicago Press, 1991.

Burt, Ronald S. *Brokerage and Closure: An Introduction to Social Capital*. Oxford: Oxford University Press, 2013.

Buschmann, Arno. "Estor, Pütter, Hugo – Zur Vorgeschichte der Historischen Rechtsschule." In *Vielfalt und Einheit in der Rechtsgeschichte: Festgabe für Elmar Wadle zum 65. Geburtstag*, Vol. 136, pp. 75–103, edited by Thomas Gergen. Annales Universitatis Saraviensis. Cologne: Heymann, 2004.

Buschmann, Arno. "J. G. Estors System der *Bürgerlichen Rechtsgelehrsamkeit der Teutschen*." In *Wirkungen europäischer Rechtskultur*, pp. 77–98, edited by Gerhard Köbler and Hermann Nehlsen. Munich, 1997.

Caenegem, Raoul C. van. "The *Rechtsstaat* in Historical Perspective." In *Legal history: A European Perspective*, pp. 185–200. London; Rio Grande: Hambledon Press, 1991.

Carsten, F. L. *Princes and Parliaments in Germany, From the 15th to the 18th Century*. Oxford: Clarendon Press, 1959.

Cerutti, Simona. "Law Merchants: a Model for an Egalitarian Society in 18th Century Europe." Paper presented at the Conference on Political History: Recent Trends in International Perspective, Bielefeld, December 10–12, 2009.

Chang, Ha-Joon. *Kicking Away the Ladder: Development Strategy in Historical Perspective*. London: Anthem, 2002.

Chown, John F. *A History of Money: From AD 800*. London; New York: Routledge, 1994.

Confino, Alon. *The Nation as Local Metaphor: Württemberg, Imperial Germany, and National Memory*. Chapel Hill: University of North Carolina Press, 1996.

Conte, Emanuele. "Modena 1182, the origins of a new paradigm of ownership: the interface between historical contingency and the scholarly invention of legal categories." *Glossae: European Journal of Legal History* 15 (11/1 2018): 4–18.

Conte, Emanuele. "The order and the *Volk*. Romantic roots and enduring fascination of the German constitutional history." *De rebus divinis et humanis Essays in honour of Jan Hallebeek* (2019): 37–53.

Cordes, Albrecht. "The search for a medieval *Lex mercatoria*." In *From lex mercatoria to commercial law*, pp. 53–68, edited by Vito Piergiovanni. Comparative Studies in Continental and Anglo-American Legal History. Berlin: Duncker & Humblot, 2005.

Cusine, Sheriff Douglas J. "Res merae facultatis: Through a Glass Darkly." In *Essays in conveyancing and property law: In honour of Professor Robert Rennie*, pp. 185–202, edited by Frankie McCarthy, James Chalmers and Stephen Bogle. Cambridge: Open Book Publishers, 2015.

Darnton, Robert. "The High Enlightenment and the Low-Life of Literature in Pre-Revolutionary France." *Past and Present* 51 (1971): 81–115.

Davies, Glyn. *A History of Money: From Ancient Times to the Present Day*. 3rd, revised ed. Cardiff: University of Wales Press; Julian Hodge Bank Limited, 1994.

Davies, Norman. *Heart of Europe: a short history of Poland*. New York: Oxford University Press, 1984.

Davis, Richard W., ed. *The Origins of Modern Freedom in the West*, The Making of Modern Freedom. Stanford: Stanford University Press, 1995.

Demandt, Karl E. "Die hessischen Landstände im Zeitalter des Frühabsolutismus." *Hessisches Jahrbuch für Landesgeschichte* 15 (1965): 38–108.

Demandt, Karl E. *Geschichte des Landes Hessen*. 2nd, expanded ed. Cassel: Bärenreiter, 1972.

Demsetz, Harold. "Toward a Theory of Property Rights." *American Economic Review* 57, no. 2, Papers and Proceedings of the Seventy-ninth Annual Meeting of the American Economic Association (May 1967): 347–59.

Deneen, Patrick J. *Why Liberalism Failed*. Politics and Culture. New Haven: Yale University Press, 2018.

Desan, Christine. *Making Money: Coin, Currency, and the Coming of Capitalism*. Oxford: Oxford University Press, 2014.

Diestelkamp, Bernhard. *Das Reichskammergericht in der deutschen Geschichte: Stand der Forschung, Forschungsperspektiven.* Quellen und Forschungen zur höchsten Gerichtsbarkeit im alten Reich. Cologne: Böhlau, 1990.

Diestelkamp, Bernhard, ed. *Die politische Funktion des Reichskammergerichts.* Cologne: Böhlau Verlag, 1993.

Dietz, Alexander. *Frankfurter Handelsgeschichte.* Reprint ed. 4 vols. in 5 vols. Glashütten im Taunus: D. Auvermann, 1970. Originally appeared in 1910–1925.

Dietze, Gottfried. *Two Concepts of the Rule of Law.* Indianapolis: Liberty Fund, 1973.

Dreitzel, Horst. *Absolutismus und ständische Verfassung in Deutschland: Ein Beitrag zu Kontinuität und Diskontinuität der politischen Theorie in der frühen Neuzeit.* Mainz: Verlag Philipp von Zabern, 1992.

Eddie, Sean A. *Freedom's Price: Serfdom, Subjection, and Reform in Prussia: 1648–1848.* Oxford: Oxford University Press, 2013.

Endemann, Wilhelm. *Studien in der romanisch-kanonistischen wirthschafts- und rechtslehre bis gegen ende des siebenzehnten jahrhunderts.* 2 volumes published as 1 volume. Berlin: J. Guttentag; D. Collin, 1874–1883.

Epstein, Richard. "Reflections on the Historical Origins and Economic Structure of the Law Merchant." *Chicago Journal of International Law* 5, no. 1 (2004): 1–20.

Fasolt, Constantin. *The Limits of History.* Chicago: University of Chicago Press, 2004.

Fasolt, Constantin. "Quod omnes tangit ab omnibus approbari debet: the words and the meaning." In *In iure veritas: Studies in Canon Law in Memory of Schafer Williams,* pp. 21–55, edited by Steven Bowman and Blanche E. Cody. Cincinnati: University of Cincinnati College of Law, 1991.

Forman-Barzilai, Fonna. *Adam Smith and the Circles of Sympathy: Cosmopolitanism and Moral Theory.* Ideas in Context. Vol. 96. Cambridge: Cambridge University Press, 2011.

Foucault, Michel. *Power.* Edited by James D. Faubion. New York: New Press, 2000.

Fox, George Thomas. "Studies in the Rural History of Upper Hesse." Ph.D. thesis, Vanderbilt University, 1976.

Fox, George Thomas. "Land Tenure, Feudalism and the State in Eighteenth-Century Hesse." In *Themes in Rural History of the Western World,* pp. 99–140, edited by Richard Herr. The Henry A. Wallace Series on Agricutural History and Rural Studies. Ames: Iowa State University Press, 1993.

Franz, Eckhart G. "Der Finanzplatz Frankfurt und die Hof- und Staatsfinanzen der Hessischen Fürstenstaaten." *Blätter für Deutsche Landesgeschichte* 125 (1989): 43–62.

Friedeburg, Robert von. "Landgemeinde, adlige Herrschaft und frühmoderner Staat in Hessen-Kassel nach dem Dreißigjährigen Krieg: Merzhausen 1646–1672." *Hessisches Jahrbuch für Landesgeschichte* 41 (1991): 153–76.

Friedeburg, Robert von. "Natural Jurisprudence, Argument from History and Constitutional Struggle in the Early Enlightenment: Gottlieb Samuel Treuer's 1719 Anti-

Absolutist Polemic." In *Early modern natural law theories: Contexts and strategies in the early Enlightenment*, Vol. 186, pp. 141–67?, edited by T. J. Hochstrasser and Peter Schröder. Archives internationales d'histoire des idées; International archives of the history of ideas. Dordrecht; Boston, 2003.

Friedman, Milton. *Capitalism and Freedom*. Chicago: University of Chicago Press, 1962.

Fustel de Coulanges, Numa Denis. *The Ancient City: A Study on the Religion, Laws, and Institutions of Greece and Rome*. Translated by Willard Small. Boston; Ann Arbor: Lee and Shepard, 1874. Originally appeared in 1872.

Galéra, Karl Sigmar von. *Vom Reich zum Rheinbund, 1713–1806*. Die Riedesel zu Eisenach: Geschichte des Geschlechts der Riedesel Freiherrn zu Eisenach, Erbmarschälle zu Hessen. Vol. 5. Neustadt an der Aisch: Degner, 1961.

Geary, Patrick J. *Before France and Germany: The Creation and Transformation of the Merovingian World*. New York: Oxford University Press, 1988.

Gebhardt, Bruno. *Handbuch der deutschen Geschichte*. Edited by Herbert Grundmann. 8th ed. 4 vols. Stuttgart: Union Deutsche Verlagsgesellschaft, 1954. Originally appeared in 1891.

Gelderen, Martin van. "Liberty, Civic Rights, and Duties in Sixteenth-entury Europe and the Rise of the Dutch Republic." In *The Individual in Political Theory and Practice*, pp. 99–122, edited by Janet Coleman. The Origins of the Modern State in Europe: New York, 1996.

Gerber, David J. "Law and Economics in Wilhelmine Germany: Examining the Dynamics of the Relationship." In *Grundlagen des Rechts: Festschrift für Peter Landau zum 65. Geburtstag*, edited by R. H. Helmholz, Paul Mikat, Michael Stolleis and Jörg Paul Müller. Paderborn: F. Schöningh, 2000.

Golder, Ben, and Peter Fitzpatrick. *Foucault's Law*. Milton Park; New York: Routledge, 2009.

Gorski, Philip S. *The Disciplinary Revolution: Calvinism and the Rise of the State in Early Modern Europe*. Chicago: University of Chicago Press, 2003.

Graeber, David. *Debt: The First 5,000 Years*. Brooklyn: Melville House, 2011.

Grunert, Frank. "The Reception of Hugo Grotius's *De jure belli ac pacis* in the Early German Enlightenment." In: *Early Modern Natural law Theories: Contexts and Strategies in the Early Enlightenment*, edited by T. J. Hochstrasser and Peter Schröder. Dordrecht: Kluwer, 2003.

Grünhut, Carl Samuel. *Grundriss des wechselrechts*. Grundriss des österreichischen Rechts. 2nd, corrected ed. Leipzig: Duncker & Humblot, 1903.

Haakonssen, Knud. "German Natural Law." In *The Cambridge history of eighteenth-century political thought*, pp. 251–90, edited by Mark Goldie and Robert Wokler. Cambridge: Cambridge University Press, 2006.

Haberkern, Eugen, and Joseph Friedrich Wallach. *Hilfswörterbuch für Historiker; Mittelalter und Neuzeit*. Berlin-Gruenwald: Verlag für Staatswissenschaften und Geschichte, 1935.

Habermas, Jürgen. *The Structural Transformation of the Public Sphere: An Inquiry into a Category of Bourgeois society*. Studies in Contemporary German Social Thought. Cambridge: MIT Press, 1989. Originally appeared in 1962.

Hagen, William W. *Ordinary Prussians: Brandenburg Junkers and Villagers, 1500–1840*. New Studies in European History. Cambridge: Cambridge University Press, 2002.

Hasnas, John. "The Myth of the Rule of Law." *Wisconsin Law Review* 199 (1995): 199–233.

Hayek, Friedrich August. *The Constitution of Liberty*. Chicago: University of Chicago Press, 1960.

Head, Randolph C. "Documents, Archives, and Proof around 1700." *Historical Journal* 56, no. 04 (2013): 909–30.

Heideking, Jürgen, and James A. Henretta, eds. *Republicanism and Liberalism in America and the German States, 1750–1850*. Publications of the German Historical Institute. Cambridge: Cambridge University Press, 2002.

Heiler, Carl. "Die Matrikel der Hohen Schule zu Herborn (1725–1817)." In *Nassauische Annalen*, Vol. 55, pp. 148–84. Wiesbaden: Verein für Nassauische Altertumskunde und Geschichtsforschung, 1935.

Heldmann, August. "Die cölnische Stadt Rhens am Rhein in hessischer Pfandschaft." *Zeitschrift des Vereins für hessische Geschichte und Landeskunde* 31 (1896): 1–68.

Helfferich, Tryntje. *The Iron Princess: Amalia Elisabeth and the Thirty Years War*. Cambridge: Harvard University Press, 2013.

Henderson, W. O. "The Genesis of the Industrial Revolution in France and Germany in the 18th Century." *Kyklos* 9 (1956): 190–207.

Henshall, Nicholas. *The Myth of Absolutism*. London: Longman, 1992.

Hespanha, António Manuel. "Form and Content in Early Modern Legal Books: Bridging the Gap between Material Bibliography and the History of Legal Thought." *Rechtsgeschichte* 12 (2008).

Heusler, Andreas. *Germanentum. Vom Lebens- und Formgefühl der alten Germanen*. Heidelberg: C. Winter, 1934.

Hirschman, Albert O. *Exit, Voice, and Loyalty: Responses to Decline in Firms, Organizations and States*. Cambridge: Harvard University Press, 1970.

Hochstrasser, T. J. *Natural Law Theories in the Early Enlightenment*. Vol. 58, Ideas in Context. Cambridge; New York: Cambridge University Press, 2000.

Holborn, Hajo. *Ulrich von Hutten and the German Reformation*. New York: Harper Torchbooks, 1966. Originally appeared in 1929.

Holdsworth, William S. *A History of English Law*. Edited by Arthur L. Goodhart, Harold Greville Hanbury and John McDonald Burke. 17 vols. Vol. 9. London: Methuen, 1924.

Hollenberg, Günter, and Berthold Jäger, eds. *Hessen-Kasselische Landtagsabschiede, 1649–1798*. Vol. 5, Vorgeschichte und Geschichte des Parlamentarismus in Hessen. Marburg: N. G. Elwert, 1989.

Hollenberg, Günter. "Landstände und Militär in Hessen-Kassel." *Hessisches Jahrbuch für Landesgeschichte* 34 (1984): 101–28.

Holt, James Clarke, ed. *Magna Carta and the Idea of Liberty*. New York: Wiley, 1972.

Hölzle, Erwin. *Die Idee einer altgermanischen Freiheit vor Montesquieu; Fragmente aus der Geschichte politischer Freiheitsbestrebungen in Deutschland, England und Frankreich vom 16.-18. Jahrhundert*. Munich: R. Oldenbourg, 1925.

Hont, Istvan. "The 'Rich Country, Poor Country' Debate." In *Wealth and Virtue: The Shaping of Political Economy in the Scottish Enlightenment*, pp. 271–315, edited by Istvan Hont and Michael Ignatieff. Cambridge University Press, 1983.

Hsia, R. Po-chia. *Social Discipline in the Reformation: Central Europe, 1550–1750*. Christianity and Society in the Modern World. London; New York: Routledge, 1989.

Hunter, Ian. *Rival Enlightenments: Civil and Metaphysical Philosophy in Early Modern Germany*. Ideas in Context. Cambridge: Cambridge University Press, 2001.

Hunter, Ian. *The secularisation of the confessional state: the political thought of Christian Thomasius*. Ideas in Context. Cambridge; New York: Cambridge University Press, 2007.

Ingrao, Charles. *The Hessian Mercenary State: Ideas, Institutions, and Reform under Frederick II, 1760–1785*. Cambridge: Cambridge University Press, 1987.

Johns, Adrian. *The Nature of the Book: Print and Knowledge in the Making*. Chicago: University of Chicago Press, 1998.

de Jouvenel, Bertrand. *Power: The Natural History of its Growth*. London: Hutchinson, 1948. Originally appeared in 1945.

Kagan, Robert A. *Adversarial Legalism: The American Way of Law*. Cambridge: Harvard University Press, 2001.

Kantorowicz, Ernst Hartwig. *The King's Two Bodies: A Study in Mediaeval Political Theology*. 7th ed. Princeton: Princeton University Press, 1997. Originally appeared in 1957.

Kantorowicz, Ernst Hartwig. "Kingship under the Impact of Scientific Jurisprudence." In *Twelfth-century Europe and the foundations of modern society*, pp. 89–114, edited by Marshall Clagett, Gaines Post and Robert Reynolds. Madison: University of Wisconsin, 1966.

Keck, Hermann. *Die Entwicklung des Oberappellationsgerichts zu Kassel*. Cassel, 1906.

Kelley, Donald R. "*Tacitus noster*: The *Germania* in the Renaissance and Reformation." In *Tacitus and the Tacitean tradition*, pp. 152–67, edited by T. James Luce and A. J. Woodman. Princeton University Press, 1993.

Kessler, Amalia. *A Revolution in Commerce: The Parisian Merchant Court and the Rise of Commercial Society in Eighteenth-Century France*. New Haven: Yale University Press, 2007.

Kindleberger, Charles P. "The Economic Crisis of 1619 to 1623." *Journal of Economic History* 51, no. 1 (Mar. 1991): 149–75.

Kindleberger, Charles P. *A Financial History of Western Europe*. London, 1984.

Kindleberger, Charles P. *Manias, Panics, and Crashes: A History of Financial Crises*. New York: Basic Books, 1978.

Kleinschmidt, Arthur. "Prinz Karl Konstantin von Hessen-Rothenburg." *Zeitschrift des Vereins für hessische Geschichte* 35 (1901): 31–162.

Klemme, Heiner, ed. *Reception of the Scottish Enlightenment in Germany: Six Significant Translations, 1755–1782*. 7? vols. Bristol: Thoemmes, 2000.

Klippel, Diethelm. "Der Einfluß der Physiokraten auf die Entwicklung der liberalen politischen Theorie in Deutschland." *Der Staat* 23 (1984): 205–26.

Klippel, Diethelm. "Johann August Schlettwein and the Economics Faculty at the University of Giessen." *History of Political Thought* 15 (1994): 203–27.

Klippel, Diethelm. *Politische Freiheit und Freiheitsrechte im deutschen Naturrecht des 18. Jahrhunderts*. Paderborn: Ferdinand Schöningh, 1976.

Klippel, Diethelm. "The True Concept of Liberty: Political Theory in Germany in the Second Half of the Eighteenth Century." In *The Transformation of Political Culture: England and Germany in the Late Eighteenth Century*, pp. 447–66, edited by Eckhart Hellmuth. London: Oxford University Press, 1990.

Köbler, Gerhard. "Eigen und Eigentum." *Zeitschrift der Savigny-Stiftung für Rechtsgeschichte. Germanistische Abteilung*. 95 (1978): 1–33.

Koselleck, Reinhart. *Critique and Crisis: Enlightenment and the Pathogenesis of Modern Society*. Studies in Contemporary German Social Thought. Cambridge: MIT Press, 1988. Originally appeared in 1979.

Kreike, Emmanuel. *Scorched Earth: Environmental Warfare as a Crime Against Humanity and Nature*. Princeton: Princeton University Press, 2021.

Krieger, Leonard. *The German Idea of Freedom: History of a Political Tradition*. Chicago: University of Chicago Press, 1957.

Krieger, Leonard. *The Politics of Discretion: Pufendorf and the Acceptance of Natural Law*. Chicago: University of Chicago Press, 1965.

Krüger, Kersten. *Die Landständische Verfassung*. Enzyklopädie deutscher Geschichte. Vol. 67. Munich: Oldenbourg, 2003.

Krüger, Kersten. "Entstehung und Ausbau des hessischen Steuerstaates vom 16. bis zum 18. Jahrhundert – Akten der Finanzverwaltung als frühneuzeitlicher Gesellschaftsspiegel." *Hessisches Jahrbuch für Landesgeschichte* 32 (1982): 103–26.

Kümin, Beat, and Andreas Würgler. "Petitions, Gravamina and the Early Modern State: Local Influence on Central Legislation in England and Germany (Hesse)." *Parliaments, Estates & Representation* 17 (1997): 39–60.

Kümin, Beat A. *Imperial Villages: Cultures of Political Freedom in the German Lands, c. 1300–1800*. Studies in Central European Histories. Boston: Brill, 2019.

Landes, David S. *The Wealth and Poverty of Nations: Why Some are so Rich and Some so Poor*. New York: Norton, 1998.

Lange, Tyler. "Property Rights." In *Cambridge History of Rights, Volume 2: The Middle Ages*, forthcoming.

Leeson, Peter T. "One More Time with Feeling: The Law Merchant, Arbitration, and International Trade." *Indian Journal of Economics and Business* special issue (2007): 19–34.

Legendre, P. *La pénétration du droit romain dans le droit canonique classique: recherche sur le mandat (1140–1254)*. 1957.

Leoni, Bruno. *Freedom and the Law*. 3rd ed. Indianapolis: Liberty Fund, 1961.

Lerch, Hans. *Hessische Agrargeschichte des 17. und 18. Jahrhunderts*. Hersfeld: H. Ott, 1926.

Levy, Ernst. "Natural Law in the *Institutes*." In *Proceedings*, pp. 43–72, edited by Alfred L. Scanlan. Indianapolis: University of Notre Dame Press, 1948.

Levy, Jacob. "Not So *Novus* an *Ordo*: Constitutions without Social Contracts." *Political Theory* 20 (2009): 1–27.

Levy, Jacob. *Rationalism, Pluralism, and Freedom*. Corby: Oxford University Press, 2014.

Lichtner, Adolf. *Landesheer und Stände in Hessen-Cassel, 1797–1821*. Göttingen: Vandenhoeck & Ruprecht, 1913.

Lindemann, Mary, and Jared Poley, eds. *Money in the German-Speaking Lands*. Vol. 17, Spektrum: Publications of the German Studies Association, 2017.

Linebaugh, Peter. *The Magna Carta Manifesto: Liberties and Commons For All*. Berkeley: University of California Press, 2008.

MacIntyre, Alasdair C. *Whose Justice? Which Rationality?* Notre Dame: University of Notre Dame Press, 1988.

Maine, Henry Sumner. *Ancient Law*. Dorset Press, 1986. Originally appeared in 1861.

de Malafosse, Jehan. *L'interdit momentariae possessionis: Contribution à l'histoire de la protection possessoire en droit romain*. anastatica, 1967.

Maruhn, Armand. "Duale Staatsbildung contra ständisches Landesbewusstsein. 1655 als Epochenjahr der hessischen Landesgeschichte." *Zeitschrift für Hessische Geschichte* 109 (2004): 71–94.

Maruhn, Armand. "'Justiznutzung' und ihre Grenzen wie der Landauer Bürger David Bick 1592 Graf Franz III. von Waldeck herausforderte." *Geschichtsblätter für Waldeck* 94 (2006): 56–75.

Marx, Karl. *Capital: A Critique of Political Economy*. Vol. 1. Harmondsworth: Penguin Classics, 1976. Originally appeared in 1867.

Maza, Sarah. *The Myth of the French Bourgeoisie: An Essay in the Social Imaginary, 1750–1850*. Cambridge: Harvard University Press, 2005.

Meinecke, Friedrich. *The Age of German Liberation, 1795–1815*. Edited by Peter Paret and Helmuth Fischer. Berkeley: University of California Press, 1977.

Menk, Gerhard. *Georg Friedrich von Waldeck (1620–1692): Eine Biographische Skizze*. Vol. 3, Waldeckische historische Hefte. Arolsen: Waldeckischer Geschichtsverein, 1992.

Menk, Gerhard. "Die Hochschul- und Wissenschaftslandschaft zwischen Main und Weser in der frühen Neuzeit." In *Wege der Neuzeit: Festschrift für Heinz Schilling zum 65. Geburtstag*, pp. 585–620, edited by Stefan Ehrenpreis. Vol. 85, Historische Forschungen. Berlin: Duncker & Humblot, 2007.

Merten, D. "Friedrich der Grosse und Montesquieu. Zu den Anfangen des Rechtsstaates im 18. Jahrhundert." In *Verwaltung im Rechtsstaat. Festschrift für Carl Hermann Ule*, pp. 187–208. Cologne, 1987.

Metz, Wolfgang. "Zur Sozialgeschichte des Beamtentums in der Zentralverwaltung der Landgrafschaft Hessen-Kassel bis zum 18. Jahrhundert." *Zeitschrift für Hessische Geschichte* 67 (1959): 138–48.

Milosz, Czeslaw. *The Captive Mind*. New York: Knopf, 1953.

Moeller, Bernd. *Imperial Cities and the Reformation: Three Essays*. Durham: Labyrinth Press, 1972.

Mohnhaupt, Heinz. "'Jura mercatorum' durch Privilegien: Zur Entwicklung des Handelsrechts bei Johann Marquard (1610–1737)." In *Wege europaeischer Rechtsgeschichte*, pp. 161–71, edited by Gerhard Köbler. 1987.

Monateri, Pier G. "Black Gaius: A Quest for the Multicultural Origins of the 'Western Legal Tradition'." *Hastings Law Journal* 51, no. 3 (2000).

Monateri, Pier G. "Deep Inside the Bramble Bush: Complex Orders and Humanities." *Rechtsgeschichte* 11 (2007): 172–79.

Moran, Bruce T. *The Alchemical World of the German Court: Occult Philosophy and Chemical Medicine in the Circle of Moritz of Hessen, 1572–1632*. Vol. 29, Sudhoffs Archiv Beihefte. Stuttgart: F. Steiner, 1991.

Morstadt, Carl Eduard. *Commentar über das Handelsrecht Deutschlands und Frankreichs*. Vol. 1. Heidelberg: Verlag von Julius Groos, 1849.

Müller, Andreas. *Der Regensburger Reichstag von 1653/54: eine Studie zur Entwicklung des Alten Reiches nach dem Westfälischen Frieden*. Europäische Hochschulschriften Reihe III, Geschichte und ihre Hilfswissenschaften. Frankfurt am Main; New York: P. Lang, 1992.

Muller, Jerry Z. "Justus Möser and the Conservative Critique of Early Modern Capitalism." *Central European History* 23 (1990): 153–78.

Neal, Larry. *The Rise of Financial Capitalism: International Capital Markets in the Age of Reason*. Studies in Monetary and Financial History. Cambridge: Cambridge University Press, 1990.

Nehls, Almut. *Alte Gewohnheit und Stadtrecht zu Kassel in Erbfällen: Ein Beitrag zur Rezeptionsgeschichte*. Vol. 6, Hessische Forschungen zur geschichtlichen Landes- und Volkskunde. Cassel: Bärenreiter, 1967.

Nehlsen-Von Stryk, Karin. "Die Monopolgutachten des rechtsgelehrten Humanisten Conrad Peutinger aus dem frühen 16. Jahrhundert." *Zeitschrift für Neuere Rechtsgeschichte* 10 (1988): 1–18.

Nicholas, Barry. *An Introduction to Roman law*. Oxford: Clarendon Press, 1962.

Niederquell, Theodor. "Im Kampf um die Reichsunmittelbarkeit: Die Geschichte der Deutschordensballei in Hessen vornehmlich im 16. Jahrhundert." *Hessisches Jahrbuch für Landesgeschichte* 5 (1955): 193–232.

Nietzsche, Friedrich Wilhelm. *On the Genealogy of Morals*. New York: Vintage Books, 1967.

Nitzan, Jonathan, and Shimshon Bichler. *Capital as Power: A Study of Order and Creorder*. RIPE Series in Global Political Economy. London: Routledge, 2009.

Noack, Winfried. *Landgraf Georg I. von Hessen und die Obergrafschaft Katzenelnbogen (1567–1596)*. Darmstadt: Historischer Verein für Hessen, 1966.

North, Douglass C., and Robert Paul Thomas. *The Rise of the Western World: A New Economic History*. Cambridge: Cambridge University Press, 1973.

North, Douglass C. "The Paradox of the West." In *The Origins of Modern Freedom in the West*, pp. 7–34, edited by Richard W. Davis. Stanford: Stanford University Press, 1995.

Oakley, Francis. "Legitimation by Consent: The Question of the Medieval Roots." *Viator* 14 (1983): 303–35.

Oestreich, Gerhard. *Geist und Gestalt des frühmodernen Staates. Ausgewählte Aufsätze*. Berlin: Duncker & Humblot, 1969.

Oestreich, Gerhard. *Neostoicism and the Early Modern State*. Cambridge Studies in Early Modern History. Edited by Brigitta Oestreich and H. G. Koenigsberger. Cambridge: Cambridge University Press, 1982.

Ogilvie, Sheilagh C. *Institutions and European Trade*. Cambridge: Cambridge University Press, 2011.

Ogris, Werner. "Besitz." In *Handwörterbuch zur deutschen Rechtsgeschichte*, Vol. 1, pp. 389 ff., edited by Adalbert Erler and Ekkehard Kaufmann. Berlin: E. Schmidt, 1971.

Olden, Rudolf. *The History of Liberty in Germany*. London: V. Gollancz Ltd., 1946. Originally appeared in 1939.

O'Neill, John. "The Disciplinary Society: From Weber to Foucault." *The British Journal of Sociology* 37, no. 1 (1986): 42–60.

Orlow, Dietrich. *A History of Modern Germany: 1871 to Present*. 8th ed. London; New York: Routledge 2018.

Ostrom, Elinor. *Governing the Commons: The Evolution of Institutions for Collective Action*. Political Economy of Institutions and Decisions. Cambridge: Cambridge University Press, 1990.

Ozment, Steven E. *The Age of Reform (1250–1550): An Intellectual and Religious History of Late Medieval and Reformation Europe*. New Haven: Yale University Press, 1980.

Padgett, John Frederick, and Walter W. Powell, eds. *The Emergence of Organizations and Markets*. Princeton: Princeton University Press, 2012.

Paisley, Roderick. "Right to Make Roads and *res merae facultatis*." *Edinburgh Law Review* 11, no. 1 (2007): 95–99.

Pedlow, Gregory W. *The Survival of the Hessian Nobility, 1770–1870*. Princeton: Princeton University Press, 1988.

Pettit, Phillip. *Republicanism: A Theory of Freedom and Government*. Oxford political theory. Oxford; New York: Oxford University Press, 1997.

Philippi, Hans. *Landgraf Karl von Hessen-Kassel: Ein Deutscher Fürst der Barockzeit*. Veröffentlichungen der Historischen Kommission für Hessen. Vol. 34. Marburg: Elwert, 1976.

Piergiovanni, Vito. "Genoese Civil Rota and mercantile customary law." In *From lex mercatoria to commercial law*, pp. 191–206 Comparative Studies in Continental and Anglo-American Legal History. Berlin: Duncker & Humblot, 2005.

Pitkin, Hanna Fenichel. *The Concept of Representation*. Berkeley: University of California Press, 1967.

Planitz, Hans. *Deutsches Privatrecht*. 3rd ed, 1948.

Pocock, J. G. A. *The Ancient Constitution and the Feudal Law*. Cambridge, 1957.

Polley, Rainer. "Retraktsrecht und Weinkauf im Hochstift Fulda. Zur Bedeutung des Volksgewohnheitsrechts im 18. Jahrhundert." *Hessisches Jahrbuch für Landesgeschichte* 33 (1983): 239–56.

Popper, Karl. *The Open Society and its Enemies*. London: Routledge, 1945.

Posner, Richard. "The Economic Approach to Law." *Texas Law Review* 53 (1975): 757–63 or so.

Preussischen Akademie der Wissenschaften, Deutsche Akademie der Wissenschaften zu Berlin, and Heidelberger Akademie der Wissenschaften. *Deutsches Rechtswörterbuch*. Weimar: H. Böhlaus Nachfolger, 1914.

Rabb, Theodore K. *The Thirty Years' War*. University Press of America, 1981.

Raeff, Marc. "The Well-Ordered Police State and the Development of Modernity in 17th- and 18th-Century Europe: An Attempt at a Comparative Approach." *American Historical Review* 78, no. 3 (1975): 1221–43.

Raeff, Marc. *The Well-Ordered Police State: Social and Institutional Change through Law in the Germanies and Russia, 1600–1800*. New Haven: Yale University Press, 1983.

Ranieri, Filippo. *Recht und Gesellschaft im Zeitalter der Rezeption: eine rechts- und sozialgeschichtliche Analyse der Tätigkeit des Reichskammergerichts im 16. Jahrhundert.* Quellen und Forschungen zur höchsten Gerichtsbarkeit im alten Reich. Köln: Böhlau, 1985.

Ranieri, Filippo. "Die Juristen im Alten Reich des 17. und 18. Jahrhunderts: ein Forschungsprojekt." In *Stände und Gesellschaft im Alten Reich*, pp. 231–44, edited by Georg Schmidt. Veröffentlichungen des Instituts für Europäische Geschichte Mainz. Abteilung Universalgeschichte. Beiheft. Stuttgart: Franz Steiner Verlag, 1989.

Redlich, Fritz. "Contributions in the Thirty Years War." *Economic History Review* 12 (1959–1960): 247–54.

Reichert, Folker. *Landesherrschaft, Adel und Vogtei: Zur Vorgeschichte des spaetmittelalterlichen Staendestaates im Herzogtum Oesterreich.* Vol. 23, Beihefte zum Archiv für Kulturgeschichte. Cologne; Vienna, 1985.

Reid, John Phillip. *Rule of Law: The Jurisprudence of Liberty in the Seventeenth and Eighteenth Centuries.* Dekalb: Northern Illinois University Press, 2004.

Riesenberg, Peter N. *Inalienability of sovereignty in medieval political thought.* Columbia Studies in the Social Sciences. New York: Columbia University Press, 1956.

Rogers, James S. *The Early History of the Law of Bills and Notes: A Study of the Origins of Anglo-American Commercial Law.* Cambridge: Cambridge University Press, 1995.

Rommel, Dietrich Christoph von. *Geschichte von Hessen.* 9 vols. Cassel: Theodore Fischer, 1853.

de Roover, Raymond A. *Money, Banking and Credit in Mediaeval Bruges: Italian Merchant Bankers, Lombards and Money-Changers.* Cambridge: Mediaeval Academy of America, 1948.

de Roover, Raymond A., and Lorenz Laubenberger. "Wechsel, Wechselrecht." In *Handwörterbuch zur deutschen Rechtsgeschichte*, Vol. 5, pp. 1179–84, edited by Adalbert Erler, Ekkehard Kaufmann and Wolfgang Stammler. Berlin: E. Schmidt, 1998.

de Roover, Raymond A. "New Interpretations of the History of Banking." In *Business, Banking, and Economic Thought in Late Medieval and Early Modern Europe*, pp. 201–38, edited by Julius Kirshner. Chicago: University of Chicago Press, 1976.

de Roover, Raymond A. "What is Dry Exchange?" In *Business, Banking, and Economic Thought in Late Medieval and Early Modern Europe*, pp. 183–99, edited by Julius Kirshner. Chicago: University of Chicago Press, 1976. Originally appeared in 1944.

de Roover, Raymond A. "Cardinal Cajetan on '*Cambium*' or Exchange Dealings." In *Philosophy and Humanism. Renaissance Essays in Honor of Paul Oskar Kristeller*, pp. 423–33, edited by Edward P. Mahoney. New York: Columbia University Press, 1976.

Rosenberg, Nathan, and L. E. Birdzell. *How the West Grew Rich: The Economic Transformation of the Industrial World.* New York: Basic Books, 1986.

de Ruysscher, Dave. "Innovating Financial Law in Early Modern Europe: Transfers of Commercial Paper and Recourse Liability in Legislation and Ius Commune (Sixteenth to Eighteenth Centuries)." *European Review of Private Law* 19, no. 5 (2011): 505–18.

Samtleben, Wolfgang. *Die Idee einer altgermanischen Volksfreiheit im vormärzlichen deutschen Liberalismus*. Hamburg, 1935.

Schefold, Bertram. "Die Bedeutung des Freihandels in wirtschaftstheoretischen Debatten in Deutschland während des 19. Jahrhunderts." Paper presented at the Völkerrecht und Weltwirtschaft im 19. Jahrhundert, Frankfurt am Main, September 2009.

Scherner, Karl Otto. "Zum Sonderrecht der Kaufleute bei Johann Marquard." In *Usus modernus pandectarum: Römisches Recht, Deutsches Recht und Naturrecht in der Frühen Neuzeit; Klaus Luig zum 70. Geburtstag*, pp. 199–218, edited by Hans-Peter Haferkamp and Tilman Repgen. Cologne: Böhlau, 2007.

Schindling, Anton. *Die Anfänge des Immerwährenden Reichstags zu Regensburg: Ständevertretung und Staatskunst nach dem Westfälischen Frieden*. Beiträge zur Sozial- und Verfassungsgeschichte des Alten Reiches. Mainz: P. von Zabern, 1991.

Schmelzeisen, Gustaf Klemens. "Eigen und Erbe." In *Deutsches Privatrecht*, Vol. 22, pp. 65–101 Schaeffers Grundriss des Rechts und der Wirtschaft. Leipzig: Schaeffer-Verlag; E. L. Hirschfeld, 1935.

Schmidt, Georg. *Geschichte des Alten Reichs: Staat und Nation in der Frühen Neuzeit, 1495–1806*. Munich: Beck, 1999.

Schmidt, Georg. *Wandel durch Vernunft: Deutschland, 1715–1806*. Munich: C. H. Beck, 2009.

Schmitt, Carl. *The Concept of the Political*. Chicago: University of Chicago Press, 1996. Originally appeared in 1976, 1932.

Schmitt, Carl. *Constitutional Theory*. Durham: Duke University Press, 2008. Originally appeared in 1928.

Schmitt, Carl. *Political Theology: Four Chapters on the Concept of Sovereignty*. Studies in Contemporary German Social Thought. Cambridge: MIT Press, 1985. Originally appeared in 1922.

Schneider, Jürgen. "Hat das Indossament zum Niedergang der Wechselmessen beigetragen?" In *Geldumlauf, Währungssysteme und Zahlungsverkehr in Nordwesteuropa 1300–1800: Beiträge zur Geldgeschichte der späten Hansezeit*, edited by Michael North. Cologne: Böhlau, 1989.

Schormann, Gerhard, ed. *Rintelner Studenten des 17. und 18. Jahrhunderts*, Schaumburger Studien: C Bösendahl, 1981.

Schulze, Winfried. "Die Entwicklung des "teutschen Bauernrechts" in der frühen Neuzeit." *Zeitschrift für Neuere Rechtsgeschichte* 12 (1990): 127–63.

Scott, James C. *Seeing Like a State: How Certain Schemes to Improve the Human Condition have Failed*. Yale Agrarian Studies. New Haven: Yale University Press, 1998.

Scribner, R. W. "Communalism: Universal Category or Ideological Construct? A Debate in the Historiography of Early Modern Germany and Switzerland." *The Historical Journal* 37, no. 1 (1994): 199–207.

Sedatis, Lutz. *Über den Ursprung der Wechselstrenge: Eine historischdogmatische Untersuchung der Lehre vom rigor cambialis*. Duncker & Humblot, 1967.

Sheehan, James J. *German History, 1770–1866*. Oxford History of Modern Europe. Oxford: Clarendon Press; Oxford University Press, 1989.

Sheehan, James J. *German Liberalism in the Nineteenth Century*. Chicago: University of Chicago Press, 1978.

Simmel, Georg. *The Philosophy of Money*. London; New York: Routledge, 1978. Originally appeared in 1900.

Simmonds, Nigel E. "Reason, History and Privilege: Blackstone's Debt to Natural law." *Zeitschrift der Savigny-Stiftung für Rechtsgeschichte. Germanistische Abteilung* 105 (1988): 200–13.

Skinner, Quentin. *Liberty Before Liberalism*. Cambridge: Cambridge University Press, 1998.

Small, Albion W. *The Cameralists: The Pioneers of German Social Polity*. 606 vols. Chicago: University of Chicago Press, 1909.

Sonenscher, Michael. *Capitalism: The Story Behind the Word*. Princeton, New Jersey: Princeton University Press, 2022.

de Soto, Hernando. *The Mystery of Capital: Why Capitalism Triumphs in the West and Fails Everywhere Else*. New York: Basic Books, 2000.

Spector, Horacio. "Four Conceptions of Freedom." *Political Theory* 38 (2010): 780–808.

Stahl, Friedrich Julius. *Die Kirchenverfassung nach Lehre und Recht der Protestanten*. Erlangen: Bläsing, 1840.

Steinberg, S. H. *The Thirty Years War and the Conflict for European Hegemony, 1600–1660*. New York: Norton, 1967.

Stollberg-Rilinger, Barbara. *Des Kaisers alte Kleider: Verfassungsgeschichte und Symbolsprache des Alten Reiches*. Munich: Beck, 2008.

Strieder, Friedrich Wilhelm, Ludwig Wachler, Karl Wilhelm Justi, and Otto Gerland, eds. *Grundlage zu einer hessischen Gelehrten und Schriftsteller Geschichte, seit der Reformation bis auf gegenwärtige Zeiten*. 21 or more vols. Cassel; Gotha: J. J. Cramer; Barmeier, 1985. Originally appeared in 1781–1863.

Taylor, Charles. *Modern Social Imaginaries*. Duke University Press, 2004.

Taylor, Peter K. *Indentured to Liberty: Peasant Life and the Hessian Military State, 1688–1815*. Ithaca: Cornell University Press, 1994.

Tellenbach, Gerd. *Church, State, and Christian Society at the Time of the Investiture Contest*. Oxford: Basil Blackwell, 1940. Originally appeared in 1936.

Theibault, John. "Community and *Herrschaft* in the Seventeenth-Century German Village." *Journal of Modern History* 64, no. 1 (Mar. 1992): 1–21.

Theibault, John. *German Villages in Crisis: Rural Life in Hesse-Kassel and the Thirty Years' War, 1580–1720*. Studies in German Histories. Atlantic Highlands: Brill, 1995.

Thieme, Hans. "Landsiedel." In *Handwörterbuch zur deutschen Rechtsgeschichte*, Vol. 2, pp. 1570–74. Berlin: E. Schmidt, 1978.

Thudichum, Friedrich von. *Wettereiba. Eine Gau-Geschichte*. Giessen: Alfred Töpelmann, 1907.

Thudichum, Friedrich von. *Zur Rechtsgeschichte der Wetterau*. 3 vols. Vol. 2. Tübingen: H. Laupp, 1874.

Tierney, Brian. "Hierarchy, Consent, and the "Western Tradition"." *Political Theory* 15, no. 4 (Nov. 1987): 646–52.

Tierney, Brian. *The Idea of Natural Rights: Studies on Natural Rights, Natural Law, and Church Law, 1150–1625*. Emory University Studies in Law and Religion. Atlanta: Scholars Press, 1997.

Tierney, Brian. "Freedom and the Medieval Church." In *The Origins of Modern Freedom in the West*, edited by Richard W. Davis. Stanford: Stanford University Press, 1995.

Tigar, Michael E., and Madeleine R. Levy. *Law and the Rise of Capitalism*. New York: Monthly Review Press, 1977.

Tilly, Charles. *Coercion, Capital, and European States, A.D.990–1992*. Cambridge: Basil Blackwell; Wiley-Blackwell, 1992.

Tribe, Keith. *Governing Economy: The Reformation of German Economic Discourse, 1750–1840*. Cambridge; New York: Cambridge University Press, 1988.

Trivellato, Francesca. "Credit, Honor, and the Early Modern French Legend of the Jewish Invention of Bills of Exchange." *The Journal of Modern History* 84, no. 2 (2012): 289–334.

Trossbach, Werner. "Power and Good Governance: The Removal of Ruling Princes in the Holy Roman Empire, 1680–1794." In *The Holy Roman Empire, Reconsidered*, edited by Jason Philip Coy, Benjamin Marschke and David Warren Sabean. Spektrum: Publications of the German Studies Association: Berghahn Books, 2011.

Ullmann, Hans-Peter. "Der Frankfurter Kapitalmarkt um 1800: Entstehung, Struktur und Wirken einer modernen Finanzierungsinstitution." *Vierteljahrschrift für Sozial- und Wirtschaftsgeschichte* 77 (1990): 75–92.

Umbach, Maiken. *Federalism and Enlightenment in Germany, 1740–1806*. 2000.

Vann, James Allen. *The Making of a State: Württemberg, 1593–1793*. Ithaca: Cornell University Press, 1984.

Van Kley, Dale K., ed. *The French Idea of Freedom: The Old Regime and the Declaration of Rights of 1789*, The Making of Modern Freedom. Stanford: Stanford University Press, 1994.

Voegelin, Eric. *The New Science of Politics: An Introduction*. Chicago: University of Chicago Press, 1952.

Volckart, Oliver. "Politische Zersplitterung und Wirtschaftswachstum im Alten Reich, ca. 1650–1800." *Vierteljahrschrift für Sozial- und Wirtschaftsgeschichte* 86, no. 1 (1999): 1–38.

de Vries, Jan. *Die geistige Welt der Germanen*. Darmstadt: Wissenschaftliche Buchgesellschaft, 1963. Originally appeared in 1943.

de Vries, Jan. *The Economy of Europe in an Age of Crisis, 1600–1750*. Cambridge: Cambridge University Press, 1976.

Wakefield, André. *The Disordered Police State: German Cameralism as Science and Practice*. Chicago: University of Chicago Press, 2009.

Walker, Mack. *German Home Towns: Community, State, and General Estate, 1648–1871*. Ithaca: Cornell University Press, 1998. Originally appeared in 1971.

Walker, Mack. *Johann Jakob Moser and the Holy Roman Empire of the German Nation*. Chapel Hill: University of North Carolina Press, 1981.

Walker, Mack. "Rights and Functions: The Social Categories of Eighteenth-Century German Jurists and Cameralists." *Journal of Modern History* 50, no. 2 (Jun. 1978): 234–51.

Wallerstein, Immanuel. *World-Systems Analysis: An Introduction*. Duke University Press, 2004.

Weber, Hans Heinrich. *Der Hessenkrieg*. Giessen: O. Kindt, 1935.

Weidhaas, Peter. *A History of the Frankfurt Book Fair*. Translated by Carolyn Gossage and Wendy Wright. Toronto: Dundurn Press, 2007. Originally appeared in 2003.

Weiske, Julius, Julius Merkel, and Philipp Bopp, eds. *Rechtslexikon für Juristen aller Teutschen Staaten, enthaltend die gesammte Rechtswissenschaft*. 16 vols. Leipzig: O. Wigand, 1839.

Welkoborsky, Gerhard. "Das Solmser Landrecht." *Archiv für hessische Geschichte und Altertumskunde* 30 (1967–1970): 1–66.

Wenz-Haubfleisch, Annegret. "'... damit die Landes-Bürden hinfüro mit gleichen Schultern getragen werden.' Ziele und Durchführung der Rektifikation des landschaftlichen Steuerstocks in der Landgrafschaft Hessen-Kassel im 18. Jahrhundert." *Hessisches Jahrbuch für Landesgeschichte* 39 (1989): 151–203.

Whitman, James Q. "Long Live the Hatred of Roman Law!" *Rechtsgeschichte* 2 (2003): 40–57.

Whittle, Jane. "Individualism and the Family-Land Bond: A Reassessment of Land Transfer Patterns among the English Peasantry c. 1270–1580." *Past and Present* 160 (1998): 25–63.

Wieacker, Franz. *A History of Private Law in Europe with Particular Reference to Germany*. Translated by Tony Weir. Oxford: Clarendon Press, 1995. Originally appeared in 1952.

Wilberforce, Robert Isaac. *A Sketch of the History of Erastianism: together with two sermons on the reality of Church Ordinances, and on the principle of Church Authority*. London: John Murray, 1851.

Wilder, Colin F. "Property, Possession and Prescription: The Rule of Law in the Hessian and Rhine-Main Region of Germany, 1648–1776." Ph.D. thesis, University of Chicago, 2010.

Wilder, Colin F. "Teaching Old Dogs New Tricks: Four Motifs of Legal Change from Early Modern Europe." *History and Theory* 51 (2012): 18–41.

Wilder, Colin F. "TL;DR, or, an experimental application of text analysis and network analysis to the study of historical library collections, in particular the title catalogs of four libraries in the western Holy Roman Empire in the period 1606–1796, accompanied by some methodological speculations and ideas for further research." In *New Technologies in Renaissance and Medieval Studies*. Toronto, 2019.

Wilder, Colin F. "The Importance of Beginning, Over and Over: The Idea of Primitive Germanic Law." *Intersections*, Vol. 25, edited by Minou Schraven and Maarten Delbeke. Brill, 2011.

Williamson, Oliver E. "The New Institutional Economics: Taking Stock, Looking Ahead." *Journal of Economic Literature* 38, no. 3 (2000): 595–613.

Willoweit, Dietmar. *Deutsche Verfassungsgeschichte: Vom Frankenreich bis zur Wiedervereinigung Deutschlands: ein Studienbuch*. 5th, expanded ed. Munich: C. H. Beck, 2005.

Willoweit, Dietmar. *Rechtsgrundlagen der Territorialgewalt: Landesobrigkeit, Herrschaftsrechte und Territorium in der Rechtswissenschaft der Neuzeit*. Cologne: Böhlau, 1975.

Wilson, Peter H. *The Holy Roman Empire, 1495–1806*. Studies in European history. 2nd ed. Houndmills, Basingstoke, Hampshire: Palgrave, 2011. Originally appeared in 1999.

Wilson, Peter H. *The Thirty Years War: Europe's Tragedy*. Cambridge: Belknap Press, 2009.

Witte jr., John. "Rights, Resistance, and Revolution in the Western Tradition: Early Protestant Foundations." *Law and History Review* 26, no. 3 (2008): 545–70.

Zmora, Hillay. *State and Nobility in Early Modern Germany: The Knightly Feud in Franconia, 1440–1567*. Cambridge Studies in Early Modern History. Cambridge: Cambridge University Press, 1997.

Zywicki, Todd. "The Rise and Fall of Efficiency in the Common Law: A Supply-Side Analysis." *Northwestern University Law Review* 97 (2003): 1551–633.

Index

www.ingramcontent.com/pod-product-compliance
Lightning Source LLC
LaVergne TN
LVHW010542300926
849162LV00002B/210